INSIDE THE MIND OF BTK

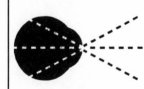

INSIDE THE MIND OF BTK

THE TRUE STORY BEHIND THE THIRTY-YEAR HUNT FOR THE NOTORIOUS WICHITA SERIAL KILLER

JOHN DOUGLAS

AND JOHNNY DODD

THORNDIKE PRESS

An imprint of Thomson Gale, a part of The Thomson Corporation

Detroit • New York • San Francisco • New Haven, Conn. • Waterville, Maine • London

THOMSON

GALE

LIBRARY OF CONGRESS CATALOGING-IN-PUBLICATION DATA

Douglas, John E.
  Inside the mind of BTK : the true story behind the thirty-year hunt for the notorious Wichita serial killer / by John Douglas and Johnny Dodd. — Large print ed.
    p. cm.
  Includes bibliographical references and index.
  ISBN-13: 978-0-7862-9931-7 (hardcover : alk. paper)
  ISBN-10: 0-7862-9931-2 (hardcover : alk. paper)
  1. Rader, Dennis, 1945– 2. Douglas, John E. 3. Serial murder investigation — Kansas — Wichita — Case studies. 4. Serial murders — Kansas — Wichita — Case studies. 5. Serial murderers — Kansas — Wichita — Psychology. 6. United States Federal Bureau of Investigation — Officials and employees — Biography. 7. Large type books. I. Dodd, Johnny, 1963– II. Title.
HV8079.H6D684 2007b
364.152'30973—dc22

                                                2007027430

Published in 2007 in arrangement with John Wiley & Sons, Inc.

Printed in the United States of America on permanent paper
10 9 8 7 6 5 4 3 2 1

In memory of my mother, Dolores A. Douglas, February 9, 1919–March 4, 2006.
Mother and my biggest fan — with love.
— John Douglas

To my father, a man of few words, but many books. Long may you read.
— Johnny Dodd

CONTENTS

ACKNOWLEDGMENTS

I am indebted to the heroic people who shared their insights, professional experiences, and, in many cases, their lives with me — particularly the men and women of the Wichita Police Department and the Kansas Bureau of Investigation, who worked so long and so hard and so well to see this case through and see justice done. They have the undying gratitude of us all. Thank you.

This book was a team effort, and it would not have been possible without the support of our literary agent, Liza Dawson; our intrepid editor, Alan Rinzler; my entertainment attorney and good friend, Steve Mark; and of course Johnny Dodd, who became an extension of my life and personality in writing this book. Thank you all.

Finally, I would like to pay tribute to my mother, Dolores Douglas, who died in an accident while I was writing this book. She was my biggest fan and supporter, and I

miss her dearly.
— John Douglas

An extra special thanks to Liza Dawson, the best agent an ink-stained wretch could ask for. To John Douglas for his patience and trust in allowing me to tell his story. To Alan Rinzler and his editorial cat o' nine tails (the scars have almost healed). To Kris "It's So Over" Casarona for literally everything. To Ken Landwehr, Larry Welch, and Bernie Drowatzky for all their help. And to all those who knew Dennis Rader (or thought they did) for agreeing to share their stories with me.

A shout-out of gratitude to Evan and the staff at Peet's at 14th and Montana. To Bill "Deer Hunter" Lischak and Diamond Joe Bruggeman for always being there with an open ear and a shoulder. To Ron Arias for his words, wisdom, and advice. To Lizz Leonard for once again being so absolutely Lizz Leonardesque. To Diana for picking up the domestic slack and then some. To Mother Antonia for her prayers of protection, her insight, and her lorca. To my various friends who spent fourteen months listening to my rants and nightmares. To Jamie Lee for her wordsmithing. To Champ Clarke, Oliver Jones, and Lorenzo Benet for allowing me to constantly pick their gray matter. To T-lu for her motherly advice and proofreading prowess. To Julie for helping me shape every single word. And to Christian and Ella, my two little rays of sunshine: remember always to do your best.

— Johnny Dodd

INTRODUCTION

It began in the autumn of 1974 while I was working as a "street agent" in the FBI's Milwaukee field office. I was twenty-eight years old and had spent the past three years working with the bureau. One afternoon while I was chewing the fat with a couple of homicide detectives from the Milwaukee Police Department, somebody mentioned a serial killer in Wichita, Kansas, who called himself "the BTK Strangler."

BTK. Just those initials. What did they stand for? I didn't know then, but the moment I heard them I felt a little jolt of electricity shoot through me. I yearned to know everything I could about this murderer. Little did I realize how far my search for answers would take me and how entwined my life would become with this violent, elusive killer.

It was during this period of my life that I started on my quest to understand what motivated someone who seemed to enjoy perpetrating acts of violence upon complete strangers. This was what made serial killers so difficult to identify — they rarely killed anyone whom they knew intimately, and their crimes often appeared to have no motive.

As a young FBI agent, I made it my personal mission to find out what drove these vicious, heartless killers. I wanted to know how they viewed the world, how they perpetrated their crimes, how they selected their victims. If I could get the answers to those questions, I told myself, I'd one day be able to help police around the nation identify serial killers long before they got the chance to leave a long, bloody trail in their wake.

So after work that evening back in 1974, I went digging through the Milwaukee Public Library and located some old newspapers from Wichita. I read every word that had been written about the quadruple homicide this killer had committed in January 1974 and learned that BTK stood for "bind, torture, and kill." His self-chosen nickname perfectly summed up his modus operandi. He somehow managed to waltz his way into his victims' homes, tie them up, and torture them in the same way a schoolboy might torment an insect. Then, when it suited him, he snuffed out their lives. He was an equal opportunity killer who had claimed the lives of a man, a woman, and children.

That was a hectic, busy time in my career. When I wasn't working bank robberies and fugitive and kidnapping cases, I could be found at the University of Wisconsin, where I'd enrolled in graduate school, studying educational psychology, pushing myself to understand what made someone like BTK perpetrate such heinous, brutal acts.

Some nights I'd lie awake asking myself, "Who the hell is this BTK? What makes a guy like this do what he does? What makes him tick?"

At the time, the FBI's Behavioral Science Unit (BSU) was operated out of the FBI Academy in Quantico, Virginia. It served primarily as an academic unit. The word *profiling* had yet to find its way into the bureau's investigative vocabulary. But it would one day soon — I just knew it. And I promised myself that after I earned my graduate degrees, I would transfer into the BSU and spend my days profiling the minds of violent serial offenders full-time.

By June 1977, I did just that. I was selected and transferred to the FBI Academy as an instructor for the BSU and quickly began teaching courses in hostage negotiation and criminal psychology. Most of my hours were spent working as an instructor, but I occasionally thought about BTK, wondering if he'd ever been identified and arrested.

One afternoon in March 1978, while researching another case, I again dug up what I could on BTK and was surprised to learn that since 1974, he had somehow still eluded police and now claimed responsibility for seven murders. By this time in 1978, he'd already sent two taunting letters to local newspapers — the first in October 1974, the second in February 1978 — daring the police to try to catch him.

By 1979, I was in the midst of my serial murder research program, conducting what would eventually become in-depth interviews with three dozen serial killers, including Charles Manson, Arthur Bremmer, Richard Speck, John Wayne Gacy, David Berkowitz (aka Son of Sam), and others, each of whom had murdered three or more victims with some sort of cooling-off period between their crimes.

In the autumn of 1979, the phone rang in my office, which at that point was located in the basement of the FBI Academy library. On the other end of the line was a homicide detective with the Wichita Police Department. "I heard about the work you've been doing out there," he said. "Was wondering if you could help us on a case we've been working on."

"Tell me about it," I said.

"We got a serial killer out here," he said. "Goes by the name of BTK. You heard of him?"

"Only what I've read in the papers."

Over the next few minutes, he walked me through the BTK murders, detailing the twists and turns of the investigation and re-iterating his claim that police would welcome any assistance the FBI's BSU could lend.

"If you can get out here," I told him, "I can give you a day. Bring everything you've got. We can go through it, and I'll put together an analysis for you."

One week later, Wichita police lieutenant Bernie Drowatzky arrived at Quantico. I walked him upstairs to a quiet corner of the library, and Drowatzky spread his crime scene photos across the table. "Let's go through this murder by murder," I said. "The only caveat is that you can't tell me about any potential suspects you might be looking at."

The veteran cop frowned and, in a subdued voice, said, "We don't have any suspects."

Drowatzky remained silent as I thumbed

through the grisly photos. The fact that he'd traveled all this way to seek my help told me one thing: the Wichita Police Department was grasping for anyone or anything that could help steer them in a direction they hadn't thought of.

"We've never run across anything like this before," Drowatzky said. "We normally solve our murders in Wichita."

At the time, my colleagues and I were trying to acquire answers to the formula of Why + How = Who that I believed could help investigators crack these often frustrating, hard-to-solve cases.

Why, we wondered, would someone want to kill multiple victims over a period of days, months, and, in the case of BTK, many years? Why do they target certain types of victims? How do they prepare for their crimes? What sort of impact do their actions have on them?

Are they born to kill? Did some childhood trauma warp them, causing them to turn violent? Or is their homicidal appetite a combination of these two factors? What factors led to their identification and arrest? Did they get sloppy, or was their capture a result of stellar detective work? Our interview protocol involved thousands of questions and stretched fifty-seven pages in length. The insight we gleaned from these killers provided us with a priceless understanding of how the mind of a serial killer worked.

From what police had been able to piece together from BTK's crime scenes, it was clear that this killer maintained a high level of control over his victims. This form of dominance over another person appeared to be a big turn-on for BTK. He tied his victims up, using rope or whatever else was handy at the scene. When it came time to kill, his preferred method involved either a garrote or a plastic bag tied over the head. He often arranged the bodies of his victims in poses reminiscent of a detective magazine cover. Before fleeing, he would sometimes masturbate on or near his victims.

Among other things, in the pages of the analysis I wrote in 1979, I emphasized to police that BTK's ego would eventually lead to his downfall. Their job, I wrote, was to stroke his ego in public whenever possible, to show him the respect he craved, in the hopes that he would continue to communicate with them. The way I saw it, the best chance that law enforcement had to get a handle on this killer was to keep him talking. Exactly what police did with my analysis, I have no idea. I had to jump to the next case on the front burner. If they needed me, all they had to do was pick up a phone and call me.

In October 1984, the Wichita Police paid a second visit to my office. Seven years had passed since BTK's last known murder, and police still weren't any closer to taking this sick killer off the street.

The Wichita Police Department had recently formed an eight-person BTK task force, known as the Ghostbusters. The longtime chief was retiring, but before leaving his post, he wanted the case solved and closed. So he assembled a team of six crack investigators, a captain, and a lieutenant and instructed them to reopen the files and sift through the mounds of crime scene photos, witness statements, police and autopsy reports, and even the analysis I'd written on the case five years earlier. After three months, they were desperate to ensure that the investigation didn't hit another brick wall, so they reached out again to our BSU. A week after telephoning to ask if my unit could offer any assistance, two task force detectives — Paul Dotson and Mark Richardson — arrived at the FBI Academy toting several pounds of new crime scene photos and various reports. I met them in the lobby of the forensic science building, where my office was located. At the time, I oversaw a staff of six criminal profilers.

"Let's go to the conference room," I told them. "Several of my colleagues are waiting there for you. I want you to walk us through the case."

As Dotson and Richardson passed out the grim, gritty eight-by-ten photos and readied the slide projector, I explained just how far we'd come with our criminal profiling program since the last visit by a Wichita homicide detective. Then, for the next eight hours, they outlined the basic facts of the case, describing the victims, communiqués the killer had sent, medical examiner's reports, and the various neighborhoods where the murders had occurred.

I listened to their presentation, yet when they'd finished I had many more questions than answers. Despite being considered one of the nation's foremost experts on serial murderers, I'd never encountered a case quite like BTK's.

Six years had passed since he had written to police, gloating over one of his murders. How, I wondered, was this publicity-starved psychopath able to go underground for so many years? Was he still killing? What specifically did he do sexually, physically, and psy-

21

chologically to his victims? Why hadn't he been apprehended?

Together with four of my colleagues, I ingested the information from our briefing. A few days later, we sat down with the detectives again, and, during a marathon skull session, we provided them with a detailed verbal profile of what we had concluded about BTK, given the limited information we had at that point, along with some proactive ideas that we believed might work to flush him out.

The Ghostbusters task force was disbanded in 1987. Because BTK was only one of thousands of cases I worked on during those years, I never learned exactly how many of the ideas generated from our analysis were actually ever used in the investigation. But one fact was frustratingly clear: by the time I retired from the FBI in June 1995, the unknown subject (UNSUB) in Wichita had yet to be identified. Was he dead? Was he incarcerated for another crime? Had he moved away from Wichita? Or was there another reason to explain why he'd gone underground?

I'd begun to believe that I'd never get the answers to my questions until one evening in March 2004, when a former colleague telephoned. At the time, my wife, Pam, and I were living together with our oldest daughter, Erika, twenty-nine, who was living at home, studying to become a nurse. Her sister, Lauren, twenty-four, was finishing up her third year of law school. My son, Jed, eighteen, was getting ready to graduate from high school. My family had just finished dinner, but I was seated at my desk in the study, talking to a rape victim who had contacted me through my Web site. No sooner had I ended my conversation with that sobbing, shell-shocked woman than my phone rang.

"He's back," said the voice on the other end of the line. It belonged to a FBI profiler I'd hired and trained shortly before leaving the bureau.

News that BTK had resurfaced and had just sent the local newspaper a packet containing a photo snapped of a murder he'd committed in 1991 both excited and disappointed me. My gut told me that it would be just a matter of time before he tripped himself up and police nabbed him. But I also knew that because I was no longer employed by the FBI, I'd have to wait years before I'd ever get a crack at interviewing him.

Over the next eleven months, Wichita police used a technique I'd first tried out in the 1980s to solve a murder in San Diego. It involved creating what I called a "super-cop," the kind of law enforcement officer who could stand up at press conferences and talk directly to the UNSUB, eventually building up such a rapport with the suspect that he allows himself to take chances and risks he wouldn't take otherwise.

Which was exactly what happened with BTK. He let his guard down. He began to believe that he and the police were, in a sense, comrades and colleagues. He made the mistake of believing that he could trust them to tell him the truth, and that led to his downfall. In February 2005, police arrested Dennis Rader, a seemingly mild-mannered, married, churchgoing father of two grown children. He was a municipal employee; he worked for the city of Wichita as a compliance officer, handing out tickets to people when their lawns grew too high or they held a garage sale without obtaining the necessary permits. And, just as we feared, he had continued to kill. His body count had climbed to ten victims.

Six months after his arrest, I watched intently as Rader spoke at his televised sentencing hearing, calmly detailing whom he had killed and how. But what I really wanted to know was *why*.

Several years had passed since I'd written a

book. I'd been waiting for the right kind of story to come along, something that I could use to tell readers about how the inside of a serial killer's head works and how other serial killers might be stopped. As I watched Dennis Rader's performance in court on that day in August, I knew I'd finally found my inspiration. It was the kind of story that comes along once in a career. BTK was one of the very first serial killers I encountered whose appetite for death set me on a journey into the heart of darkness. His career spanned mine. He was always there, always lurking on the periphery. So when the opportunity came to finally put the pieces together, I jumped at the chance.

Yet for all the years of study and analysis I'd done on serial killers, nothing about Rader made sense to me: Who was this guy? Why did killing mean so much to him? How could he be married, raise two kids, and also be such a heartless monster, such a sick sexual pervert? Why did he go underground for so many years? How was it that this killer could be elected president of his church? Why was no one able to glimpse his real identity? Is there anything that could have been done during all those years that would have led sooner to his arrest? Why did he finally come out of hiding and get caught?

So I picked up the phone, called my literary agent, Liza Dawson, and told her all about BTK, detailing my involvement with the case and how, with my police contacts on both the local and state level, I'd try to secure a prison interview with Rader. Within weeks, she made an arrangement with Jossey-Bass, an imprint of John Wiley & Sons, to publish the book, and I soon embarked on my odyssey into the dark, twisted mind of Dennis Rader.

At the time, I had no idea just how rough that journey would be. It quickly became plagued by so many problems — both personal and political — that I began to lose hope of ever getting my questions answered. My supposedly perfect story soon emerged as the most arduous, frustrating one I'd ever experienced, researched, and written.

Yet by the time it was all over, I'd become the only author to talk to Rader. Part of the reason was that Rader wanted to talk to me. He knew me and my work very well and was anxious to communicate about it.

I found out that during the years Dennis Rader had been leading his Jekyll-and-Hyde existence, he'd read many of my books. In one of them, *Obsession,* published in 1998, he had read my profile of BTK.

He apparently found what I'd written intriguing, and nine months after his arrest, he wrote a critique of my analysis. I eventually read it while I was researching this book; it proved both fascinating and disturbing.

What you're about to read is a story of a haunting journey through the mind of one of America's most elusive serial killers. In researching this book on BTK, I was handed the keys and invited into the kingdom of his convoluted, empty, and horrific inner world. I entered his life, his point of view, his relationships, and the world he lived in. Besides speaking with his friends, confidants, and others whose lives intersected with Rader's, I spent a year getting to know a number of law enforcement officials who had tracked this killer for decades. They led me through the actual places — Rader's home and office, the rooms and streets, the basements and automobiles and phone booths — and every aspect of their investigation into the killings that terrorized the Wichita community.

But most revealing of all, they granted me a rare glimpse into the reams of evidence seized from Rader's house and office after his arrest. Never in my career had I been given access to such an enormous stash. It was mind blowing. The material, which included Rader's personal journals, drawings, Polaroid snapshots, and written accounts of his crimes, provided me with a startling, often sickening look at this cold, calculating killer.

Climbing inside the heads of monsters is my specialty. It was something I did on a daily basis during my twenty-five-year tenure with the FBI. My work there — along with the research I continue to do — allowed me to understand killers like Rader far better than they themselves could ever hope to. With this book, I've pushed my criminology skills in entirely new directions in order to do the following:

1. Tell the story of why Rader started killing
2. Describe how he was able to so effectively compartmentalize his life
3. Explain why — at the peak of his ability to terrorize — he seemingly disappeared into the shadows
4. Detail how the police caught him and what we've learned from him that can help us catch serial killers sooner, before they can become the next BTK

If you've read my books before, you know that education and prevention are the cornerstones of my writings. I want people to understand that Rader — and those like him — don't happen overnight. As he told me in our exclusive prison interview, he not only had become obsessed by violent thoughts at a very young age but had already begun acting them out while still a young boy.

I truly believe that parents and teachers should be able to recognize certain behavioral "red flags," alerting us that a potentially dangerous problem is festering.

In the end, Rader proved a horrifying but fascinating study, allowing me to glimpse an altogether new variation of the homicidal mind. Having said that, it makes me sick that he was able to escape the ultimate punishment he deserved and not be executed for his heinous crimes.

Shortly before noted serial killer Ted Bundy was electrocuted in 1989, a group of behavioral scientists wanted me to make a public announcement that Bundy should be studied and not put to death. They were less than thrilled when I told them, "It would only take a few days to study Ted Bundy. After that, he should receive his just rewards."

I'm glad Dennis Rader lived long enough to speak with me and provide me with the answers I first started asking back in 1974.

But about what happens to him now, I truly could not care less. Perhaps he'll commit suicide? Or maybe a fellow inmate, hoping to acquire a bit of notoriety in prison circles, will snuff out his sad, empty life?

Whatever fate awaits Rader, the chronicle of his days, the exclusive account of his crimes, and the exploration into his mind are waiting for you in the pages of this book. I trust you'll find the odyssey of this enigmatic killer both terrifying and enlightening.

It's a story I've been waiting to tell for more than three decades.

■ ■ ■ ■

ACT ONE
MY LIFELONG HUNT
FOR BTK

■ ■ ■ ■

1

Somewhere inside my head, the murder played itself out the way it always did in my dreams. His hands were wrapped around her throat — patiently, relentlessly squeezing the life away from her. Blood vessels in the whites of her eyes ruptured from the pressure building up inside her head, creating hemorrhages that resembled faint red and yellow flowers.

She never thought it would end like this. But then who really does? And still he continued to squeeze. His hands and fingers were powerful enough to prevent the blood from flowing through the carotid arteries that snaked up either side of her neck. But to compress the vertebral arteries that allowed the blood to drain from her brain, he needed to twist her head at just the correct angle. So he lifted her torso a few inches off the mattress and went about his business. It was almost over — even amid the chaos, she could

sense this. So she used what remained of her strength to try to claw his face. But he'd already considered that option and had tied her arms and legs to the wooden bedposts. She never laid a finger on him.

After a few more moments, her hyoid bone cracked. The sound was similar to that of a twig snapping. It was only a matter of time now. A spasm-like shudder rippled through her nude body, followed by a trickle of blood dripping from her nostrils . . .

"Jesus," I muttered, sitting up in bed, wiping the sweat from my eyes. "I gotta get a grip."

My heart was pounding, thumping madly. For a moment, I wondered if I was having a heart attack, but the vision of the strangled woman's face quickly returned. Just another god-awful nightmare.

That face — I'd been seeing that face and hundreds like it for the past couple years now. Almost every night they came to visit me when I fell asleep. Each was in the midst of being brutally murdered — strangled, stabbed, shot, beaten, poisoned. All of them were people I'd come to know only after they'd been killed.

Welcome to my life, circa October 1984. For the past five years I'd worked myself to the point of physical and mental exhaustion

while helping create the FBI's elite criminal profiling unit. Back when I started with the bureau in 1970, criminal profiling was seen as a bunch of snake oil, something spoken about only in whispers. But over the course of the next decade and a half, I and a few other visionary, bullheaded souls like Bob Ressler and Roy Hazelwood had worked tirelessly to prove that criminal personality profiling could provide a legitimate, effective crime-fighting tool. Investigators from police departments around the globe turned to me and my unit after they'd hit a brick wall. We examined crime scenes and created profiles of the perpetrators, describing their habits and predicting their next moves.

I was addicted to my job as the leader of the FBI's Investigative Support Unit (ISU) and over the years had immersed myself in thousands of the nation's most grisly homicides and other violent interpersonal crime cases. I'd poured over mountains of crime scene reports and scrutinized stacks of photos that sometimes made me physically ill. I hunted some of the most sadistic and notorious criminals in the nation — the Trailside Killer in San Francisco, the Atlanta child murderer, the Tylenol poisoner, and the man who hunted prostitutes for sport in the Alaskan wilderness.

In an effort to understand the motives and motivation of the killers we were trying to catch, I — along with my colleagues — met face-to-face with dozens of serial murderers and assassins, including Charles Manson, Sirhan Sirhan, Arthur Bremmer, Richard Speck, John Wayne Gacy, David Berkowitz (Son of Sam), and James Earl Ray. The findings of these interviews became part of a landmark study into what makes serial killers tick and, in 1988, it was published as a book: *Sexual Homicide: Patterns and Motives.*

Up until then, no one had ever thought to undertake this type of research from an investigative perspective. It had always been done by psychologists, psychiatrists, or parole officers. But I was convinced that those of us with a police background had the ability to understand the mind of an incarcerated felon far better than any psychologist or psychiatrist. We possess a type of street smarts that can't be learned out of a book or a classroom. We can listen to a suspect's words, but we also know how the mind of the criminal works.

I worked much like a physician — only all my patients had usually either been murdered or raped by the time I got to them. And instead of studying their medical history in an effort to cure their disease, I reviewed crime scenes, forensic evidence, and the victim's background (this work is known as victimology), trying to better understand what kind of person could have committed a particular crime. It was only after we answered those questions that we could prescribe a course of action that investigators should take.

Over the years, our work helped police crack plenty of cases and put countless sick, dangerous people behind bars. But it wasn't without a heavy price. I could never turn down any request for help on an investigation. My caseload quickly became so overwhelming that I worked myself past the point of exhaustion.

In early December 1983, while in the Seattle area trying to come up with a profile of the so-called Green River serial murderer, I collapsed in my hotel room from viral encephalitis. For three days, unbeknownst to anyone, I lay on the floor in a coma, my body racked by a 105-degree fever with a Do Not Disturb sign hanging on my door.

After they found me, I hovered in that strange purgatory between life and death. The right side of my brain had ruptured and hemorrhaged. I wouldn't survive the high fever raging within my body, the specialists explained to my wife.

A grave was reserved for me at Quantico National Cemetery. A priest administered my last rites. But I somehow managed to hold on to life. My family, along with friends and fellow agents, kept a weeklong vigil in my hospital room, occasionally encircling my bed and holding hands while praying for me.

After I emerged from my coma, the left side of my face drooped, my speech was horribly slurred, and blood clots formed in my lungs and legs. In an effort to control my seizures, I was given phobarital, then Dilantin. After I left the hospital and returned home to Virginia, my body slowly went to work mending itself.

Yet before long I began to sense that something was different about me; something seemed amiss. I'd awoken from my coma a different man. I found myself looking at the world in a new way. It wasn't obvious to anyone but me. It was so subtle at first that I barely realized what was happening.

I'd begun to identify with the victim. I still wanted to catch the monsters and slap them behind bars. But it was my newfound propensity to identify with the victim of violent crimes that began changing the way I looked at the world. I started seeing things through the eyes of those who, for whatever reason, had their lives stolen away from them by another. It wasn't long before I began to understand — viscerally, from the inside — the horror that comes with being murdered, beaten, or raped.

This newfound shift in perspective hardly came as a surprise. In my own way, I'd become a victim of my own obsessive-compulsive way of doing my job. Weeks after arriving home from the hospital, I still felt vulnerable, weak, and overwrought with emotion that something like this could happen to *John Douglas.* A few months before, I was at the top of my game — thirty-eight years old, strong as an ox, focused, motivated, and driven. I had a beautiful wife and two adorable little girls, and I felt blessed to be forging a name for myself in a career I loved. Nothing could stop me. Or so I thought. On that cool autumn night in October 1984 when I woke from my nightmare, I was on the mend. After a few unstable months, I could now walk, run, and lift weights.

My mind, however, was another story. As much as I hated to admit it, I was a psychological wreck. A few weeks before, I'd begun driving out to Quantico National Cemetery to sit by the grave where I was supposed to have been buried, wondering who had taken my spot in the ground. Try as I might, I couldn't shake my anger at the FBI for not giving me the support I'd needed to perform my job, for fostering a work environment where you had to literally drop from exhaustion before anyone would ever step forward to help you.

I pushed myself up from the bed, shoved my feet into a pair of slippers, plodded downstairs into my study, and closed the doors behind me. It had been a long day, and it was turning out to be another long, sleepless night. I collapsed into my leather chair and polished off what remained in the wine glass on my desk. I'd returned to my job at Quantico the previous April, but I was still a raw nerve, still trying to come to grips with the inescapable fact that my brain couldn't work the way it used to.

Earlier that afternoon, two detectives from the Wichita Police Department arrived at FBI headquarters, hoping I might have some answers for them. They'd read my 1979 analysis of the BTK case and wanted to discuss the latest developments in my research that would allow them to finally nab this heinous killer. We sat down in a conference room, and they walked me through a case that had stumped their department for the past decade. Almost seven years had passed since his last known murder.

As I listened, I felt my focus and confidence return. For the next eight hours, my brain ran on autopilot, soaking up every fact and bit of data the two detectives tossed at me. The sensation wouldn't last, I knew. But it was nice, all the same — it reminded me of who I used to be.

Despite my having recently returned to work after months of being on sick leave, I already had an enormous caseload. So did the six wannabe profilers assigned to me, whom I'd handpicked because of their impeccable reputations as investigators. But I could sense how much pressure the Wichita police were under from their community to take this killer off the street, so I decided we owed it to them to carve out some time in our overcrowded schedules to see how we could help.

The facts behind BTK's killings went like this:

In January 1974, he strangled Joseph Otero, thirty-eight; his wife, Julie, thirty-four; and son Joey, nine. The partially nude body of Josephine, eleven, was discovered hanging from a water pipe in the basement. A large amount of semen was found on her leg.

In October, the local paper received a detailed letter from someone claiming to have killed the Otero family. In March 1977, Shirley Vian, twenty-four, was found strangled, with her hands and feet bound. The killer had locked her children in the bathroom. In all likelihood he would have killed them, but was scared away by a ringing telephone. In December 1977, BTK telephoned a police dispatcher to inform police about his latest murder — twenty-five-year-old Nancy Fox, whose body was found strangled on her bed. The next month, the killer sent a letter about the killing to the local paper — although it wasn't discovered for almost two weeks. In February 1978, he sent another letter to a local TV station, gloating over his killing of Vian and Fox, along with another unnamed victim.

In April 1979, he waited inside the home of a sixty-three-year-old woman, but eventually left before she returned home. Not long afterwards, he sent his intended target a letter, informing her that he'd chosen her as his next victim, but had opted not to kill her after growing tired of waiting for her to arrive home.

The local cops had exhausted all their leads. But in the five years since I'd last reviewed the case, investigators had managed to link another homicide to him. In April 1974, three months after the Otero killings, Kathryn Bright, a twenty-one-year-old assembly line worker, was stabbed to death in her home. Despite being shot twice in the head, her nineteen-year-old brother survived the attack. The detectives briefing me believed that having another case to link to BTK, especially one with a survivor, might help shed some new light on the UNSUB responsible for the murders.

From my knowledge of the case and of the Wichita Police Department, widely regarded in law enforcement circles as one of the most progressive in the nation, I was confident that the police hadn't botched this investigation. Yet the killer was still on the loose, and this worried everybody.

Why, everyone wondered, had he stopped killing? What had happened to him? I sensed he was still out there. But he'd become a ghost, which was why the task force created by Wichita police a few months before, in July 1984, had been named the Ghostbusters. I had a hunch that the only way we could catch this ghost would be to find some way to flush him out, to develop some sort of a strategy to force him out into the light where we could finally see him.

■ ■ ■ ■

I rummaged through a few drawers in my hopelessly messy desk, looking for the criminal profile I'd written for police back in 1979, but I couldn't locate it.

"Probably back at the office," I mumbled to myself.

And then it suddenly came rushing back to me — the memory of that night three years ago in 1981, when I used BTK to help pry information out of the head of one of the nation's most notorious serial killers. It happened in a pale green interrogation room deep inside the Attica Correctional Facility, with fellow FBI profiler Bob Ressler.

It was evening, the loneliest time inside a prison. We'd arrived unannounced, on a fishing expedition of sorts, hoping to convince David Berkowitz, aka the Son of Sam, to help us with our criminal profiling study, which involved a fifty-seven-page interview questionnaire. We wanted answers to such questions as *What was his motive? Was there a trigger that set him off on his murderous spree? What was his early childhood like? How did he select his victims? Did he ever visit the grave sites of his victims? How closely did he follow the press coverage of his crimes?*

His answers would help us better understand the killers we were hunting.

Berkowitz was three years into his 365-year prison term after trying unsuccessfully to convince a jury that his neighbor's Labrador retriever had commanded him to gun down his six victims. He looked surprised to see us when the guards led him into the tiny interrogation room.

"Who are you guys?" he asked the moment he spotted us seated at the far end of the only piece of furniture in the room — a linoleum-covered table. As planned, the guards had quickly exited before Berkowitz had a chance to tell us to take a hike.

"We're FBI agents, David," I told him. "We'd like to talk to you. We're hoping you might be able to help us." Berkowitz wheeled around toward where he expected the guards to be, but because they were no longer there, he begrudgingly took a seat.

"It's like I always say," I explained, "if you want to learn how to paint, you don't read about it in a book. You go straight to the artist. And that's what you are, David. You're the artist."

I was laying it on, but, I hoped, not too thick. Berkowitz stared at me with his aquamarine eyes. He didn't smile. He didn't even blink. Inside his head, he was trying to figure out some way to get something in return for talking to us.

"I'll speak to the warden," I said, trying to head off his question. "I can't make any promises. But if you agree to talk to us, I'll tell him how helpful you've been."

He nodded slightly, looking past us at the cinder-block wall behind our backs. I didn't have much time. He seemed about thirty seconds away from shouting out to the guards to get back in here and take him back to his cell.

"Why me?" he asked. "I ain't no artist."

"What in the hell are you talking about?" I laughed. "You're famous. You're huge. You had all of New York City scared shitless. In a hundred years, no one will remember my name. But everybody will still know who the Son of Sam was." Berkowitz listened, but he didn't seem all that impressed with the bull-shit I was spoon-feeding him.

Like all the killers I'd interviewed, he longed to have his ego stroked — the prob-lem was, I wasn't particularly stroking him the way he liked. I was losing him. He turned to see if the guards had returned yet, but of course they hadn't. So he spun back around and fixed his gaze on me.

We stared at each other in silence for a few moments. The fluorescent lights overhead cast a green tint on Berkowitz's pale, pudgy skin. A year earlier, another inmate had slit his throat with a razor. The scar, which snaked a jagged path across his neck, had required sixty stitches to close. It glowed an unhealthy shade of pink.

"You know, David, there's a serial killer out in Kansas, a guy responsible for the deaths of at least six people, who idolizes you," I told him. "He's mentioned you in the letters he writes to the police. He fancies himself just like you. He even wants a name like you."

Berkowitz's eyes were suddenly ablaze with curiosity. His look of boredom had been replaced with a smirk.

"Is he shitting me?" he asked, glancing over at my partner.

"It's the truth," replied Ressler, quietly.

"He calls himself BTK," I explained.

"BTK?" Berkowitz said. "What's that for?"

"Bind, torture, and kill. That's what he does to his victims."

Berkowitz nodded. "And this BTK, he's still out there?" he asked. "You guys haven't caught him yet?"

"No," I said. "But we will."

Berkowitz laughed, and I slowly walked him through BTK's various murders, describing how he'd kill and then disappear for years at a stretch. He listened, spellbound, unable to fathom how someone so blood-thirsty could exhibit such restraint. I could tell by the way his eyes locked onto me that he was soaking up every word I told him. *How can this guy control his appetite like that?* he appeared to be thinking. To a killer like Berkowitz, whose reign of terror lasted a mere thirteen months, this serial killer in Wichita was a criminal with enviable endurance — a virtual marathoner of mayhem.

After a few minutes spent listening to BTK's exploits, the man we'd come to interrogate turned to putty in our hands. Over the next five hours, he walked us through every dark, twisted corner of his sad life, sharing details he'd never told anyone, confiding that he'd made up all the crap about demons in order to be able to cop an insanity plea if he ever got caught. By the time Ressler and I emerged from the interrogation room, our heads were spinning. And we owed it all to some deranged killer in Wichita.

The clock on my bookshelf read two-thirty. Upstairs, my wife slept like a baby. My two little girls were tucked away in their beds. The house was so quiet that even down here in my study I could make out the soft rhythm of my wife's breathing. It reminded me of surf breaking on the beach where I used to hang out as kid, growing up on Long Island.

I was jealous of her peace. And as I sat there listening to the make-believe waves, I felt another pang of jealousy rise up inside me. *How,* I wondered just like Berkowitz, *could a guy like BTK just turn it on and off like he did?*

I'd already concluded that one of the reasons he'd managed to elude us was his consummate ability to compartmentalize his life — to appear normal on the outside and keep his perverted, murderous alter ego locked up inside. He'd somehow found a way to prevent his dark inner world from seeping out and infecting his outer world.

I was dying to know how he'd managed to do it. *When they catch this son of a bitch,* I thought to myself, *I'm gonna look him up and get him to tell me.*

Inside my briefcase were the notes I'd penciled from my meeting earlier that day with the two detectives from Wichita. Together with a group of my profilers and a handful of the agency's top criminologists, we listened as the men walked us through the case. This time they'd come to us looking not so much for a profile of the UNSUB, but for some proactive techniques they could use to flush the killer out into the open.

After we listened to the presentation, the one idea that came to mind was that police should organize a community-wide public meeting where the BTK murders would be discussed. The purpose of the gathering, held in a location central to all the crime scenes, would be to get the UNSUB to attend. From my experience with many of the serial killers I'd hunted in the past, I knew that their enormous egos and feeling of invincible superiority make it difficult for them to stay away from such meetings.

My plan was that investigators would covertly photograph those in attendance and identify all the vehicles outside the community hall. And because I was convinced that the killer was a police buff, I suggested that an announcement should be made that the authorities were looking for potential volunteers "if the need should arise in the future when the police might need help." The only requirements were that the applicants needed their own transportation and some law enforcement training or education.

The two detectives from Wichita scribbled down my suggestion, but it ate at me that there was something more that could be done, something altogether new.

■ ■ ■ ■

Sitting there in my study, all I could think about were the eyes of Josephine Otero, BTK's eleven-year-old victim in his first series of murders, the one he'd hung from a pipe in the basement of her family's house, after strangling her parents and younger brother. Nothing in my career could ever prepare me for what I imagined this innocent little girl must have endured before finally dying of asphyxiation. I'd worked more child homicide cases than I cared to remember, but something about this one was different.

This killer didn't feel human to me. All the guys I'd chased and studied were monsters, but even with the worst of them I usually sensed something familiar and human. No matter how horrific their butchery, I found some shred of fragility within them. But I didn't get that with this killer in Wichita. Just when I thought I'd studied and classified every variation of evil, along comes this freak. He resided in a class all by himself.

I wandered back upstairs and climbed into bed. Before long, I felt myself begin to drift, but I fought the urge, trying to remain in that strange region between wakefulness and sleep. It was a place where I'd sometimes retrieved the information that helped me put together a profile. I waited for my mind to unearth something on the ghost I was chasing, but nothing came.

After a few minutes, my lids grew unbearably heavy. *How does someone like this start?* I whispered to myself as I began to fade. *And how can I put an end to him?*

2

The sun had yet to appear in the sky when I awoke the next morning, a few hours after finally drifting back to sleep. Out of habit, I quickly rolled over to check the legal pad sitting on my bedside table. Years before, I'd trained myself to dream about whatever case I was working on. More often than not, in the middle of the night, still half asleep, I'd open my eyes, fumble for a pen, and scribble cryptic notes on the pad, clues culled from the depths of my subconscious. My wife, Pam, hated this habit of mine because it always woke her up.

But on this chilly fall morning, the top page appeared blank. I switched on a lamp, just to make sure my eyes weren't playing tricks on me. Pam moaned. I turned off the light, got dressed in the darkness, and drove the winding twenty-one miles to my office at Quantico, located on the main floor of the agency's forensic science building. The location was a definite upgrade from the previous home of the Behavioral Science Unit — in the basement beneath the FBI Academy's library. But the downside was that my office was constantly awash with nauseous, chemical fumes from the various laboratories in the building. On any given day, researchers attempting to develop more reliable, valid methods for testing crime evidence would tinker with various types of acid, iodine fumes, and gunpowder. Explosions and eye-burning smoke were commonplace. So were clanging fire alarms and evacuations of our building.

I was the first guy in the office as usual, making it to my desk by 6:30 A.M. The first thing I did was close my office door so that no one would think I was there. I lived for the cases and loathed the unavoidable administrative duties that came with running a unit that was on the verge of mushrooming to forty-three people, including twelve FBI agents and twenty-one support personnel. I was constantly at odds with the paper-pushers above me, but the men and women of my unit knew I'd do anything for them. In between hopping from one brush fire to the next, I often spent hours each day either helping them with their work or providing a shoulder to cry on.

It was nearly noon by the time I began rifling through my filing cabinets, trying to locate the profile I'd written on BTK back in 1979. As I dug through my files, I thought back to that day in fall 1974 when I first heard about BTK from a couple of veteran homicide detectives who worked for the Milwaukee PD. Although it wasn't part of my job description, I was itching to gain experience in the science of murder investigation. That night in 1974, I dug up what I could find on this unknown killer in Wichita at the public library. I was amazed that news of his murders hadn't received more play in newspapers outside of Kansas and noticed that the local cops appeared to be keeping a tight lid on information about the case.

A few months afterwards, I wrote about BTK in a research paper for one of my graduate courses in abnormal psychology. In it, I noted that other mass murder cases, such as Charles Whitman (the Texas Tower sniper in Austin) and Richard Speck in Chicago, garnered national headlines, whereas the Otero family homicides received precious little play. I found myself seeing parallels to professional sports and how the athletes all want to play in the big media venues like New York, Chicago, and Los Angeles. I wondered if BTK felt slighted by the lack of attention his killings were receiving and frustrated that he lived in such a backwater media market.

I eventually unearthed my BTK file from beneath a sheaf of similar profiles penned over the past few years. Three pages long, with a cover sheet stapled on top, it read, "The attached analysis is only as good as the information that has been provided. In addition, it may be necessary to totally change or modify this analysis if new information is developed — such as additional victims, more forensic evidence, or new information obtained from research."

I rolled my chair up tight against my desk and laid the pages down on top of the clutter. As I began reading the words I'd typed years before, I felt it all coming back to me:

MULTIPLE HOMICIDES. WICHITA. The murders of the BTK Strangler are the result of a fantasy acted out. A fantasy where for the first time in his life, he is in a position of importance and dominance. He is an inadequate type, a nobody, who, through his crimes, has placed himself into a position of importance. The BTK Strangler is now a somebody who is receiving the recognition he feels is long overdue him. To show his inadequacies, he is not even very original in his crimes. He must pattern himself after other notorious killers such as the .44 caliber killer, better known as the "Son of Sam" in New York City. Much of the verbiage that your subject is using (in his letters) probably comes out of recent publications in detective magazines.

Your subject is alienated, lonely and withdrawn. He would not be expected to have any lasting relationships with others and would lead a solitary existence dominated as mentioned above — by fantasy and magical thinking. His killing is an attempt on his part to find affection and acceptance. He fears everyone, including himself. He would not be expected to have ever enjoyed any normal relations with women and probably has never had a normal heterosexual relationship with one. When he is not killing, he experiences intense fear that he is not "normal" and therefore kills to cope with his disorder in an attempt to escape from his own fantasies. Thus, he can be expected to kill again and to do so in a compulsive repetition of the pattern he has already established. His victims can be anyone either male or female, who are both loved and outgoing. His victims will be in a position of vulnerability, one where he can totally render them helpless. His victims represent his own feelings of helplessness and hopelessness. His own life has been disruptive. He probably comes from a background where his family was broken. He was raised by an overbearing mother who was inconsistent with her discipline. His father probably left home, either by marital separation or death, when he was a youth. Your subject may have been raised by foster parents.

Your subject was an average student in the classroom. However, he was more adept at disrupting the class by using profanity and pranks. His language and statements make us believe that he has some military experience and/or is a police buff. He probably has had run-ins with police in the past, such as assault, and/or breaking and entering (B&E). His involvement with B&Es will show that the items taken were of insignificance. Items taken were more for reason of a fetish or a strong urge to obtain an article of clothing that he is fond of — or the thrill of committing a crime that will leave little evidence to investigating officers. The BTK Strangler may have a history of voyeuristic activities and he may have an arrest record for same. He hunts his victims by selecting neighborhoods where he can peruse different homes without being detected. Furthermore, his victims will live in an area where, if need be, he can have an easy escape route, such as a neighborhood park, where he can secrete himself to elude the police.

His killings are impulsively motivated and without elaborate planning. He seeks out targets of opportunity. Such individuals of this type are frequently mechanically adept. They suffer from insomnia and thus would find difficult to hold steady employment. Control of himself and of his environment is essential for such a person. Although he is gaining in confidence, he is still shy, withdrawn, asocial and isolated. Such persons have typically been raised in overly strict and religious fashions.

As a counter strategy technique, your department must not make any statements concerning the killer's mental condition. That is to say, don't allow the media to label him as some psychotic killer. If they have already done so, your best strategy would be to align yourself with the killer and not the psychiatric experts. Any press releases should clearly state that he is a killer who must be apprehended and that he is not a psychotic animal, if the press has already painted him to be this. This approach may reduce the killer's anxiety concerning his own psychiatric health and reinforce his own guilt feelings by removing the rationalization of the excuse of psychiatric cause and hence non-responsibility for his acts.

Extended periods between his murders may be for reasons when he was absent from the area either as a result of military service, schooling, incarceration, or mental treatment. It is not uncommon for subjects such as yours to frequent police hangouts in an attempt to overhear officers discussing the case. Furthermore, such offenders will be at the crime scene observing detectives investigating the case and looking for clues to the homicide. All this allows the murderer to fulfill his ego and gain a feeling of superiority. He may go so far as to telephonically contact your department and provide information relative to the crime.

Your advantage in this case is that his very strong self-centered attitude will be his downfall. He will provide information to a friend or an acquaintance in a local tavern concerning information that he knows about the case. He may even pretend to be an officer working the case. If the BTK Strangler reads police detective magazines, he probably sent away for a "police badge" that he carries on his person. In fact, he may even use this MO to gain admittance into his victims' homes. He probably flashes his badge whenever opportunity lends itself. (Example paying for a drink in a tavern.) His egocentricity keeps him in your city and he will probably kill again.

Reading an analysis I'd written five years before was nerve wracking. Of course, it was just a thumbnail sketch of what I'd told police when I'd contacted them on the phone, shortly after I'd sent it back to Wichita in 1979. Even though I firmly believed I'd nailed this guy dead-on, I was constantly asking myself if I'd missed something or placed too much the emphasis on the wrong bit of evidence. The pressure to get it right was overwhelming. Knowing that what I wrote could send investigators off in the wrong direction, which could indirectly result in more dead bodies, weighed heavily on me. It was one of the reasons I was so obsessive about my work.

The key to writing the kind of analysis that actually helps investigators do their job is deceptively simple, but it's something that takes years to teach. In fact, it was only after five years of in-depth training and analysis that I considered one of my wannabes to be an expert. The most important thing is not just to regurgitate back to the police the data they already know.

My profiles were rarely more than five pages. I always ended them with a simple request that investigators pick up the phone and call me. This was why I never inserted any proactive techniques — on how to catch the bad guys — into our reports. I feared that whatever I wrote might get leaked to the press.

In this case, however, I had a hunch that the best use of my expertise would be to develop some proactive recipes to flush this killer out of the woodwork. He'd manipulated the police and the community long enough. The time had come to return the favor and begin messing with his mind. The only question was, *How the hell do we do it?*

I decided to skip lunch, gather up all my notes on the case, and walk over to the third floor of a nearby building on the FBI campus. This was where the bureau's legal unit did all its research, and I loved to sit up there in the library and gaze out through the massive windows at the green, rolling Virginia countryside. The view of all those oak and maple trees, along with all that sunlight, was definitely a hell of a lot more conducive to clear thought than an often foul-smelling office in the forensic science building. Up there, surrounded by all that blue sky and those green treetops, things just felt different.

I organized the crime scene reports and my extensive notes in front of me in neat piles on the table — one stack for each series of murders. I knew that somewhere within those stacks of paper there existed a single, simple fact, a piece of evidence — either physical or verbal — that I might be able to use against the UNSUB. It wasn't enough for me to simply serve up some ideas that I believed might prove useful in the case. I was consumed by the idea of helping police find a way of taking this killer down. Before coming up with an effective proactive strategy, I wanted to force-feed all the gruesome, mundane details of the case into my brain one last time. The white eight-by-twelve-inch piles bulged off the table, resembling four freshly dug graves covered with snow.

The first thing that came to mind was that the cops in Wichita had done everything right. They'd interviewed thousands of people and tracked down countless potential suspects (including a former police officer), none of whom turned out to be the right guy. For the past four months, the department's recently assembled task force, composed of six detectives, had sifted through the mountains of old case files that had accumulated over the last decade, familiarizing themselves with every convoluted twist and turn the case had taken.

One thing was certain: our UNSUB was in the driver's seat. Not only that, he had grown smarter with every kill and seemed to enjoy toying with the police. But perhaps the most unnerving thing about BTK was how he seemed to defy so much of what we took for granted about serial sexual killers. The one thing different we knew about him now that we didn't in 1979 was that three months after the Otero homicides, he had been responsible for the messy, nearly botched murder of Kathryn Bright.

Kathy Bright's brother, Kevin, who miraculously survived the attacked despite being shot twice in the face, described how his sister's killer attempted to convince them that he was a fugitive. He would, of course, need to tie them up, BTK told them. But all he really wanted was some food, money, and their car keys. Then he'd be on his way. Rader lived only a short distance from Kathy and

Kevin, and had no intention of leaving them unharmed.

Having a living witness provide a firsthand account of the killer's technique for calming and lulling his potential victims into allowing him to tie them up gave us a priceless bit of insight into how the UNSUB carried out his crimes. His homicides were difficult to pigeonhole because they possessed elements of both organization and disorganization. He was a control freak who came prepared, often arriving at the homes of his victims with rope, gags, guns, and a knife. He didn't use force to convince his victims to go along with him. He used bullshit. He pretended to be a relatively harmless thug, using words to manipulate his victims into allowing themselves to be tied up, usually without any struggle.

But he also left some things to chance. If his intended victim wasn't available, he would strike the next best target he could find. On several occasions, it appeared he had difficulty controlling his victims. And he was hardly the neatest killer I'd encountered, leaving behind semen near the bodies of two of his kills.

Then there was his peculiar way of posing his victims. I'd never come across another killer who did it the way he did. He primped and preened the bodies in erotic positions, clothing, and bindings as fuel for his masturbatory fantasies. But he had also laid out and displayed nearly all the bodies of his victims — except for Kathy Bright, who died of stab wounds — for the investigators who arrived at his crime scenes long after he'd fled.

It was as if he positioned the corpses the way a florist might arrange flowers. He wanted to shock, yet his visual statements were also fairly tame and modest — at least in terms of the work I'd seen other sociopathic serial killers leave behind. Compared to those maniacs who left severed heads propped up on TV sets or their victims spread-eagled on the floor with various objects inserted into their vaginas or rectums, UNSUB was downright juvenile and soft core. Nevertheless, he used his victims as inanimate props, posing them to resemble a scene out of the pages of a detective magazine, leaving them out in the open so that the first person to discover the body would practically trip over it when entering the front door of the victim's home.

Without a doubt, BTK was a sadist who inflicted unfathomable horrors upon his victims. Yet he also differed from all the other sexual sadists I'd studied, guys who needed to inflict physical torture in order to be sexually satisfied. He got off by employing a form of torture that was predominantly mental, not physical. Although he seemed obsessed with physical torture, it wasn't part of what's referred to as his "signature," which is what a killer must do to satisfy himself psychologically. BTK's signature was bondage — not physical torture.

BTK never penetrated any of his victims. It would have been easy to interpret this type of behavior as though he were trying to say *You're not even good enough for me to rape.* But I knew better.

His decision to not rape his victims or engage in necrophilia actually told me that despite BTK's sexual obsessions, deep inside his mind he felt hopelessly inadequate. His opinion of himself was so low — and his fear of women so great — that he could never bring himself to thrust himself so intimately into any of his victims. They were used purely as props. Masturbation was the only sexual activity he enjoyed during his binding, torture, and killing.

When I thought of the UNSUB as a boy, I couldn't imagine that he had ever raped anyone, which was unlike a lot of sexual predators. I did imagine him learning his craft as a Peeping Tom. If nothing else, this youthful pastime gave him a priceless crash course in surveillance techniques. Monitoring and studying his victims were absolutely crucial to him. He seemed to love the thrill of the hunt probably even more than the actual killing. By the time he actually did strike, he'd spent so much time fantasizing over what he intended to do to his victim that he'd convinced himself that he controlled every aspect of their environment.

As for his victims, he told police in the handful of taunting communiqués he'd sent over the years that he chose them based on both planning and spur-of-the-moment opportunity. His intended victims had to be available when the overpowering urge to kill struck. If they weren't, he moved on to another target.

There was something else: judging from the way he managed to keep his crime scenes so relatively free of fingerprints and other incriminating evidence, he was an extremely well-organized person, someone fixated on detail. Inwardly he was an insecure, self-hating wreck. Outwardly, however, he exuded a pompous attitude that made it appear as though he possessed a grandiose opinion of himself. It was another one of his crazy, sick paradoxes.

What I also found interesting were those communications he'd sent police over the years, boasting of his prowess as a killer and his ability to elude law enforcement. From the language he used, he was obviously both fascinated by cop subculture and investigative procedure and quite familiar with them. I was convinced that he was either employed in some form of law enforcement, probably low down in rank or status, like a security guard or parking violation officer, or just got off dreaming about the power such a job could bestow on him.

As is often the case with serial killers, his slayings were the most important undertakings of his life, imbuing his otherwise empty existence with meaning. From his letters, it seemed obvious that he was a nobody who, because of his unfathomable savagery, suddenly felt like a celebrity. He'd become addicted to seeing his crimes written about in the newspaper and discussed on TV. I bet that hearing others discuss his killings proved almost as thrilling and satisfying as committing the crimes themselves.

Although he had killed men and children, it seemed obvious that women were his primary targets. Everyone else just happened to be in the wrong place at the wrong time. I believed that deep down, he loathed women. Whatever conflicts he'd had with them, as well as with society, were released through the murders he committed. Within his troubled mind, he took no responsibility for his actions. He was clearly in some state of depression, unable to genuinely love or be loved. As a result, his life was one in which he must seek out excitement and drama in order to feel alive. And although he was able to put up a good front to others, the world he lived for — and lived in — had nothing to do with reality. It was based purely on the sadistic fantasies inside his brain.

By his own admission, BTK took trinkets from the homes of his victims. He used them as fuel for his fantasies. I felt confident that they were one of the few things that quieted his head, which is why he needed to collect and preserve the trophies of his conquests, taken from his crime scenes. Having the personal possessions of his victims reminded him of his "glory days." I imagined that all he needed to do to relive one of his kills was hold his victim's belongings in his hands. Each homicide brought with it a psychological high that would quickly evaporate, always leaving him alone with his depressed thoughts. His trophies and keepsakes no doubt proved a bit more effective at keeping the depression away. But the peace these ghostly mementos brought never completely removed his feelings of depression and anxiety.

The question that stumped me and everybody else involved in the case was this: *Why had so many years lapsed since his last murder?* I couldn't understand it. Every time I pondered the question, I came up with another theory. All of them made sense. None of them I could prove.

Perhaps he'd been picked up on some unrelated charge and was now rotting in a prison cell or mental institution? Or could the police have gotten too close to him during one of the various phases of their investigation? Maybe they even interviewed him as a potential suspect, and the experience might have proved too unnerving for this otherwise unflappable sociopath?

One thing was certain — serial sexual predators don't wake up one morning, decide to turn over a new leaf, and start their lives over. For all I knew, he could have been killed in a car wreck, although I had a hunch that we weren't going to get off that easy. Someone as sick and dangerous as BTK will stop killing only when he is killed or gets locked behind bars. My research had proven to me that this is the only way to rein in these guys. Rehabilitation is a fairy tale.

Which I suppose was the most unbearable

part of being involved in this case — knowing in my gut that that if he were alive, BTK would resume his killing. Somewhere out there, there was a family whose future was on the verge of becoming a living hell. If you've ever seen the blank, numb look on the face of someone whose loved one has just been murdered, you know that it stays with you forever. Just as BTK had stayed with me throughout my career at the FBI.

I joined the agency in 1970, four years before the first BTK killings, a twenty-five-year-old rookie agent working the streets of inner-city Detroit. Like most idealistic young agents (and I was one of the youngest ever hired), I'd convinced myself that I was going to make Motor City safer by helping put the bad guys behind bars, a crusade I imagined the citizens would applaud. It didn't take long before I realized how the residents living in my "beat" felt about my presence in their neighborhood.

The Detroit area had been nearly leveled by the 1967 race riots that left forty-three people dead. When I joined the FBI three years later, the place still exuded the desperate, forgotten aura of a second-generation war zone. Whenever my partner and I drove through the area in our so-called "bucar" (short for bureau car), the locals would flip us off and shout, "DOWN WITH THE PIGS."

One afternoon in 1971, while en route to stake out a bookie joint, I asked myself, *Is this really how you want to spend the next twenty-five years of your career?* Before an answer could come to me, an empty bottle bounced off the roof of my car, shattering on the asphalt just outside my open window. I stomped on the accelerator, muttering to myself that the only way I'd ever last in the FBI would be to find some specialty in the science of criminology, then hurl myself into it with everything I had.

By 1972, shortly after the new FBI Academy opened in Quantico, Virginia, I learned about an agent named Howard Teten who was dabbling in criminal profiling, using it to catch violent criminals. And I started on the path that led me to this library, to these stacks of paper that told the story of how seven people in Wichita had come to be murdered.

3

I glanced back down at the police and autopsy reports, yellowed press clippings, and black-and-white crime scene photos on the table and took a deep breath. I lifted the top page from the stack, adjusted my glasses, and began reading.

Years spent pouring through countless reports just like these had enabled me to develop the ability to transform the facts and images appearing on these pieces of paper into a series of moving pictures loosely resembling a movie. All I needed to do was absorb the information, and, before I knew it, scenes and images were spilling out inside my head. The sensation was similar to watching TV — only most of what I glimpsed was much more violent.

It all began on a frigid Tuesday morning around 7:50 A.M. The date was January 15, 1974. That was the moment the city of Wichita underwent a transformation because of what took place in a white house with black shutters in a lower-middle-class, predominantly white neighborhood in the southeast part of town.

When the man responsible for the event fled the dwelling at 803 North Edgemoor Street around noon, the residence sat quiet for over three hours. A furnace rumbled in the basement, and the family's German shepherd paced anxiously through the snow in the backyard, letting out an occasional bark.

Shortly after 3:30 P.M, fifteen-year-old Charlie Otero and his brother, Danny, fourteen, and sister, Carmen June, thirteen, walked home from school and discovered the bodies of their mother and father in their bedroom. Charlie tried calling for help from the kitchen wall phone, but he couldn't get a dial tone. So he ran to the house next door, shouting that his father was dead.

A moment later, the neighbor sprinted back to the family's residence, ran down the hallway to the master bedroom, and poked his head inside. He spotted Julie Otero's body sprawled atop the bed. Nearby, on the floor, lay her husband, Joseph, with a butcher knife beside him and his bound ankles propped up on a briefcase. The neighbor had no idea that the knife was there because the Otero children had used it to cut the bindings off their father. So, in a flash, he assumed the worst: Joseph had murdered his wife, then killed himself. That was what he told police a few minutes later when he telephoned them from his kitchen.

By the time rookie Wichita Police Department patrolman Robert "Bob" Bulla arrived at the Otero house less than five minutes later, the three or four inches of snow carpeting the lawn had begun turning to slush. Dispatch had radioed him that there was a possible murder-suicide at 803 North Edgemoor. Charlie was on the front lawn when Bulla pulled his cruiser up to the curb. The teary-eyed teen was desperately yanking on the arms of the ambulance crew who had arrived a few minutes before Bulla. Charlie pleaded with the paramedics to go inside, to see if they could revive his parents, but all they could do was apologize and explain that they had to wait for police to give them the OK.

Bulla made his way up the walkway, chatting with the ambulance crew for a few moments as Charlie sent his brother and sister off on a mission to fetch the two youngest members of the family. He believed they were on their way home from elementary school. Being the protective older brother he was, he didn't want them arriving back at the house and having to look at the bloody, swollen bodies of their parents.

Bulla entered the house and made his way into the master bedroom, where he spotted the bodies of Joseph and Julie. He gently touched their skin with his fingertips, trying to gauge the temperature of their flesh. Their skin was cold, and their limbs were already stiff from rigor mortis. They'd been dead for many hours, he concluded.

Joseph lay on his back on the floor; his feet, clad in white socks, were bound tightly together by rope at the ankles. Strips of cord, each tied in complex knots, lay next to the bodies. Charlie told officers that he sliced the bindings off of his father after discovering him in the bedroom. Next to Joseph was a plastic bag that had been pulled off his head. Blood was smeared around his mouth and nose. His thick, strong hands were swollen to the size of baseball mitts.

Julie's face was also grossly swollen, and dried blood was caked around her nose and mouth. Carmen June had used fingernail clippers to cut the gag out of her mother's mouth, along with her many bindings. The white nylon cord that had been snipped away from her body had formed a thin necklace-like bruise around her neck. She was barefoot and dressed in her powder-blue housecoat. Her ankles were still bound by a single loop of white cord. Sitting on a nearby dresser was a framed photo of a pensive, smiling Julie in her wedding gown. Most of the drawers had been pulled open, and it appeared someone had rifled through the contents.

Additional officers arrived at the home, and before long they discovered the body of Joey, the youngest of the Otero siblings. The boy, who wore maroon corduroy pants and a shirt covered with dragons, lay on his side on the floor of his bedroom, beside the bunk bed he shared with his brother Danny. Next to his head was a Wichita phone book. His ankles were bound by cord. Another cord extended up behind his back and was knotted to his wrists. The cord that bound his hands behind his back was cinched so tight that the boy's tiny wrists were bruised. Like those of his father, Joey's hands were engorged with blood and lymph, and had swollen to several times their normal size.

The manner in which he was bound suggested that the UNSUB either tied the boy himself or instructed another family member in how to do it, perhaps trying to create the impression that if everyone would just cooperate with him, he'd take what he needed from the house and be on his way.

A few feet away from the bunk bed sat a wooden chair. The bottom rung of the chair had been broken. Splinters from the shattered piece of wood lay atop the carpet. I glanced at the crime scene photos and imagined the killer sitting there, watching the boy die, and somehow the rung had snapped. The sick image of this killer having the wherewithal to watch Joey suffocate underscored the staggering amount of control he maintained over the Otero family . . . and himself.

The fact that there was so little evidence of a struggle meant two things to me. The first thought was that more than one offender might be involved in the murders. But this possibility had a couple of major flaws. To begin with, I'd never heard of a crime scene where the two offenders had worked together in such perfect synchrony. I'd also never seen a case where two offenders would each have bondage as their signature. Normally, each killer would have his own distinct patterns at the crime scene. More often than not, one offender will be organized and controlling, whereas the other is disorganized, leaving evidence behind. Then there was the fact that the only biological evidence recovered at the scene was semen, later determined to have come from just one person. So if just one person was involved, I believed that he must have relied on a gun, not a knife, to intimidate the members of the Otero family, who — according to police — were well trained in karate. His gun was the equalizer. It leveled the playing field in a way a knife couldn't.

But most disturbing of all about the scene was that Joey's head had been encased within a series of hoods — a white T-shirt, a white plastic bag, and a blue T-shirt. Back in 1979 when I'd initially looked at the case, the presence of the bags and shirt over the boy's head led me to believe that killing Joey was probably the most difficult murder the UNSUB committed that morning. The killer, I theorized, identified with the child. Looking at the young boy, he glimpsed himself. Lying there on the floor, Joey was helpless and hopeless in exactly the same way the killer felt helpless and hopeless in his own life.

Within the mind of the killer, all the other murders were justified — but not Joey's. I thought that was why whoever had killed him had gone to such lengths to cover his face. He couldn't bear to look at it.

In 1979, therefore, I advised the police that if they ever tracked down and were interviewing a suspect, they should provide him with a face-saving scenario, focusing only on the young boy, not the other three family members. Tell him something, I had written, like "We know you don't feel good about the death [not murder] of Joey. It was difficult for you, and you tried to soften the kill." Even though this might not be 100 percent true, what I wanted them to do was place the suspect at the crime scene.

But now, five years later, I learned that the killer had also used hoods on Joey's father and mother. Unfortunately, the officer who briefed me on the case back in 1979 had somehow omitted this fact. This unintentional oversight reminded me of an adage that has long since become my mantra: profilers are only as good as the information they receive. In other words, garbage in, garbage out.

Shortly after Joey's body was discovered, Bulla set off to search the remaining rooms in the house to determine if the killer or killers had left behind any other grisly discoveries. Because tornadoes are a fact of life in this part of the country, he knew there was a basement. He just needed to find a way to get down there.

As he walked down the hallway that led into the living room, he spied the contents of Julie's purse scattered atop the burnt-orange shag carpet. Bulla glanced around the room at the wood carvings hanging from the wall that looked as though they'd been picked up on an overseas trip. A moment later, he spotted a door in the kitchen that led down to the basement. He opened it, but all he saw was blackness, so he had to rely on his flashlight while slowly navigating the carpeted stairs. Near the bottom step, he spotted a pair of shiny black boots that looked as though they might belong to a little girl. Walking slowly across the room, he spotted a squadron of model airplanes in various stages of construction, spread out across a table, along with a rocking chair and TV set.

In an adjacent corner, a door led to a small room containing the family's washer and dryer, and a wall filled with wooden storage cabinets. Bulla walked through the doorway into the darkened room. But before he could locate a light switch, his shoulder bumped into something solid that gave way when he made contact with it. He stumbled back, aimed the white beam of his flashlight onto the object, and instantly jumped back in shock.

What he had bumped into was the stiff body of Josephine, eleven, dangling from a pipe. A noose, fashioned from the same type of cord used on the others, bit a deep hemorrhaged groove into her neck. Her hands were tied tightly behind her back. Her mouth had been gagged with a strip of towel that made her tongue bulge out above the top of the gag. It was swollen and the color of eggplant.

Josie wore a pale blue T-shirt and nothing else. Her panties had been pulled down to her ankles, just above her saggy royal-blue socks. The back strap of her bra appeared to have been sliced with a knife.

Around Josephine's body was wrapped a web of cord; this reinforced my belief that the UNSUB had arrived at the home with a large length of this cord in his "murder kit." Like some Boy Scout gone bad, he'd come prepared. Her wrists were tied together behind her back and bound to a rope encircling her waist. Another length of cord had been wrapped around her knees, followed by yet another around her ankles. The tips of her toes almost touched the concrete floor. On her leg was a milky gelatinous substance that appeared to be semen. It had run down her leg over her sock and formed a tiny puddle on the floor.

Bulla took a deep breath, shook his head, and headed back upstairs.

"We got another body in the basement," he announced to the officers and detectives who had just arrived at the scene and were busy combing through the house.

Before the discovery of Josie's body, the killings had all the makings of a revenge- or retaliation-style homicide. But now the case had taken a macabre, darker twist. It now seemed to reek of a homicide that had sexual underpinnings. This meant that police were dealing with a much more sinister, complex type of killer.

When the call about the Oteros came over his radio, Wichita Police Department detective Bernie Drowatzky had been riding through the northeast part of town, looking for a couple of suspected heroin dealers. Like Bulla, he knew only that there had been a report of a possible murder-suicide at 803 North Edgemoor. Upon arriving, he quickly learned that police had discovered four bodies, including two children.

Drowatzky, who was known as a cop's cop, didn't like what he was hearing. Over the years, he'd immersed himself in plenty of violent crimes — he'd solved grisly murders, survived bloody shootouts, taken down armed suspects using only his fists — but something about what was unfolding inside the Otero house felt deeply bizarre and disturbing.

While all the detectives and crime scene technicians were moving through the house, Drowatzky, who would eventually arrive at the scenes of three other BTK murders over the next three years, fanned out across the neighborhood with several officers. They interviewed residents about anything they might have seen happen outside the Otero house that morning. Eventually he located a witness who had caught a glimpse of the Otero family's tan-colored Oldsmobile Vista Cruiser station wagon backing out of the garage at approximately 10:30 A.M. The driver, according to this neighbor, was a short man with a "Middle Eastern" complexion.

Another neighbor also reported seeing a dark-haired stranger quickly back out of the family's driveway. Whoever was driving the car was in such a rush that yet another neighbor had to slam on his brakes to avoid plowing into him as the neighbor backed onto Murdoch Street.

A few hours later, the car was located in the parking lot of Dillons grocery. A witness at the scene told police that the driver exiting the car looked terribly nervous. His whole body appeared to be shaking.

It was hours past sunset when Charlie Stewart, the lead detective working the case, broke the news to the three surviving Otero children that their two youngest siblings weren't going to be coming home from school.

From fifteen-year-old Charlie Otero, Stewart, known for his rock-solid investigative skills, learned that the family had moved to Wichita in fall 1973 from the Panama Canal Zone, where Joseph, thirty-eight, had served the last stretch of his twenty-year hitch in the Air Force. An aviation fanatic with a penchant for bongo playing and practical jokes, he decided to move his family to Wichita, known as the "Air Capital of the World," in order to pursue a career in flying. For the past couple of months, Joseph, who had a commercial pilot's license, worked as a mechanic and flight instructor at a local airport.

Like his wife, Julie, thirty-four, to whom he'd been married for the past sixteen years, Joseph was born in Puerto Rico. The couple's five kids, ages nine through fifteen, were all well mannered and studious, and seemed to adore their parents. The only other member of the family was their often unpredictable German shepherd mix,

Lucky, a trained military guard dog the Oteros had brought with them when they moved from Panama.

The dog was pacing around the backyard when police arrived, something that perplexed detectives when they spotted boot prints near the spot where the UNSUB had cut the family's phone line. Why, they wondered, hadn't the foul-tempered Lucky started barking to sound the alarm?

After speaking with the distraught, dazed children, a picture of the family's morning routine began to come into focus, along with some rough details about what may have happened over the course of the morning.

The kitchen appeared to hold the lion's share of the clues in explaining the opening moments of the attack. From the looks of things, the kids were in the midst of preparing their lunches when the killer or killers entered. The three older Otero siblings had already departed for school. Josephine had just finished fixing a sandwich that consisted of a smear of potted meat between two pieces of white bread. She wrapped it in wax paper and placed it in a lunchbox covered with flowers, left sitting on the stove. Joey stood at the kitchen table beside his father, spreading meat on a piece of bread. His open lunchbox with pictures of policemen on it sat on the table beside him. Joseph was hunched over the table, eating pears from an open can.

Stewart and other detectives figured that it must have been just around this moment that Joseph asked one of the children to take out the garbage and place it in the trash can sitting back behind the house. Two theories emerged over what happened next. In the first scenario, Josie, who had finished with her lunch-making duties, pulled on her white mittens, grabbed the garbage pail, and walked out the back door. It was at this moment that the intruder grabbed her and forced her back into the kitchen, where he confronted the rest of the family. Police retrieved her mitten, which might have fallen off when she was jumped by the attacker, on the concrete stoop just outside the back door.

In the second possible scenario, Joey was the one who was dispatched on garbage duty. The fact that he hadn't finished making his lunch probably wouldn't have fazed his father, who had the reputation for being a taskmaster. Josie might have been giggling over the fact that her brother might not get to finish making his sandwich before heading off to school. So, in the spirit of brotherly retaliation, Joey grabbed her gloves, lovingly caressed the trash bucket with them, then headed outside, where he was quickly overtaken by the UNSUB.

Exactly what happened next also proved difficult for detectives to determine with any certainty, although a couple of facts seemed clear. It didn't appear that anything had been taken from the house, which ruled out the chance of the attack's being a botched burglary. It also didn't seem likely that this was the work of two intruders. And because the interior of the house didn't indicate that a struggle had taken place, it seemed unlikely that the killer entered the house brandishing only a knife. To maintain the kind of control that it appeared he must have had, he in all likelihood used a gun. The prevalence of ropes, medical tape, and other bindings signified to detectives that the killer had arrived prepared.

Police speculated that after the attacker somehow managed to subdue the family and tie them up, he quickly decided to get rid of Joseph. With this one wild card out of the picture, the killer could continue his work at a more leisurely pace. Exactly what Joseph must have been thinking during those final moments, no one will ever know. But this one-time champion boxer, who was also a black belt in karate, surely must have been cursing himself for not putting up more of a fight when he had the chance, before allowing himself to be tied up.

Time was another factor. Even after he managed to kill Joseph, the UNSUB would have been constantly watching the clock. He knew he had to work quickly. With that many people living at the residence, the odds were good that somebody — one of the other Otero siblings, a classmate, another parent or a neighbor — might show up at the house. Yet he still wanted to savor the sick thrill of what he was doing, reminding himself that he couldn't spend much time with Julie, Joseph, and Joey. He hadn't come for them. From what I could see, they were just appetizers. It seemed obvious that he'd been watching the family, and what he really longed for was the main course and the dessert, all rolled into one — eleven-year-old Josephine.

Judging from the abrasions on the upper portion of Julie's neck, just below her ears, she had been strangled from behind while she lay on her stomach. The killer had evidentially straddled her, lifting her torso up off the bed while choking her. Beside her, traces of semen were found on the sheets and pillow; these were eventually determined to have come from her husband. The presence of Josephine's glasses in her parents' bedroom led detectives to believe that the killer had purposely left them there to confuse investigators.

Another bit of evidence that puzzled detectives was the chair with a broken rung found in the boys' bedroom. In her interview with police, Carmen June claimed that the chair came from the bedroom she shared with Josephine. Upon learning that, detectives began to suspect that the killer had moved the chair into the boys' bedroom, then held Josephine in his lap, forcing her to watch her brother suffocate. The wooden rung could have been cracked while he struggled to hold the squirming child, who probably would have fought to keep from watching Joey die. Even though traces of bruising could be seen encircling his neck, Joey was the only member of the family to die from asphyxiation, not strangulation. With a plastic bag over his head, along with the two T-shirts, the boy probably took four to five minutes to expire.

The killer's decision to take Josie down into the basement indicated just how badly he wanted her and to what lengths he'd travel to act out the fantasies writhing inside his head. He no doubt knew that such a move would have been incredibly risky. He could have easily gotten trapped down there if someone had entered the house. Nevertheless, he was clearly eager to take the risk.

The presence of the gag in her mouth provided another window into the mind of her killer. There was really no need to gag her because the others were all dead and, due to her location in the far corner of the basement, neighbors wouldn't be able to hear her scream. Nor was there any reason to hang her to a pipe or to tie her up at all if all the suspect wanted to do was rape her. What he did was all about his need to script, direct, and produce a crime to fulfill his fantasies of dominance and control. She was no longer human, merely a prop.

After binding her wrists, thighs, and ankles, he pushed her head through the loop in the rope hanging from a water pipe and pulled it tight, careful to make sure it lifted her body just high enough so that the tips of her toes barely touched the cold cement floor. In order to prevent the rope from biting into her neck, she would have had to strain to push against the floor with all her strength. I wouldn't have been surprised if he had demanded that Josie talk dirty to him, but my guess was that she was too petrified to play along with his sick game. The one common theme I'd learned from the interviews I'd conducted with sexual offenders

was that they would script their victims —
even if they were juveniles — and coerce
them to talk in such a way that it sounded as
though they wanted to be sexually assaulted.
Perhaps Josephine was so terrified and confused about the horrible events that had just
unfolded in front of her that all she could do
was whimper and plead for her life. And that
was the last thing the killer wanted to hear.
It ruined everything. He'd come to her
house to live out a fantasy.

There was no telling how long she fought
to stay conscious. Her underwear had nearly
been pulled down to her feet, just below the
white rope he'd tied around her ankles. At
some point during the ordeal, the killer
tugged her blue T-shirt shirt down over her
left shoulder, then cut her bra strap with a
knife. Before walking back upstairs and
switching off the lights to leave Josephine
hanging in darkness, the UNSUB masturbated, ejaculating onto his victim's right leg.
By the time police arrived at the scene, the
semen had dripped onto the floor, forming a
sickening, milky puddle.

Within days of the killings, one of the city's
two daily newspapers created a Secret Witness Program, hoping to coax locals into
phoning one of the papers' columnists to

feed them tips on the case. The reward money, donated by one of the newspapers, for anyone who provided information that led to the killer's conviction eventually climbed to $7,500. Rumors about the case spread through the city like a flu virus. Not even the investigators working the homicide were immune to the tall tales.

Some of the detectives were perplexed by the seemingly large amount of semen left on the floor in the Otero's basement. Exactly how much seminal fluid was present at the scene was never established, due to the fact that it had begun to dry and spread out by the time Josie's body was discovered. If it could be proven that the volume was too great to have come from a single individual, it could help substantiate claims that more than one killer was involved. But first, detectives needed to determine just how much semen was discharged during a typical ejaculation. To do that, police reportedly approached a cash-strapped Wichita State University upperclassman with an overdue parking ticket and made him a proposition that involved an empty test tube. I was never able to determine what, if anything, the police learned as a result of their unusual offer.

For police, the investigation that ensued

over the next few weeks quickly became as convoluted and complex as those knots found in the Otero home. Nobody could remember a case quite like this. Over a thousand neighbors, coworkers, ex-cons, and friends of the family were interviewed. The local newspapers and radio and TV stations carried reports of the killings and the latest developments in the case nonstop.

The killer had forced his way into a home — into the one place where people always believed they were safe — then savagely murdered a husband and father, a wife and mother, along with their little boy and little girl. The aftershock of the murders proved disorienting to the city's collective soul, shaking loose everything Wichita stood for. In one brutal swoop, the UNSUB had managed to turn this law-abiding town upside down, causing nearly everyone to begin asking themselves, *If he could do this to the Otero family, what would stop him from doing it to mine?*

Despite the presence of Josie hanging from a pipe in the basement, detectives just couldn't shake the idea that the murders had either been an act of retaliation or — due to the family's having just moved to the area from Panama — was somehow connected with the narcotics trade. It also seemed possible that the killer had been targeting Julie and her daughter. If that were true, he was undoubtedly surprised to find Joseph at home on that morning, especially because there were no cars parked in the driveway. Little did the killer know that a few weeks earlier, two men had run Joseph off the road. The accident not only caved in the front end of his car, which was now in the shop, but also severely injured his shoulder.

By early February, none of the leads unearthed by detectives had led anywhere. In an effort to dig up some information into Joseph Otero's background, an investigative trip to Puerto Rico and Panama was undertaken by Floyd Hannon, Wichita chief of police, and Bill Cornwell, chief of homicide. They traveled there to flesh out some of the rumors they'd heard about Joseph Otero.

Could this veteran pilot have been involved in the drug trade? Might this have been a gang hit? Was it possible that the murders were a ritualistic killing performed by some religious group the family belonged to?

Other than getting a suntan and having a few run-ins with the local police, who didn't like the no-nonsense attitude of these two gringo interlopers, Hannon and Cornwell did little to crack open any new leads. By the time the two cops returned to Wichita, they were no closer to solving the murders than they had been a month before when the bodies of Joseph, Julie, Josie, and Joey Otero were discovered.

4

"One down, three to go," I told myself, sliding the stack of crime reports from the Otero murders back to its original spot on the library table.

Next up was the pile of papers containing every imaginable detail of the April 4, 1974, murder of Kathy Bright, a twenty-one-year-old assembly line worker at the Coleman Company. Owing to the fact that BTK had left behind an adult survivor who could possibly identify him, this was the one homicide for which he never directly claimed responsibility in his taunts to the media up to this point. It wasn't until almost two years after BTK's bombshell communiqué in February 1978 in which he informed the city that a serial killer was on the loose that police finally linked Bright's murder to him.

In the taunting letter, he wrote, "You guess the motive and the victim." By the winter of 1979, investigators had combed through every unsolved murder between 1974 and 1977 and finally concluded that several elements of Bright's killing bore a sick resemblance to those found in BTK's other known kills.

By now it was 3:45 in the afternoon. My legs were cramping up from sitting in this stuffy library for so long. I stood up from the hard wooden straight-backed chair I'd been camped out on for the past three hours and stretched my legs, hoping to clear my head before diving into my next batch of crime reports.

Part of me wanted to take a break, needed to drag some fresh air into my lungs. But as I stood up, I made the mistake of glancing at what lay on the top of the pile — a grainy black-and-white photograph of Kathy Bright's bedroom. Unable to control myself, I grabbed the picture and sat back down. To hell with stretching my legs, I scolded myself. I'll take a break later.

In my pocket was a pill bottle containing the blood-thinning medication that I'd come to rely on ever since emerging from my coma. I fished out two capsules and popped them in my mouth. The irony that I was attempting to catch one of the nation's most elusive serial killers while ingesting a blood-thinning drug that was essentially rat poison was not lost on me.

I began dissecting the photograph, studying the mattress, which had been moved off the metal bed frame; the shoes scattered about the floor; and the comforter, blood smeared on the corner, that lay crumpled in the corner of the room.

I'd learned long ago that the most important thing to remember when studying a crime photograph is to resist the urge for your eyes to be pulled into the center of the picture. Sometimes the thing you need to find most lies on the periphery of the photo, at the distant edges.

I was once called in to work a homicide where the victim had been raped, then stabbed ten times in the throat. Local police believed that the UNSUB had stolen the victim's engagement ring after abducting her from a rest stop near Morrilton, Arkansas, while she exercised her dogs during a cross-country car trip. The fact that her killer might be the type who collected souvenirs from his victims had spun the investigation into one dead end after another.

The morning I met with detectives in that Arkansas police station, the victim's parents were present in the room, desperate to find the man who had killed their daughter. The first thing I did was begin combing through the stack of photos snapped at the crime scene. By the time I reached the third photograph, I found myself pointing to a tiny gray object wedged between the carpet and the frame of the passenger door, situated on the far right side of the picture.

"What's this?" I asked.

The victim's aunt peered at the photo and gasped, "Oh my God — it's the ring."

This particular homicide had already been featured on *America's Most Wanted,* and the public had been advised that the killer had taken the victim's ring. That he hadn't, told me that the murderer wasn't the type who felt compelled to collect souvenirs or mementos from his victims. This meant that detectives needed to track a killer with a different psychological makeup, which ultimately changed the course of the investigation. The killer was eventually linked through DNA to cases in California and Montana.

Something told me not to expect this sort of lucky break in the BTK case. And as I stood there in that library, thumbing through the various photos snapped in the rented wooden house where Kathy Bright lived with her older sister, along with a few taken in the medical examiner's office, I saw only one thing: a vibrant, feisty young woman whose life was ripped away too soon. So I settled back into my chair at the table and began immersing myself in the sad, cold facts surrounding her murder.

It was a couple minutes shy of 12:30 in the afternoon when the front door of the white clapboard house burst open and nineteen-year-old Kevin Bright flung himself outside, staggered through the ice-crusted snow, and began running down the street. Blood had soaked through his white T-shirt. The sight of this young man stumbling through the streets, waving his arms and screaming something about his sister needing help, caught the eye of a passing driver. He slammed on his brakes. The passenger jumped out, quickly pushed the frantic man into the front seat, then sprinted to a nearby automotive repair shop and told the owner to call the cops.

A few minutes later, as the Good Samaritan drove the dazed, bloody young man to the emergency room, a Wichita police dispatcher put out a call over the radio: "Officers to a robbery at a residence, 3217 East 13th Street North. Suspect still at the scene. Armed and dangerous." Patrolman Raymond Fletcher was driving through the neighborhood. He arrived at the house three minutes later, scrambled out of his cruiser, and slowly walked up the front steps with his .38-caliber service revolver drawn. The front door was open.

"POLICE OFFICER," he yelled. "POLICE OFFICER."

When he poked his head inside, he immediately spotted twenty-one-year-old Kathy Bright lying on her side in a puddle of blood in the wood-paneled front room. Oriental carpets hung on the wall, and beer bottles crowded a makeshift table fashioned out of a cable spool. A telephone lay beside her. "Help me," she whispered in a faint, raspy voice. "I . . . I can't breath."

Fletcher knelt beside her, keeping his eyes peeled for the suspect he believed might be hiding in the house.

"I'm gonna get you a doctor," he told her. "You just gotta stay calm . . . Can you do that?"

He radioed for an ambulance while kneeling on the floor beside Bright, who appeared to be fighting to keep her eyelids from closing. Her breathing grew shallower with each labored inhalation.

"Do you know who did this to you?" Fletcher asked, stroking her head. The poor woman was in bad shape, he thought. She could barely make any sound come out of her throat, so she just shook her head back and forth. The last words she uttered were "Help me."

What Fletcher didn't know at that moment was that Bright had been stabbed eleven times in her torso and was bleeding from nearly every major organ of her body. Two of the knife wounds had sliced through a portion of her lung, causing her to slowly suffocate. Her larynx had been also crushed.

Moments later, several more patrolmen and detectives arrived on the scene. The back two bedrooms of the house were in shambles. Smears of blood could be seen on the floor. From the looks of things, Kathy had been tied to a chair with a pair of nylons, but had somehow broken free and crawled out to the phone. Because this was in the days before 911, she dialed the operator, but her assailant had crushed her larynx, so she was unable to utter anything besides a horrible raspy howl.

Shell casings from an automatic pistol that would later be identified as a Woodsman Colt .22 were found in the other bedroom. A nearby bathroom door had a hole blasted in it. A .22 slug belonging to the same pistol was soon dug out from the bathroom wall. In the kitchen, the backdoor window had been shattered and the glass swept neatly into a pile.

An ambulance took Kathy to Wesley Medical Center, the same hospital to which her brother had been whisked twenty minutes earlier. She died on the operating table five hours later.

"She lost so much blood, she really never had a chance," recalls a detective who worked the case.

Not far from where Kathy died, her brother lay in a hospital bed. Kevin was skinny as a rail, but tough as boot leather. Despite being shot twice in the head, he was eager shortly after emerging from surgery to tell detectives everything he could remember. The men pulled up chairs beside his bed and asked him questions.

Kevin had driven into Wichita from his parent's house in nearby Valley Center the previous night and crashed at the rental house where his two sisters — Kathy and Karen — lived. Earlier that morning, Kevin and Kathy had gone to a local bank to see about getting a loan to help nineteen-year-old Kevin fund an invention he wanted to turn into a business. Karen was off working the first shift at Coleman. It didn't take long for the loan officer to nix his request, so they returned to Kathy's house and had just walked through the front door when — as Kevin recalled — a dark-haired man with a slight pot belly, standing about five feet, ten inches tall, wearing a stocking cap, gloves, a white T-shirt, and a green parka, stood waiting for them in the living room. He was holding a pistol.

"Stop," the man told them. "Hold it right there."

The intruder announced that he was on the lam from police in California and trying to get to New York. "I need your car keys and a hundred dollars," he said.

Kathy told him to take a hike. The man forced the two into a back bedroom at gunpoint. In the middle of the room, he'd positioned a chair. On a nearby bed he'd laid out various ligatures and bindings made out of rope and nylons he'd apparently found in the house.

Kevin was ordered to tie his sister to a chair. Then the intruder instructed Kevin to lie on the floor, and he bound Kevin's arms and legs with pair of jeans and stockings. He placed a pillow beneath Kevin's head, then told Kathy to walk to an adjoining bedroom, which she was somehow able to do, despite being tied to a chair. The stranger darted out of the room and disappeared into another part of the house.

Kevin couldn't quite figure out what this guy, who was both forceful and almost gentle, really wanted with the two of them. Before long, he could hear him opening drawers and slamming doors.

After a few minutes, the man appeared back in the bedroom, walked directly over to Kevin, and, without a moment's hesitation, kneeled beside him and wrapped what was either a pair of nylons or a rope around his neck, then pulled it tight. The force yanked Kevin up off the floor. When Kevin suddenly realized what the intruder intended to do to him, he began squirming and twisting his hands and arms back and forth. Within seconds, the wiry youth managed to wedge his hands loose from their bindings, and he jumped up onto his feet. In a flash, the man pulled out the pistol with which he'd been threatening the Brights minutes earlier and pointed it at Kevin's forehead. He pulled the trigger. None of Kathy's neighbors reported hearing the shot — which wasn't surprising. I'd lost count of the number of homicides I'd worked involving a firearm that neighbors never heard go off.

The force of a slug hitting his skull and the sheer shock of being shot knocked Kevin backward, and he quickly crumpled onto the floor, unconscious. When he came to a few moments later, the man had disappeared into the bedroom with his sister, obviously satisfied that he'd taken care of Kevin.

"You shot my brother," Kathy was shouting. "You shot my brother."

Kevin sat up on the floor and listened as the stranger tried to calm her. "Relax," he said. "I only wounded him. He's gonna be OK."

Kevin attempted to stagger to his feet, but the noise he made must have reached their attacker. The man walked back into the room, where Kevin had just managed to untie his legs. In a flash, Kevin remembered seeing the grip of a pistol tucked into the waistband of the man's pants, lunged at him, grabbed the gun, and managed to shove it into the man's chest. He squeezed the trigger, but before the hammer could slam down on the back of a round in the chamber, the attacker wedged his fingers beneath the hammer, preventing the gun from discharging. The two wrestled for control of the pistol, and Kevin managed to squeeze the trigger one more time, but once again the gun didn't fire.

The man finally wrenched the weapon free, quickly took aim at Kevin's head and fired, but missed. He pulled the trigger again, and the bullet hit Kevin in the mouth, tearing through his upper lip, turning Kevin's face into an even bloodier mess than it already was. What the gunman didn't know, however, was that Kevin's front teeth deflected the slug. Kevin crumpled to the ground once again, and the gunman jumped on top of him in a flash, then wrapped a rope around his neck and yanked it tight.

Upon hearing the pistol shots, Kathy began screaming, and the man ran back into the other bedroom where she was still tied to a chair. Kevin blacked out for an unknown amount of time, probably just a few minutes. When he came to and stumbled to his feet, his sister was still screaming. He made a split-second decision that sent him running out the front door. The best thing he could do for Kathy, he decided, was to run and get help. Fifteen minutes later, a police cruiser pulled up in front of Bright's house.

The detectives listened as Kevin whispered his story to them, amazed at his indestructibility and moved by his devotion to his older sister. Despite his injuries, he practically had to be tied down in the hospital bed to prevent him from fleeing the hospital and hitting the street to search for Kathy's killer.

Before leaving his hospital room, one of the detectives opened up an Identi-Kit, used by police to create composite sketches of an unknown suspect. Over the next forty-five minutes, Kevin poured through the seemingly infinite number of combinations in the book and reconstructed what he could recall from his assailant's face.

He told officers that the man was a stocky twenty-five-year-old Caucasian with dark hair and a thick dark mustache. He stood about five-foot-ten, had a black stocking cap pulled over his head, which he later removed, and wore a uniform that consisted of an orange shirt and jacket. The completed picture was immediately put on the wire and distributed to law enforcement agencies in the western states, where it was believed the assailant had come from.

Despite the fact that police suddenly had what could be a good description of the Brights' attacker, the composite caused a fair bit of dissension among several of the detectives assigned to the case. A few believed that the likeness might actually help them nab Kathy's murderer, whereas others doubted that Kevin, who many suspected had suffered a concussion, could be expected to recall much of value about the suspect.

In all my years working these sorts of cases, I'd rarely heard of a witness involved in a violent crime being able to create a composite drawing that turned out to resemble the perpetrator. That's why detectives and prosecutors know that they had better have more than just eyewitness testimony to tie a suspect to a crime. Many an investigation has been sent down a dead-end road for this very reason. Nevertheless, in the absence of anything else to work with, the Wichita police quickly put out an all points bulletin, using the details Kevin provided, along with the sketch he helped create.

Other than the clothes and nylons that had been used to tie up the Brights, detectives found precious little evidence in the house. The only set of latent fingerprints that police were unable to identify was found on the back door, but these turned out to belong to Bright's landlord and he was quickly eliminated as a suspect.

Police knocked on every front door in the lower-middle-class neighborhood where the sisters lived, asking if anyone could remember seeing a suspicious-looking character shortly after the attack, but no one reported seeing anyone out of the ordinary. A bloody white nylon rope was discovered under a tarp in the bed of Kevin's rusted, decrepit Ford truck, parked on Holyoke Street. Police surmised that the killer might have tossed them in there when fleeing the scene.

About the only thing detectives had to work with was a small amount of marijuana they discovered in the house, leading them to wonder if maybe the attack had something to do with a drug deal gone awry. But then Karen Bright admitted that she and her sister were recreational pot smokers, something the cops had no problem believing because the amount found was so minuscule.

Although police weren't ruling out the possibility that a local resident could be responsible for the brutal slaying and shooting, they reached out to California authorities, trying to determine if the description given by Kevin matched any fugitives they were currently pursuing. Before long, what few leads they had to work with had grown ice cold.

Although there were a few whispers among detectives that Bright's killer might be the same individual responsible for the Otero murders, nobody wasted much time trying to link the two cases. And why would they? There appeared to be so many differences — Bright's killer didn't cut the phone line, and he'd used both a knife and a gun on his victims. Even his knots, which had been tied from jeans and nylons (as opposed to the venetian blind cord used at the Otero crime scene) were different. Kathy had been tied with granny knots, whereas the Oteros had been bound with both clove hitches and half hitches.

By the end of April, something else was clear: 1974 was turning out to be one of the bloodiest in recent memory. Six months after the discovery of those four bodies in the Otero house, another quadruple homicide rocked Wichita. Those murders, however, were quickly revealed to be the result of a drug rip-off.

But the Otero and Bright murders were different. Every homicide detective knows that good, thorough victimology — which, quite simply, is the study of the victim of a particular offender — can help crack cases. The problem with the Otero and Bright murders was that all these victims were "low risk," meaning that there was no single clue to indicate why they were destined to die a violent death. None had engaged in any personal or criminal activities that might explain the fate they met. They were all just regular people, living and working in a community where the overall crime rate was remarkably low. The fact that none of the victims had probably ever laid eyes on their killer before he struck was another reason why police were having such a rough time unearthing any solid leads. Yet there were a few detectives in homicide who believed that the same killer might be responsible for all five murders.

It wasn't until October 8 that police received what they cautiously believed might be the biggest break in the case. Gary Sebring, a local resident with a lengthy history of deviant behavior that included an arrest for having sex with a duck in Riverside Park, was picked up for molesting a five-year-old girl behind a public library. While being questioned about the incident at the police station, Sebring made an off-the-cuff comment about the Otero homicides that proved to be the equivalent of dropping a lit match into a gas tank.

"He said, 'If I was doing the Oteros, this is how I would have done it,'" recalls one officer who worked the case. "'I would have been with my brother, and we would have tied them all up and my buddy Thomas Meyers would have been with us.'"

Anyone looking at their individual rap sheets could tell that Gary Sebring and his brother, Ernest, had serious mental problems. So did Meyers. If somebody was going to give false confessions to a quadruple homicide, they were the perfect candidates. But the heat to crack the Otero murders was getting intense, and because the three had a history of sex offenses, the decision was quickly made to bring them in for questioning. Although this was five years before I first got involved with the case, if I'd been working on it, I would have told the cops not to bother. From a profiling standpoint, the Oteros' killer was far too sophisticated and careful to have a history of bestiality and attempted molestation of a juvenile on his rap sheet. It just didn't fit.

Meyers couldn't be found. But on October 9, Sebring's older brother was taken in and grilled. Instead of being booked in jail, the Sebrings were taken to a local mental hospital for evaluation. On October 18, Meyers was located after he tried committing suicide and paramedics were called to the scene. Eventually he was placed under observation in a psychiatric hospital.

Despite Gary's rambling statement about his involvement in the murders, police quickly realized they'd opened a Pandora's box due to the threesome's mental instability. Years before, my Behavioral Science Unit worked on a case with similar dynamics, involving two homicides that had occurred nearly a decade apart in northern Virginia. After reviewing the murders, we concluded that the same offender was responsible for

115

both crimes. There was just one problem. A mentally challenged man was currently sitting in jail for the first homicide at the time the second murder had occurred. We eventually discovered that police interrogators had convinced the suspect to confess to the killing, telling him it was the only way to avoid the death penalty if convicted. The real killer, it turned out, was a career burglar who committed the murders during his probationary stints in half-way houses. He was later found guilty of the killings, and the governor exonerated the first man and ordered him released from prison.

None of the three men in Wichita were ever charged with any crime, but media coverage of these new unnamed suspects in the Otero case evidently began to annoy the real killer. The fact that three poseurs were getting ink and airtime for what he considered to be the crowning achievement of his life proved more than he could bear.

Late in the morning on October 22, he telephoned the Otero murder hotline set up by one of the city's two daily newspapers — the *Wichita Eagle* and *Beacon.* When columnist Don Granger picked up the phone, the voice at the other end of the line got right to the point.

"Listen and listen good because I'm not

going to repeat it," he growled, explaining that the man who killed the Oteros had stuck a letter inside a mechanical engineering textbook on the second floor of the Wichita Public Library.

That was all he said. Then he hung up, as if really annoyed.

Granger immediately telephoned Floyd Hannon, the chief of police, and told him the news. Within minutes, Detective Drowatzky was combing through the aisles of the library, located across the street from police headquarters, searching for the book. He eventually found a white envelope with the name Bill Thomas Killman, which police would eventually realize was an acronym for BTK, typed in the upper left-hand portion of the envelope.

Drowatzky's first impression upon reading it was, "It was jumbled up to make everyone think he was an idiot, which he was. But it also became apparent that he had a certain sick intelligence to him."

The letter had been typed and was laced with butchered syntax and numerous misspellings, grammatical mistakes, and misconjugated verbs. Of the detectives who poured over it, no one was quite sure whether the errors were unintentional or added simply to fool police into believing

117

they were dealing with an imbecile.

It had been my experience that offenders who communicated with police generally attempted to disguise their writing and throw investigators off by purposely misspelling words or by using improper grammar. But one thing was clear: whoever created this one-page letter didn't seem concerned about sending police the original rather than a photocopy. He had to know that forensic specialists would comb through every square inch of the letter with a microscope. He had to know there was a good chance that it contained a crucial piece of physical evidence that might allow investigators to trace the letter back to him. It was also risky because it provided investigators with their first real glimpse into his cold, savage mind. Even if everything he wrote was a lie, from that point onward he was no longer an invisible phantom. His image, albeit still terribly murky, had begun to take some semblance of shape and form. And he was OK with that. His ego obviously allowed him to believe the risk to be worth it.

Here was what the letter said:

OTERO CASE
I write this letter to you for the sake of the taxpayer as well as your time. Those

twothree dudes you have in custody are just talking to get publicity for the Otero murders. They know nothing at all. I did it by myself and no ones help. There has been no talk either. Lets put it straight . . .

Joe:
Position: Southwest bedroom, feet tie to the bed. Head pointed in a southerly direction.
Bondage: Window blind cord.
Garrote: Blind cord, brown belt.
Death: The old bag trick and strangulation with clothesline rope.
Clothed: White sweatshirt, green pants.
Comments: He threw up at one time. Had rib injury from wreck few week before. Laying on coat.

Julie:
Position: Laying on her back crosswise on the bed pointed in southwestern direction. Face cover with a pillow.
Bondage: Blind cord.
Garrote: Clothes line cord tie in a clove hitch.
Death: Strangulation twice.
Clothes: Blue housecoat, black slack, white sock.
Comments: Blood on face from too

much pressure on the neck, bed unmade.

Josephine:
Position: Hanging by the neck in the northwest part of the basement.
Dryer or freezer north of her body.
Bondage: Hand tie with blind cord. Feet and lower knees, upper knees and waist with clothes line cord. All one length.
Garrote: Rough hemp rope 1/4 dia., noose with four or five turns.
Clothes: Dark bra cut in the middle, sock. [For some reason BTK left out the pale blue T-shirt and panties pulled down to her socks.]
Death: Strangulation once, hung.
Comments: Most of her clothes at the bottom of the stairs, green pants, and panties. Her glasses in the southwest bedroom.

Joseph:
Position: In the east bedroom laying on his back pointed in eastern direction.
Bondage: Blind cord.
Garrote: Three hoods; white T-shirt, white plastic bag, another T-shirt, Clothes line cord with clove-hitch.
Death: Suffocation once, stranglation-

suffocation with the old bag trick.

Clothes: Brown pants, yellow-brown stripe T-shirt.

Comments: His radio is blaring.

All victims had their hands tie behind their backs. Gags of pillow case material. Slip knotts on Joe and Joseph neck to hold leg down or was at one time. Purse contents south of the table. Spilled drink in that area also, kids making lunches. Door shade in red chair in the living room. Otero's watch missing. I needed one so I took it. Runsgood. Themostat turn down. Car was dirty inside, out of gas.

I'm sorry this happen to society. They are the ones who suffer the most. It hard to control myself. You probably call me "psychotic with sexual perversion hang-up". When this monster enter my brain I will never know. But, it here to stay. How does one cure himself? If you ask for help, that you have killed four people they will laugh or hit the panic button and call the cops.

I can't stop it so the monster goes on, and hurt me as well as society. Society can be thankful that there are ways for people like me to relieve myself at time by day dreams of some victims being torture and being mine. It a big compicated game my friend of the monster play putting victims number down, follow them, checking up on them, waiting in the dark, waiting, waiting . . . the pressure is great and sometimes some times he run the game to his liking. Maybe you can stop him. I can't. He has aready chosen his next victim or victims. I don't who they are yet. The next day after I read the paper, I will know, but it to late. Good luck hunting.

YOURS, TRULY GUILTILY

P.S. Since sex criminals do not change their M.O. or by nature cannot do so, I will not change mine. The code words for me will be . . . Bind them, toture them, kill them, B.T.K., you see he at it again. They will be on the next victim.

There was no signature on the bottom of the letter. Instead, whoever penned it drew a cryptic symbol created from the letters BTK.

Judging from the way he described his crime scenes — with the attention to detail of a detective — whoever wrote the letter was clearly a wannabe cop. But he obviously needed to bone up on his Criminology 101, because plenty of criminals do change their MOs. Decades later, investigators would learn that BTK changed his modus operandi when he removed the bodies of his last two victims from their homes. What doesn't change is the killer's *signature,* which is something the offender does to fulfill himself emotionally, but that isn't necessarily needed to accomplish the crime.

In the Otero murders — and, we would later learn, in the Bright case — BTK's signature was the use of bindings and gags, along with a form of psychological torture wherein he denied his victims the courtesy of a quick death.

Not surprisingly, detectives pounced on the letter almost as soon as it landed on Chief Hannon's desk and began picking it apart, examining it for hair, fiber, and fingerprints, then sifting through every single misspelling and word usage, looking for any clue they could unearth.

The first thing that jumped off the page was the fact that whoever sent it had — when discussing the suspects being looked at by police — crossed out the word "two" and replaced it with "three." He evidently had written the letter before October 18, when Thomas Meyers was finally located. But, for some reason, he had opted to sit on his communiqué for several days before sending it. Clearly the UNSUB didn't want someone else getting credit for what he considered to be his *Mona Lisa*.

But there was another reason. He appeared to be enjoying how he was making the Wichita police resemble the Keystone Kops. The last thing he wanted was for his local law enforcement agency to garner any positive accolades from the media or the community for possibly solving the Otero murders.

The UNSUB didn't claim responsibility for Bright's murder for the simple reason that he'd left behind a living witness — her brother. Police wouldn't make that connection until the waning months of 1979. But now that I'd learned he'd been responsible for Kathy's botched, bumbling, albeit lethal attack four months earlier, it seemed quite possible that he also typed his letter to police in order to remind himself — and them — of exactly what he was capable of when he was at the top of his game. After all, here was a killer who, in the Otero case, was able to overpower and con a family of four into submission.

What was certain, however, was that his letter contained a level of detail that only the Oteros' killer could have known. It went far beyond anything that had appeared in the media after the homicides occurred. It read like a police crime report. His descriptions were so exact that I was left wondering if he'd photographed the crime scene before fleeing. How could he remember all those details if he hadn't brought a camera, or perhaps discovered one at the house and used that?

Yet for all the precise, accurate information he included in his letter, there was also something peculiar. A few of the descriptions were so off the mark that detectives were a bit stumped. For instance, at the crime scene, Joseph didn't have a bag on his head, and Julie's face wasn't covered by a pillow. The reason, police eventually learned, was that the Otero children had removed them while trying to revive their parents. Also, BTK never mentioned the pale blue T-shirt that Josephine was still wearing after her death.

In the end, however, these inaccuracies actually did more to prove that whoever penned the letter actually was the Oteros' killer. After all, he would not have known that the crime scene had been disturbed. He would have expected it to look exactly the way it did when he fled the house. Another factual error was the writer's claim that he'd used five turns of his rope to create Josephine's noose. In reality, he'd only used three. Detectives wrote off this mistake as a case of inattention due to the excitement he must have been experiencing prior to killing his eleven-year-old victim. Another perplexing aspect of the letter was the writer's reference to Josephine's glasses being left in the bedroom. Why would the killer have gone to the trouble of placing them there? Was it simply some weird way to taunt police? The answer turned out to be much more mundane, although decades would pass before investigators learned the real reason.

Over the next couple of weeks, nearly two dozen psychologists and psychiatrists were shown the contents of the letter and asked to compile a personality profile of the individual they believed might have written it. The doctors were divided over whether or not it should be released to the public, something police were hesitant to do out of fear that they'd be inundated by an avalanche of false leads they knew they didn't have the manpower to investigate.

We now know that there was an issue far more important than whether or not the department needed additional personnel to chase down leads. My belief is that police might have been more effective in their efforts if they'd been more forthcoming with the release of information to the public. Because when provided with useful behavioral characteristics of an UNSUB, the community can begin acting as a powerful tool for investigators, serving as their eyes, ears, and a type of collective data bank. Surely somebody, somewhere, may have seen something around the time of the murders, some odd bit of behavior in a friend, coworker, or relative. But until people are given some clue as to what they're supposed to have seen, they can't help connect the dots for police.

The specialists were unanimous in their assessment: the writer was "a very sick man . . . who had a fetish for bondage. His reaction, sexually, is to be bound, to bind other people," Chief Hannon eventually told reporters.

At the request of police, Granger placed a classified ad in the newspaper, which ran from October 24 to October 27, urging the killer to contact him. It read:

B.T.K.
Help is available.
Call 684-6321 before 10 p.m.

Granger never received any response from the ad. A few days later, he wrote a column in the newspaper, explaining that police were searching for "a man who needs help badly," who had information about the Otero murders. The intrepid columnist went so far as to ask the man to call him at home, but the call never came. The killer was no longer in a talkative mood. He obviously had other things on his mind.

5

It was getting late. When I looked up from the stack of pages detailing the Kathy Bright homicide, the sun had vanished, and a coating of darkness had descended on the world outside.

I decided that maybe it was time to pack it in and head home for the night. I was tired. I gathered up my stacks of crime reports, wrapping rubber bands around each individual pile, tossed them into a bag, and trudged out into the darkness to my car. A few minutes into my half-hour drive home, I realized exactly what I needed to do. It was something I hadn't done in nearly a month. So I turned the car around and steered north, toward Quantico National Cemetery, to visit the grave that had been intended for me.

Months earlier when it was assumed that I'd probably never pull out of my coma, some bureaucrat in the Veteran's Administration reserved a plot for me in this newly opened cemetery that had once served as a blockade point for Confederate troops during the Civil War. When I refused to die, my plot was given to someone else. But I knew its location and felt a kind of strange attachment to the place. There but for the grace of God, I often thought to myself.

The grass was damp with evening dew as I walked through the cemetery looking for the grave, clutching my flashlight as though it were a club. A full moon, bright as a medical examiner's lamp, had just crawled above the hickory and oak trees in the distance, helping illuminate my way. Before climbing out of the car, I had grabbed the sheaf of papers detailing BTK's next victim — Shirley Vian, murdered in her bedroom as her children, who had been locked away in a bathroom, pleaded with the killer to leave their mother alone. I didn't know what the hell I intended to do with all those papers, but it seemed only natural to bring them along for my nighttime stroll through the cemetery.

I started coming here months ago, thinking it might provide answers to all the questions my brush with nonexistence had left me. For someone who had surrounded himself with death for most of his career, cemeteries felt like a natural extension of my office. Nevertheless, something about the darkness on this particular night set me on edge. I'd never been here at night. Nor had I ever told a soul about my visits here. Why would I? No one would understand.

The last time I'd come here, I happened upon the grave of a little girl whose brutal homicide I'd once investigated. Although it was sheer coincidence that she'd been buried near my would-be plot, as I stood above her tiny body I felt a flash of panic surge through me. For years, I'd been advising cops to keep their eyes on cemeteries because my research had shown that killers sometimes visit the grave of their victims to get close to their "accomplishments." In the case of this little girl, police had a viable suspect, but they were never able to link the two-time convicted felon directly to her homicide. And this caused a tiny shiver to run up my spine.

What if the cops have her grave staked out at this very moment? I had thought, peering over my shoulders to determine if I was being observed. *They're probably looking at me right now, thinking they've finally nabbed their killer.*

But on this night, I cut a beeline straight to my plot and plopped down in the damp grass. I stared at the white headstone that appeared to glow in the darkness. The man who ended up here had served in the U.S.

Army in Vietnam. So had the men buried on either side of him. Closing my eyes, I sucked the cool evening air up into my nostrils and, before I knew it, caught myself praying, asking God to help me. *Balance your life, John,* I thought. *You're falling back into your old ways. You're losing control again. If you're not careful, you're going to end up here . . .*

From somewhere behind me, I heard a twig snap. In a split second, my fingers wrapped around the butt of the revolver that hung in the shoulder holster I wore beneath my suit jacket, then I wheeled around to confront what I imagined to be my assailant. But all I saw was a deer chewing on some dried leaves.

I stood up, fumbled for the flashlight beside me, and hit the animal with a white blast of light. It bolted toward the woods. My heart was pounding as I sat back down in the grass, chuckling over my edginess.

I looked over at the sheaf of papers I'd carried with me and decided that this was as good a place as any to begin boning up on BTK's next victim. I spread the pages out in front of me and, with the help of the moonlight and my flashlight, began reading again.

It was the early afternoon of March 17, 1977, when Wichita police lieutenant Bernie

Drowatzky pulled up to the house at 1311 South Hydraulic Street, located two miles northwest of the Otero residence. The fact that Drowatzky kept showing up at BTK crime scenes was hardly surprising. Bernie was something of a go-to guy with the Wichita Police Department, the type of cop who loved to stick his nose into just about any call from dispatch he heard come over his car radio. All he knew from the radio was that the woman who lived there, twenty-four-year-old Shirley Vian, had been strangled. As he walked up to the front door and stood on the rundown wooden porch, he couldn't help thinking how much the tired, white wooden siding reminded him of Kathy Bright's house, yet another murder he'd helped investigate. Drowatzky went inside, and a patrolman who'd arrived earlier gave him a quick tick-tock of the events as told to officers by Vian's five-year-old son, Steve.

According to the boy, a stranger had entered the house, locked him and his eight-year-old brother, Bud, and four-year-old sister, Stephanie, in the bathroom, then proceeded to murder his mother in the adjacent bedroom. No more than thirty to forty-five minutes had passed between the time the killer walked into the house and departed.

Drowatzky poked around the small, hopelessly cluttered place. Two doors, one from each bedroom, led into the bathroom. To prevent the kids from opening one of the doors, the killer looped a length of new nylon rope to a pipe beneath the sink, then tied it off around the doorknob. The first thing that struck Drowatzky were the knots.

I've seen those before. Something about them reminded him of what he'd seen at the Otero murder. It just wasn't the kind of knot that someone in the Navy or the Boy Scouts would tie. It was like someone had taken a basic clove hitch and kept tying it over and over again until he'd stumbled on this new one.

Shirley's nude body was laid out in the living room, near the opened sofa bed. Two white adhesive EKG leads were stuck to her chest, left behind by paramedics who initially thought they might be able to revive Vian. Newspapers and shoes littered the floor. A tattered overstuffed chair sat in a corner beside an ashtray heaped with cigarette butts.

Paramedics arrived at the scene a few minutes before 1:00 P.M., not long before police. A neighbor made the call after Vian's terrified son ran over to her house, screaming that his mother was dead. They found her in the bedroom, tied to the metal bed frame.

Nearby, vomit had formed a kidney-shaped puddle on the dirty carpet. Because her body was still warm (police estimated that fifteen minutes had lapsed since the killer had left) and the room was so dark, the EMS technicians cut the white nylon cords looped around her arms and legs, then carried her out into the light, vainly hoping to be able to resuscitate her.

Her face was a mess, splotchy red from cyanosis and hemorrhaging, with a haze of blue. Dried blood and vomit was caked around her nose and mouth. The rope around her neck had left a hideous rust-colored abrasion on much of her throat.

Two years after her murder, when detectives from Wichita first showed up at FBI headquarters wondering if my unit could provide any help on the case, I nearly gasped upon looking at the photos of Shirley's body. Even after the years I've spent viewing crime scene photos, she had the kind of corpse you don't forget, the kind that occasionally came back to haunt me in my dreams. That's because one of the things I do as a profiler is take that expression frozen on the face of a murder victim and work backwards. I have to place myself inside the head of both the offender and the victim at the time of the crime.

Her lips, along with much of her face, exuded a dull, cold bluish tint. Her last thoughts, I felt sure, were about her children. She'd cooperated with the intruder because he'd no doubt promised her that he wouldn't harm her three kids. But the moment she felt that rope tighten around her neck, she knew she'd made a terrible mistake. Like Joseph Otero, she lay there wracked with guilt, totally helpless, praying that the stranger who seemed so intent on killing her would leave her daughter and two sons alone, hoping that when it was all over they wouldn't be the ones to find her.

Reading between the lines of the crime reports, I sensed that Shirley was forever trying to straighten up her sad life, but never quite could. By the age of twenty-four, she'd been married twice and had three kids, all of whom lived with her. She raised them the best she could, and, just like the Otero parents, she was adored by her kids.

Her oldest boy, Bud, was thought to have a cognitive impairment. His sister, Stephanie, suffered from various learning disabilities. Steve, at five, appeared to be the only member of the family without some kind of learning or intellectual deficit. Shirley now lived with her husband, Rick Vian, who was away at his job at a construction site when the murder occurred. Her kids were frequently absent from school, and, on that particular morning, they'd stayed home because their mother had stomach flu and didn't feel up to getting them ready for class.

Earlier that morning, she'd sent Steve to a nearby grocery to fetch some chicken noodle soup and 7-Up for her queasy stomach. At the time, it wasn't that odd for a five-year-old to run an errand like that in Wichita. Vian phoned ahead and told the storekeeper to keep a lookout for her boy. She also asked Steve to pick up two money orders totaling $40. As Steve returned home, a stranger stopped him on the sidewalk not far from his house, pulled out his billfold, and showed him a photograph. He asked the boy if he'd seen either of the people in the picture. Steve told him no.

The man, who was carrying some sort of a bag, continued to question him about the identity of the two people in the photograph, but Steve insisted he had no idea who they were. Eventually, the stranger allowed the boy to pass. But as Steve walked off, he turned to watch the man continue up the street, then stop at the home of his neighbors and knock on their door.

The boy had been home about ten minutes and was mesmerized by a cartoon show on

TV when someone knocked on his door. He opened it and saw that the same man who he'd talked to out on the sidewalk was now standing on his front step.

"Excuse me, son," the man said. "I've lost my dog. Have you seen any lost dogs around here?"

"No, sir," Steve replied, as the man peered into the house.

"Is your mother home?" he asked. "Let's ask her. Maybe she can help me find my lost dog."

Steve stood there with Bud by his side as the man pushed past them and walked over and turned off the TV, which Stephanie was glued to. Next, he pulled the shades down over the two front windows. The front room instantly went dark.

The kids were confused, not quite sure what to make of this strange man who barged into their home as though he lived there. When he noticed the children staring at him, he pulled a pistol out of the shoulder holster hidden beneath his jacket and pointed it at them.

"Where's your mother?" he demanded.

"She's in there," the siblings shouted in unison.

But by then, Shirley had heard all the commotion going on in the front room. She had been lying in bed in her room, but managed to drag herself out into the front room when she heard the stranger's voice.

"What the hell are you doing?" she demanded. "Who the hell are you?"

The man walked over toward her, brandishing his pistol. "Shut up," he snapped, pointing toward the bedroom. "And get in there."

The telephone rang before she could move. Steve stared at it, but the intruder said, "Leave it alone."

Next, he glanced around the house and ordered Shirley to gather up a blanket and some toys, then instructed her to spread everything out on the bathroom floor. After hustling the kids inside, he pulled some rope out of his pocket and went to work looping it around the doorknob, then tying it to a drainpipe beneath the sink. He exited through the other door and soon could be heard sliding a bed against it, effectively sealing the kids inside. A defiant Steve threatened to untie the rope, but the man quickly made him reconsider.

"You better not or I'll blow your fucking head off," he shouted. Shirley pleaded with her headstrong son to do as the man said.

From inside the bathroom, the children heard the sound of adhesive tape being torn from a roll. Steve pushed open the door with the bed shoved up against it and peeked out. The image he saw was of his mother, lying face down on the bed, naked. Her hands had been taped behind her back, a rope tied around her neck, and a plastic bag pulled over her head.

The children had no idea how long they were stuck in that bathroom, but reported that it felt like an eternity. Then the telephone began ringing again, and Bud somehow managed to climb up on the sink and break out a tiny bathroom window with his fists. Blood quickly began streaming out from the cuts in his hand, as he screamed for help through the window. Stephanie joined him. By this point, Steve used all his strength to kick through the bottom panel of the door that the killer had tied to the sink. The boy was so angry at the man who he'd seen hurting his mother that he ran into the bedroom with his fists balled up, ready to fight. But the man had vanished.

Steve glanced at his mother, still lying on her stomach on the bed. She didn't move. He sprinted outside and was standing on his neighbor's porch a few seconds later, pounding on their door.

"MY MOM IS DEAD," he screamed. "CALL THE COPS."

The neighbor rushed over to Steve's house and found Bud and Stephanie sitting beside their mother's body, sobbing.

Paramedics were moving Vian into the front room of the house as police arrived, forcing detectives to rely on the children's memories to piece together a clearer, more detailed picture of the crime scene. Although much of it had been removed by emergency medical personnel, white nylon cord appeared to have been used to bind Vian's wrists and ankles, along with electrical tape that ascended up her legs in a pattern reminiscent of Roman army sandals. Investigators were never able to trace where the rope came from.

An autopsy revealed that she had not been sexually assaulted, nor did her hands bear the traces of any defensive wounds that she might have received trying to defend herself.

So how was the killer able to subdue Shirley?

Police reasoned that he convinced her to allow him to tie her up, promising her that if she did, he wouldn't hurt her children. After making her remove all her clothes, the killer placed her nightgown over her head, then slipped a bag over that. If the UNSUB did ejaculate while at the house, police speculated he might have done so in a pair of Shirley's panties, then taken them with him when he fled.

In between telling the detective who interviewed them about the songs their mother would sing to them when they couldn't sleep, the children did their best to describe the killer. They insisted he was a dark-haired man in his late thirties or forties with a heavy build and a "paunch." Police, however, placed little faith in the information Vian's kids provided — especially their description of the suspect.

Because the $40 in money orders that Steve picked up at the grocery had been taken from the house, investigators believed robbery may have been the initial motive for the crime. Nevertheless, the murder was classified as a sex crime. Police didn't believe at first that there was enough evidence to connect Vian's homicide to the Otero murders. The reason? The phone line hadn't been cut, the killer didn't appear to have masturbated at the scene, the victimology was different, and none of Shirley's children were harmed. That the paramedics had disturbed the crime scene, removing Vian's various bindings, meant that police had nothing to visually link the two killings. They had to rely on the memories of Vian's kids and the emergency medical technicians to reconstruct the scene.

Still, according to Drowatzky, there were a few detectives on the force who whispered about possible parallels between the homicides. That they even toyed with a connection between the two murders spoke volumes about just how deeply the Oteros' killer had wormed his way into the consciousness of the Wichita police force. But their suspicions never amounted to anything other than a collective gut hunch, certainly nothing anyone could prove — at least not until the killer penned his next letter, claiming responsibility for the killing. Over the next few weeks, nearly fifty people were interviewed by police. Because of the puzzling randomness of the murder, however, the hunt for a viable suspect quickly turned cold, and the case was put on the back burner.

Yet despite the lack of anything resembling a lead, investigators had a strong hunch that the photograph the killer displayed to Vian's son Steve was a snapshot of Cheryl Gilmore and her son. Gilmore was the neighbor on whose front door Steve saw the killer knock earlier that morning while walking home from the store.

Detectives believed that Gilmore might have been the killer's intended target. She lived alone with her son and regularly came home for lunch from her job at a nearby optometrist's office. The only reason she wasn't home when the UNSUB knocked on her door was that she had to take her son to a medical appointment.

Gilmore learned about the murders after returning home from work that afternoon. Her street was swarming with police and TV crews. The thought that she narrowly missed meeting the grisly fate suffered by Shirley spooked her horribly. But because she couldn't afford to move away from the area, she remained living in her house. Each night for the next year, she lay in bed with an unloaded shotgun, telling herself she'd use it as a club should the killer ever return.

I couldn't help but wonder what would have happened if five-year-old Steve hadn't bumped into that stranger roaming his neighborhood on that morning. The killer was obviously pumped up to murder someone, consumed with the need to control and devour another human being. When Gilmore wasn't home, I surmised, he remembered the boy he'd just spoken to and decided to see if there was anyone home at his house who might make a worthwhile victim. It was a bold, stupid maneuver that could have gotten him caught, but he somehow pulled it off.

It was close to midnight when I finally decided to pack up my paperwork and head home from the cemetery. The moon shone bright, but the beam of my flashlight had turned a weak yellow. I felt a bit calmer, more in control.

The more I thought about the Vian case, the more I could sense that the UNSUB was probably kicking himself over how this killing had unfolded. Three years had passed since his botched, haphazard attack on Kathy Bright and her brother. The incident had no doubt spooked him, causing the part of him that hungered to murder to retreat and slink back underground in hiding. For three years, he no doubt plotted and fantasized over taking another victim. After his experience at Bright's house, I would have expected to see a smarter, savvier killer the next time he surfaced.

But that wasn't really the case. For the most part, he bulldozed his way into Shirley Vian's house by fast-talking a five-year-old boy, then got out by the skin of his teeth. He was calculated and determined, but more than anything else, the killer was lucky.

When I tried to imagine what transpired in Shirley Vian's bedroom on the afternoon the UNSUB stole her life, I caught glimpses of him standing in Shirley's bedroom over her body, drinking in the image of her wrapped up with all that cord and electrical tape. All the while he was probably attempting to masturbate.

But the children seemed intent on ruining everything with their incessant screaming and their pounding on the bathroom door and shattering of glass. He yearned to kill them, but first he needed to take care of business before the situation completely went south. So he continued masturbating, and when the phone in the front room started ringing, he finally decided he'd had enough and fled. Police were never able to ascertain who had been calling, but whoever placed the call no doubt saved the lives of Vian's three kids.

What was going through his head, I wondered, as he departed Vian's house? He'd obviously gone there because his intended target, the one who had consumed so many of his waking hours, wasn't at home. But the urge to kill was too strong, so he'd changed directions in midstream and struck out at random. Because of his inability to completely control his environment, however, he committed a less-than-perfect crime. What resulted was anything but the fantasy world he'd yearned for, a realm where he called all the shots and yanked all the strings.

Nevertheless, he'd pulled it off and also managed to gather plenty of raw material to feed his ravenous imagination in the months and years that followed. After all, that was one of the real motives behind why these guys kill. From my work spent interviewing these monsters, I'd learned that for many, the act of killing was tantamount to putting money in the bank. They committed their brutal crimes not only to live out their fantasies but also to provide fuel for future fantasies. The more visual memories they could "bank," the larger the cache they could draw on during those long days and nights when killing someone wasn't an option.

Despite what I'd learned about this dark netherworld from the serial murderers I'd interviewed, I realized I was just scratching the surface in my understanding of the strange powers this parallel universe held. But whether I understood it or not, there was no denying one thing: for most of these guys, their fantasy world, populated with victims — real, imagined, and of the soon-to-be variety — often felt more real than the world they dwelled in during their waking hours.

Consequently, what's really important to these guys is that they develop an effective, consistent way to access this inner world. Judging from the precise way the UNSUB described his crime scenes, he seemed to be a very visually oriented person. That told me he would probably be the type to rely on drawings or perhaps photographs snapped at his crime scenes to help open this trap door leading to his dark fantasy realm.

Not all serial killers are visual types. Plenty of these guys make audiotapes of their torture and murder sessions. Afterwards, they listen to the recording of their victims screaming, begging for their lives — and in a few cases pleading to be killed — much like a normal person would listen to a piano concerto by Mozart on their stereo. The sounds transport them to that other world.

I kept several of these cassette tapes in a drawer of my desk. Listening to them never failed to make the hair on the back of my neck stand straight up. I've sat in a room with hardened veteran homicide detectives who could endure only a few minutes of these recordings before wincing and quickly exiting the room, shaking their head.

I once worked a case involving two truly savage murderers who used sound as a way to relive their killings. Lawrence Bittaker, convicted of assault with a deadly weapon, and rapist Roy Norris became pals while incarcerated at the California Men's Colony at San Luis Obispo. Shortly before their release from prison, they hatched a plan to kill teenage girls, one for every "teen" year from thirteen to nineteen. They yearned to record their crimes on audiotape. By June 1979, they'd purchased an old Ford van, nicknamed "Murder Mack," and set out to fulfill their dark fantasy.

In quick succession during that summer, they brutally raped, tortured, and killed four young girls. When police finally caught up with them, they quickly discovered the duo's collection of audiotapes. I'll never forget the afternoon I listened to one of their cassettes in preparation for an interview that I and a female agent did with Bittaker, who was sentenced to death for his crimes and sent to San Quentin State Prison.

During the recording, his cohort was driving the van while Bittaker — whose nickname was "Pliers" because this was his favorite instrument of torture — scripted the frightened, moaning fourteen-year-old girl, telling her exactly what he wanted her to say as he slowly mutilated her. Just as the BTK posed his victims in order to see their bodies in his imagination, Bittaker needed to hear just the right combination of words in order to keep his victims alive within his head.

The afternoon we finally sat down with this sad excuse for a human being in a San Quentin interview room, he was more than happy to spill his guts to us. The only glitch was that he refused to look at my female colleague when she asked him questions. That was how much he hated women. By the time our session was over, he was sobbing. Of course, his tears were for himself — not his victims.

Walking back to my car through the moon-beam-lit cemetery, I caught myself thinking about the letter BTK sent to police in October 1974. In it, he wrote, "Since sex criminals do not change their M.O. or by nature cannot do so, I will not change mine."

I could only assume that he'd written this out of ignorance, because every criminal justice student with even the slightest bit of frontal lobe activity knows that killers *do* change their MO. It is their most malleable and fluid quality, a skill that is constantly evolving and changing to the point of perfection.

BTK's method of killing appeared to be evolving. Instead of becoming more cautious, as one might have expected, he was taking more chances. His crime scenes re-vealed a high degree of organization, and he still seemed to be planning out his murders, but he'd begun developing a new skill. He now appeared comfortable with the idea of improvising when one of his victims didn't show up, which is what led to Shirley Vian's death. What I couldn't explain was the source of this impulsiveness. Was it born out of an inability to control his homicidal urges, of grandiose thinking, or of just plain care-lessness?

Then again, was it something else, some-thing none of us in the criminology business had encountered before? My twenty-minute-old sense of calmness and compo-sure began to evaporate. There was just so much I didn't know, so many unanswered questions. What on earth could have com-pelled the UNSUB to tackle such high-risk targets in the middle of the day? It didn't make sense.

Yet.

6

The next morning, I awoke at 5:15 and got dressed for work. Pam was breathing softly, her head buried in her pillow. I watched her in the mirror while knotting my tie, thinking about how her stillness resembled that of a corpse. My job was devouring me, the violence was eating a dark hole inside me, and there seemed little I could do to escape it.

A few days before, I had taken my two daughters — Erika, eight, and Lauren, four — to a wooded park near our house, but found myself constantly peering off into the brush, looking for the body of a murder victim that I tried to convince myself had been dumped there, then covered over by leaves. Two weeks before that, while making love to Pam, a flashback had washed over me, and I suddenly found myself staring into the dying face that belonged to a woman whose torture slaying I was trying to help solve.

On my way out of the bedroom, I bent

down and brushed my lips across Pam's forehead, then walked downstairs and crept into my little girls' room and stood there, listening to the faint sound of their breathing, held spellbound by the way their tiny faces quivered as they slept.

I was back at the office by 6:15. This was the only way I could ever get any work done, especially now that I was still having problems getting my post-coma brain to resume firing on all eight cylinders. I told myself I'd get to the next installment of BTK's homicides — this one involving what the killer surely must have considered to be his most satisfying murder — later in the afternoon. In the meantime, piles of file folders that desperately needed my attention were spread across my desk.

This dynamic between organized and disorganized, chaos and order, proved to be a constant source of tension in my life. I was embarrassed to admit it, but I had the unshakeable feeling that the man responsible for these unsolved killings in Wichita could probably teach me a thing or two about organization.

BTK's murders employed elements that were both uniquely organized and disorganized. He could be sloppy at times, such as when leaving behind biological evidence at his crime scenes. But it was the razor-sharp control that he obviously maintained after his murders that perplexed and astounded me. I wasn't sure what he did for work or even if he was married, but I felt confident that he never allowed his inner world — which seethed inside him like a bubbling cauldron — to bleed into his outer world.

In the analysis I wrote in 1979, performed on the heels of his two last known murders, I thought we were looking for someone who resembled a monster. But five years had passed, and now I began to glimpse another element of his character.

One of the reasons he was able to place so much time between his kills was because he'd somehow developed the ability to blend in to his environment. It would be far too much to expect him to stand out in his community. The reason we couldn't see him was that we were looking past him, not at him.

Shortly before lunch, I'd plowed through my paperwork, played Dear Abby to a couple of men in my unit, and was happily back at it up in my quiet corner of the law library, digging and sifting though the stack of reports that detailed BTK's last known murder, which occurred during the night of December 8, 1977.

Clearly, this was the UNSUB's most perfect kill, no doubt producing the kind of memories that might just have been tiding him over for these past few years. It began to unfold to the outside world with a phone call to an emergency dispatcher at 8:20 the next morning.

For Wichita firefighter Wayne Davis, it had been shaping up to be a typical morning. Like plenty of his coworkers, he supplemented his income by working side jobs. On this particular chilly morning, he was sent to pick up a truck that was supposedly parked on St. Francis Street and drive it across town. But there was just one problem — Wayne couldn't find the damn thing. So when he spotted a pay phone outside a market on the corner of St. Francis and Central Streets, he decided to pull over and call the guy who'd hired him. He hopped out of his car, shoved his hand in his pocket, and quickly realized he had no change.

Just my luck, he shrugged, as he hurried inside the market to break a dollar bill. A man was using the pay phone, speaking quietly into the receiver, but Davis barely noticed him.

In those few moments that Davis was inside the store, a brief, chilling exchange took place between the caller and two police dispatchers. "You will find a homicide at 843

South Pershing," the man told the dispatcher. "Nancy Fox."

"I'm sorry, sir," she replied. "I can't understand you. What is the address?"

At that point, another dispatcher, who had been monitoring the call, interrupted: "I believe 843 South Pershing."

"That is correct," the man said. Then the phone line went quiet.

By the time Davis made it back to the parking lot, the caller had vanished, and the receiver dangled in midair. Davis grabbed it, placed the phone against his ear, and, when he didn't hear a dial tone, said, "Hello?"

The voice on the other end of the line inquired if he was the same person who she'd just been speaking to. "No," he replied. "Some other guy was using the phone."

"Wayne, is that you?" the dispatcher asked, recognizing his voice because emergency calls were often routed through the fire department and the two regularly spoke to one another.

"Yeah, it's me," he said. "What's going on?"

A moment later, Wichita homicide captain Al Thimmesch jumped on the line. The two men and their wives were longtime square dance buddies. "Wayne," Thimmesch asked, "did you get a look at the guy on the phone?"

"Not really," he said. "What's all the fuss about?" Thimmesch quickly filled him in on the details. When it became apparent that Davis could recall precious little about the caller's appearance, Thimmesch asked if he'd object to undergoing hypnosis at police headquarters.

"No problem," Davis replied.

But there *was* a problem. The killer had surfaced again. For seven brief seconds and in fifteen words, he'd broken his silence and risked everything to let the local authorities know he'd returned.

Shortly before 8:30, two patrol cars pulled up to the curb beside the pink duplex identified by the caller. The two officers who arrived at the scene quickly surveyed the exterior of the house. A back window had been shattered, they observed, and the phone line leading into the dwelling had been cut. The front door was unlocked. The officers entered the house and were hit by a blast of hot air.

A moment later, twenty-five-year-old Nancy Fox was found lying face down on the neon-blue paisley bedspread, wearing only a pale pink long-sleeved sweater. The tips of her toes, which hung over the edge of the mattress, had turned black. The nails of her long, slender fingers were pink. Something about the way they were positioned — partially extended, partially curled — looked deceivingly peaceful, beatific. Nylon stockings tightly bound her wrists behind her back. Her violet-colored panties had been pulled down around her hips, just above her knees. A cream-colored yellow nightgown had been tied around her ankles.

When police rolled Fox over, they saw that the left side of her face had also turned black. In her mouth was stuffed a gag fashioned out of various colored panty hose, and her dark tongue was swollen to many times its normal size. Wisps of sandy blonde hair covered much of her face, but beneath it smears of blood could be seen caked around her nose and mouth. Another pair of panty hose had been cinched tightly around her neck.

"Whoever did this was a real pervert," recalled one homicide detective who arrived at the crime scene a few minutes later. "You could just see the sexual perversion all over that poor girl. . . . The whole thing really just aggravated me."

Dumped on a coffee table were the contents of Nancy Fox's purse. The killer, it was believed, had taken her driver's license as a souvenir. On the dresser beside the bed sat a picture of Fox's bowling team — she and four friends stood there beside their bowling balls, goofy grins plastered on their faces. On either side of the picture, two jewelry boxes appeared to have been rifled through.

On the bed next to Fox's body, the contents of her lingerie drawer had been dumped. Police speculated that the killer had been searching for suitable bindings and gags. They also theorized that he'd turned up the thermostat in order to compensate for the cold air that had entered the dwelling through the window he'd shattered.

Semen was found at the scene in a blue nightgown, left at the head of the bed. Crime scene technicians were able to retrieve enough of a sample to send it quickly to the state crime lab in Topeka and have it analyzed. This was a decade before the advent of DNA testing, and the only thing police could hope to glean from the sperm sample was the blood type of the person it came from.

What they learned did little to help investigators focus their efforts, for the sperm had come from someone classified as a PGM-1 non-secretor. In layman's terms, this meant that the UNSUB had just hit the genetic jackpot. Because if you were going to leave sperm behind at a crime scene, you could only hope to be a PGM-1 non-secretor, as this made trying to pinpoint your blood type physically impossible.

The search for other types of evidence also proved less than fruitful. In an effort to determine if the killer left behind any fingerprints on Fox's body, investigators employed what was, at the time, considered to be a newfangled forensic technique.

A week before the murder, the department's fingerprint technician had just attended a seminar on "fuming," which involved erecting a makeshift plastic tent over the bed and pouring a chemical known as cyanoacrylate (commonly referred to as super-glue) into a ceramic bowl, then heating it at a low temperature. Over the next two hours, the chemicals vaporized inside the tent and adhered to any of the oils left behind by fingerprints, which were visible when viewed under a black light. When the process was finished, a portion of several fingerprints and part of a palm print were detected on Fox's body, but they weren't sufficient in helping police locate any suspects.

By late that afternoon, Fox's body was wheeled out on a gurney and driven to St. Francis Hospital, four miles way. An autopsy determined that she died from strangulation. Yet the coroner found that despite partially undressing his victim and binding her, the killer had not raped or penetrated her.

As a battery of tests were being run on Fox's body, detectives were busy interviewing her friends, family, and coworkers, enabling them to reconstruct her final hours.

They learned that shortly after 9:00 P.M., Nancy Fox left her job at Helzberg's Jewelry Store at the Wichita Mall, where she worked as an assistant manager. On her way home, she grabbed a burger at a drive-thru fast-food joint, then continued back to the duplex where she lived alone in a quiet, relatively crime-free lower-middle-class neighborhood. Detectives postulated that once inside, Fox had had a smoke, downed a glass of water, then undressed for bed, neatly folding her tan skirt over a wooden chair. It was at this point, police believed, that the killer, who had been hiding in Fox's bedroom closet, appeared and forced her onto the bed.

Although I had no way of proving it, I speculated that the killer masturbated into Fox's nightgown only after his victim had died. His inability to rape or penetrate any of his victims told me that he was so fearful of women that a woman's lifeless but partially naked body would represent the ultimate sexual turn-on.

Once dead, she became the perfect object,

nonthreatening, no longer human, nothing more than a flesh-covered mannequin — all the things he dreamed about. Which was why the man responsible for Fox's death went to such lengths to pose the body of his victim, much the way a painter or sculptor might pose a model. Everything about her positioning on the bed, the tilt of her head, the way her panties were pulled down to her knees, her various bindings and gags fashioned from panty hose, revealed to me that the killer wasn't posing his victim merely as a way to shock police who arrived at the scene.

Just as he did with the body of Shirley Vian, the UNSUB posed Fox because he had to. The images he created at his crime scenes were similar to a cache of food. He needed to pose Fox in order to take mental "snapshots" of her body, then use that memory to get him through those long, lean periods when killing wouldn't be an option.

Harvey Glatman, billed as the nation's first modern serial killer, went to similar lengths when displaying the bodies of his victims. A hardcore bondage freak, he documented his many kills in diaries and with countless photographs he snapped and later developed in his darkroom. But Glatman wasn't content merely to take pictures of his victims' bodies after murdering them. He used his camera to chronicle his killings, capturing the look of terror on the faces of his victims before garroting them with a piece of rope. More than anything else, Glatman got off on preserving in a photograph that empty, glazed look of primal fear and hopelessness in the eyes of those he killed.

I often wondered what sort of a role model this sick man had been for BTK — they were both consumed by bondage, and, because of his detailed crime scene descriptions, I believed BTK was also photographing his victims.

As a child, Glatman possessed an insatiable obsession with bondage and ropes. In his early teens, he'd spent hours masturbating in the attic, hanging himself from the rafters in an effort to heighten his orgasms. A family doctor told his concerned parents to ignore their son's strange hobby because he'd one day outgrow it.

By the time Glatman turned sixteen, he used a cap gun to force a girl to undress. He was quickly arrested and, upon being released on bail, traveled to New York. Not long afterward, he was arrested for robbery and sent to jail for five years. After his release in 1951, Glatman moved to Los Angeles and opened a TV repair shop. To the outside world, he lived a fairly quiet life and did his best to keep away from women.

Then, one sweltering afternoon in July 1957, the dam broke, and Glatman's self-imposed exile from the opposite sex ended. An avid amateur shutterbug, he convinced a nineteen-year-old model he met while on a TV repair job to pose for him, telling her he made extra cash shooting pictures for detective magazines. She showed up at his house a few days later, eager to pocket the $50 he promised her for the photo shoot. Within minutes of her arrival, he raped her at gunpoint, then drove her out to a remote expanse of desert outside Los Angeles. He stripped the hysterical woman to her underwear and, before strangling her, shot pictures of her pleading for her life. Over the next year, he killed two other women using his photography ruse in order to win them over.

Glatman wasn't caught until one of his would-be victims, whom he'd already shot through the thigh, grabbed his pistol while he drove her on a one-way ride out to the desert. When taken into custody, Glatman gleefully provided officers with detailed accounts of each of his killings. He was executed by cyanide gas in San Quentin's death chamber in 1959.

BTK could very well feel a kinship with a sick killer like Glatman. After all, he seemed to possess a fantasy life every bit as intense and consuming as Harvey's. Yet Glatman's main problem was his inability to harness this invisible world inside his head. If he had been able to do so, that world might have provided sustenance for him during those stretches when he should have been lying low. Which was, it appeared, what Nancy Fox's killer had been doing for the nine months since his murder of Shirley Vian — he'd managed to restrain himself. And it was also what he did for the next two months after Fox's death. He retreated back into the shadows and no doubt did his best to resume his day-to-day life.

The brazenness of Nancy Fox's killer both sickened and intrigued the community — at least for a week or two. To murder an innocent young woman was terrible enough. But to actually pick up a phone and notify police about the killing seemed unfathomable. What in God's name would he have to gain by doing that, most people thought, other than to flaunt his handiwork?

At this point, the crime still hadn't been connected with any of the UNSUB's previous killings. Police focused much of their efforts on three of Nancy's former boyfriends, but this quickly led nowhere. To nearly everyone but her grieving family and friends, her death began to feel like nothing more than a terribly random, isolated act of violence.

And this, I believe, must have irked the UNSUB. The rush brought on from Nancy's killing would have faded in a matter of weeks. True, the murder would have provided him with plenty of sick memories, but something told me that Fox's murder just wasn't receiving the kind of attention BTK had hoped and yearned for.

Media interest in the killing quickly waned, especially because police didn't have any real suspects other than the mysterious man who phoned in to report the murder. A recording of his voice was played over and over on local radio and TV stations, but no one could identify the man behind the voice. FBI voice analysts were unable to uncover anything of value from the seven-second audio clip, such as whether or not the caller had attempted to mask his voice.

The only thing police knew about the caller came from information fireman Wayne Davis provided. The man was six feet tall, blonde-haired, dressed in a gray industrial uniform and wearing a hat with earflaps. Davis also reported that the man might have driven a late-model van with some sort of writing on its side. After undergoing four sessions with a hypnotherapist, that was all Davis could retrieve from his subconscious. The general consensus among detectives was that he was "blocking" due to a very primal emotion — fear.

"It wasn't that he didn't want to help," said one officer working on the case. "I think he was just scared."

On the last day of January, BTK's desire to stir things up appeared to get the better of him. He penned a pithy Valentine's poem to his latest victim, then sent it to the local newspaper. It wouldn't be discovered for nearly two weeks. By this point, police still hadn't made the connection between Shirley Vian's murder and Fox's. Nor had they established any links with either of those homicides and the killing of Kathy Bright and the Otero family. But that was about to change when BTK decided the time had come to stick the knife in and twist it just a bit. And in one terrifying moment, the murders of the Oteros, Vian, and Fox would be irrevocably linked, although several more years would pass before the identity of Bright's killer would be understood.

All hell broke loose in Wichita on the morning of February 10, 1978, when BTK surfaced again, setting in motion a chain of events that finally garnered for him the type of attention he craved.

A receptionist at the offices of the local ABC affiliate, KAKE TV-10, opened an envelope that morning and discovered four pages of photocopied material that included a letter and a poem (both filled with punctuation and spelling errors) and a drawing of a woman bound, gagged, and lying face down on a bed. This communiqué was the killer's most prolific public confession to date and a chilling taunt. It also provided me with a revealing glimpse into his brain.

I find the newspaper not wirting about the poem on Vain unamusing. A little paragraph would have enough. Iknow it not the media fault. The Police Cheif he keep things quiet, and doesn't let the public know there a psycho running around lose strangling mostly women, there 7 in the ground; who will be next?

How many do I have to Kill before I get a name in the paper or some national attention. Do the cop think that all those deaths are not related? Golly -gee, yes the M.O. is different in each, but look a pattern is developing. The victims are tie up-most have been women-phone cut- bring

some bondage mater sadist tendencies-
no struggle, outside the death spot-no
wintness except the Vain's Kids. They
were very lucky; a phone call save them.
I was go-ng to tape the boys and put
plastics bag over there head like I did
Joseph, and Shirley. And then hang the
girl. God-oh God what a beautiful sexual
relief that would been. Josephine,when I
hung her really turn me on; her pleading
for mercy then the rope took whole, she
helpless; staring at me with wide terror
fill eyes the rope getting tighter-tighter.
You don't understand these things because your not underthe influence of factor x). The same thing that made Son of
Sam, Jack the Ripper, Havery Glatman,
Boston Strangler, Dr. H.H. Holmes
Panty Hose Strangler OF Florida, Hillside Strangler, Ted of the West Coast and
many more infamous character kill.
Which seem s senseless, but we cannot
help it. There is no help, no cure, except
death or being caught and put away. It a
terrible nightmarebut, you see I don't
lose any sleep over it. After a thing like
Fox I ccome home and go about life like
anyone else. And I will be like that until
the urge hit me again. It not continuous
and I don;t have a lot of time. It take time

to set a kill, one mistake and it all over. Since I about blew it on the phone-handwriting is out-letter guide is to long and typewriter can be traced too,.My short poem of death and maybe a drawing;later on real picture and maybe a tape of the sound will come your way. How will you know me. Before a murder or murders you will receive a copy of the initials B.T.K., you keep that copy the original will show up some day on guess who?

May you not be the unluck one!

P.S. How about some name for me, its time: 7 down and many more to go. I like the following How about you? "THE B.T.K. STRANGLER", "WICHITA STRANGLER", "POETIC STRANGLER", "THE BOND AGE STRANGLER" OR "PSYCHO" THE WICHITA HANGMAN THE WICHITA EXECUTIONER, "THE GAROTE PHATHOM", "THE ASPHIXIATER".

#5 You guess motive and victim.
#6 You found one Shirley Vain lying belly down on a unmade bed in northeast bedroom-hand tied behind back

with black tape and cord. Feet & ankles with black tape &legs. Ankles tied to west head of the bed with small off white cord, wrap around legs, hands, arm, finally the neck, many times. A off white pla stic bag over her head loop on with a pink nitie was barefooted. She was sick use a glass of water and smoke I or Two cigarette-house a total mess- kids took some toys with them to the bathroom-bedagainst east bathroom door. Chose at random with some pre-planning. Motive Factor X.

#7 One Nancy Fox-lying belly down on made bed in southwest bedroom-hands tied behind back with red panty hose-feet together with yellow nitie-semi-nude with pink sweater and bra small neckless-glasses on west dresser-panties below butt-many different than the hosery. She had a smoke and wbnt to the bathroom before the final act-very neat housekeeper& dresser-rifled pursein kitchen-empty paper bag — white coat in living-room- heat up to about 90 de-grees, Christsmas tree lights on- nities and hose around the room- hose bag of orange color it and hosery on bed-driver licence gone-seminal stain on or in blue women wear. Chose at random with little

171

pre-planning, Motive Factor "X"

#8 Next victim maybe: You will find her hanging with a wire noose-Hands behind back with black tape or cord -feet with tape or cord-gaged- then cord around the body to the neck -hooded maybe- possible seminal stain in anus-or on body. Will be chosen at random. Some pre-planning-Motive Factor "X".

Enclosed with the letter was a poem and a pencil sketch that closely resembled the scene officers saw when they entered Nancy Fox's sweltering apartment on the morning of December 9, 1977. The poem, titled "Oh Death to Nancy," was based on an Appalachian folk song called "Oh Death."

What is this taht I can see
Cold icy hands taking hold of me
for Death has come, you all can see.
Hell has open it,s gate to trick me.
Oh! Death, Oh! Death, can't you spare me,
    over for another year!
I'll stuff your jaws till you can't talk
I'll blind your leg's till you can't walk
I'll tie your hands till you can't make a
    stand.
And finally I'll close your eyes so you can't
    see

I'll bring sexual death unto you for me.

When KAKE news producer Ron Lowen delivered the packet to police chief Richard LaMunyon, it proved to be the final straw that forced the top police department official in town to do the very thing he dreaded most — go public with the news that a serial killer was stalking the streets of Wichita and that police, despite their best efforts, had been so far powerless to stop him.

For someone in LaMunyon's position, having to stand up in front of the community that entrusted him to protect it and admit that a predatory sexual killer was on the loose is tantamount to screaming "Fire!" in a packed theater. The reaction, he knew, would be predictable and swift — panic, widespread fear, perhaps a touch of civil chaos, followed by anger, finger pointing, and a flood of useless tips inundating police. But despite this inevitable reaction, clearly the genie could no longer be kept in the bottle. He'd grown too bold and lethal.

By midafternoon on Friday, February 10, a few hours after the Fox letter was dropped on his desk, LaMunyon put out the word that a press conference would be held that evening at city hall. What he was about to tell the city's media made headlines around the nation.

By the time reporters began filing into the building, a tense buzz hung in the air. Something big and ugly was afoot. The sun had set, snow was piled in the gutters of downtown, and the air held a cold sting to it, reminiscent of that winter day four years before when four bodies were discovered inside the Otero home.

"The purpose of this news conference is to advise the public of an extremely serious matter involving a series of murders which have occurred in our city," he said slowly, pausing every few words to allow the gravity of his message to sink in.

"As you know, in January 1974, four members of the Otero family were murdered. In March of 1977, Shirley Vian was killed. And in December 1977, Nancy Fox was also murdered. Earlier today KAKE-TV received and immediately brought me a letter wherein the author took credit for the Otero, the Fox, and the Vian murders. In addition, whoever wrote this letter has taken credit for a seventh victim. . . . We are convinced without a doubt that the person who claims to have killed the Oteros, Miss Fox, and Miss Vian is in fact the same person. I want to restate that there is no question in our minds but that the person who wrote the letter killed these people. This person has consistently identified himself with the initials BTK and wishes to be known as the BTK Strangler. Because we are sure this man is responsible for seven murders, we wish to enlist the assistance of each citizen of this community.

"Our police department has already begun special efforts, which are as follows: (1) Additional uniformed officers are already on the street. (2) A special detective task force involving the major case squad has been established. (3) A special phone number for citizens to call has been established — 269-4177. This phone will be staffed twenty-four hours a day. (4) We have solicited the assistance of the district attorney, the sheriff, and of professionals in the field of human behavior and would welcome assistance from any person regardless of their expertise. . . . I know it is difficult to ask people to remain calm, but we are asking exactly this. When a person of this type is at large in our community, it requires special precautions and special awareness by everyone."

The one thing that struck me about LaMunyon's press conference was how honest he was with the residents of Wichita. Hearing him admit that his investigators had no solid leads in the case made my head spin for one simple reason: it let the killer off the hook far too easily. And that was the last thing the authorities should have done. In my opinion, their best course of action was to keep the heat turned up on the UNSUB, to force him to continue looking over his shoulder, asking himself when police were going to come crashing through his back door.

Not surprisingly, LaMunyon's announcement sent a collective shudder through the community, especially when, several days later, an unfounded rumor began sweeping through the city. BTK, it seemed, targeted only the occupants of residences "located on the west side of a north- and south-running street with a house address containing a number *three* within it." Even if this had been true, I would have written it off to coincidence. Serial killers, I'd learned, are far more interested in finding a victim who — because of his or her various traits and attributes — satisfied them psychologically, rather than one who has a certain number in his or her street address.

BTK's habit of cutting the outside phone lines of his victims was also mentioned in the press conference. That evening, thousands of residents throughout the city began a ritual that would last for years: the first thing they did upon entering their home was check to see if the phone worked. Others made it a habit — before entering their house — to dial their home number from a pay phone, to see if their phone rang.

Within days, the sale of guns soared. So did the demand for additional door locks and peepholes and Mace. Because anyone could be the killer, nobody felt safe, and every stranger seemed like a suspect. Paranoia swept through the community like fire through a prairie grassland — which certainly must have sent shivers of ecstasy up the UNSUB's spine.

Because, at its core, BTK's letter was no different than the ones the Son of Sam used to pen during his one-year killing spree that began in July 1976. Like the Son of Sam, BTK wasn't seeking notoriety initially, but he soon took that direction when the press began running stories. Both offenders relished the publicity, and each felt good about the terror and fear they were creating and causing to unfold in their respective communities. Both had become the bogeyman, a role to which they quickly became addicted.

Police were initially stumped about the way BTK opened his communiqué, complaining about "the newspaper not writing about the poem on Vain." Of course, it didn't take Sherlock Holmes to understand that the killer was referring to Shirley Vian. Within hours of LaMunyon's press conference, the full answer became apparent when an employee of the *Wichita Eagle* discovered that a three-by-five index card, which arrived in the newsroom on January 31, had mistakenly been routed to the newspaper's advertising department.

Because the cryptic message on the card was printed in children's block letters from a rubber stamp, whoever first spotted the card believed it to be a personal ad, not a poem based on the murder of Shirley Vian. It was based on an eighteenth-century Mother Goose nursery rhyme, titled "Curley Locks."

SHIRLEYLOCKS SHIRLEYLOCKS
WILT THOUGH BE MINE
THOU SHALT NOT SCREEM
NOT YET FEEL THE LINE
BUT LAY ON CUSHION
AND THINK OF ME AND DEATH
AND HOW IT IS GOING TO BE.

At the bottom of the card, he printed the message, POEM FOR FOX NEXT.

The UNSUB waited fourteen months before surfacing again, although initially police had their doubts that it was actually him. Just after 10 P.M. on the cool spring night of April 28, 1979, a sixty-one-year-old widow named Anna Williams returned home after a night of square dancing. She lived at 615 South Pinecrest, roughly one mile from Nancy Fox's house. Friends dropped her off at her house and watched as she fumbled for her keys on the front porch. But just before unlocking the door, she decided to reconsider their offer of a cup of coffee at a local café. She dropped her keys in her purse, climbed back in their car, and was whisked away into the night.

An hour later, she once again returned home and quickly discovered that one of her basement windows had been shattered. Rope, a broom handle, and several pieces of undergarments were found lying beside a bed in the basement guest room where her granddaughter often slept. Williams walked back upstairs and noticed that several scarves, pieces of jewelry, various articles of clothing, and $35 in cash were missing. A half roll of toilet paper had also been used, she realized. Most frightening of all, when she tried to telephone police, she couldn't get a dial tone. She hurried next door to a neighbor's house and phoned police.

A few minutes later, a squad car pulled up to the house, and two patrolmen began asking the badly shaken Williams questions. She'd been in poor health ever since the recent death of her husband, and this near disaster seemed on the verge of pushing her over the edge. One of the officers, who poked around the backyard with a flashlight, spotted the reason why her phone was dead — the line had been cut. Burglary investigators combed through the house, searching for fingerprints and traces of semen, but nothing was found. A crime report was taken, but it quickly disappeared into a file cabinet, and, because there was no reason to do so, it was never shared with homicide detectives in the police department's burglary unit.

No mention of the incident appeared in the local newspaper. Williams, however, never believed a random burglar was responsible for the break-in. In her heart, she believed it to be the work of BTK.

In his heart, the individual responsible for the break-in couldn't stand it that news of his most recent surfacing didn't make headlines. On June 15, a manila envelope, printed in neat block letters, arrived at Williams's home and was opened by her daughter. It contained her mother's pilfered scarf and jewelry. Also stuffed inside the envelope was a typed photocopied poem and a drawing of a bound, nude woman lying face down on her bed; a broomstick had been inserted into what appeared to be either her vagina or anus. Williams's daughter telephoned police without ever showing the letter to Anna.

Two days later, the *Wichita Eagle* ran the headline BTK IS BACK; INTENDED VICTIM GETS POEM on the front page. True to his word, BTK had chosen his eighth victim. The only problem was, she never bothered to show up. In his nineteen-line poem titled "Oh Anna, Why Didn't You Appear?" he aired his frustration at being denied the pleasure of getting to snuff out another life.

T'was perfect plan of deviant pleasure so
    bold on that Spring nite
My inner felling hot with propension of the
    new awakening season
Warn, wet with inner fear and rapture, my
    pleasure of entanglement, like new vines
    at night
Oh, Anna, Why Didn't You Appear
Drop of fear fresh Spring rain would roll
    down from your nakedness to scent to
    lofty fever that burns within,
In that small world of longing, fear, rapture,
    and desparation, the game we play, fall

181

on devil ears

Fantasy spring forth, mounts, to storm fury, then winter clam at the end.

Oh, Anna Why Didn't You Appear

Alone, now in another time span I lay with sweet enrapture garments across most private thought

Bed of Spring moist grass, clean before the sun, enslaved with control, warm wind scenting the air, sun light sparkle tears in eyes so deep and clear.

Alone again I trod in pass memory of mirrors, and ponder why for number eight was not.

Oh, Anna Why Didn't You Appear

Although the UNSUB possessed the poetic sensibility of a love-drunk college freshman, his communiqués reinforced my belief that he possessed an eye for detail. I couldn't shake the idea that he'd snapped photographs of his victims, crime scenes, and — in Anna Williams's case — his intended crime scene. Either that or he had a photographic memory, which seemed unlikely.

His sketches, moreover, weren't half bad — detailed and reasonably well drawn. They weren't Michelangelo, but he drew a helluva lot better than I did. Although his subject matter was a bit limited, I sensed that he'd honed his ability to draw gagged, scantily clad women bound up in rope by staring at the pages of pulp detective magazines sold up through the mid-1970s in almost every mom-and-pop convenience store around the nation.

We in the criminal profiling business referred to the violent offenders who read these magazines as "collectors." These glossy publications, which usually bore a cover photo of a hog-tied, frightened woman with a gun or knife pressed against her breast or temple, served as virtual textbooks for budding killers. Criminologists like myself had long suspected that killers studied the exploits of those savages who'd come before them, soaking up every detail of true or fictional crimes wherever they could find it — magazines, books, movies, and TV. Long before any of these animals ever claimed their first victim, they'd spent a lifetime nurturing the dark dreams festering inside their heads by devouring publications with names like *Master Detective, Official Police Detective, Front Page Detective,* and *Startling Detective.*

Do the words and images contained in the pages of these magazines create violent criminals? Certainly not. But clearly they fuel their sick fantasies. The way I see it, precious few people who read true (or fictional) crime books harbor some latent desire to go out and kill someone. People read them for the same reason they rubberneck when driving past a bloody automobile accident. They want a glimpse of horror, but they don't want to get too close to the blood and gore. Others consume these books and magazines in order to understand a violent offender's background, to grasp what makes him so different than the rest of us — particularly when they seem to so closely resemble us.

Did BTK read these magazines? I would have bet my FBI pension on it. The one thing that this violent media didn't do, however, was cause these individuals to become killers — it only fueled their already deeply embedded fantasies and provided literal models of horrible acts in vivid detail.

For me, the killer who drove home the idea that violent offenders learn the tools of their trade from their elders was a balding, gaunt serial killer named Joseph Fischer. On the evening I showed up at Attica State Prison to speak with him, back in 1981, it was hard to imagine how this former transient could have killed six women during his wanderings across the nation. Yet Fischer, who insisted that he'd actually murdered thirty-two people, put this killer-nurturing-killer concept into perspective for me in a way that none of the other murderers I'd interviewed before had.

"It's kinda like guys who follow baseball or football," he told me in that dimly lit prison interrogation room. "They know all the batting averages, yards per game, interceptions versus touchdowns, where the players went to high school. They know every stat about all their favorite players."

Fischer took a deep breath and began tracing an imaginary circle into the top of the table that separated the two of us.

"Well, those other guys got their games, and guys like me, we got our games. I didn't grow up wanting to hit home runs. I grew up wanting to kill people. And I used to soak up every bit of information I could find on the guys who were good at playing my kind of game."

It always made me sick to my stomach when guys like Fischer referred to their habit of killing innocent people as a game. But clearly that's what it had become for BTK — a deadly game that nobody had yet been able to stop. And by the summer of 1979, when the locals in Wichita learned that the serial killer living in their midst wasn't going away, BTK finally graduated from rookie player to coach, from pupil to teacher. He'd finally achieved what he craved most — the chance to be somebody.

These last communications had revealed that in his mind, he'd transcended to the next level, in terms of his ability and proficiency as a killer. And now he yearned for some degree of recognition for his "accomplishments."

The buzz from all the mayhem he created must have been intense, but it wouldn't last forever. That giddy sensation of self-worth would eventually fade, just as everything else that sustained him did. And when that emptiness and self-loathing returned and grew too intense, we'd hear from him again.

The only question was when.

7

How do you trap a shadow? Where do you even start? You can't shine a light on it. Shadows dwell in darkness. They disappear in the presence of light. The police in Wichita had thrown plenty of light in the direction of the UNSUB, but had found nothing. He'd remained hidden, revealing himself only to his victims, then vanishing.

If the authorities had managed to get close to him, he'd never let on. Now it was 1984, and ten years had passed since what he claimed were his first grisly series of murders.

After combing through hundreds of pages of crime reports, photos, and other documents detailing his murders, I'd slowly come to the conclusion that perhaps the only way to catch this killer was to let him catch himself. That was really all I had to offer. The UNSUB seemed to hold all the cards — a fact that both he and the police were well aware of. This meant we might have to wait years before he let his guard down enough to slip up.

But he'd done it before. Besides leaving traces of semen behind in the Oteros' basement and in Nancy Fox's bedroom, he'd felt compelled to send his revealing, potentially evidence-laden communiqués to police. But it had been five years since he'd felt the need — and taken the risk — to type out another letter.

Sitting in my file-strewn office one afternoon a few days after my second visit from the Wichita Police Department, I thought back to a case near San Diego that I'd been called in to work on the previous year.

The victim had apparently run out of gas on a fairly busy highway during the early evening. Her nude body was later discovered in some nearby foothills. A dog collar had been cinched tightly around her neck. Shortly before her murder, she'd been raped.

To help the local police find the killer, I tried to imagine how the events leading up to her death had unfolded, picturing the interaction between the killer and his victim. It quickly became obvious that this tragedy was another example of someone's being in the wrong place at the wrong time. She'd run out of gas, but felt safe because of the abundance of traffic. Surely no one would be crazy enough to harm someone in front of so many potential witnesses, she told herself.

The more I thought about it, the clearer it became that the very thing the victim believed would protect her could be used to coax her killer out of hiding and into the investigation — not because he wanted to, but because he felt he had to. By walking in the shoes of the UNSUB, I could "see" him driving past the stranded motorist on that busy highway and suddenly realizing that he'd just stumbled on the perfect victim of opportunity. The only glitch was how he could pull it off, especially in the presence of so many possible eyewitnesses.

His answer? He'd approach the victim, exuding every bit of friendliness he could muster, offering her a ride to a nearby service station. But as soon as she sat in his vehicle, he no doubt pulled out a gun and ordered her to lie down on the floorboard. Next, he drove her to an isolated area he was familiar with because he either worked or resided in the immediate vicinity.

With all that in mind, my advice to police was to create three press releases. The first would provide readers and listeners with the basic facts of the case and end with police reaching out for potential witnesses. A day or two later, they'd advise the community about the positive responses they'd received, which were generating some solid investigative leads. The last release would inform the community that they'd developed information about a vehicle observed by several witnesses as well as a description of an individual standing next to the victim.

I suggested that they should say they were uncertain if this person was a suspect or just someone who stopped to lend a helping hand.

A few days later, our "Good Samaritan" took the bait and stopped by police headquarters to inform them that he may have been the person seen by some of the witnesses. And, yes, as a matter of fact, he had stopped by to help the victim, but for some reason she'd declined his assistance. Bingo! Suddenly, the police had someone they could place at the scene, and investigators could go to work doing a thorough background check of the suspect, along with attempting to link him to the crime.

The so-called Good Samaritan was later convicted when police were able to match up hair and fibers on the dog collar, along with biological evidence in the form of sperm.

When it came to the murders in Wichita, we didn't have a busy highway or a plethora of potential witnesses. But we did have something else. We knew our UNSUB had a weak spot.

In the past, BTK had risked everything for the chance to thumb his nose at police by writing letters, which for all he knew might inadvertently contain a few incriminating scraps of forensic evidence or intimate clues about his psychology. If he was going to slip up again, my hunch was that it might be because of this unquenchable need to communicate, to reach out and share the secret he had to keep locked up inside his brain.

I just had one question: *How do we force his hand?*

A few afternoons later I still didn't have an answer. So I decided to spend my lunch hour going for a mellow jog through the woods that surrounded the FBI Academy. I'd often done this in the past when working on a case. I'd head out onto a trail at a slow ten-minute-a-mile pace, allowing my mind to drift wherever it wanted. The process was similar to what I did at night when I forced myself to dream about a case. My technique led to plenty of heart-stopping nightmares, but the insight I gleaned made it worthwhile. The network of running trails that weave and crisscross their way through the dense woods at Quantico have achieved near mythic lore among agents. Many a promising rookie has emptied the contents of his stomach on these trails as a result of pushing himself past his physical limits. Because it's so easy to get disoriented on the meandering paths (as I once did for several hours when I first arrived at Quantico), fitness instructors long ago began marking the way with yellow bricks. Ever since, the running course has been known as the Yellow Brick Road. On that warm, hazy autumn afternoon, I soon found myself trotting over a dirt trail that bore the name "We're Not in Kansas Anymore."

Just a few minutes into my run, the full weight of those five words hit me — this could have been the BTK's mantra. From what I recalled from a college literature class, Dorothy uttered that famous phrase to Toto in *The Wizard of Oz* for good reason. Kansas was a symbol of Dorothy's outer world. But thanks to a tornado and a knock on the head, she suddenly embarked on an inner journey to a place she called Oz, a world that dwelled deep within her subconscious.

For Dorothy, Oz was filled with everything from a loveable Cowardly Lion and cute Munchkins to a hideous-looking Wicked

Witch and a squeaky Tin Man. My hunch was that years before the UNSUB committed the Otero murders in January 1974, this aspiring killer had begun a similar journey. But for him, Oz was a much more sinister, violent realm, a dark fantasy world where he retreated on a daily basis to relive his kills.

While I was mulling over all this, thinking about how much Dorothy reminded me of Josie Otero, the vision of an ultracool black man in a suede trench coat flashed into my head. The juxtaposition of these disparate, seemingly random images proved jarring. *Where the hell is this going?* I laughed.

Then suddenly I remembered the night before when Pam and I were channel surfing. After a few minutes, she stumbled on a rerun of an early 1970s flick, starring Richard Roundtree, about a no-nonsense, ass-kicking inner-city black detective named John Shaft. The movie's theme song thundered out of the tiny speaker in our TV set.

"Oh, I remember this movie," she said, flipping to another channel.

"Turn it back," I pleaded. "I gotta watch this."

Pam moaned, switched back to the movie, then snuggled up next to me. "OK, you win," she said. "But if you start sobbing over this the way you did over that Lassie movie two weeks ago, I'm turning off the TV."

She had a point. Ever since emerging from my coma ten months before, I'd been an emotional basket case, bursting into tears at the strangest moments — commercials for used cars, sunsets, even a *Lassie* rerun.

"I think I can handle this," I replied.

For the next ninety minutes I stared into the flickering TV screen, not exactly sure why I was so mesmerized by the movie. But somewhere in the back of my head, a voice told me to sit back, pay attention, and enjoy the show. I liked Shaft. He kicked a lot of butt, bedded a bunch of women, and still managed to look like a million bucks the whole time. Something about his no-holds-barred approach to cracking that kidnapping case so crucial to the movie's plot felt strangely inspiring.

"I bet *he* could catch BTK," I mumbled. "Maybe I oughta call up the task force in Wichita and tell them that what they really need is Shaft, super-detective."

The sheer absurdity of Richard Roundtree running around the streets of Wichita trying to crack a serial murder case made me smile.

Maybe the idea wasn't so absurd. The local police didn't need a super-detective. What they really needed was a *super-cop,* someone who could crawl inside our UNSUB's mind and gently steer him in the direction we wanted him to go.

What I began to envision was a John Wayne–like twist on the standard concept of a police spokesman, typically used to brief the media during ongoing high-profile cases. That individual's job is to stand up in front of the cameras and microphones and update reporters on the status of the investigation. Sometimes they even give descriptions of the suspect or suspects. It's hardly cutting-edge criminology. Police agencies around the nation have been using spokespeople for decades. Sometimes the person tapped for the role is the chief or the sheriff. Other times, a lead detective on the case is used. More often than not, the honors go to one of the department's public information officers.

But now, out here on that running trail, an idea took shape and began to unroll itself inside my head like thread off a spool. We'd tweak the standard-issue police spokesperson concept just a bit. We'd turbocharge this otherwise predicable symbol of law and order, and transform it into a psychological crime-fighting tool who would be the perfect counterpart of BTK's grandiose vision of himself. How would we do this? For starters, it was obvious that part of the UNSUB's motive was a desire to thumb his nose at police. He wanted the world to know that he was smarter than the cops trying to catch him. At the same time, his detailed descriptions of his crime scenes told me that he was also a wannabe cop, someone who would have probably given anything to have a job in law enforcement. I wondered if he'd ever applied for a job with police and been turned away. Or yearned to apply, but knew that if they ran a fingerprint check on him they might stumble on a print he'd left behind at one of his crime scenes, which police had collected but never made public.

David Berkowitz (aka Son of Sam) had a bit of this same type of confused love-hate relationship with police festering inside him. On April 17, 1977, after shooting ten people and killing five, he pumped four .44-caliber bullets into two Bronx teenagers necking in a Mercury Montego. The event marked the latest chapter in his pathetic, senseless murder spree. But what made this one different was that before fleeing the scene, he left a note behind, marking the first time he'd felt compelled finally to reach out to the world and explain who he was. The note was addressed to Joseph Borrelli, the Bronx police captain who had been investigating Berkowitz's earlier homicides.

In the note, which has become one of the most infamous examples of the workings of a deranged homicidal mind, he wrote, "I am deeply hurt by your calling me a woman hater. I am not. But I am a monster. I am the 'Son of Sam.' . . . When father Sam gets drunk he gets mean. He beats his family. Sometimes he ties me up in the back of the house. Other times he locks me in the garage. Sam loves to drink blood. 'Go out and kill,' commands Father Sam."

BTK penned loosely similar-sounding rants to police, hinting at the dark, unstoppable forces that dwelled within him. But the more I thought about it, I realized that part of the key to influencing his behavior was getting a better understanding of whom he was really thumbing his nose at when he wrote his communiqués. Was he directing his taunts at a specific officer whose identity only he knew? Or were the police merely some ambiguous, fuzzy concept inside his troubled mind, a collection of faceless, nameless men in blue? If the latter were the case, I wondered why we couldn't provide him with a single image he could latch on to. Because if we could begin to control the mental picture he maintained of the police, we might just have a chance of controlling him.

Which is exactly where our so-called

super-cop would enter the picture. He would become the face that the UNSUB would picture whenever he thought of the police. He would become, in a sense, BTK's partner in crime, the devoted acolyte who tracked every move the killer made. The trick, of course, would be to locate someone whom BTK could not only identify with but also feel comfortable opening up to, the kind of law enforcement professional who could begin to harness BTK's self-inflated sense of his own importance, power, and intelligence that covered up his deep-seated feelings of inferiority and self-hatred. This meant that our super-cop couldn't be just anyone. That he might be a detective working the case or some high-ranking officer in the department wouldn't be good enough. What mattered most was that they be made of the kind of stuff that we could mold into the proper façade. Image would be everything.

Our super-cop would have to mouth words that sounded something like this: "If it takes me my whole career or even my lifetime, I will solve this case. I will look and search in every corner, every dark alley, and every crack in the sidewalk until I can identify the individual responsible for these homicides — and that's a promise to you."

Would it work? Could my idea help nab a

killer as elusive as BTK? It seemed worth a try.

A few afternoons later I was seated in a first floor conference room in the FBI's forensic science building, not far from my office. With me at that massive rectangular oak table were two other agents, along with the two detectives from Wichita who had traveled to Quantico looking for answers. Behind us were a handful of rubber-neckers, camped out in the back of the room to catch a glimpse of what was about to unfold during the next few hours.

We were going to toss out ideas about what sort of person might be responsible for those seven unsolved murders in Kansas, how police might track him down, and ways they could get him to crack once they had a possible suspect.

To my left sat Roy Hazelwood, a rail thin, chain-smoking forty-seven-year-old FBI instructor, widely regarded as one of finest minds in the study of interpersonal violence. A truly brilliant researcher and homicide investigator, Hazelwood was a former Army major who was first introduced to detective work while serving in the military police. Beside him sat Ron Walker, a clean-cut thirty-five-year-old former FBI field agent from

Colorado, brought into my unit shortly after my collapse from viral encephalitis. A veteran Air Force pilot, Walker was whip smart, highly organized, and in the midst of learning the ropes of profiling from me. He was proving to be an exceptionally quick study.

In many ways, our goal here felt similar to what musicians do when they get together and jam. Only instead of sound, we were bouncing our thoughts off one another, working with ideas based on clues BTK had left us at his murders and in his letters. Sometimes we chased a thread spooled out by someone else. At other moments, one of us would dart off in a fresh, new direction, watching to see if anyone followed. Much of what we would offer up would be insightful, some of it not so. We didn't always agree with what the others said, yet we were smart enough to know that this was part of the process, part of the journey.

The objective of our session was to keep moving forward until we ran out of juice, until we were tapped out. It was up to the two detectives from Wichita to take notes, jotting down whatever elements they found helpful. Whether anything we came up with at this table would ever get implemented was up to the task force. Our unit's caseload was far too crowded to allow the luxury of monitoring how our ideas were used in a particular investigation.

I decided to kick off the discussion by spending a few minutes rehashing the case for those present, hoping to refresh everyone's memories.

"Here's where I'm at with this guy," I said, pulling off my suit jacket and draping it over my chair. "Back when he started in 1974, he was in his mid- to late twenties. It's now ten years later, so that would put him in his mid- to late thirties."

"How'd you come up with that figure?" Walker asked.

"I started with the age of twenty-five because that's what our research is finding to be the median age when most of these guys start killing," I said. "Then I tacked on a few more years because of the level of criminal sophistication evident in the Otero murders and his apparent knowledge of police and criminology."

Walker nodded.

I turned toward the two detectives seated at the far end of the table. "If you haven't already, you guys should check and see if Nancy Fox's driver's license had her picture on it," I said. "If it did, it seems logical to assume that he took it as a type of trophy to help him relive her kill later. If not, perhaps he removed it in order to have enough facts on hand so he'd have something to read to the police dispatcher."

I paused for a moment to collect my thoughts. Since nobody opened his mouth, I continued. "If this is all a game to him, he's doing it to fulfill his ego," I said. "It's a challenge thrown at police. His victims are all so different. He may have a preferential victim, but when it's time to go on the hunt, the person he hits is the first one to come into his sights. The significance for him is his ability to get away with the crime and flaunt his skills. The only torture I'm seeing with his kills is psychological torture."

Hazelwood, a serious caffeine addict, polished off what was left of his coffee and then said, "But in his mind, he is torturing his victims. That's why he uses the bags. He wants to see the terror in their eyes as he places it over their heads."

Hazelwood stopped talking, but Walker and I knew better than to speak — he was just getting started. "He's definitely a sexual bondage practitioner and a collector of bondage magazines and detective magazines. He's also got an interest in criminology or psychology. He's probably pretty well known to adult book store operators in the area."

"Yeah," said Walker. "This guy is definitely into psychological torture. That indicates a higher level of sophistication and a higher level of intelligence than the average Joe on the street. The more physical the torture, the more primal and reactive the person inflicting it is. Not much intelligent thought goes into physical torture."

All of our heads nodded in unison.

"What we're finding from our research is that most of these guys have an IQ range between 105 and 145," I said. "The average falls between 115 and 120. Average for the normal population is 100. What this is showing us is that most of these guys are able to move around in society fairly easily. We catch the dumb ones quickly. The smarter ones take longer. . . . And so do the lucky ones.

"I think it's pretty clear that this guy is able to spend a bit of time at his crime scenes. This is something that appears important to him. He seems to want to have some kind of dialogue with his victims. It isn't a blitz-type scenario. As we learned from the Bright murder, he attempted to diffuse the situation and make everyone feel that if they'd just cooperate with him, he'd leave. They had no way of knowing that this was part of his MO. So he's capable of maintaining that type of control relationship. In a group kill, he's smart enough to go after strength first. He uses the stronger victim to tie up the others. Then he gets rid of that strong figure and, as he said in one of his letters, he saves the best for last."

As I spoke, I rubbed the tip of my index finger over the raised monogram on one of my gold cufflinks. "I've often wondered if the reason he took eleven-year-old Josie Otero to the basement was that she'd begun to get hysterical and loud after seeing her family killed," I said. "He was taking a chance by forcing her down there, but he may have been losing control of her at that moment and was concerned about the neighbors hearing her. It was a chance he was willing to take. And the way he tied her up with all those bindings felt like he was attempting to make his crime scene appear more complex than it really was. It was his way of turning it into an Ellery Queen mystery, forcing detectives to waste their time and scratch their heads, asking, 'Why would he do this?' "

Walker seemed to think he knew one of the reasons why. "The fact that we didn't see any signs of penetration, or any clear sign of fondling, says we're looking at a guy who has an inadequate, immature sexual history," he said. "Her bra was probably cut in order to expose the breasts for voyeuristic kicks rather than touching. There's just so much emphasis on substitute sex with this guy. I think we should be looking at a lone-wolf type of personality. But he's not alone because he's shunned by others — it's because he chooses to be alone. His social and sexual life will reflect this. He wants to be alone. He can function in social settings, but only on the surface. He may have women friends he can talk to, but he'd feel very inadequate with a peer group female."

Hazelwood sensed something else. "This guy is a sexual sadist," he said. "He's sexually inadequate, but he will have relationships with women. To a sexual sadist, the act of sex isn't important. What is important are the acts and activities leading up to the sexual act. That's why we haven't seen any penetration of his victims. He's the type who is heavily into masturbation, having oral sex performed on him, ejaculating onto his partners, tying them up, blindfolding them, or choking them. Women who have had sex with this guy would describe him as aloof, uninvolved, the type who is more interested in her servicing him than the other way around."

I listened to what Hazelwood was saying and decided to follow his lead. Unlike

Walker, I believed our killer had managed to rack up a bit of sexual experience in his troubled lifetime. But I sensed his partners were probably the type whom he could easily manipulate and control.

"The women he's been with are either many years younger, very naïve, or much older and depend on him as their meal ticket," I said. "Therefore, even if she suspected something about him, she'd put up with his imperfections because she needs him in order to survive. Bondage is very important to him and I'd think there's a good chance he may have tried to get a prostitute to allow him to bind her up. But most would be afraid. The police might get a lead by checking with prostitutes to see if anyone has come into contact with a guy who's heavily into bondage." Hazelwood drummed his fingers on the side of his empty coffee cup. "He definitely will like older women because he can manipulate them in exchange for their affection," he said. "I also think he'll have the ability to interact with others on a peripheral level. He's got what I'd call a 'service personality.' People will know him, but they don't really know him. The idea of him being a lone wolf is a good description. In terms of employment, I think we'll find he does well in his job, but doesn't like to stay in any one position for very long. He doesn't like anyone being over him. I also think he'd love to drive and would probably have a fairly decent automobile. In fact, people would associate him with driving."

"His car will probably be a nondescript type of vehicle," I said. "Perhaps a sedan that will smack of law enforcement. He might have even purchased it at an auction from law enforcement. He's image conscious, so there would antennas on the car, along with a scanner and a CB."

As I spoke, Walker stared out the massive glass windows at the far end of the room. He appeared transfixed by the trees and freshly-trimmed grass that stretched off into the distance. "I think he's apt to be an under-achiever — that's what his supervisors will say," Walker blurted out. "They'll tell you he's a smart guy who has the ability to do better than he's doing. But he refuses to work up to his potential on the job. The reason is that he probably feels he's better, more intelligent than his supervisors. Why should he bust his ass when he's smarter than his boss? He's egotistical with an exaggerated sense of self-importance."

I sat there listening to Walker, thinking about how fascinated BTK was with the world of law enforcement, telling myself that if he ever did become a police officer, he would have been one of those heavy-handed cops who carried a service revolver, along with another handgun in an ankle holster. Then, just to play it safe, he'd also stash a couple of knives in his various pockets. He'd be the type of cop who would have racked up a file cabinet full of complaints from those he came in contact with while performing his duties.

"I think our UNSUB would have been openly critical of the investigation," Hazelwood said. "Not openly so, but more in terms of his saying, 'Those damn cops, they don't know what they're doing.' He holds the police in disdain because they've been unable to solve the case, in spite of the tremendous amount of clues he believes he left them, clues they should have been able to pick up on. He tells himself that if he were a cop working the case, he would have picked up on these clues. I'd say there's a good chance he's already been interviewed by police and found to be cooperative. He may have even phoned in with additional information, perhaps telling detectives about something he 'just remembered.' "

"I keep thinking that early on he might have been married to someone who would have allowed him to get away with some of the stuff he enjoys — bondage and sexual exploration," I said. "But now at his age, I'm wondering if maybe he's divorced."

Hazelwood shook his head. "When they're married, sexual sadists will act out their fantasies on their spouses," he said. "They can't control it. They have to be in control. When they're dating, they're often very charming, manipulative, and very attentive. When having sex, they may act out superficially, asking things like, 'Can I hold your arms? Do you mind if I tie you down?' But after they get married, they get into it heavily. One option might be to take the list of suspects and find out who is divorced. Then interview the ex-wives to find out about their ex's sexual sadistic activities during their marriage."

Ex-wives, I'd learned long ago, could provide a wealth of information for investigators with the right touch. "You might also ask these exes if they were ever the recipients of souvenirs or other items taken from victims," I said. "Ask them if, when they were together, did the suspect ever give them gifts of used jewelry or other items missing from our crime scenes. Ask them if he ever spoke about BTK or his kills? Did he ever take them to where the murders had occurred or to the cemeteries where his victims were buried? And, if so, did he act strange when he got there? You might even release information to the media that serial killers often become obsessed with coverage of their crimes and intensely follow them. This information might prompt a spouse or former spouse to come forward."

"Ex-wives could prove very important to police," continued Hazelwood. "They could tell us if their ex-husbands had more than a normal interest in the media coverage of the killings. They could also detail their interest in pornography, detective magazines, and bondage restraints like blindfolds, gags, and hoods. I'd expect someone like this to be an outdoorsman, a gun and knife collector. He might own a large dog like a Doberman and have a pseudo-mercenary soldier-of-fortune type of mentality."

I decided to shift gears just a bit and focus more on how this guy went about killing. "It's not important to us if he killed before in another community," I said. "What's important to us is those first one or two kills in Wichita. That's why Otero and Bright are important. In that first kill, he selects an area where he feels a great deal of comfort. He knows deep down that he can get away with his crime there. To do what he has to do, he needs a great amount of time and to do that he must feel safe. I think there's a strong possibility he knew his first victims at least casually or had observed them. Although now, ten years later, I believe he's no doubt changing his MO."

"All it might take for him to feel comfortable about a certain area," said Hazelwood, "is to drive through it a sufficient number of times."

"With the breaking-and-entering type of mentality, they select an area where they always feel in control," I added. "I still think it's significant that he ventured into the Otero's basement on his first kill."

"The reason he was so successful with the Oteros is that he'd played out these bondage fantasies before, most likely with prostitutes," Walker said. "He's got a very rigid, methodical personality. It's possible that the Oteros were his first nonconsenting victims. But he'd already played those acts out in his mind over and over again. So when he walked into that house, he knew exactly what he was going to do. He'd planned on his victims being passive. The mere threat of a weapon, he believed, may have been enough to overcome victim resistance. If the Oteros were his first kill, look at Bright and determine if that was out of character from his other cases. He may have felt so successful on his first murder that he was surprised when confronted with resistance on his second one."

Hazelwood nodded his head in agreement. "This guy has been fantasizing about sadistic acts since he was a young child," he said. "He had fun at the Oteros and the reason he didn't shoot anyone is that he likes to have hands-on kills where he can choke, suffocate, and strangle. He used a weapon just to control the Otero family, not to kill them."

"If we want to see what happened to the Otero household, just look at the victims at the Bright residence," Walker said. "That's what happened at the Oteros. He would have said the same things, using his gun, but also reassuring his victims. That's his method of control — reassurance and a gun. Mr. Otero wasn't going to resist because he probably was afraid of what would happen to his children if he had."

"Or maybe he used a different ruse," I said. "He went in and grabbed a young child and held a gun on them. That would cause Mr. Otero to comply, to not resist. The daughter was the main attraction and her brother was the main distraction. Everyone else at the scene, except for the girl, were secondary victims."

As I spoke, I was reminded of something else. "A long rope is his fantasy," I said. "It's his imagery. He talks about this in his letters. He's a writer. But he can also draw his fantasies. Look at his doodling. Part of his trophies is in the form of images he takes from his scenes. It's what helps him relive his kills. I still think he photographed his scenes."

Hazelwood nodded in agreement, so I continued: "Since we know he rifles through the drawers and purses of his victims, but doesn't seem to be taking monies or property, I think that's indicative of not needing money. So he must have an income to sustain himself."

"Going through drawers is a sophisticated, extended means of voyeurism," said Walker. "You can bet that as a juvenile he had a voyeuristic history."

"In his late teens he might have hung or strangled feminine animals like cats or cows," said Hazelwood. "He would have done this close to his home, so he could watch how the people around him reacted. The police might go back and check if they ever had any reports of that sort of thing."

"I see this guy as being in the lower-middle class," I said. "He's not going to have much cash. Because of that, I don't think he'd have the income to pay a mortgage. So I'd expect he'd be living in a rental property."

"Yeah," said Walker. "He'd have a lower-paying white collar job, as opposed to blue collar. But he's a quasi-professional. Not poor, but not middle class either."

Hazelwood didn't buy this. "I see him differently," he said. "He's middle class, intelligent, articulate, but he's also an underachiever. He selects victims he feels superior to, so I'd expect him to be killing victims in a class just below him."

The smell of gunpowder, no doubt the result of some forensic experiment gone awry in a nearby lab down the hall, seeped into the conference room. For some reason at that moment, the odor triggered a memory of my days spent in basic training, back in the Air Force. And this reminded me of another thought I'd had a few days earlier, something I couldn't shake.

"He's connected with the military," I said. "Possibly the Air Force. I know there's an Air Force base near Wichita. Maybe he worked security there. If he's still in Wichita, that could be the reason. Maybe he was recently discharged and stuck around for a while. Perhaps he was taking college courses in criminology at Wichita State University in 1974, using the GI Bill to foot the bill. There's a professor out there who might have known him. When he was a student, he probably talked to him, even borrowed books from him to write a term paper. I can see him working on one that dealt with famous people who have killed. This is a guy who really wants to be in law enforcement, but maybe he can't make the grade because of some physical handicap, speech impediment, or bad eyes. But his application should be on file with the local police, reserve police, perhaps even as an emergency room ambulance driver."

Hazelwood interrupted my reverie to bring us back to what he felt was important about the UNSUB's relationship to his victims. "He's angry at women, but not angry at the people he killed," he said. "He's unemotional and detached from them. They are nothing but props. He feels emotionally and intellectually above them."

Walker nodded as Hazelwood spoke, but he seemed interested in following the thread I'd begun to weave regarding BTK's possible military background. "The Air Force seems logical to me because of that base in Wichita," he said. "He probably enlisted to avoid the Vietnam draft out of high school. This guy is basically a coward. He won't be the type to project a macho image and definitely not the Marine Corps type. I could see him using the two Otero kids as a shield. He threatened to harm the children if the parents didn't cooperate. When he was in the service, he'd be seen as a nondescript under-achiever. His performance rating would be average. His officers would say he completes a task when it's given to him, but he could have done a better job. He's probably a little lazy and somewhat rebellious. Those who came in contact with him in the military or college might say they remember him, but didn't really know much about him."

I liked where Walker was heading and decided to see what I'd find if I began to move my thoughts in that direction. "He's always going to be frustrated because he's not in the position that he thinks he should be in," I said. "That could have caused problems with his superiors and it would have affected his promotions. At tops, when this guy got out of the Air Force, he would have had an E-4 rating. His lackadaisical attitude might have led to him getting the boot from the service. He's not a team player. He's definitely got that lone-wolf mentality."

"He's a now person," added Hazelwood. "He wants instant gratification. He has short-lived interests. He'll pursue a hobby, but then lose interest. Like a small child, he needs constant gratification."

"His downfall will be ego," I said. "If he's incarcerated, he'll tell his cellmates about the case. He won't say he did it, but he'll talk about it in the third person, bragging about the person who did it, how they're beating the inept cops."

Something else just occurred to me, something I'd thought about before, but hadn't paid much attention to until now. "This guy is into autoerotic asphyxiation," I said. "We found evidence of that in the Otero basement when he hung Josephine. Police need to be on the lookout for any accidental cases where someone died while doing this. If they searched the scene, they might find materials at the location that would have identified him as BTK. These would include writings, photos, and sketches. It would be in an area that was easily accessible to him — a footlocker or a drawer. He would never destroy these things, even if he felt the police were moving in. What he'd do is hide it."

"His spouse might have stumbled onto this material," said Hazelwood. "She might have stumbled onto one of his trophies. But he would have explained it away. Reminds me of that deputy sheriff down in Florida, who killed all those women. Happened a few years back. His wife found the driver's license of one of his victims at their house and when she asked him about it he told her, 'Oh, I kept it by mistake. Thanks for finding that. I gotta return it to our files at the office.' Three days later, she found the license again and told him she'd take it back to the office for him. 'No,' he said, snatching it away from her. 'I'll do it.' Not long after that, he showed her a box filled with used jewelry and asked her to toss it in a swamp not far from their house. She did and didn't come forward about it."

"Yeah," I said. "Marriage isn't going to stop this guy — even if he has the most willing, pliable mate in the world. It's not going to be enough for him. He needs to be taking all the time. He has to always be in complete and absolute control. . . . But why has he stopped? If he has stopped. If he left town and is still killing, he probably has modified his MO. He won't use the BTK handle or correspondence anymore, but his kills would still include some sort of element of bondage."

Walker slapped his hand down on the table. "The NYPD got some guy about six months ago," he said. "He strangled a bunch of prostitutes, then bound them up in rope."

Hazelwood and I both nodded. Probably worth following up, we both thought. I glanced across the table and saw one of the detectives scribbling a note to himself on the legal pad in front of him.

"In all probability, this guy isn't dead, unless it was from some accident or he was killed while committing a burglary," I said. "He might be in jail in connection with a burglary, one where he was picked up with a weapon on him. Burglaries are often a major first step when a perp is planning an indoor rape or a homicide."

"This guy will not stop killing," Hazelwood said. "He's either still killing or is stuck somewhere where he can't kill."

"He's emulating other crimes he's read about in detective magazines," I said. "He cut phone lines because he read about that somewhere. He's adding bits and pieces of other crimes into his crimes. . . . When I listen to his voice on that tape, when he called in to report the Nancy Fox murder, I can't get over how controlled and cryptic his words were. He gave just enough information to get his point across. The phrases he used reminded me of conversations you hear when dispatchers speak among themselves. He sounded like he had some experience talking on the radio."

Keep things moving, I told myself. But stay alert. The one thing I'd learned about these skull sessions was that I couldn't allow my mind to drift. Not even for a second. Do that and I'd miss something crucial. And at that point in our session what was crucial was to steer straight toward the last element on our agenda. Namely, how could police — after pinpointing a credible suspect — cause him to crack.

"You need to break him down during that first interview you'll get with him, the first time you bring him in," I said. "You need to disrupt his life and make him lose sleep. Make sure he notices you in his neighborhood, so he'll begin to see you even when you're not there. When he starts to look disheveled, when you realize he's starting to turn to drink and soft drugs to cope with the pressure, when you can tell he's starting to lose sleep, then yank him in. Don't give him time to prepare. Bring him in when he's not ready.

"A night-time interview would be best, between the hours of eight or nine, in a confined area. Make sure the place where you hold the interview is stacked high with mounds of information in order to project your extreme level of thoroughness. The best place would be in the task force offices. Let him see a bunch of flow charts in the background and a file drawer with his name on it. Have some of the evidence present, items that could link him to the crime, something significant that he'll react to. But don't show him any crime scene photos. Because of what he's written in his communiqués about being controlled by evil forces, he's no doubt layered a strategy for the insanity defense. Show him those photos and his defense attorney will say he's unstable and only offered up what he saw in the pictures.

"Don't trick him to try to play games because he's enough of a police buff to know what's going on. Be rested and ready for a long interview. You want him to be the one who fades out. In the end, he may be looking for some sort of face-saving scenario. Don't bring up his killing of young children because he doesn't want to be known as a child killer. That's not a healthy reputation to have in prison. Get him thinking that maybe he was in a trance when he committed his murders. If he's arrogant, then be very nonchalant. Let him speak in the third person, if he wants.

"At the same time as your interview, you need to be performing a simultaneous search of his residence. If he gets tipped off in advance that this is what you're going to do, he won't destroy his stash, but he will move it. Drill it into his head that you're not going to stop going until you solve this case because you know it is solvable. What you want is for him to become extremely rigid. That's going to mean he's losing control and you're gaining control."

As I spoke, Pierce Brooks walked into the conference room and took a seat at the table. A veteran LAPD homicide detective, Brooks was something of a legend, made famous for his role in Joseph Wambaugh's crime classic *The Onion Field*. For years, Brooks used to pour over out of town newspapers searching for violent crimes that might be similar to cases he was investigating in Los Angeles. After coming to the FBI, he'd begun developing a computer program, known as VICAP. The idea was for police around the nation to enter data from open cases into a centralized computer, allowing cops to better track violent crimes where the same UNSUB might be responsible.

When Brooks heard me talking about interrogation techniques, he said in his strained, whisper-like voice: "Be ready to go with the polygraph at the right moment. But be careful. Do it the wrong way and you might just get an inconclusive unless the questions are designed in a way that will be more distressing to him. For instance, the killing may not upset him, but the fact that he was soiled by the victim's blood could cause a reaction. He may respond to the Bright case because he screwed up. In the

Otero case, he might respond more to the boy because he feels bad about him. Don't expect him to break down."

I had to force myself not to interrupt Brooks. Walker looked at me and grinned. He knew how I felt about polygraphs. I hated them, especially when it came to cases involving violent offenders. The way I saw it, whenever you resort to using a polygraph, you're basically tipping your hand to the suspect, informing him that you don't have anything on him, so your only hope is to rely on this primitive Buck Rogers type of device to determine if he's telling the truth.

Walker felt the same way. "If this guy passes his polygraph, he's going to sit back and smirk," he said. "He's going to feel that he's beaten you. But I like the idea of telling him that you're executing a search warrant of his home while he's at the station talking to you. That would cause him a lot of stress. Which is what you need to do during your questioning. Create stress, then give him the benefit of doubt. Watch how he responds to the stressors, figure out why he reacts that way, then go after him.

"Use two interviewers, one peeling off the other. You have to come off professional, thorough, but low key. Show him you mean business and you're not going to stop until he caves in. He'll be more vulnerable to that. And play up the notion of the task force being created just for him, just to catch him. He'll like that he's being taken seriously, that he has these select super-cops trying to catch him. He'll like it that he's not considered just some small case."

As I listened to Walker's words, something else just occurred to me. It didn't come to me in the form of an image. It was a sense, almost a knowing.

"I wouldn't be surprised if, in the job he's in today, that he's wearing some sort of a uniform," I said. "When you bring him in for questioning, make sure he's not wearing his uniform. He'll feel shielded by it, protected by it. Don't insult him by canceling the interview if he arrives wearing it, but plan things so that it's unlikely he'll arrive in his work clothes. If he still walks into headquarters wearing it, that might tell you something.

"Don't insult his intelligence directly by saying something like, 'That was a stupid thing to do.' All that's going to do is make him react defensively or get hostile because the bottom line is that he thinks he's pretty smart. But you do want to attack him indirectly by pointing out mistakes at the crime that led you to him. This would be easy to do

DIAGNOSIS MURDER: THE LAST WORD

DIAGNOSIS MURDER: THE LAST WORD

LEE GOLDBERG

BASED ON THE TELEVISION SERIES
CREATED BY
JOYCE BURDITT

THORNDIKE
CHIVERS

This Large Print edition is published by Thorndike Press, Waterville, Maine, USA and by BBC Audiobooks Ltd, Bath, England.
Thorndike Press is an imprint of The Gale Group.
Thorndike is a trademark and used herein under license.

The text of this Large Print edition is unabridged.
Other aspects of the book may vary from the original edition.
Set in 16 pt. Plantin.

LIBRARY OF CONGRESS CATALOGING-IN-PUBLICATION DATA

Goldberg, Lee, 1962–
    Diagnosis murder. The last word / by Lee Goldberg.
      p. cm. — (Thorndike Press large print mystery)
    "Based on the television series created by Joyce Burditt."
    ISBN-13: 978-0-7862-9860-0 (hardcover : alk. paper)
    ISBN-10: 0-7862-9860-X (hardcover : alk. paper)
    1. Physicians — California — Los Angeles — Fiction. 2. West Nile virus — Fiction. 3. Murder — Investigation — Fiction. 4. Los Angeles (Calif.) — Fiction. 5. Large type books. I. Rebeta-Burditt, Joyce. II. Diagnosis murder (Television program) III. Title. IV. Title: Last word.
PS3557.O3577D535 2007
813'.54—dc22   20070242096

BRITISH LIBRARY CATALOGUING-IN-PUBLICATION DATA AVAILABLE

Published in 2007 in the U.S. by arrangement with NAL Signet, a member of Penguin Group (USA) Inc.
Published in 2008 in the U.K. by arrangement with NAL Signet, a division of Penguin Group (USA) Inc..

U.K. Hardcover: 978 1 405 64296 5 (Chivers Large Print)
U.K. Softcover: 978 1 405 64297 2 (Camden Large Print)

Printed in the United States of America on permanent paper
10 9 8 7 6 5 4 3 2 1

To Dick Van Dyke,
the one and only Dr. Mark Sloan

ACKNOWLEDGMENTS

I would like to thank my wife, Valerie, and my daughter, Madison, for their love and support during the long days and nights it took me to write this book. I thought I'd never finish it and I know that they did, too. I'm also grateful to Dr. D. P. Lyle, Diane Stavroulakis, Robin Burcell, Paul Bishop, Karen Dinino, Joel Goldman, Colleen Casey, and Peter Keane for their advice and wise counsel. Whatever medical or legal errors I've made or creative liberties that I've taken are entirely my own.

The story you are about to read picks up characters and events from my previous books in this series as well as the *Diagnosis Murder* episodes "Retribution," "Obsession," and "Resurrection," which I cowrote with William Rabkin, with whom I produced the TV series.

Fair warning: If you haven't read the previous *Diagnosis Murder* books, you might want to set this one down until you have, because I spoil some of the surprise endings in this novel.

I've been associated with *Diagnosis Murder,* on-screen and in print, for well over a decade and it has been one of the highlights of my career as both a TV writer and a novelist. I've enjoyed every minute that I've spent with Dr. Mark Sloan, and I hope that you have, too. Let me know at www.diagnosis-murder.com.

CHAPTER ONE

Carter Sweeney was a pale, slight man with a receding hairline and a meticulously groomed goatee. He wore a loose-fitting bright orange jumpsuit and sat in a stiff-backed stainless-steel chair. His wrists and ankles were in irons, which were looped around his waist and strung through an eye-bolt in the concrete floor.

Despite these restrictions, Sweeney seemed completely relaxed, as if he were lounging on a beach instead of sitting in the chilly, sterile visitation room at Sunrise Valley State Prison, home to extremely violent offenders. That's because the visitation room was a luxury suite compared to solitary confinement in his twelve-by-seven-foot cell, where his bed, writing shelf, and stool were all made of poured concrete.

During his first year at Sunrise Valley, he was allowed outdoors for only one hour each day, by himself, in a concrete cavern known as the Dog Run. After three years of incarceration, he was allowed three hours per day in the Dog Run with two other prisoners. With continued good behavior, that was the most sunlight and social interaction he could expect to enjoy until his execution.

So the opportunity to spend time in the visitation room with someone from the outside world was truly an experience to be savored for as long as possible. Unfortunately for Sweeney, his reluctant guest didn't share his eagerness to prolong the visit.

"You don't call. You don't write. I was beginning to wonder if you still cared about me," Sweeney said in the smooth, calming voice that had made him a Los Angeles talk radio star at one time.

Dr. Mark Sloan sat across from Sweeney in a stainless steel chair that felt like it had been carved from a block of solid ice. He was shivering from the cold, but he couldn't let Sweeney see it. Sweeney would interpret the shaking as fear and use it as a psychological weapon against him.

Mark knew it would be foolhardy to underestimate Sweeney simply because he was chained and imprisoned. Sweeney was the most dangerous man Mark had encoun-

10

tered in his forty years as a homicide consultant to the LAPD.

It wasn't that Sweeney was a violent man, at least not physically. As far as Mark knew, Sweeney had never hurt anyone with his bare hands. His preferred method of killing was an explosive encased in an ornately crafted, hand-carved wooden box. Sweeney and his younger sister, Caitlin, had learned their bomb-making and wood-carving skills from their father, Regan, a furniture maker who set off bombs all over Los Angeles after his store was condemned by the city to build a new freeway.

But Carter Sweeney's true weapon was his mind, which Mark was sure the years of near-solitary confinement hadn't broken. He was a brilliant analytical thinker, with the frightening ability to manipulate others into doing exactly what he wanted, often without them ever being aware of it.

"I didn't come here to play games with you," Mark said, despite knowing full well that he was deluding himself. Simply by showing up, he was already playing whatever game Sweeney had begun.

"Of course not," Sweeney said. "We both know how much you dislike games — unless there's a corpse involved."

"You kill people," Mark said. "I don't."

"So that must have been a different Dr. Mark Sloan I read about a few months ago," Sweeney said. "*That* Mark Sloan gunned down a woman in his own home."

"It was self-defense," Mark said. "Not premeditated murder."

For an instant, that horrible moment played out in front of Mark's eyes again. He was in bed, helpless, recovering from a head injury. She was going to smother him with a pillow. He had to shoot. But the first shot didn't stop her. *She just kept coming —*

He blinked hard, willing the image away, but he knew it was a temporary reprieve. The memory of that blood-soaked night would haunt him for the rest of his life.

"But you knew she would show up," Sweeney said. "If you didn't intend to kill her, why were you waiting for her with a loaded gun?"

"I tried to reason with her," Mark said. "I didn't want her to die."

"Sure you didn't." Sweeney winked at him.

So was *that* what this visit was about? Mark wondered. Did Sweeney want to revel in Mark's deadly misfortune? If that was it, Mark wasn't going to play along.

"You're in no position to judge me or anybody else," Mark said. "You're a mass murderer. You blew up a hospital, maiming and killing dozens of innocent people."

"Come now, Mark. You know I didn't do that. My poor, disturbed sister, Caitlin, planted those bombs. You saw her there yourself, right before the hospital fell on top of you."

"She was acting on your orders," Mark said. "You wanted revenge against me for sending your father here."

"You killed him."

"I *caught* him," Mark said. "The State of California executed him."

Within days of Regan Sweeney's execution, Carter Sweeney embarked on a copycat bombing campaign to make it appear that Mark had framed an innocent man. Sweeney also used his popular radio program to expertly turn public opinion against Mark, the LAPD, and the district attorney's office. But Carter ultimately failed, undone by his own arrogance, which Mark used to trick him into incriminating himself in the bombings.

But Mark didn't know that Carter's sister was also involved in the plot. She remained free and blew up Community General Hospital, trapping Mark, his son, and many of his closest friends in the flaming rubble.

That was just the beginning of the nightmare for Mark Sloan.

Caitlin joined the Revolutionary Order for Armed Rebellion, or ROAR, a white supremacist group, using them to hijack the bus that was taking her brother to prison. Together, Carter and Caitlin kidnapped Mark and forced him to help them steal a hundred million dollars from the Federal Reserve.

But Mark outsmarted them once again. Now the Sweeneys were finally imprisoned, and Carter was sentenced to death by lethal injection. Like father, like son.

"As much as I enjoy reliving your downfall," Mark said, "I'm sure you didn't invite me here to rehash your history of violence."

"I'm an innocent man," Sweeney said.

"Oh spare me," Mark said.

"I couldn't possibly do that," Sweeney said with a gleam in his eye. "I wanted you to hear the good news directly from me. I'll be out of here in a few weeks."

"The only way you're leaving prison is in a coffin," Mark said. "All your appeals have been denied."

"Not all," Sweeney said. "The court has granted my writ of habeas corpus. There's going to be a hearing soon. I have a feeling it's going to go very well. I might even be freed in time to cast my vote for mayor. But

14

it's such a difficult choice. Do I vote for John Masters, the police chief whose department unjustly arrested me? Or Neal Burnside, the district attorney who railroaded me into this hellhole?"

"The evidence against you is overwhelming and irrefutable. No court will ever overturn your conviction," Mark said. "But go ahead — enjoy your fantasy. I'm sure it makes the hours pass more swiftly in your cell."

"I won't be the second innocent Sweeney wrongly put to death because of you."

"You're wasting your act on me," Mark said. "We both know the truth."

Sweeney broke into a broad grin. "Haven't you heard? Clinton never had sex with that woman and Iraq has weapons of mass destruction. The truth doesn't matter anymore. Truth is so last century. The new currency in our culture is perception. And everyone's perception of me is about to change."

"Not mine," Mark said.

"I'm counting on that," Sweeney said. "So tell me, Mark, how's your health these days? I heard you took a nasty fall."

"I'll live."

"That's good, because I want you to enjoy a very long life."

"It's too short to waste any more of it here with you," Mark said. "Make your point."

"I already have. Weren't you listening? Let's have lunch when I get out. How do you feel about Chinese food?"

"This is the last time we'll be seeing each other." Mark rose from his seat. "At least until your execution."

"Now *that's* more like the Mark Sloan I know," Sweeney said. "You never miss an opportunity to see someone die, do you?"

Mark went to the door and pounded on it a little too urgently.

"Guard, I'm ready to go."

"What's your hurry? There are so many of your friends in here. You should really say hello to them before you leave. I know they'd love to see you."

"I'll pass," Mark said.

The serial killer known as the Silent Partner was here. So was former councilman Matt Watson, psychiatrist Gavin Reed, Detective Harley Brule, Mob accountant Malcolm Trainor, and many others Mark had helped capture. He didn't need to see how the years of incarceration had taken their toll on the minds and bodies of all those murderers.

He took no pleasure in their suffering, even though they deserved it. His investigations weren't about vengeance. They were about seeing that justice was served, but he'd come to accept the fact that that wasn't his primary motivation. It was the chase. It was the intellectual challenge of the hunt, the methodical piecing together of the clues that led to the killer. *That* was what drove him.

Mark never wanted to see the faces of the killers he'd caught again, not in the flesh or in his memory. And yet here he was, in a room with Carter Sweeney, the worst of them all.

What was he thinking, coming here?

Why was it taking so long for the damn door to open?

"Think of all the vacancies they'd have in here if not for your diligence, Mark. They should really have named this prison in your honor," Sweeney said. "Maybe they're just waiting until you die."

Finally, Mark heard the electronic hiss of the locks opening automatically inside the thick steel door. A guard stepped in, eyed Sweeney warily, and escorted Mark out. The big door closed behind them, the locks sliding into place with a heavy, satisfying *thunk.*

Carter Sweeney was chained in place behind a steel door. He couldn't do Mark, or anybody else, any harm ever again. Even so, it took every ounce of self-control Mark possessed not to run all the way out of the prison.

CHAPTER TWO

Mark was almost at the door of his car, which he had parked at the far end of the prison lot, when he was overwhelmed with nausea. He dashed to the nearest garbage can and vomited, heaving until his stomach was empty and his throat was raw, trying to purge the past hour from his life.

He staggered to his Lexus SC 430, opened the door, and slumped into the driver's seat, too light-headed at the moment to drive, too dazed to care about the burning sting of the sunbaked leather upholstery against his back.

There was a bottle of water in the cup holder. He took a sip of hot water, swished it around in his mouth, and spit it out on the cracked asphalt. He watched the water evaporate almost instantly in the dry July heat and wished he'd never come here.

When Sweeney's lawyer had called yesterday to relay his client's invitation, Mark had flatly refused to see the killer.

That should have been the end of it.

But it wasn't.

Mark couldn't stop thinking about the call. What was Sweeney up to? Why did he want to talk to Mark?

His curiosity about Sweeney was too strong to ignore, just as Sweeney had known it would be. Mark knew he was being manipulated, which only made it harder for him to decide whether or not to go.

Which reaction was the one that Sweeney was expecting? Which one would play into his scheme, whatever it was?

He found himself second-guessing every decision he had made and wondering if that, too, was part of Sweeney's plan. He hadn't even spoken with Sweeney again and already the killer was playing with his head.

Mark thought about getting his son Steve's advice, but he knew what it would be: Don't go. Don't give Sweeney the pleasure of toying with you again.

Steve was the homicide detective who'd arrested Sweeney. He believed that once murderers were imprisoned, their existence was no longer worth acknowledging. They deserved no one's care or attention. So he certainly wouldn't have approved of Mark paying a visit to Sweeney.

Mark considered getting an opinion from Dr. Amanda Bentley, the adjunct county medical examiner and Community General's pathologist, but she'd nearly died in the hospital blast, and she wouldn't approve of Mark's consenting to any request from the man who'd almost killed her.

The only one of Mark's friends who might have told him to visit Sweeney was Dr. Jesse Travis, the young ER resident whose enthusiasm and curiosity often trumped his common sense and better judgment. In fact, Jesse would probably have insisted on tagging along with Mark.

So, after a day of indecision, Mark decided it would be easier just to face his adversary and get it over with than to continue obsessing over what Sweeney might be up to.

And now that the visit was over, Mark sat baking in his car outside the prison, a concrete island amidst a sea of cotton fields two hundred miles north of Los Angeles. He went over their conversation again, word for word. The exercise didn't provoke any fresh insights, only another wave of nausea, which thankfully passed quickly.

Mark was no closer to understanding Sweeney's reasons for wanting to see him than he had been before the visit. But he was sure Sweeney hadn't summoned him

merely to announce his latest legal maneu-
vering.

So what message was Sweeney actually
trying to convey?

And why now?

He told himself to let it go; the answers
didn't matter anyway. Unlike Carter
Sweeney, Mark still had a life to live.

CHAPTER THREE

Corinne Adams did everything she could to ensure that she would have a long, healthy life. The blond-haired twenty-four-year-old didn't smoke, drink, or do drugs. She was even reluctant to take Advil for a headache, preferring massage, meditation, or a bracing cup of herbal tea as a way of relieving her pain.

She ran for thirty minutes each day on her treadmill, which was strategically placed in front of the TV in her one-bedroom apartment. She watched *House Hunters* while she exercised, dreaming of what she would buy when she finally sold one of her screenplays and gave up secretarial work forever.

She was a vegetarian and brushed her teeth after every low-cal, low-fat, organic meal. She was the thinnest, healthiest member of her obese family, none of whom had ever stood on a scale and seen the needle point to anything below two hundred pounds.

One night four years ago, when Corinne still lived at home in Woodland Hills, the whole family went out to dinner at Home Sweet Home Buffet. It was seafood night. Her mother, Noreen, was going back for thirds when she dropped dead of a massive heart attack. The other diners paused, confused, in their lemminglike march to the fried shrimp, until management stepped in and ushered everyone to the opposite side of the restaurant.

The tragedy at Home Sweet Home Buffet had a profound effect on Corinne. She moved out of the house, went on a strict diet, began exercising regularly, and earnestly pursued her dream of becoming a screenwriter. All of her scripts, regardless of their plots, were titled "Home Sweet Home Buffet," which made it difficult, even for her, to tell her screenplays apart without reading the first few pages.

The scripts, which were either family dramas or romantic comedies, had nothing to do with her mother's death. Corinne just thought "Home Sweet Home Buffet" sounded clever, and she liked all the meanings that could be read into the title.

She'd written all of her screenplays with

Reese Witherspoon, Julia Roberts, or Sandra Bullock in mind, because they played characters who were just like her: spunky, adorable, independent, and desirable.

A big part of her desirability came from her new breasts. She'd had to work three jobs for two years to save up enough to get them. It wasn't an issue of vanity, but rather a matter of basic survival. In LA, having a nice rack meant she would get better jobs, better pay, better health benefits, and better men.

But so far the only men she seemed to date were her miserable screenwriting instructors at UCLA's extension school. They were hack writers who never got the money or recognition they knew they deserved, so now, for a measly $1,500 a quarter and a healthy serving of irony, they taught other people how to compete against them. Corinne couldn't help wondering if her instructors were taking her money and intentionally sabotaging her scripts with bad advice.

Even so, that didn't stop her from sleeping with her instructors, who, in the absence of recent screen credits, measured their self-worth by how many students they could seduce.

She didn't mind that. The part she didn't

like was sitting in the classroom with nineteen other wannabes, their desperation to break into the Industry as palpable as body odor. Ben Bovian, the instructor on this particular night, was no less desperate, though his aspirations were focused on breaking into Corinne's pants.

That wasn't going to happen, partly because Corinne was bored with his fumbling foreplay, which consisted of sticking his tongue in her ear while they watched his unforgettable episodes of *Sue Thomas F.B-.Eye,* and his postcoital whining six minutes later about all the less talented, but more successful, screenwriters who were getting all the work.

But mostly Ben wouldn't be going to bed with her tonight because Corinne would never sleep with anyone again, though she didn't know that at the time.

The first hour of class was spent giving notes to Jeremy Glatz, a thirty-four-year-old travel agent, on his 257-page, handwritten, epic screenplay about a thirty-four-year-old travel agent who was irresistible to women.

Ben went through the atrocious script page by page, commenting in detail on lame lines of description and inept dialogue. It was an excruciating and pointless exercise, Corinne thought. The most constructive advice Ben could give Jeremy would be to chuck the whole screenplay into the trash and give up the idea of ever becoming a writer.

By the time the ten-minute break came around, Corinne was so eager to escape Jeremy's horrendous writing and Ben's hungry glances that she bolted out of the third-floor classroom and rushed down the stairs, taking them two at a time.

That was a mistake.

She missed a step on the second flight and went tumbling down the stairs with a shriek, banging off the steps, the walls, and the handrails until she finally landed headfirst on the linoleum floor of the lobby with a sickening, bone-cracking *smack*.

But she didn't hear it.

She didn't feel it either.

She was past hearing or feeling anything ever again.

CHAPTER FOUR

It was a slow night in the emergency room at Community General Hospital. Dr. Jesse Travis sat in the waiting room, his feet on a coffee table, watching an episode of *Grey's Anatomy* and eating a bag of Cheetos. His wife, Susan, an ER nurse, sat next to him, her head on his shoulder.

Jesse liked the weight of her, the pressure of her, the warmth of her against him. He couldn't imagine how he could ever survive without it. And he didn't think he was just romanticizing his need for her. He'd read about studies done on monkeys that died, despite terrific diets and comfortable environments, because they were deprived of the "contact comfort" of other monkeys.

A full bag of Cheetos and a big-screen TV weren't enough for him anymore. He needed Susan, too.

He'd become one of those monkeys.

He was a love monkey.

Jesse was about to tell Susan what he was thinking, but then he thought better of it. He had a feeling that telling Susan that he realized they were just like monkeys wouldn't strike her as the most romantic thing he'd ever said.

He and Susan were newlyweds and spent most of their waking hours at the hospital. Home was just the place where they slept, showered, and changed clothes. So the ER waiting room had become their family room, one they reluctantly shared with the general public and, on occasion, a few homeless people seeking shelter from the elements.

Jesse gestured to the TV. "This is a show about the worst doctors in America."

"But that Dr. McDreamy guy is cute," Susan said.

"Every one of those oversexed doctors is guilty of malpractice, unethical behavior, and unbelievable stupidity."

"But they're cute," Susan said.

"So nothing else matters."

"It's television, Jesse."

"Tens of millions of people watch this show," Jesse said. "They think that's how doctors are supposed to behave. No real doctor could make the mistakes that they do on a consistent basis and still be allowed to practice medicine."

"Real doctors aren't nearly as entertaining," she said. "Or cute."

"What about me?"

"I married you, didn't I?" she said.

"That's not an answer," Jesse said.

She kissed him on the cheek. "You'll just have to live with it."

"The patients would be better off operating on themselves with garden tools," Jesse said. "That hospital is a death trap."

"Full of cuties," she added.

"I had no idea you were so superficial," Jesse said.

"I thought that's what attracted you to me," Susan said.

"No, it was your body," Jesse said.

"At least you're not superficial," Susan said.

"I've got so much depth that people have been known to fall to their deaths just looking into my eyes."

"I can vouch for that," Susan said.

An ambulance pulled up outside. Jesse and Susan got up, put on surgical gloves, and met the paramedics as they came in, wheeling their bloody patient on a gurney.

The paramedics were two stocky men who looked like they needed to catch up on sleep. One of them was pumping an Ambu bag to keep the patient breathing. The other paramedic gave Jesse the rundown on their patient, who had a cervical collar around her neck, a cardboard splint around her left wrist, and an IV line in her right arm.

"The victim's name is Corinne Adams, age twenty-four. She took a header down a staircase," the paramedic said. "And I mean a header. Cracked her skull open like an egg. She's also got a broken wrist. She's not breathing on her own. Her blood pressure is one hundred over fifty, pulse one-twenty-five, her sats are ninety-five percent on four liters. We started an IV of D-five with lactated ringers."

Jesse lifted her eyelids and shined a light in both of her eyes. Her pupils were wide open, big and black. It was like staring into the eyes of a Barbie doll.

It wasn't a good sign.

"Let's get her into trauma one," Jesse said, leading the way. "Anyone contact her family?"

"The police are on it," the paramedic said.

They wheeled her into the trauma room. Jesse, Susan, and the paramedics lifted Corinne onto the table and transferred her IV bag to a stand. Several more nurses spilled into the room. They started getting the things that they knew from experience

Jesse was going to ask for. Susan took over pumping the Ambu bag to keep Corinne Adams breathing.

Jesse listened to Corinne's heart and lungs, which she'd worked so hard to keep healthy and strong. They hadn't failed her now. She had good heart and breath sounds. The organs were working.

He palpitated her belly, the one she'd kept flat and firm with diet and exercise, checking for internal injuries and unusual masses. It was clear.

"I need blood gases, CBC, SMA-seven, and type and cross for four units of blood in case we have to do some surgery." Jesse rattled off the orders to the nurses while he tapped Corinne's right elbow and knees with a tiny rubber hammer, checking her reflexes. She didn't have any. "Get me a skull X-ray, cross-table lateral C-spine, and a CT of the head. Make it fast."

One of the nurses hurried out. Susan looked across Corinne's body to Jesse, who was preparing to intubate the patient and put her on a ventilator that would take over her breathing.

"What do you think?" Susan asked.

"Check her driver's license," Jesse said. "We need to find out if she's an organ donor."

from people informing me that although they realized the story was set in a fictional town, the suspect I described reminded them of someone they knew or had known. Most wondered whether I might be interested in following up on their tip or knew of a detective they could pass their information on to.

To promote the book, I traveled from city to city, giving lectures and readings and signing copies. I never could quite the shake the feeling that BTK might be sitting out in the audience at one of these engagements, especially the ones held in Kansas.

Did I fear for my safety? Hardly. The one thing I did know with certainty was that this guy was an absolute coward. He'd never in a million years be able to summon up the nerve to attempt any violence in such a public setting. His brand of terror was reserved solely for his victims, and he revealed it only when he knew they were completely helpless.

9

Close to two hours had passed, and still no sign of Ken Landwehr.

That didn't surprise me. When a case breaks open, you do what you gotta do. There was many a night while I still worked for the FBI when I'd be sitting down to dinner with my family and the telephone would ring. A moment later I'd hear one of my daughters shout, "Dad, it's for you . . . Somebody from your office needs to speak to you. NOW!"

I'd answer it, and the next thing I knew I'd be sitting on an airplane. Three days would pass before I returned to my home.

I got up from the bed, walked across the room, and grabbed Landwehr's CD off the desk and stared at it. It was tucked inside a white plastic envelope. I sat down on the chair next to the desk and stared at it, wondering what it might tell me about Dennis Rader.

In the weeks before my arrival in Wichita,

I'd begun piecing together some of the facts about Rader's life that had gradually emerged through the police investigation and my own research. I'd located a number of his friends after obtaining a copy of the Wichita Heights High School yearbook from 1963, the year Rader graduated. I made a list of his classmates and began doing computer searches on each of the names in order to track down their phone numbers. After countless phone calls, I began to hit pay dirt.

A handful of Rader's former friends, most of whom had never spoken publicly about Dennis, began offering up snippets from his life that hadn't appeared anywhere in the police work or the media, little snapshots that I hoped to piece together into a massive collage that would give me a better understanding of the man who became BTK.

One person led me to the next. A few of his old friends cried as they dredged up their memories for me. All of them sounded dazed, dumbfounded, and horribly saddened by the nightmarish mess their one-time friend had made of his life.

A few more minutes passed.

I decided to slide the disc out of its plastic case.

"What the hell," I mumbled. "Probably

wouldn't hurt to take a peek."

I tapped the space bar on my laptop, awakening it from its slumber. I pushed the CD into the tiny slot, and a second later a folder icon appeared on my desktop. I opened it, saw dozens of other folders, and began clicking my way from one to the next. There didn't seem to be any rhyme or reason to the order of the files in each folder. Some contained scanned copies of drawings of women strapped to torture devices. Others held what appeared to be journal entries scrawled in blue ballpoint ink on scraps of notebook paper.

Scattered among all the folders were Polaroid snapshots. Rader had snapped most of them himself while engaged in various activities, most of which involved ropes tied around his neck, arms, and legs and gags shoved into his mouth. Sometimes he wore frilly dresses, blonde wigs, and clear plastic Halloween masks with large, pouty lips. Sometimes he wore only white briefs, pulled up high and tight on his otherwise naked, soft, pudgy body, as he dangled from the branches of trees barren of leaves.

The images were disturbing, a bit frightening, and ridiculous.

But what I was most interested in were Rader's words. So I began reading.

■ ■ ■ ■

The feelings and thoughts that set him apart from the rest of the world began when he was around three years old. According to one of his journal entries, that was when Dennis Rader's first memory wrapped itself around him like a vine and began to squeeze and choke him.

Rader wrote that he never could recall all the details — at least not with the precision he could maintain with each of his ten murders. All he could remember was that he was about three years old when he walked into his mother's bedroom and found her struggling on the bed, hopelessly entangled in the twisted bed sheets wrapped around the wrought-iron headboard.

He had discovered her wrapped up in the sheets, her arms extended above her head, writhing, sobbing, and struggling to free herself. He claimed to have stood there in the doorway for what seemed like an eternity, watching her, feeling helpless, powerless to do anything about her situation.

How on earth could she have gotten caught up in such a predicament? Even after all the years that had elapsed between the event and when he wrote about it in his journal, he never could answer that question.

But clearly, he acted out some facet of this memory in each of his murders. This image of his mother, lying in bed, half dressed, writhing and twisting in desperation, became his visual mantra.

In another folder, I spotted the transcripts from Rader's interrogation session. The way Dennis Rader remembered it a few hours into his grilling by police, there had always been Raders in this section of the country. There probably always will be, he said. Unless, of course, they all decide to pack up and move out of the region because of what he did. He certainly wouldn't blame them if they did. That was something he sometimes wondered about, during the last part of his life — the impact his actions might have on the ones he left behind.

His ancestors came over from Bavaria back in the 1800s. Rader's kinfolk were good, solid people. They worked hard, farming the rich soil, trying to follow God's word as best they could. The family's name, derived from the German noun *rat*, means wheel. The earliest Raders, it seems, were employed as wheelwrights. When he was a boy and on into adulthood, Rader often drew pictures of those same large wooden wheels that his ancestors used to build. Only Dennis didn't want to employ them for transportation. He dreamed about lashing women to them, then torturing his victims.

Dennis Lynn Rader was born just outside the tiny town of Columbus, Kansas, on March 9, 1945. When I typed the date into Google, I learned that at almost the exact moment of his birth, 350 B-29s dropped 1,500 metric tons of incendiary bombs onto Tokyo, resulting in a firestorm that killed over 100,000 people.

Dennis was the first of the four sons of William, a former U.S. Marine, and Dorothea Rader. His parents grew up in the area — William had served as the captain of the high school football team, and Dorothea had been chosen as the school's head cheerleader. Dennis was baptized at the Zion Lutheran Church in Pittsburgh, Kansas. His first four or five years were spent living on the wheat, dairy, and cattle farm owned by his paternal grandparents, who also happened to be cousins. Space was tight, as the entire brood lived under the same roof.

It was here, roughly 110 miles west of Wichita, that Rader first began to think that he might be different from other people. It was here the secrets began. Sitting on the back porch of the farmhouse, he would often watch his grandmother go through the ritual of twisting the heads off chickens, before frying them up for dinner. The headless fowl would dance about the dusty yard, blood spurting from the empty socket at the top of their neck.

Rader wrote in his journal that the spectacle caused a curious sensation to flutter up inside his stomach — vaguely sexual and thoroughly enjoyable. The more he thought about it, the more it seemed to him that the feeling was something akin to standing on the edge of a high-rise rooftop, one without any guardrail, and peering over into the blurry void below.

Perhaps, I thought to myself, that was when it started. In the impressionable young synapses of Rader's developing brain, he began to equate death and its various associates with the intoxicating mystery of sexual arousal. One became inextricably linked to the other.

I learned from a source that Rader often spent his summers at the family farm of his cousin, Larry Sutherland, in Columbus, Kansas. Sutherland's father, according to one of Rader's close friends who — like many of my sources — would speak to me only on the condition that I kept his name out of my book, became the first true figure of authority in Rader's life. He worked as the town's sheriff, and Rader recalled that he carried himself with the confident swagger of Clint Eastwood in his spaghetti western days. Rader looked up to his son, also named Larry, who was five years his senior, as the older brother he never had.

Larry was a bright kid, and the two of them would often build model airplanes together and fantasize about one day becoming pilots. But there was something else about Sutherland that forever intrigued Dennis. According to what Rader told one of my sources, it involved an incident that occurred one sweltering summer afternoon on Larry's farm. As a boy, Rader claimed to have heard his parents speak about it in hushed tones, and, like the image of his mother trapped in her bed, it became a powerful source of mystery for Dennis. It marked his first true brush with death. According to my source, Sutherland was allegedly swimming with another friend in a pond on the family property. At some point during that afternoon, the other boy disappeared beneath the water and never returned to the surface. What happened next Rader claimed to have pieced together from listening to his parents' brief conversations on the matter. According to Dennis, when cousin Larry returned back home, his folks demanded to know where his friend had disappeared to.

"He dove down into the pond," Larry explained.

"And then what?" his father the sheriff had asked.

"I walked back home," the boy replied.

"But what happened to your friend?" he demanded.

"He didn't come back up," Sutherland told him. "He stayed underwater, I guess."

The boy's body was allegedly later found floating just below the surface of the water.

For the rest of his days, whenever Rader embarked in the pages of his journal or with police on one of his half-assed quests for the roots of what made him so different, he always stumbled back to that memory of cousin Larry. How, he wondered, could someone be so nonchalant about the death of another human being? Or at least that was how Dennis perceived it.

Time and time again, I'd asked myself that same question, trying to understand the relationship between how a particular incident in someone's life might have led to his decision to kill. Long ago, I realized that the biggest mistake I could make when analyzing a case was to assume that the sexual predator I was trying to catch possessed the same feelings and thinking processes as mine. He doesn't. Yet I sensed that perhaps what was so interesting about this episode in Rader's childhood was that it marked the first time he'd ever witnessed someone else acting out in a manner that he thought mirrored his own mixed-up feelings, feelings he had never been able to express.

One of Dennis's childhood friends told me that when Rader was around five, his family moved to Wichita, which had become something of an industrial boomtown since the end of World War II.

Little Dennis's father, William Rader, was a big man who expected his boys to be decent and respectful to their elders. He landed a job at the Kansas Gas and Electric power plant, located about ten minutes from the family's house. He worked long hours, sometimes pulling double shifts or working graveyard, doing maintenance around the plant and perpetually monitoring the myriad gauges that sprouted out of the walls and pipes. Rader looked up to his old man. In his mind, he was tough, but fair. He wrote that his only complaint was about the times when his dad would return home from working one of his crazy shifts, disappear into his bedroom, and shout for everybody to pipe down so he could get some shut-eye.

Dennis's pals from that period in his life told me they recalled that his mother, Dorothea, had a certain movie-star quality about her. When she got dressed up, which she always seemed to for her job as a bookkeeper at Leeker's Family Foods, the neighborhood kids thought she bore an uncanny resemblance to Natalie Wood. To catch a glimpse of her sitting at her desk in the middle of the grocery, elevated up on a little platform above the floor, made them feel as though they'd suddenly been plunked down in the middle of a Hollywood movie set. Rader, according to various sources, has both confirmed and denied that on the rare occasions that Dorothea resorted to spanking, he experienced that same familiar sensation in his crotch that he'd first felt while watching his grandma wring the necks off chickens.

By all accounts, the young Dennis Rader fit in well with the simple, don't-rock-the-boat sensibility so prevalent in Kansas's largest city in the 1950s. By the time third grade rolled around, no one was surprised when he was picked to play Joseph for the Riverview Grade School's Christmas play.

The Rader family lived in a three-bedroom house in the 4300 block of North Seneca

Street. Despite being located on the north-western edge of town, the neighborhood had a fairly rural feel to it. Rader hung out with a close-knit group of nearly a dozen kids. When school let out, they'd could often be found walking home together and exploring the sandy banks of the Little Arkansas River, which snaked its way through town. On nearly every afternoon, most of the boys played baseball in a nearby empty field.

But not Dennis. He wasn't much of a sportsman. By the time he was nine years old, his friends told me, he wasn't much of anything — other than a quiet kid who seemed to have a knack for never standing out. And that was why his absences from those neighborhood ball games never felt odd. Even if he had participated in those games, chances are that nobody would have noticed him. He kept to himself, but not because he was shy. Rader had other reasons. Reasons that only he knew about.

Rader wrote in his journals that by that point in his life, he was obsessed with strings and cords. There was just something magical about them. It was hard for him to put it into words.

In an effort to add to his collection, he was forever scouting the back alleys of his neighborhood and the rubbish bins behind local stores. He also loved to draw pictures of mummies, like the ones he'd sometimes see chasing archeologists during the Saturday matinees at the local theater.

Something about being wrapped up tight in all those strips of cloth, feeling the pressure of all those bindings, just seemed so wonderful. All he had to do was think about it for just a few seconds, and he'd get an erection.

The fantasies were beginning, although the details were still fuzzy and unresolved in his mind. All he knew was that he possessed an insatiable need to find a pretty girl, then bind her arms and legs together. Sort of like a mummy, he told himself, only it would be different.

The young Rader instinctively wanted his victim to be alive. After a while, this longing to either wrap up a victim or have someone wrap him up grew inside him like a tumor. One afternoon, his journals reveal, he placed some of his precious ropes into his pocket and wandered to the distant outskirts of his neighborhood, out to a hedgerow. He scouted the area like a soldier, searching to make sure he was alone.

Eventually, after determining that all was safe, he lay down in the warm dirt and awkwardly wrapped string around his ankles, yanked it tight, then tied it off with a quick knot. The next step was a little trickier, but he managed to pull it off. After placing his wrists together, he passed his hands through a slipknot and, with the string clenched between his teeth, pulled his bindings tight. He lay there hidden away from the world, the hot afternoon sun warming his skin, feeling himself get aroused in a way he never had before. Off in the distance, a tractor rumbled, but he didn't pay it any mind.

Then one afternoon, during one of his solo bondage sessions, it happened: after a few minutes, he ejaculated. He'd never felt anything like it. The sensation was so euphoric that he sneaked out of his house the next afternoon and did it again. It wasn't long before he was tying himself up whenever he could find a few minutes alone. He wrote about enjoying imagining himself to be helpless and weak, always just minutes away from death, completely at the mercy of some bad stranger who possessed complete control over him. It was even better than the fantasies he used to drum up in his head after rifling through his mother's lingerie drawer, then stealing a pair of her underwear and disappearing into a nearby barn with it to masturbate.

■ ■ ■ ■

One afternoon, when Rader was in sixth grade, a snowstorm blanketed Wichita under a pile of white. I learned from one of Rader's friends that because the weather was so nasty outside on the playground, his teacher, Mrs. Hadon, made all the kids stay inside for recess. According to the friend, Dennis and two of his buddies got a sheet of paper, grabbed some pencils, and decided to pass the time by drawing what Rader referred to as a "girl trap."

Both his pals thought it sounded like a good idea. After all, plenty of the girls they knew had the tendency to be pretty annoying, always showing off by winning the class spelling bees and arithmetic contests. Rader had other reasons for wanting to trap girls, but he kept them to himself, and within minutes the group was busy drawing.

The first thing Dennis did was sketch out a giant castle, like the one he'd heard about in Chicago, built in the early 1890s by Dr. Henry Holmes, a wealthy physician later convicted of butchering over twenty-seven people. (Some estimate that his total number of kills may have reached two hundred.) Rader had become fixated on Dr. Holmes ever since he'd read about the details of the hotel Holmes had built — filled with trap doors, secret passageways, and a hidden dungeon where he performed experiments on his victims.

The three boys sketched the interior of the hotel while Rader drew the various contraptions, which included massive combines and threshing machines that he imagined would subdue his unsuspecting prey. As Dennis worked on his drawing, one of his friends noticed that something peculiar was happening to him. While Dennis was drawing the blades on his threshing machine, along with the steel cages and the flames that shot out of the walls to roast his victims, a look washed over his face. It was an expression that went far beyond intensity or passion for the task at hand.

It seemed more like a possession.

On that afternoon in sixth grade when Mrs. Hadon walked up to the table where the three boys were putting the finishing touches on their girl trap, Dennis was clearly excited. His face was lit up like a Christmas tree doused in kerosene. When the boys were asked about their drawing, his two friends grew embarrassed by their little house of horrors. A tiny voice inside them, my source said, seemed to be telling them that what they were doing was . . . something they probably shouldn't be proud of.

Both boys grew quiet under the gaze of Mrs. Hadon.

Not Rader, though. He began jabbering nonstop about all the intricate details of his diabolical creation — how the unsuspecting girls would enter through an ordinary front door, only to be quickly bound by a web of ropes. In the depths below lay a labyrinth of dungeons and subdungeons where the bewildered victim would be transported via conveyor belt. His imagination went wild, spinning out dark scenarios so intricate that his friends' mouths hung open in dumbfounded amazement. But they were embarrassed by what Rader was telling Mrs. Hadon, who looked bewildered and shocked by what she heard.

The friend explained that he carried the memory of that strange, intense look with him for the next five decades. The haunting vision of his friend's face always made him uneasy in a way he never could quite put his finger on. And on more than a few occasions after BTK's murders had begun, he would quietly tell himself that this image held the key to some enormous mystery — although he was never quite sure what it was.

"I know this sounds crazy, but back during the height of all the BTK hysteria, I used to tell myself that I knew who BTK was," said Rader's old friend. "I knew who he was, but I just couldn't remember his name. It was like I had amnesia."

Rader's friend sobbed uncontrollably as he told me this, unable to fathom that he had once been close friends with a serial killer. "I don't understand how any of this could have happened. I'm buffaloed by the whole thing. As long as I live, it'll never make sense to me."

According to an entry I read in his journal, Rader's family bought their first TV set in 1955, when Rader was around ten years old.

The Rader boys loved watching *The Mickey Mouse Club.* But Dennis enjoyed the Mouseketeers for reasons other than their zany songs and adventures. By the time he entered junior high, he'd developed an obsessive and violent crush on America's newest teen sweetheart — Annette Funicello. He told Landwehr about how he longed to drive out to California, kidnap her, tie her up in ropes, then take her to an abandoned house — always situated atop a lonely hill outside of town. He loved to shut his eyes and think about the *sexual things* he'd do to her, relishing the frightened look she'd wear once she realized that her fate rested in his hands.

Rader's notes about that period of his young life never make it quite clear what these *sexual things* would entail. I doubt Rader even knew. Yet. He didn't particularly want to kill Annette, although she usually had the tendency to expire at the end of his imagined torture sessions. More than anything, he loved the feeling of having total and absolute power over another. He'd begun to realize that nothing could compare to it.

By eighth grade, Rader could usually be found sitting in the back row of class, losing himself in the increasingly dark world that festered inside his head. School was boring, he wrote, probably because it took him away from his fantasies. Although he possessed a vivid imagination, he never quite figured out how to put it to use in school. He would rather use it to create dungeons, living mummies, and torture devices. He did fairly well in mathematics, but no matter how hard he tried he could never get his mind around his English classes — despite his enjoyment of penning poorly structured limericks. The only problem was that his verbal creations weren't the types of things he could ever show a teacher. Here is one I found in his notes:

There once was a girl who had all the right curves
and a large tummy.
All the better to wrap up tight
and make a mummy.

Rader did the minimum amount of work necessary for him to slide through school, saving the rest of his neural activity for other tasks. He'd often sit there in class, half asleep, allowing himself to be pulled away to all those dark places he fantasized about. No one really paid attention to him back there, and he got the biggest kick out of watching how his teachers would come unglued when one of his fellow students slipped up and got caught nodding off in class. He loved how it would cause the teachers to smash their rulers down on the offending student's desk.

Despite telling himself that he was bored out of his wits, Rader wrote that he always plastered a perpetually attentive, serious look on his face, as if he were following every word the teacher uttered. He wrote that one of his favorite pastimes was to stick the tip of his pencil through the middle of a ruler and spin it around like a propeller. Something about the spinning motion lulled and calmed him, allowing that wall that existed between his mind and his fantasies to dissolve. All he needed to do was stare into that blurry rotor for a few moments, and all those things inside his head felt much more real. He wrote that it was as if his thoughts were a snowball rolling down a hill, gathering speed and energy with every inch it moved. In his journal, he wondered if this sensation was one of those so-called hypnotic . . . *stances?* He knew that wasn't the correct term, but it never occurred to him to try to figure out just what the proper word actually was.

That wasn't how his brain operated.

So he'd sit there in class, daydreaming about the girls seated around him, wondering what it would feel like to capture one, two, or three of them, then tie their hands and legs together with a heavy rope. Next, he yearned to bind their bodies to the icy cold iron train tracks.

I rubbed my eyes for a moment, leaning back in the chair I'd pulled up to the little desk in my room, staring at the screen of my laptop, not quite believing what I was reading. It felt as though I'd taken a radial saw and sliced away the top of the skull of this man I'd been chasing for decades, and now I was peering inside. The view was ugly, but was helping me understand how this monster evolved.

He loved to imagine how the ropes would bite even deeper into the girls' soft flesh, causing their wrists and legs to turn a bloody shade of pink. But the best part was when the locomotive came into view. And as it bore down on his victims, he grew so excited that his heart would practically rip out of his chest. The pitiful way they'd attempt to raise their heads in order to catch a glimpse of the thousand-ton steel monster hurtling toward them was absolutely priceless.

But the best part came at that moment when his victims realized that he'd bound their necks so tight to the tracks that their heads couldn't move. All they could do was listen as the locomotive drew closer and closer. It was all so wonderful, he told himself. They were his captives, completely at his mercy. And when they tried to scream (they always tried to scream at the end), when they attempted to make their voice heard through the gag he'd tied across their mouths, all he ever heard was a soft mumble. Because by then the train was on top of them, and it was too late.

Sometimes he'd get so worked up over the scene that he'd hold it in his mind until he went to bed later that night, then travel back to those tracks and masturbate to the image of those hopeless girls. Before long, he later confessed to police, he began to think of it like a picture show — only he had the power to put himself inside the action. He not only served as the producer and director but also got to star in it. He created entire worlds inside his head, all of them bad, hurtful, and thrilling. Yet he never told a soul about them. He kept it all locked up inside his head. The only people who knew were his female costars, but they weren't talking.

They all had gags in their mouths.

10

I couldn't get over it. I'd never seen a stash of material like this. Not ever. As I clicked my way through the countless folders on the CD Landwehr had left in my hotel room, I realized that in all my years studying violent offenders, I'd never glimpsed a collection of diaries, journals, notebooks, scrapbooks, photographs, drawings, and other confessional materials from a serial killer such as these. The only killer I could think of who came close to being such a prolific diarist was David Berkowitz, aka the Son of Sam. His journals documented the majority of the nearly two thousand "nuisance" fires he ignited in trash cans around New York City in the years prior to his homicidal spree.

But Rader's writing was different, darker and move convoluted. Any time you read a diary or other type of personal writing, you're more than likely being granted an intimate look into the subconscious of whoever wrote it. Some humans just seem to express their feelings, needs, and desires on paper more freely than they ever can to another person. Which is why they put those little locks on diaries. In fact, if anyone's diary ever deserved to have a lock on it, it was Rader's.

One of the things I learned from reading his words was that by the time high school rolled around, he had become quite adept at knowing how to stay just below the radar. He may not have been fully conscious of what it was he was doing, but by then he had emerged as an expert at fooling all the people all the time.

According to another of his friends who didn't want their name to appear in print, Rader was one of that rare breed of youth who often caused the parents of other kids in his neighborhood to exclaim, "Why can't you be like Dennis Rader?" His personality was so predictably even-keeled that many of his classmates at Wichita Heights High School wrote him off as hopelessly boring.

Clearly Rader did not fit the mold of the typical serial killer. In most of the cases I've looked at, teachers and neighbors often tell me that they were already predicting that a certain child would grow up to be a violent offender long before he was old enough to graduate high school. For generations, the mantra among mental health professionals has been, "The best predictor of future behavior is past behavior." Yet sometimes this dictum doesn't hold true — at least not in the case of a burgeoning killer like Rader, who never allowed anyone to glimpse his real mind or his secret behavior.

The teenage Rader would much rather be boring than draw any sort of attention to himself. Trouble, it seemed, was for the careless. Rader didn't have much time for that sort of sloppiness. As a kid, he'd gotten in a few tight scrapes, and they had left their mark on him. One of his friends told me about the afternoon Rader and some of the other neighborhood kids stuck pennies on the train tracks near his home. One of his pals got carried away and stuck a baseball bat on the tracks; this ticked off the railroad dicks, who hunted the kids down. They knocked on the Rader family's front door and told his mother that if she couldn't keep her boy in line, they'd be happy to do it. Their threat rattled Dorothea, and after that, I was told, Rader thought twice about pulling the kind of stunts that might land him in hot water. It wasn't worth the hassle, he told himself.

In reading his journal, I began to sense his

preternatural concern over his parent's reaction to his behavior. This paranoia was wonderful training for the young serial killer, providing him with a skill that would come in handy after he began killing. It taught him to never let his guard down.

Yet I wondered just what caused him to be so hypervigilant. Was it due to respect, or was there some other cause? Over the course of reading through his journals and speaking with childhood friends, I have never been able to find any evidence of abuse — either sexual or physical — in the family. During his interrogation, Rader steadfastly denied that he'd ever been molested or beaten as a boy. Whatever the answer may be, he came across as a skittish youth, one who became a quick study in the fine art of maintaining a low profile. He rarely did the normal outlandish things kids do that cause others to pay attention to them.

But, of course, Rader didn't need to. He had other outlets for all that crazy, pent-up energy percolating inside his teenage body. By then he'd become quite adept at conducting a secret life. He would creep out to one of the dilapidated old barns located a mile or so from his house. Sometimes he'd go there to tie himself up. Other times, he'd take a bit of rope from his collection and go hunting for a stray cat or the occasional dog, which he'd carry with him to the barn.

Once inside, he'd loop a stretch of rope around the animal's legs, then cinch it tight and knot it off. If he didn't do that, if he didn't control the animal from the get-go, the damn thing would do its best to bolt. Even a four-legged critter with a brain the size of a walnut had enough sense to know that Rader was up to no good.

After a while, he began tie his victim to whatever post or beam looked sturdy enough to hold it. He found that to be the best way. It couldn't move. He'd wrap it up like a mummy in rope, thrilled to observe the wild look that would come over the animal — its eyes wide open in watchful terror, waiting to see what he'd do next. It was just like what he imagined would happen to a person. Eventually, he'd encircle its neck with baling wire and slowly twist it tight — not enough to tear into its flesh, but enough to cut off the blood supply to its brain. He'd sit there in the dirt and watch the animal squirm, tightening the wire ever so slightly, loosening it up and then twisting it taut all over again.

I had a fairly good idea of what happened next. Other serial killers I have interviewed over the years have described to me the ritual they'd go through when killing an animal. Rader would be no different, I told myself. Because his crimes had a sexual component to them and were directed against women, he struck me as the type who would kill cats, as opposed to dogs. But if he really concentrated, he could transform the animal into something else. He'd stare into its eyes and watch as it changed itself into a human girl.

Then he'd whisper to it, telling it all the terrible things he was going to do to it. And as the animal's brain slowly died from lack of oxygen, Rader would masturbate, then probably try to ejaculate on the body. When it was all over, he'd untie the animal and, on the way back to his house, toss it in a ditch or leave it on the side of the road. Leaving it strung up inside the barn would have been far too risky.

One of the things Rader would have enjoyed best about killing animals was how powerful he felt afterward, how high it made him. Because he had no other way to achieve that rush of power, he had to steal it away from others. So he started with animals. He loved the sensation of it. It made up for all the ways he felt different from the other kids. It not only leveled the playing field but made him feel better than everyone else.

Over the years, I've learned that many serial killers escalated their violence, moving from inanimate objects to animals and then to people. In fact, torturing and killing animals is a type of prep school for potential sex offenders and killers.

Despite his love of violence, Rader wasn't much of a fighter. This wasn't because he was scared to trade blows with other kids. His reticence had more to do with his always seeming to have other uses for his energy. Besides, from what he'd observed in the past, fights rarely went down the way they did in the movies. Physical altercations were messy affairs. In a fight, one risked losing control — the last thing Rader would ever want to have happen. He'd worked far too hard, spent far too much time crafting his image, to let down his guard like that.

Most of the time, Rader was content to use words instead of his fists. Years later, as BTK, he used this same approach when convincing victims to go along with him and allow him to tie them up. He used words rather than a blitz attack because he wanted his victims to be conscious when he played out his bondage fantasies.

One of his high school chums told me about the time when another student cut in front of Rader in line; he never lost his cool. One morning when everyone was lined up in front of the cafeteria for lunch, the school's biggest jock butted in front of Rader and his buddies. One of Rader's pals recalled how the group quickly decided not to make a big deal out of the incident. But Rader wasn't the type to ignore such an obvious infraction of the social code. So he tapped the guy on the shoulder and informed him, in the most matter-of-fact way, that he didn't like the jock's cutting in front of him. Rader didn't have a mean look on his face, said the friend. And he never raised his voice. But before anyone knew what had happened, the interloper mumbled a terse apology and walked to the back of the line.

Rader would also do the same thing to anyone who bothered his youngest brother, Paul, who his friends all referred to as Paulie. If there was ever a time when Rader's softer side came out, it was around Paulie, who was always a small child. That was why his older brother often seemed to have him at his side. He reportedly couldn't stomach the thought of the other kids razzing Paulie because of his size. On more than one occasion, Rader walked straight up to one of Paulie's tormentors and, with his usual calm and level voice, stared unblinkingly into his foe's eyes and said, "I don't appreciate you teasing Paulie . . . You need to stop now, or I'm going to have to do something about it." After a while, kids no longer bothered teasing the youngest Rader boy. Nobody, it seemed, wanted to endure Rader's unnerving, matter-of-fact routine.

There may have been another reason why Rader's words seemed to carry such weight. The other kids understood that if he had no alternative, Dennis actually did know how to use his fists. According to a friend, back when Rader was in grade school, his father gave him a bit of advice about how to handle those clowns who seemed hell-bent on picking a fight. If he ever encountered one of those guys, old man Rader instructed his eldest son, he needed to learn how to defend himself. So one afternoon, he showed his son how to punch and where to aim his blows on the other guy's body.

It wasn't long after that, when Rader was in eighth grade, that the class bully set his sights on the him. All morning long, he picked on and badgered Dennis, calling him names and shoving him around in front of the other kids. Rader finally snapped shortly after lunch, after retreating into a restroom with a buddy, partly to get away from the bully who had decided to make his life hell.

It wasn't long before his tormentor discovered him and quickly resumed picking on him. And it was then, according to one of his childhood friends, that Rader remembered his father's advice.

He balled up his fists and announced, "That's enough."

The fight reportedly didn't last long, but Rader matched the kid blow for blow. And after all the punches had been thrown, nobody had won or lost, but nobody else ever picked on Rader again.

Back when Rader was in grade school, Friday nights were always a big deal for him. That was the night the local TV station, KAKE, played all those old horror movies. The show was called *Rodney and the Host,* and it centered around a guy who looked like Boris Karloff, known as the Host, and Rodney, who resembled some sort of a hunchback.

According to his friends, Rader loved being scared. Back then, there were nights when he and his buddies would see who could stand being scared the most. Rader always seemed to win. The other guys would be forced to shut their eyes, but Rader couldn't get enough. The next week at school, when his friends would still be having nightmares, Rader would be carrying on about all the monsters and evil doctors he'd watched on that previous Friday night. For the rest of the week, he was beside himself trying to imagine what horrors Rodney and his sidekick would serve up for their next show.

A few years later, when high school rolled around, his buddies no longer wanted to spend their Friday nights watching horror flicks. By then, they'd moved on to other pursuits, such as the regular Friday night ritual of hanging out at a place known as "The Big Spot." That was where a lot of the guys in town would end up after telling their parents they were spending the night at a buddy's house. They'd drive out to a shallow bend on the Little Arkansas River, build a big bonfire, and drink beer. Often a bunch of local girls would join them. Around midnight after the girls went home, the guys would drink more beer, shoot the shit, then fall asleep on the sand.

But friends recall that Rader never seemed interested in showing up at the popular hangout, which at the time didn't seem all that odd because he was always working at a nearby grocery. Then again, there was something peculiar about his absence, because he certainly would have been welcome there.

After all, Rader wasn't one of those typically hopeless social basket cases. Although he certainly did seem . . . well, different. He was one of those guys you could convince yourself you knew. But deep down, if you ever bothered to really think about him, you'd have to admit that you had no idea who he really was — and that was just the way he liked it.

Still, Rader was hardly an automaton. He enjoyed a good laugh, but he wasn't the type to tell a joke. Yet he knew how to make his buddies laugh. It's just that the gags he employed were a bit . . . well, dark. And the laughter that followed always had more to do with a sense of relief than with hilarity.

One of Dennis Rader's favorite gags, according to a friend, involved a trick he would play on his buddies while cruising around town in his old Chevy, the one he spent so much time tinkering on. It always happened the same way. He'd have a few of his pals with him, and he'd be driving beside the railroad tracks that ran through town. Everybody would be carrying on, yakking away, not paying a lick of attention to the scenery rolling by outside.

Nobody, of course, except Rader.

He always knew exactly where he was. And when the moment was just right, he'd crank the wheel and drive over the railroad crossing. Only just before his front tires would come in contact with the rails, Rader would let out the kind of fake train whistle that not even Boxcar Willie could match. It sounded just like the ear-splitting sonic blast a diesel locomotive might make seconds before it came tearing through the side of your car, annihilating everything in its path. It was enough, recalled one of his friends, to make the hair on the back of everyone's neck stand straight up.

Afterwards, Rader would roar with laughter, chuckling over the wide-eyed look of panic he glimpsed on the faces of his pals, who believed they were seconds away from death. It was all too perfect. Nobody ever saw it coming.

If Dennis Rader's childhood was spent exploring the landscape of that dark, violent world within his head, his teenage years were consumed with another type of passion — hiding it.

By the time he was a teenager, he'd sensed that whatever this thing was that lurked inside him, it needed to be hidden. To let it out in front of others would be tantamount to suicide. Which was why he loved retreating to the empty barns near his house, where he could not only dream of his bondage fantasies but also act them out on animals.

When it came to cloaking his true identity, Rader was a quick study, a natural. This was when he first began to feel like a spy, as though he had two identities, his ostensible life as a straight shooter and his secret life as a perpetrator of violent sexual fantasies. Keeping the two lives and two identities separate wasn't really that hard to pull off, if he really focused on it. Still, there were a few moments when he slipped up and let his guard down in front of someone else, when he allowed himself to get so caught up in the excitement of the moment that the next thing he knew, the darkness inside his head had grabbed hold of him and carried him away. It scared him when that happened, when he lost control like that and allowed someone else to glimpse that secret part of him.

According to one of his high school friends, this happened one evening when he and Rader were driving back from a youth group gathering at their church.

Rader loved to drive. His friends told me that acquiring a driving permit was incredibly important for him. The reason, I realized, wasn't so much that he equated a license with freedom. It had more to with the fact that driving represented power and control. It meant he could borrow his folks' car and, in a few sweet minutes, vanish from the world he believed was always watching him. He could drive out into the country and do all those secret things he so enjoyed.

The night of this incident, patches of thick fog rolled over the fields outside Wichita like smoke. Rader had just attended a church youth group meeting and was driving down the road with one of his friends, who recounted the story to me during an interview the week before my arrival in town.

The friend told me that Rader was usually a careful driver, always in control and strangely serious about the responsibilities that came with operating a vehicle. But something odd happened on that particular night as he and Rader were driving down a deserted country road near Wichita. A group of guys who'd also been at the church pulled up next to him in another car. They started honking and flashing their lights.

Rader looked at them and laughed as the other vehicle shot off ahead, disappearing into the darkness. The glowing red of taillights were just visible in the fog covering the empty dirt road.

It was at that moment the change occurred. All at once, Rader's face tensed. His eyes, which had begun to bulge, burned with an intensity that his friend sitting in the passenger seat had never seen before. Rader stomped on the accelerator, gunning the engine in his parents' '58 Plymouth station wagon so hard that his buddy felt as though he were sitting in a rocket.

"SLOW DOWN, DENNIS," he yelled.

But Rader didn't hear him. He was clenching his teeth so tightly that the muscles in his jaws were visible. His buddy couldn't understand what was happening, couldn't figure out where Rader had gone. What on earth had happened to him? he wondered. They were barreling down the bumpy road at over seventy miles per hour by the time they caught up with the other car, then flew past it.

"OK, SO YOU PASSED 'EM," his friend shouted, hoping Rader would come to his senses. "YOU CAN SLOW DOWN NOW."

But Rader was still hunched over the wheel, squeezing it so tightly that he seemed to be trying to crush it. His buddy just sat there, wishing to God he were somewhere else.

"COME ON, CUT IT OUT," he pleaded. "THIS IS CRAZY, DENNIS. CAN YOU HEAR ME? YOU GOTTA STOP NOW."

The headlights of the other car had long

ago faded away behind them in the fog. Yet Rader kept his foot pressed firmly down on the accelerator, even as the road began to kink and weave in increasingly unpredictable directions. Something bad was on the verge of happening, his buddy thought to himself. There was no getting through to Rader. The lines were all down. So he just gave up trying to talk any sense into him. And because they were moving far too fast for him to jump, he braced for the worst.

A few minutes later, Rader missed a turn in the road, and the station wagon careened over a dirt embankment and plunged into a shallow ditch, caving in the right side of the vehicle. The impact caused his pal to slam his head into the ceiling, temporarily knocking him out. By the time he felt himself coming to, he saw Rader staring at the bashed-in grillwork, hysterical, sobbing.

A few minutes later, they sat together on the roadside, waiting for their friends to catch up. All Rader could talk about was the hell he would surely catch upon arriving home and breaking the news to his folks.

Roughly forty-five minutes later when the group pulled up in front of the Rader family home, Rader jumped out of the car, wailing and frantically shouting about how he'd wrecked the family station wagon. He failed to mention anything about his injured friend. The other kids sat there watching him go to pieces in the front yard, then they left him there and drove his dazed passenger to a nearby hospital, where doctors treated him for a concussion.

His injured buddy told me that he never could make sense out of Rader's strange behavior that night. How could anyone be that oblivious to another person's pain, he wondered. It was as if nothing else mattered to Dennis Rader other than Dennis Rader.

The incident was one of the most revealing moments in Rader's young life. Yet it would take decades before the rest of the world understood just how selfish a person he actually was.

Besides his church youth group, Rader was active in Boy Scouts. He liked the structure of the organization, the order and predictability. I bet he liked the uniforms too. Rader showed a lifelong propensity for paramilitary, police, or, as in his case, low-level municipal enforcer uniforms. He felt safe in the Boy Scout culture and environment. He slowly but systematically worked his way from one merit badge to the next.

Scouting also allowed him to put his fascination with string and bindings to productive use, especially when it came time to begin learning how to tie knots. Before long he was showing the same kind of enthusiasm for his knots as he had on that snowy afternoon in sixth grade when he sketched out his ghastly, deadly girl trap. Those close to him couldn't help but notice how proud he appeared to be of his skills, once displaying them on a board at a meeting, the names of each creation written out on tiny pieces of paper pinned beneath each knot.

His favorite, according to one of his friends, was the clove hitch.

"It's one of the most elementary types of hitch knots," he once explained. "But what I like about it is that it's quick to tie and easy to slip over something. Additionally, it's one of the easiest to untie, even after a load has been applied."

One summer, Rader traveled to New Mexico's Philmont Scout Ranch with his troop and embarked on a fifty-mile hiking expedition through the Sangre de Cristo Range of the Rocky Mountains. Yet Rader, who was a stickler for details and for following instructions, just couldn't bring himself to abide by one of the most stringent requirements: nobody's backpack could weigh more than forty-five pounds. The way his friend interpreted it, Rader had clearly taken the Boy

Scout motto of always being prepared to heart, insisting on bringing a pack filled with nearly seventy pounds of gear and supplies. The troop leaders were hardly thrilled by the young hiker's enormous pack, but they told him he could bring it — provided he carry it during the entire trek.

He did. And if it was ever too heavy, he never let on.

But then, Rader hardly divulged much of what was going on inside him to anyone. God only knows what he had stashed away inside his pack. I have a hunch it wasn't survival gear he carried, but gear for his own self-pleasure. Because the one thing I knew about Rader was that, even at this young age, he'd developed a serious yearning for isolation. It's likely he anticipated that this trip might provide him the opportunity to act out his self-bondage fantasies while others slept.

During most of his time in high school, Rader put in long hours at Leeker's Family Foods, working as a bagboy, trying to save up enough money for a car. Working was hardly a sacrifice, as deep down he never felt particularly comfortable hanging out with the other kids. It required too much effort. Yet on some occasions, he actually enjoyed the company of others.

Sometimes at night, Rader and a buddy would drive out to the city dump and blast rats with their .22s. This sort of hunting required plenty of patience, because rats are easily spooked. So the first thing they'd do after shutting off the engine was to kill the headlights. According to the friend, they'd sit there in the darkness, waiting for the city's vermin to delude themselves that all was safe, that the danger had passed and it was OK to come out of hiding. While passing the time, the two friends would talk about things, whispering — so that the rats couldn't hear them — about what they wanted to do with their lives.

Like any other teenager, Rader had dreams and ambitions — although to his friend who reported this to me, they sometimes seemed a bit unrealistic for someone with his lackluster student record. For a while there, he was telling his buddies that he wanted to be a rocket scientist when he got older, a profession that seemed so beyond his capabilities that it was hard not to laugh. To most people who knew him, he seemed most likely to end up being some sort of city worker, perhaps a bus driver. If he got lucky and knew someone, maybe he could get hired on somewhere as a cop, they thought.

One of his friends said that by the time high school was finishing up, Rader was contemplating becoming a game warden — which made sense to those who thought they knew him. After all, he certainly seemed to be fond of animals. He was also an avid outdoorsman, the kind of guy who appeared at home in the woods with a shotgun or fishing rod in his hands, just happy to be out there walking through the mud, surrounded by all those elm and poplar trees. Whenever he was hunting for dove, quail, or rabbit, one hunting buddy said, he was the type who always took the "kill" shot. He went out of his way to make sure that none of the animals he shot suffered. And over the years, he'd matured into one of those hunters who didn't just venture out into the woods in order to bag as many birds as his permit would allow.

Sure, he still loved to hear his gun go boom. And he still enjoyed getting a good shot in from time to time. But more than anything else, Rader just appeared to have an ease about him when he put on his hunting jacket and flannel cap. According to a friend, he didn't need to be killing something in order to appear content when he traveled into the woods. It was enough to just be out there with his shotgun, going through the rituals of a hunter.

They usually had to wait only about twenty minutes before the rats would come scurrying out into the open. To become a proficient rodent killer, you had to trust your gut and work with your partner as a team. You had to sense exactly when to hit the headlights, which would cause the pupils of any rodent within their reach to glow red as the tip of a cigarette.

Then, for a few brief, glorious moments, time would slow down, and the animal, surprised by the blinding burst of light, would freeze. And it was at that moment the two friends would pull the triggers on their rifles, then scramble out of the car and go poking through the piles of rubbish, plucking out the bloodied carcasses. Afterwards, they'd climb back inside, kill the headlights, and wait for the rats to return.

Rader was good at the waiting part, his friend told me. That type of patience came naturally to him. What his friend didn't know at the time was that this trait would serve Rader well when he began hunting other things besides rats.

11

My computer screen pulsed and glowed. Hours had seeped by, but I couldn't pull my eyes away.

The hotel room had long ago grown dark, so I sat in the blackness. The only light was leaking out from the disturbing words and images on my monitor. My vision had begun to grow blurry, so I stood up, turned on a lamp, and walked to the bathroom to fetch a washcloth. I allowed the warm water from the sink to flow over the cloth, then I wrung it out and pressed it over my eyes, hoping to wash away the residue of what I'd just read. But I knew it wouldn't work. And deep down, I didn't want it to. After all, I'd come to Wichita to wallow in Dennis Rader, to open up his sick head and dive into his swamplike mind in order to answer the questions I'd begun asking decades before.

"You've got miles to go before you sleep, buddy," I mumbled to myself. "Now get back at it."

I tossed the washcloth in the sink, trudged dutifully back to my computer, and resumed reading.

Shortly after graduating from Wichita Heights High School in June 1963, Dennis Rader yearned to feel *it*. He was desperate to experience that sensation he'd been wondering about for all those years, and he figured the time had finally come to up the ante just a bit and do something that involved a bit more risk.

Pulling off a bold crime was something he later confessed to fantasizing over ever since he'd heard about how those two guys walked into the Clutter family farmhouse, tied up mom, dad, and the two kids with ropes, then blew everyone away with a shotgun. The killings took place in Holcomb, Kansas, just two hundred miles down the road from Wichita. Rader was fourteen years old when it happened. From time to time he'd read about the matter in the local paper or hear people talking about it on the radio. Two years after Rader graduated, Truman Capote would explore every facet of the Clutter murders in his harrowing classic *In Cold Blood*.

The summer after earning his high school

diploma, Rader began to wonder how it would feel to strike deep into enemy territory like those two guys did when they broke into the Clutter farmhouse. They just waltzed in there and took charge. That had to be a wonderful feeling, he told himself. After all, it was one thing to strangle a cat in an old run-down barn or start an occasional fire in some random dumpster. The risk was fairly low that he'd ever get caught doing something like that. And even if he did, he figured that nobody would probably give a damn.

"He's just going through a phase," they'd say. "That's all it is. Boys can be like that."

But those murders in Holcomb, now that was plain bold with a capital B. He just couldn't shake it loose from his mind. And once he'd graduated, Rader figured he had nothing to lose anymore. He'd managed to fool everyone for all those years, and now nothing could hold him back. So he cooked up a little stunt that he told himself might hold a bit of promise. It wasn't anything like what those killers in Holcomb did. But still, it had its merits.

For much of that summer, he went to work rehearsing every element of it, over and over again in his head, plotting out every move, every variable that he might encounter.

Sometimes, in an introspective moment, he'd ask himself why he'd want to do something like this. And, as he told police after his arrest in February 2005, he'd hear himself answer: just for the hell of it.

But deep down, part of him knew that wasn't the full reason. Deep down, he knew that this was the only way he could feel the excitement, the rush.

One night he up and did it. On his way home from work at Leeker's, he parked his car a few blocks away from his old high school and went for a walk. A few minutes later he arrived outside his former alma mater. The place looked pitch black inside. He walked around the building, just to make sure that no janitors were lurking around the property. When he finally decided that all was safe, he clambered up onto the roof, popped open one of the skylights, and jumped down into the darkness. The moment his shoes hit the floor, a wonderful sensation coursed through his body. It made him feel like a spy, an interloper, the ultimate invader who had dared to go somewhere he didn't belong. He walked through the darkness for a while, soaking up the feeling. It was indescribable, vaguely sexual. Eventually, he wandered into one of his old classrooms, managed to locate a piece of chalk in the nearly pitch-black room, and scribbled some profanities on the board.

A half hour later, he was back home and getting ready for bed.

It was in the first few months of 1965 that one of his acquaintances convinced him that if he ever wanted to do anything in life other than work as a clerk at Leeker's, he needed a college degree. Rader realized that he was probably right. By that point, he'd grown so frustrated and restless since graduating from high school that he began looking at colleges. But instead of opting to attend one of the lower-priced state schools in the region, he picked Kansas Wesleyan, a four-year college run by the Methodist Church, located ninety miles north of Wichita in Salina. I never was able to ascertain exactly how someone with Rader's lackluster high school GPA could have gotten accepted to a school like Wesleyan. But something told me that Rader's longtime involvement with his church youth group might have helped convince school administrators that what he lacked in smarts he made up for in faith. Whatever the reason for his admission, Rader soon realized that he had made a bad choice.

Because his parents could afford to cover

only a portion of the relatively steep tuition, Rader was constantly strapped for cash. He was so desperate for money to live on that he would drive ninety miles back to Wichita in order to work his old job at Leeker's, always earning just enough to barely get him through the next week of school. Before long, he began sneaking around at night and jimmying open soda machines and stealing the pop bottles. After dumping the pop out, he'd drive around to area groceries and collect the deposit money on the bottles. Although he enjoyed the covert nature of his scam, breaking into soda machines definitely lacked the buzz that his earlier brush with crime provided.

Nevertheless, escaping the insular atmosphere of Wichita was good for Rader. Even though his grades were just shy of abysmal, his year-and-a-half-long stint at Kansas Wesleyan did help him acquire one of his most sorely needed qualities: how to be an extrovert. He joined a fraternity and quickly became a regular fixture at the beer parties around campus. Before long, he started to enjoy the feeling of allowing himself to emerge from the shell he'd constructed around himself.

As much as it frightened him to give up that kind of control, he assured himself it would be okay. No one really knew him on campus; no one knew the Dennis Rader who'd grown up in Wichita. To everyone concerned, he was a blank slate, a young man with no past. And it was always fascinating, he told himself, to see how his peers reacted to whatever it was he decided to write on that slate. So much of high school was spent trying to hide what was inside of him. He had always been on the defensive. Now he was on the offensive. Despite all the admonitions against doing so, people truly did judge books by their covers. And he was creating the perfect cover.

All he needed to do was smile and laugh, and people just naturally assumed him to be the kind of guy who always smiled and laughed. They were such sheep. At times, he felt like a painter — only instead of creating illusions on canvas, he used his face. For the first time in his life, he began consciously constructing a cover for himself that was far different than the one he'd assumed back in his hometown, back where everyone knew him only as Dennis Rader, the perpetual face in the crowd, the guy who blended in with any background he happened to stand up against. In a few short months, he transformed himself into something of a third-rate midwestern bon vivant. Even more important, his new guise was just one more thing in his empty life that he could control and have power over — which is what he loved most of all.

How easy it was to do and how utterly simple to pull off. All he need do was crack a goofy smile, and nobody was the wiser, nobody had a clue about all the dark things festering inside his head. Why hadn't he thought about doing something like this before?

It wasn't too long before he summoned up enough nerve to ask out a few of the Wesleyan coeds, although nothing much happened on his dates — at least not from his perspective. Because when it came to sex, Rader was an inexperienced rube. Despite spending so much of his life intensely daydreaming and fantasizing about it, despite all his drawings and writings about the things he yearned to do to women, despite his occasional Peeping Tom sessions in the bedroom and bathroom windows around town, . . . despite all that, Rader was clueless about the nuts-and-bolts workings of how to be intimate with a woman.

Back in high school, he later confessed, the only advice his father had given him on the subject was, "If you're ever alone with a girl, don't lie down on the sofa with her."

For Chrissake, he often thought to himself, *what was that supposed to mean?* He never had the nerve to ask any of the guys he ran with about it. So he just went back to his world of journals and drawings, filled with imaginary torture rooms, populated with scantily clad sobbing young girls all begging for their lives, pleading for him to make the pain go away. If sex was anything like that, he told himself, he couldn't wait to try it. Yet even someone as dense as Rader understood that he was going to be hard pressed to find a partner who would allow him to tie her up and torture her — at least in Salina or Wichita it would.

Getting away from the confines of Wichita also emboldened Rader to begin thinking bigger thoughts when it came to his world of fantasy. Because much of his mental energy was consumed by the need to scrounge up spending money, he had yet to act on one of his most powerful desires — stalking women. And he had many other secret fantasies. By 1966, Rader had begun referring to all the petty crimes he desperately yearned to undertake as "projects." It wasn't long before he'd put together an entire list of them.

His so-called Project Mountain No. 1

emerged as his boldest crime to date. With it, he hoped to re-create the rush he experienced several years before when he crept into his old high school. This time, however, he picked out a home in Salina. When he was sure the owners were gone, he broke inside.

Wandering through the house, he was euphoric over the way he was violating someone else's space. But he was also nervous, which added to his excitement. Being in this place where he shouldn't be felt vaguely sexual. It also made him feel strong because, just by being there, he imagined himself to be stealing power from the people who owned this house. As he walked from room to room, he sensed the stirrings of that fluttery thing inside his stomach he'd first felt long ago as a boy.

He was becoming aroused. In one of the bedrooms, he spotted a dresser and began rifling through the drawers until he found exactly what he'd come looking for — a stash of women's underwear. He snatched a handful out from the drawer and stuffed them in the pocket of his jacket. As he was leaving, he spotted some car keys lying on a table near the sofa. He grabbed them, walked out the front door, and within minutes was speeding down the street in a car that didn't belong to him. He couldn't remember the last time he'd felt so alive — every molecule in his body seemed to be ablaze. He wanted to explode. Before leaving the car on a side road outside of town, he masturbated in the front seat, then hoofed it back to his '58 Chevy.

As oblivious as Rader could sometimes be when it came to the world around him, not even he could ignore the mess unfolding on the other side of the world in Viet Nam. Because the military needed young bodies to go fight the Viet Cong, the draft had begun to kick into high gear. Rader knew that with his dismal grades — consisting of mostly D's and C's — he might as well hang a sign on his back that read: Draft Me. Getting drafted was the last thing he wanted to have happen. Because deep down Rader was a coward. Of course he loved violence. But, I knew, just like others with his twisted psychological hardwiring, he enjoyed only the kind of violent encounters where he stood no chance of getting hurt. His later crimes would reflect this when he went out of his way to target small children and older women over whom he could have dominance with little struggle. Nearly all the serial killers I'd interviewed were psychologically weak individuals who picked the most vulnerable victims they could find.

He loved the kind of violence where his victims were weaker than he was. From what he knew about war, it was a frightfully messy, unpredictable business, filled with all sorts of uncertainties. He may have been drunk with dark fantasies, but he clearly understood the difference between make-believe and reality. (If he hadn't, he wouldn't have gone to such lengths hiding his fantasies away from those around him.) Besides, for a pathological control freak like Rader, war was to be avoided at all costs. He'd love to shoot someone, but if there was a chance that the other guy might shoot back, forget it. Let some other guy go crawl through the jungle and bayonet communists; he had other fish to fry.

So one afternoon in August 1966, he drove down to the local Air Force recruiting station and signed up. Better to enlist and have some say over which branch of the military he went into than be drafted. Because he didn't intend to be a pilot, chances were he wouldn't end up seeing any real fighting. Not long afterward, he underwent basic training at Lackland Air Force Base in San Antonio, Texas. In October, he was sent to Sheppard Air Force Base in Wichita Falls, Texas, where he attended technical school, specializing in radio communications. Before long he was clambering up 120-foot-high radio towers, adjusting antennas and fixing malfunctioning radio equipment. After another stop at Brookley Air Force Base in Mobile, Alabama, he launched into a three-year globe-trotting odyssey, living out of a suitcase while traveling from one base to the next in Turkey, Greece, Japan, Okinawa, Korea, and Japan.

The Air Force gave him his first taste of what it felt like to have subordinates. It also reminded him of one of the things he loved most about Boy Scouts — he got to wear a uniform. After a few years, when he became a sergeant, Rader was allowed to supervise men, and the sensation of being able to control people like that proved both intoxicating and addicting.

Rader wrote in his journal that these were good years for him, the one period in his life when he considered himself to be a bona fide "lone wolf." He would often think back to his Air Force days with a fondness and sick jealousy. In his mind, the lone wolf stood at the top of the food chain. He took what he wanted, answered to no one, lived only for himself, roamed indiscriminately, and killed whenever the urge hit him. Then he moved on. Nothing and nobody could ever stop a lone wolf.

Rader took his newly acquired skills as an extrovert and picked up where he'd left off in Salina. He drank a lot of beer, even letting down his guard on a few occasions and allowing himself to get drunk. Whenever he could, he enjoyed hanging out at the bars near whatever base he was stationed at. He did this because bars were a gathering spot for prostitutes. Rader had quickly become a big fan of prostitutes, especially Asian ones. His journals hint that this was how he lost his virginity. Sex with prostitutes, however, was probably something of a disappointment for him because, like all psychopaths, he would have abhorred a willing or compliant woman. For him, it was the hunt and the thrill of controlling a woman, forcing her to perform some sexual act against her will, that would have turned him on.

He claimed to have fallen in love with one of the prostitutes. In one of his diary entries, he listed her name as Tina. Reading between the lines, I got the sense that Tina gave him the equivalent of a graduate school education in sex. For a while there, he convinced himself that he wanted to marry her. But the relationship eventually went south, so he found another bar girl and picked up where he'd left off.

More than anything, he yearned to experience the feeling of binding somebody up, then having sex with her. He felt as though he'd been dreaming about it for most of his life. Sometimes in the middle of sex with some prostitute, he'd make his move and quickly attempt to tie the women up. But the prostitutes he frequented were far too seasoned for that sort of kinky nonsense. Whenever he attempted such a stunt, they sent him packing, which wasn't any big deal because he had access to more prostitutes than he knew what to do with.

He had other hobbies, too. While in Japan, he picked up a macho-looking big-barreled .22-caliber semiautomatic Woodsman Colt. The pistol, he wrote, had the craziest hair trigger he'd ever felt on a gun. The damn thing spooked him. He used to joke that all he had to do was look at it wrong and it would go off. When he bought it, he told himself he wanted it as a target shooter. But that other part of him knew it would make a helluva weapon if the shit ever started hitting the fan. On those days when he had nothing better to do, he used it to blast cans, and he was a decent enough shot. After his arrest, he told Landwehr that at twenty-five yards, he rarely missed.

Rader also bought a camera at a base store

and spent some of his off hours snapping photos of the prostitutes he'd bedded, then developing the pictures in a base darkroom. Sometimes he'd draw a noose around the woman's neck, a gag over her mouth, and ropes across her wrists and ankles. He could look at those photographs and masturbate for hours. But, he later claimed, his favorite activity involved clipping pictures of women out of newspapers and magazines, then sketching all manner of bindings around their bodies. He loved the way it felt to pick his victims at random from the pages. No one was safe. And everyone was so unsuspecting, so oblivious to what lay waiting for them. He took whomever he wanted, clipped them neatly from their paper home, and glued them to index cards.

He called his little cards "slick ads." He did that for two reasons — they were often printed on glossy paper stock, and most of his victims were in the midst of modeling something when he snatched them. He would hold them in his hands, whispering to them all the things he wanted to do to them . . . that was pure bliss. *Some guys have baseball cards,* he'd laugh to himself, *but I have these — my fantasy cards.* He quickly got so addicted to his paper prisoners that he continually felt the need to add to his stable.

After a while, they always lost their zing. He tried using the pictures he'd clip from the local newspapers he had access to, but something about those women never quite worked for him.

One night, he grew so desperate for a fix of what he considered to be American-looking models that he claimed to have smashed a window on the side of the base library, crawled inside, and stolen a stack of magazines. He quickly stashed them away deep in his locker. Whenever he felt the need to go trolling for victims, he'd retrieve one of his pilfered magazines, grab a pair of scissors, and go to work. The break-in marked something of a dark milestone for Rader. His decision to steal the magazines during a high-risk, high-stakes late-night burglary — instead of simply sneaking them out when the library was open — showed that he was beginning to have a tough time controlling his impulses.

Some nights, however, not even his slick ads could help Rader scratch his itch. So he'd wander out in the woods near his base, wrap himself up in rope, lock his wrists together with the pair of handcuffs he'd purchased during his travels, then pretend to be one of his imagined victims. The handcuffs were the latest addition to his arsenal. For the first few months he had them, they helped ease some of his sexual frustrations. Yet, as satisfying as they could be, his self-bondage eventually failed to satisfy his urges. Which was why he finally decided it was time to step up his game to the next level.

One night, he waited until nightfall, then jumped the fence surrounding the Tachikawa Air Base, located about forty miles northeast of Tokyo. I read in his journal how he spent the next half hour hailing down taxis and hopping buses, trying to get as far away from the base as possible, working his way deeper and deeper into the maze of tiny, crowded streets. He considered this to be a little game. He was going on a pretend hunt.

He stuck out like a bandaged thumb, out there in those neighborhoods. He knew that, but he didn't care. That thing inside him was getting stronger now — hungrier, too. I'd learned from other killers that their fantasies were like watching a movie over and over again. Pretty soon, no matter how exciting it once was, the story line grows boring, and the killer has to try to find something new. Rader's having access to the prostitutes was similar. After a while, his sex sessions did little to satisfy his real appetite, the one that demanded torture and pain. This new little game of his was the only way he knew how to feed it.

In the pockets of his coat, he carried rope, gags, a knife, and his Woodsman Colt. He wanted to find just the perfect woman, then tail her through the darkness wherever she went. He told himself that he'd walk through the darkness until he spotted that special someone who looked just right, then who knows what might happen. He'd walk behind his target, licking his lips, whispering to himself all the things he yearned to do to her. Sometimes the words and images that slithered out from his head surprised even him. He was so close, he told himself. But he was in control. He hadn't crossed over the line. Not yet. He called the shots. Not the monster inside him. It was all pretend. Nobody ever got hurt. He never once so much as touched any of the women he followed through the night. So it was all okay. Kind of like a hobby.

Where would it all lead? Sometimes that thought drifted through his mind as he walked back through the night to the safety of the base. As I read in his journal, he always reckoned he'd put it all behind him when he finally returned stateside. After all, what sort of a future was there in this sort of thing? Not much. He told himself that when he got back to Wichita, he'd get a job, find a wife, start a family, and settle down. He'd renew his faith in God. He'd purge all this from his system.

He told himself he could do it. And deep down he almost believed it. That was the way most of the serial killers I'd interviewed were. At times, they possessed the ability to fool everybody — even themselves.

12

The mouse pad on my computer had grown alarmingly hot, so I shut the machine down for a few moments to let it cool off. If only I could do the same thing for my brain.

I stared into the emptiness of my hotel room. The quiet at this hour of night was deafening. Thoughts were swimming around inside me like piranhas. After a few moments one of them surfaced, and it occurred to me that Dennis Rader and I had something in common. He too was a profiler. The difference was that he profiled in order to feed his appetite as a sexual predator.

He reminded me of a lion out on the Serengeti, scanning the plains for prey — weak, lame, or old. Why work up a sweat by going after some young, swift antelope when he could find others much more vulnerable? Yet the comparison only went so far, because lions hunt for survival. They kill to feed themselves and their cubs. Men like Rader kill as a form of recreation. They're predators. They live for the hunt. Like the lion, they search for easy targets. But their biggest turn-on is the chance to play God, to have absolute control and dominance over another human being. It was enough to make me sick. That is, of course, if I didn't find it so goddamned interesting.

The clock was ticking for Dennis Rader.

Even if I hadn't known the tragic, terrible outcome of his story, I had gained enough of an understanding about serial killers over the years to know that he had reached an age when there was no turning back. Even though he had yet to take a life, it was only a matter of time. Even though he told himself he was going to put his dark urges behind him, those urges were just too powerful. And growing stronger every day.

Reading this portion of Rader's journal entries was like watching an impending train wreck.

The year was 1970. Shortly after Rader returned to Wichita following his four-year hitch in the Air Force, his mother announced, "You need to come to church with me. I met a nice girl there who I think you'd like."

She was right. Her name was Paula Dietz,

and she'd graduated from Wichita Heights High School in 1966, the same year Rader went into the service. Paula had grown up in a quiet little suburb of Wichita known as Park City. Physically, she was a wet dream come true for Rader — tall and blonde, with brown eyes. She was a looker, he told one of my sources, but in a proper and sweet way. The two began dating shortly after meeting, and by May 1971 they were married. Before long, they'd purchased a home in Park City that was practically next door to the house where Paula's parents lived.

Rader wasn't in love, of course. Serial killers lack that ability. But they can fake it with the proficiency of a veteran actor. And Rader knew even then that having a wife was the honorable, normal thing to do. Having a wife, he no doubt sensed, would provide the perfect cover, allowing him to remain hidden and inconspicuous.

By all accounts, Paula is a quiet, simple, hard-working woman. Her faith and her family are her passion. Even today, no one in the area will say a single disparaging word about her. In fact, people who know her basically refuse to say anything at all about her to strangers. Shielding her from the glare of inquisitive outsiders has become something of a community project.

Yet in this entire horribly depressing saga involving her husband, she has emerged as a truly fascinating character. One can't help but wonder, *How was it that she could not know?* Of course, only Paula holds the answer to that question. What *is* known is that on the surface Dennis and Paula Rader were the picture of marital bliss. Friends have reported that Dennis could often be seen doting on his wife at church, opening and closing doors for her as she climbed in and out of the car, helping her on and off with her coat. During his interrogation, Rader admitted that he had "real good sex" with his wife, although he quickly confessed that their relationship would have been "more fun if it [the sex] was different."

One thing seems clear: marriage helped focus Rader. In 1972, he landed a job as an assembler at the Coleman Company and began to immerse himself in the goings-on at Park City's newly created Christ Lutheran Church, where Paula and her mother sang in the choir. By the summer of 1973, he was working on the assembly line at the Cessna Aircraft Company, which seemed perfect because Rader had reportedly begun toying with the idea of becoming a pilot. At this same time, he and Paula were trying to start a family, although they weren't having much luck yet.

By November, the oil crisis was wreaking holy hell across the nation. Gasoline jumped from thirty cents a gallon to more than fifty cents. Every time he flipped on the TV, Rader had to listen to another news report about some plant laying off workers. It wouldn't happen to him, though — that's what he told himself. After all, he'd been so good. He'd tried so hard to stop thinking all those bad thoughts. Before long, though, he began hearing rumblings that the suits who sat around all day in their air-conditioned offices had panicked. Because of the huge jump in gas prices, they figured the small plane business was all washed up.

So one crisp autumn morning, Rader showed up at the Cessna plant and learned that he and about five hundred other workers had been sacked. He couldn't believe it. It wasn't fair. All because of some phony oil crisis cooked up by a bunch of guys living out in the desert. His head was spinning around. He felt as though someone had plunged a Buck knife into his heart. Sure, he'd been working on the line for only four months, but he loved the job. The money was good. He was even taking night classes at Wichita State University (WSU). He felt like a person with a future. Now it had been destroyed.

He climbed into his '62 Chevy Impala and poured on the gas out of the parking lot. He told himself that somebody was going to pay for making him feel so small, so powerless. The monster began to squirm inside him. Rader might have deluded himself that it was dead, but it turned out that it had always been in there, lying low, hibernating, gathering strength for the day it would one day reappear.

Rader later told Landwehr that minutes after getting his pink slip he realized he was on the verge of doing something weird, something bad. Paula wasn't home at that hour of the morning. She wouldn't return from her bookkeeping job at the VA hospital until late that afternoon. So Rader decided just to drive the streets of Wichita, trying to pretend he didn't know what was going to happen next.

When he finally spotted a house a few miles away from the Cessna plant that looked as though the owners were away, he stopped his car, strode up to the front door, and rang the doorbell. When no one answered, he walked into the backyard and broke inside. His heart was going crazy in his chest. Yet standing inside that stranger's empty home not only calmed him but made him feel alive in a way he hadn't for years. He didn't stay long. When he finally left, he took only one thing with him — a hatchet. He walked straight back to his car, shoved it beneath the front seat, and drove home.

He felt good.

The next few weeks were bad ones. He couldn't shut off his head. The yearning to hurt someone wouldn't go away. He couldn't shake it. For years he'd fantasized about this sort of thing. But this was different. The urge was so much more powerful now, and was growing more so with each passing day. And now that he didn't have a job to occupy him, he had nothing to do all day but think.

He could control his urge if he wanted to — that was what he told himself. The thing was, he didn't want to control it anymore. Why should he? He'd done that all his life. He'd kept his secret under wraps. He'd hidden it away. He'd played by everybody's rules, and where had it had gotten him? Out of work, living off his wife's salary, and collecting unemployment, with Christmas just around the corner.

Shortly before getting laid off, Rader decided to surprise Paula with a trip to Las Vegas. But after getting his pink slip, he didn't want to go. The people at the airline, however, didn't seem to care that he'd just lost his job, he later said. They weren't going to give him his money back, so he had no choice but to use the tickets. He told himself he'd make the best of it, and before long he began to wonder what Sin City would look like from the window of his jet, those millions of flickering incandescent bulbs and miles of neon tubes setting the night sky aglow.

Yet on the evening they flew into Las Vegas, all he saw was darkness. There must be some mistake, he thought. Had their flight been diverted to another city?

When he asked a stewardess about it, she just shrugged. It was all because of the oil shortage, she told him. A couple of days before, they'd decided to turn off all the lights in town because it had gotten too expensive to power them. Rader stared down at the blackened city in angry disbelief. He never wrote another word about the trip in his diary, so I can only imagine that his visit to Vegas was both uneventful and disappointing.

A few days later, he returned to their tiny house in Park City in a foul, anxious mood. Every morning, he'd drive Paula to work, then return home to thumb through the stash of detective magazines he kept hidden away on a top shelf of the guest bedroom closet. He loved to stare into those pages, reading the stories over and over again, pausing every so often, allowing the headlines to seep deep inside him: "He Was into Kinky Sex . . . and Kinkier Kills: Weird Case of the Hog-Tied Hookers." "Rape-Strangler's Two-Year Terror Reign." "Dog-Leash Strangler Hung Victim from Doorknob!" "The Autopsy Showed That Besides Hog-Tying His Victim, the Pervert Used His "Torture Kit" on Krista!"

Rader would close his eyes and masturbate, imagining himself to be right there in the middle of whatever scene he'd just read about. He'd always be the bad guy, and he loved the way the women in these magazines would watch his every move, the way their little eyeballs would dart about in their sockets, never blinking, following him as he walked about the room with his ropes and knives. He was the one with all the power, all the control. There was no denying that. He was in charge. It was sheer ecstasy. He couldn't get enough of it.

Winter came early that year. The ground froze up hard as concrete, and the sky always looked gray. Paula was the one bringing home the bacon now. Rader didn't like thinking about that. It made him feel weak. Some mornings after dropping Paula off at work, he'd write in his journal, something he continued to do on an erratic basis for the remainder of his life as a free man. Lately, his entries had begun to detail his newfound habit of driving the streets of Wichita, allowing his mind to drift from one dark thought to the next.

He'd begun noticing things in a way he never had before — coeds from the local university, mothers and little girls, women walking by themselves on the sidewalk. They were all his for the taking, he told himself. And that made him feel good. Sometimes he'd park his car and watch them stroll past his window. Other times, he'd follow them home, paying close attention to where they lived. Up until then, he'd always felt somewhat ashamed of all those thoughts he used to have, but something was different now. The gloves were off. He was sick of pretending. There was a comfort that came with all this thinking, a sense of belonging, of being part of a universe where he called the shots. He didn't need to hide his thoughts and feelings anymore, to be embarrassed. He could go for hours at a stretch and not do anything but let that TV set between his ears play and play and play. Oh, the places it took him.

One morning, after arriving back at the house, he pulled his old typewriter out of the closet in the back bedroom and rolled a piece of paper into it. Over the past few days, he'd been starting to notice that the buzz he got by looking at his magazines wasn't enough anymore. He'd begun to grow bored reading about all the grand adventures all those other guys were having. He decided it might be nice to create a story of his own, one in which he, not somebody else, got to be the bad guy. He'd certainly never considered himself to be much of a writer, but now it seemed as though the words and sentences were bursting out of him so quickly that he wondered if he'd be able to peck them out on his typewriter quickly enough. It almost felt as though someone were dictating them to him.

According to an entry I read in his journal, the first time he tried it, he sat there for a moment and thought about what he wanted to write, what he needed to say. He'd never done that sort of thing before. Yet he had so much going on inside his head that he needed to get out. So he started off by coming up with a title — if he could just get the right title, the rest of the story would come to him.

So he typed out the words, THE CHILD

KILLER WHO DRESSED LIKE A WOMEN.

Something about the word *women* didn't look right to him, he later told my source, but he couldn't figure out why. Lord knows he had to be one of the world's worst spellers. Nevertheless, he liked the way his headline floated there at the top of the page. It looked professional, he told himself.

Then, all at once, the story he needed to write exploded inside his brain. He began typing:

It was suppertime in Wichita, Ks. The streets were nearly deserted. The scene presented, peaceful winter setting for to young girls walking down the street. There was no reason for concern as the two girls walk along happy with Christmas thought only a few day away. And neither girls notice the yellow two door Chevy following them. Inside the Chevy, a woman or someone dressed like a woman peered nervously from the steering wheel and fingered the cold steel handcuff on the seat next to her. Inside her pants suit a small revolver was cocked and fitted with a silentier. She adjusted her sunglass and move forward toward the girls. When the girls reached the corner of the street she pulled up and rolled the window down, "Girls do want a ride up the street?" The two girls look at each other for the answer, but since this was a woman driving they felt that no harm would come to them. "Sure," they both answer at about the same time, and slid in. Jessica reached out and shut the door, and the car sped away.

The story was catalogued on the disc in my computer. Rader's creation went on for four single-spaced pages. He had yet to finish page one when his main character pulled a pistol out from his waistband and thrust it against Amelia's temple. Rader wrote that the killer commanded her in a gruff voice to fasten a pair of handcuffs around her friend's wrist, then fastened the other cuff around her wrist. The car sped off into the darkness that was dropping over the city like a shroud. Next stop, a deserted farm on the edge of town.

Neither girl uttered a word during the drive. They both knew they'd been tricked by the man who dressed like a woman. Eventually, the group ended up inside a dusty old tack room located in a corner of an empty barn. The two girls were chained to a post. Next, Rader had his cross-dressing main character retrieve a suitcase from the trunk of his car. From it, he pulled a hemp rope.

The girls were seated on a hay bale, whimpering, while the man went into the main part of the barn and tied a slipknot in the rope and threw the other end over a thick wooden beam. He watched as the rope dangled in space, six feet above the hard-packed dirt floor, then returned to the tack room clutching a knife and ordered Amelia to remove her clothes. Rader wrote that the girl froze with fear, but the sharp end of the knife persuaded her to do as she was told. He placed a red gag in her mouth and bound her wrists with nylon cord. She began sobbing. He did the same thing to Jessica, then took pictures of the two frightened girls with his camera.

Outside, a full moon hung in the dark sky. The man who dressed like a woman walked out to his car and fetched a shovel from his trunk. A moment later, he stood in a nearby field, awash in the incandescent glow of moonlight, and dug two three-foot-deep holes in the cold Kansas earth, one beside the other. He returned the shovel to his trunk and wrapped it in a plastic bag, then grabbed the kerosene heater he'd brought with him and carried it into the tack room, to make it warm for the two shivering girls.

He unchained Amelia and marched her into the barn, prodding her with the tip of his knife. But she couldn't see the rope he'd prepared for her because of the darkness. After forcing the trembling child onto the ground, he tied her ankles together and pulled the slipknot over her head.

"Fear then struck her and she twisted in her rope and cried," he wrote.

She was still struggling to get free when he carried her over to the hay bale and drew the slack rope tight. She froze with fear and closed her eyes as he dropped his pants, wrapped her panties around his penis, then kicked the hay bale out from beneath her. Instantly, her head turned slightly upward and to the side, her legs kicked, her body twitched. The killer took a few pictures of her swinging back and forth in the cold barn, then he cut her down and carried her warm corpse out to the grave he'd just dug. Before rolling her into the hole, he removed Amelia's blouse and training bra.

By the end of the story, the killer who dressed like a woman encircled a loop of baling wire around Jessica's throat and ordered her to perform fellatio on him. "Suck badly on it real hard," Rader wrote. "Do you understand me pronto, he screamed."

Eventually, the killer garroted the girl,

marveling at how her face became bloated with blood and the wire buried itself beneath her flesh. He tossed her into grave beside her friend, tidied up the barn, then drove home. A few days later, after reading about the disappearance of the two girls in the newspaper, he was able to track down where their parents lived. The killer mailed them their daughters' panties, which he enclosed with a little note.

"MERRY CHRISTMAS TO YOU ALL," Rader wrote. "As the letter went on, to say, he hope this small present of goodwill will brighten your day up, for now you know that the girl in not in her pants, so where is she? Have a good day."

As an extra touch, Rader had his main character sign his letter with four capital letters — DTPG, which stood for Death To Pretty Girls.

End of story.

Over the next few days, Rader mused in his journal about his curiosity over what it would be like to take that next step. True, he'd often thought about that sort of thing, but now he was fantasizing about it in a different way. It all seemed so within the realm of possibility now, so close to happening. As if all he'd have to do is reach out his hand; he could wrap his fingers around it and squeeze. It was his for the taking now. His entire life had prepared him for this moment — all those drawings he'd been making since he was a kid, all those daydreams, all those cats and dogs out in the barn . . .

The fire inside him seemed to be growing hotter, igniting everything around it. Such a fine line seemed to exist between creating a fantasy in his head and unleashing one in real life.

Christmas came and went. None of the things he used to do could put out that fire now. He'd never wanted something so badly before. He'd crept up to the edge of the abyss and peered over so many times that he told himself he was finally ready now. All he needed was the right situation, and he'd know exactly what to do and how to do it.

According to his journal, one night after Paula went to sleep, he crept out of the house and drove into the sticks, parked his car, and walked to an all-night grocery. He pretended to be talking on the telephone, but he was really studying the women who wandered into the store and then emerged a few minutes later carrying a sack or two of food. It was 11:30 by the time he finally spotted the woman he wanted. She'd parked her car in the corner of the lot and walked into the store. He waited for her to disappear inside, then hung up the phone and casually walked over to her vehicle and tried opening the back door. It wasn't locked.

Only the Lord knew how desperately he wanted to climb inside and lie down on the floor in the shadows, behind the front seat. He'd rehearsed it over and over again in his mind. Inside his head, it always played out the same way. She'd place her groceries in the front seat, start the car, and pull out onto the highway, and he'd surprise her by pressing his .22-caliber handgun against her temple.

"Drive out into the country," he yearned to order her.

Once they arrived at that perfect spot he had in mind, he'd bind her, rape her, strangle her, and dump her body out into a culvert. But as he stood there in the parking lot of the market, he suddenly realized there were variables he'd never considered before that moment. *What if she spotted him lying there and started screaming? What if she asked a clerk to help load her groceries into the car?* He'd never get away with it, he told himself. So he walked back down the highway to his car and drove home.

But that was hardly the end of it. He now understood that he needed to be much more systematic in his planning. If he was going to pull off a bold crime, he needed to anticipate every single worst-case scenario imaginable. Nothing could be left to chance. All those guys he read about in the detective magazines — they might have pulled off big rapes, kidnappings, and mass murders, but they'd all gotten caught because of some foolish mistake. They were lazy. He vowed not to let that happen to him. He would be different. He was always an organized guy — a detail freak. He couldn't help himself. He was the type of guy who would walk into a room and want first thing to straighten it up, organize it, put everything back in order. Suddenly it dawned on him that he could use this trait to his advantage. He'd use his love of order to help him kill. The devil, he thought, really was in the details.

So he spent the next few days plotting, fantasizing. After dropping Paula off at work each day, he began hanging out in the parking lot of the Twin Lakes Mall, he later confessed, studying the girls as they walked to and from their cars. He'd lose himself in his daydreams, shutting his eyes and trying to imagine all the powerful things he could do with victims. He wanted one so badly.

One morning it came to him. He'd snatch the thirty-something-year-old brunette he'd

342

often seen walking across parking lot, the one who he knew worked in a bank located in the mall.

"I can do this," he told himself. "I can do this. People kidnap people and hold them for ransom all the time."

Rader knew, however, that he wasn't going to bother with any of that ransom nonsense. He'd bind her, force her to have sex with him, then garrote her. Afterward, he'd toss her body on the side of a highway outside of town. A few days earlier, he'd begun driving around with his bowling bag filled with his pistol, some ropes, and a hunting knife; he referred to the bag as his "hit kit" because that was the slang term that all those killers in his detective magazines used to describe the tools of their trade.

According to the entry I read in his journal, it was early evening when he finally decided to make his move. The brunette always seemed to depart the bank at about 5:35 P.M. and walk to her car. So he left his car on the other side of the parking lot, walked across to where she parked, and waited. When she appeared, he pulled the hood of his parka down over his head, walked up to her, and grabbed her, which was how everyone seemed to do it in the pages of his detective magazines. But everything went wrong.

The moment he lay his hands on her, she began screaming and punching at him. He couldn't control her arms. She'd gone insane on him. He didn't realize that a woman could be so strong. So he shoved her down onto the asphalt and ran like hell back toward his car.

"That was a big mistake," he muttered to himself while heading back home to Park City.

Dennis L. Rader, from boy to family man to convicted serial killer.

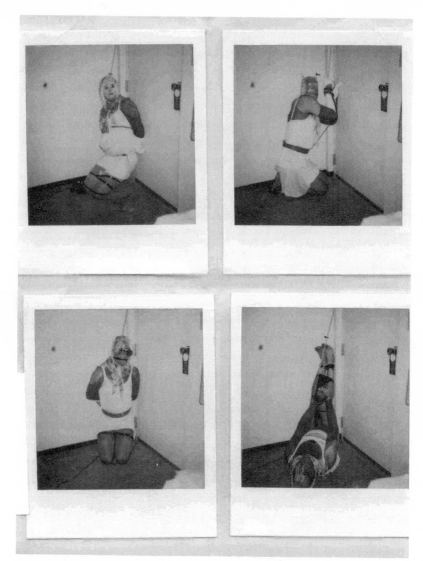

Dennis Rader took these photos of himself in the late 1980s during one of his so-called motel parties. One of Rader's favorite pastimes was to check into a motel, dress up in women's clothing, then bind his arms and legs in ropes and handcuffs.

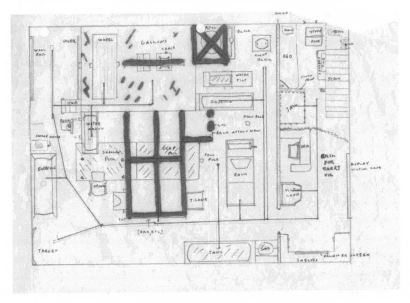

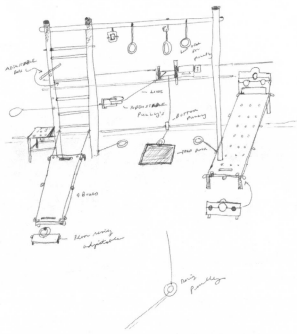

Two examples of Dennis Rader's hand-drawn torture chambers where the serial killer fantasized about taking his victims. Rader kept these drawings with his enormous stash of photos taken of his victims, sketches, and journal entries.

Police and KBI agents stand over Dennis Rader, moments after his arrest shortly after noon on February 26, 2005. Rader was driving to lunch when dozens of law enforcement agents in unmarked cars swooped in to arrest him, not far from his home in Park City. COURTESY OF THE WICHITA POLICE DEPARTMENT

The Park City home where Rader lived with his wife for more than three decades. The residence was demolished by the city in March 2007 to provide an access-way to the park located behind the property. JOHNNY DODD

Members of the Kansas Bureau of Investigation's BTK Task Force, from left: KBI Assistant Director Larry Thomas, KBI Director Larry Welch, DNA expert Sindey Schueler, and Senior Special Agent Ray Lundin, with Wichita Police Department Lt. Ken Landwehr (second from right). COURTESY OF THE KANSAS BUREAU OF INVESTIGATION

Kris Casarona, who began meeting with Dennis Rader shortly after his arrest in 2005 in an effort to write a book about him, seated with John Douglas (right) and coauthor Johnny Dodd (left) in Wichita. JOHNNY DODD

John Douglas, with coauthor Johnny Dodd, pictured below a guard tower in the parking lot of the El Dorado Correctional Facility, shortly after interviewing serial killer Dennis Rader. JOHNNY DODD

John Douglas at the entrance to the prison where Rader began serving his ten life sentences in August 2005. Because the state of Kansas did not have the death penalty when Rader committed his ten murders, he escaped lethal injection. JOHNNY DODD

13

The conversations in my head had begun. After spending hours clicking my way through the digital remains of Dennis Rader's secret inner life, I'd begun conversing with myself, giving myself instructions.

Fight it, I said. *Fight the urge to hate Dennis Rader. You don't have time for that. Just keep reading, keep moving downward through all his words. Think of those he killed. That's really why you're here,* I reminded myself. *Think of how he decided to make them suffer before stealing their lives away. Don't think about how badly you'd enjoy burying your fist squarely into the middle of his face, hitting him with the type of punch that drives the cartilage of a man's nose into the base of his brain, sending him packing to the next world.*

Don't think about those things, I ordered myself. *It'll only cloud your judgment, preventing you from glimpsing all the things you need to see, facts you might have overlooked decades ago. Your job now is to determine what you missed, what you could have done differently.*

Then I shut the hell up and kept reading.

In an entry from early January 1974, Rader wrote that Paula didn't like driving in the snow and ice. The stuff just made her nervous. So whenever the city got a dumping of snow or the streets were glazed with ice, Rader became the designated chauffeur, often carting her to and from work. He didn't mind. Deep down, there was something soothing about sitting behind the wheel of a car. It made him feel more powerful, more in control. It was one of the few socially acceptable activities he could engage in that possessed the necessary juice to quiet his mind whenever all the clamor started.

According to his journal, it was during one of those drives in the first week of January 1974 that he first spotted them — a mother and three or four kids, climbing into a station wagon and backing out of the driveway. He couldn't quite make out their nationality, but the moment he spotted their dark skin, his brain flew into overdrive. The fantasies started.

There was just something about dark-skinned people that turned him on, he told one of my sources. *What was it?* he wondered. Something about their dark eyes and dark hair. A few of the prostitutes he'd been with in the service were Hispanic, he recalled. Then again, some of his favorite detective magazines sported pictures of sexy-looking dark-skinned models on their covers. So maybe that was it?

According to what Landwehr told me, Rader was never quite sure why he'd targeted the Otero family — other than that they were in the wrong place at the wrong time.

Whatever the reason, that next morning he drove back to their neighborhood, parked down the street from their house, and waited. It was almost 8 A.M. Sure enough, just like clockwork, the mother and children climbed into a station wagon and drove away. He began to daydream about all the terrible things he wanted to do with the mother and her daughter. A couple of days later, he followed the family station wagon on its morning drive to school and back. He did this for several days. One afternoon, he later admitted, he drove over to the public library and used a reverse directory to look up the Oteros' phone number and identity. He even dialed their number a few times and listened to who answered the phone. He was desperate to figure out if any males lived at the residence. The last thing he needed was some guy to waltz onto the scene and ruin what was shaping up to be the perfect fantasy. It wasn't that he didn't believe he could overpower any man — that had nothing to do with it, he told himself. He just didn't need the hassle.

And then one day it happened. He told himself that *it* would be OK. The dark-skinned woman with the three or four children offered the prime setup. From what I knew about these sorts of violent killers, I could almost read Rader's mind. He convinced himself that it would be just she and the kids. Which was a good thing. It meant that she'd comply with his demands in order to protect her children. Even the location of her house was perfect: it was situated on a corner lot; there was a garage set off from the house, a fenced yard, and plenty of space between the neighbor's house and the back door. This time, he told himself, things would turn out differently than they had a month before. This time everything would go down just as he'd planned.

Rader typed up his chilling, utterly heartless account of what happened on that day in January, not long after it all went down. It was part of the stash on the disc in my computer.

He wrote that he awoke early that morning, drove over to the mall parking lot, and started walking. A light dusting of snow was tumbling out of the gray sky. *Damn, it was cold out,* he muttered to himself. He couldn't remember feeling a cold quite like it ever before. He pulled his Air Force parka up tight around his face and started walking toward the house in the 800 block of North Edgemoor Street. Once he got there, he walked straight toward the backyard, jumped a fence, and crouched down in the snow next to the house. That was when he spotted the dog pawprints in the snow. For a few brief moments, he panicked. Why hadn't he ever stopped to consider that the family might own a dog? Part of him wanted to get the hell out of there, but whatever it was that had control of him wouldn't hear of it. There would be no backing out now. He'd come too far for that.

In his journal, Rader wrote that he made a few soft whistling sounds, trying to flush out the dog. But the backyard seemed clear, and before he knew it, he was reviewing his three plans. The first involved waiting until the mother left to take her kids to school, then creeping into the garage. When she returned, he'd force her into the house. His second idea was to hide in the garage and overpower the mother and her two kids when they attempted to leave for school, then force them back inside. The last scenario had him sitting tight out there in the snow, then waiting for someone to open the back door, which was when he'd force himself inside.

He didn't have much time. If a neighbor glanced out a back window, he was a sitting duck. He decided he'd take the three of them in the house, and crept up next to the door. He reached his hand out and tried to quietly open it, but the door was locked. Pulling a pair of wire cutters from his pocket, he snipped a nearby telephone line, then pulled a black nylon ski mask over his face. From another pocket, he retrieved his knife and pistol. A few minutes later, at 8:40, the back door opened and a young boy appeared, clutching a bag of garbage. Rader bolted toward the door before the boy spotted him; he grabbed the child.

The next moment, Rader wrote in his journal, he was standing inside the kitchen, sizing up the scene. The boy whose shoulder he clutched, along with his sister who sat at a nearby table, had been making their lunches just moments before he burst inside the house. Their coats were piled beside their lunch boxes. They were just about to leave for school. Standing beside the stove was his worst nightmare — the father.

Where the hell did he come from? he wondered. *Why didn't I know about him?* The man stood there watching Rader with a grin on his face.

In his account of the murder penned a few days later, Rader recalled Otero saying, "Did my brother-in-law put you up to this? Come on, tell me."

Rader held up his pistol and took aim at his head. His wife shrieked.

"Don't hurt us," she stammered. "We . . . we don't have any money. Take anything you want. Anything. Just don't hurt us."

The little boy stood beside his parents, his mouth hanging open, looking as though he'd just seen the devil. Tears were beginning to streak down his sister's cheeks. Rader ordered them to walk into the front room, then told them the story he'd cooked up to keep them calm.

"I just broke out of the penitentiary," he said, as the children started crying. "The cops are after me. I need a car, money, and food."

His gun hand was shaking. He was nervous, and the father knew it. So Otero tried to quiet his family down, telling them that everything would be okay if they'd settle down. Rader ordered the father to place his wallet on the washing machine, then motioned for them to go into the family room. From out of nowhere, a mean-looking Heinz-57 mutt came running into the room, barking.

"Get the dog out of here," he told the father. "But don't even think about trying any funny tricks. This is an automatic, filled with hollow-points. You ever seen what they can do to someone?"

I read how Mr. Otero tried to reassure Rader that if he'd let him put the dog out, everything would be fine.

"He hates the cold," he said, grabbing the animal by the scruff of his neck. Rader allowed him to open up the kitchen door and dump the dog into the backyard, but he watched Otero like a hawk all the while. At first he wanted to tie them up in the family room, but when he spotted the back bedroom, he ordered the family to walk back there and lie down on their stomachs on the bed with their hands behind their backs.

Landwehr told me that Rader originally had fantasized about having sex with the mother and daughter, then strangling them. But as Rader stood there in the family's home, he wasn't so sure. He knew only that he needed to do something, fast. Lying there face down on the bed, they were beginning to panic again, and it scared him to think what might happen if he lost control of the situation. He couldn't let that happen. He stood behind them, watching them, especially the father. At any moment, they were going to turn on him. He could feel it.

"I gotta get out to California," he said while fumbling around in his oversized pockets for his rope, gags, and tape. "If I can get out there, I'll be safe . . . I'm gonna have to take your car."

"Take it," the mother pleaded. "You can have it. We want you to have it."

He was desperate to keep things from unraveling, to stay in control. That was what he wanted more than anything else — to finally have absolute and total control over another human being, to bind another person up the way he felt bound and hemmed in by his rotten life, then to cinch those ropes up tight. It was what he'd always dreamed about. And at that moment, after more than two decades of fantasizing, he realized that all his dreams and more were on the verge of being realized.

He worked on the father first, ordering him off the bed and onto the floor. He wrapped tape around his wrists, over and over again. When he was confident that Otero couldn't break free no matter how hard he tried, he moved his attention to the mother. Rader knew there was little risk of the father's attempting to run from the house for help. Because Otero feared for the safety of his wife and children, the last thing he'd want to do was be seen as a threat to the man who'd burst into his home brandishing a pistol. And this made Rader feel just a bit calmer. With the father out of commission, he felt his confidence return. And as he wrapped the tape around the mother's delicate wrists and ankles, he began to talk to them, asking them to tell him their names, where the father worked, and what was the best way to get out of town.

The mother's name was Julie. Her husband was Joseph. Their children were Josephine and Joey. Knowing their names made Rader feel better. They felt more real that way, more vulnerable. For as long as he could remember, whenever he fantasized about all the terrible things he yearned to do to his victims, he had known that details like names were important.

For the children, he employed cotton cord, the type used for venetian blinds, purchased at a hardware store near his house. The kids were both crying, but trying their best to act brave. Afterwards, he tied what was left of the cord around Joseph's wrists and ankles.

When he finished, he stepped back and stared down over the family lying beneath him, tied up like farm animals. Nobody was going anywhere, he thought.

"My . . . my hands are going numb," Julie told him. "Is there any way you could loosen this just a bit?"

According to his journal entry, Rader apologized, somewhat embarrassed that he'd resorted to so much force. He peeled off the tape and asked her to wiggle her fingers a little. In his pocket, he located another cord and wrapped it around her wrists. Joseph explained that his ribs hurt because of a car accident he'd just had. He wondered if there was some way Rader might let him change his position on the floor. Dennis untied him and let him scoot across the floor just a bit. He placed a coat beneath Otero, then retied his wrists together.

"You can tie my feet up to the bedpost," Joseph suggested. And that was just what Rader did. He gagged the family with strips he cut from a pillowcase he found in a closet. The little girl was sobbing now, tears rolling down her cheeks. Her hair was so long that he had a tough time tying the gag into place. No matter how he tried, her locks kept getting tangled up in the strip as he tried to tie it off.

"I'm sorry for pinching your hair," he wrote that he told the young girl.

Most people reading Rader's words might be struck by what appeared to be an almost gentle, compassionate streak, as if perhaps he was somehow concerned about the well-being of his victims. Unfortunately, that would be the wrong assumption. Rader's tactic was the same calculated MO used by other violent offenders I'd spoken with. The goal is to lull victims into believing that if they'll cooperate with their attacker, they won't be hurt. Nothing, of course, could be further from the truth.

Julie's purse sat on the dresser, and he began rifling through it, searching for her car keys. Things were becoming clearer now. He could feel the ideas jelling inside his head. He'd entered into this thing with a vague idea of the outcome, but now things were taking shape faster than he could control them. One thing was certain — when *this* was all over, he'd escape from their house using their car.

"Take whatever you want," Julie called to him from the bed. "We have a typewriter. Take that. You can pawn it."

He didn't say a word. He just walked over

and fished out the car keys he'd spotted in Joseph's front pocket. Joseph tried to make eye contact with him as he removed the keys, and Dennis stared at him, unblinking.

In his journal, Rader described walking out into the living room and standing there, staring at their belongings, much of which were still packed up in cardboard moving boxes, as if the family had just moved into the house. It was quiet out here, away from the chaos and panic in the bedroom. He could hear himself breathing and the thumping of his heart.

Decision time, he told himself, drumming his fingers on the side of his head. *Decision time . . . Decision time.*

He plunged his hands into his pockets and dumped everything out onto the sofa — the plastic bags, the cords, his knife and gun. *They're going down . . . They're all going down.* He grabbed what he needed and hurried back into the bedroom. Everyone except Joseph was sobbing. Rader walked over to Joseph, pulled a plastic bag down over his head, looped his preknotted cord around his neck, and pulled tight. He did the same thing to the boy. Joseph was attempting to shout at him through his gag. His words were horribly muffled, but Rader could still make out what he was saying.

"What are you doing?" Otero cried. "What are you doing?"

And that was when all hell started to break loose. They were on to him now. There was no use pretending any longer. Everyone began screaming.

"BE QUIET," Rader ordered. "EVERY-BODY SHUT UP."

Dennis didn't like this one bit. Nothing he'd read in those detective magazines of his had prepared him for this. He'd always considered those articles to be vocational primers for the kind of work he'd dreamed about doing. But now it turned out that all those stories had been painted with deceivingly broad strokes.

Why was this turning out to be so difficult? The boy was thrashing about on the floor, and so was Joseph. His head was rocking back and forth in quick, violent spasms. If his feet hadn't been tied to the bedpost, there's no telling where he would have moved to.

Meanwhile, up on the bed, the mother and daughter shrieked so loudly that the noise seemed to fill every inch of the house. Rader slammed his gloved hand down on top of them, then attempted to cover their gagged mouths with his hands. They both begged him to take the bags off Joseph's and Joey's

358

heads. For some reason, Rader reached down and yanked the bag off the boy's head. Joey's eyes were closed, and he was still. The father appeared to have rubbed a hole in the bag. Vomit was smeared around his face, and his chest was moving up and down in slow, labored movements. When Rader glanced over, he was surprised to see that the boy's eyelids were fluttering open.

"Please," Josephine cried. "Please go. You can leave. We won't tell. We won't tell anyone. Nobody will say a word."

He stood there and surveyed the scene, trying to catch his breath and calm his head. For a brief instant, he thought about getting the hell out of there. But then he realized they could identify him. They'd seen his face. If he left now, he might as well drive straight to the cops.

From out of his pocket, he pulled a coil of thin rope. When Julie saw it, she began screaming again, begging him to stop all this. He quickly looped the rope around her neck, pulled tight, and began to strangle her slowly.

"Mommy," Josephine cried out. "Mommy, I love you."

"Be calm," Rader told the girl, according to his journal. "She'll pass out soon . . . She'll go to sleep."

Julie was gasping now, staring straight up into his eyes. Not blinking. "Mama," the little girl cried out. "What are you doing to my mama?" Then, all at once, Julie's eyes shut, and she passed out. Afterwards, Rader removed the rope, slipped it around Joseph's neck, and yanked it tight.

"Be careful," the little girl whispered when she saw what he was doing. "Please be careful."

"He'll go to sleep, too," he told the girl. "Once he stops fighting the rope, he'll go to sleep."

Rader wrote that his hands hurt by the time he finally finished off the father. And that surprised him. He never thought that killing someone would be so difficult.

The little girl, he noticed, watched without a trace of emotion as he yanked the rope from her father's reddened neck, then looped it over hers. Her eyes began to bulge as he pulled on it. Rader recalled that she called out, "Mama . . . Mama . . . Mama." Then her tiny lids dropped, and she passed out. He was staring down at the girl's body when he noticed that her mother's head was moving from side to side. He tied a clove hitch in the rope, then slipped it over Julie's head. Just as he was about to tighten it, her eyes fluttered open wide and stared straight into his.

"May God have mercy on your soul," she whispered.

He couldn't believe what he'd heard. What a helluva thing to say, he thought while tugging on the rope with all his strength. Blood vessels burst in her eyes from the pressure. Blood trickled from her mouth and nose. The sight spooked him so that he grabbed a nearby pillow and covered her face.

In the corner of the room, he spotted the boy's body, twitching. It struck him that Joey was pretending to be asleep. Rader walked out into the living room, found two more plastic bags, and returned to the bedroom. After wrapping a T-shirt around Joey's head, he covered the boy's head with a plastic bag, then another T-shirt. He finished the job off with a rope and clove hitch.

"I can't breathe," Joey shouted when Rader tightened his makeshift noose. "I can't breathe."

Picking the boy up, Rader carried him into his bedroom and lay him down on his bed so that he could watch him suffocate and not be disturbed by the others in the bedroom. But Joey's body was convulsing so, struggling against the inevitable, that he quickly rolled off the mattress and dropped onto the floor. Rader didn't bother picking him back up and decided to let him die there. Afterward, he returned to the others and decided that the prudent thing to do would be to place a plastic bag over Joseph's head, which he then cinched tight with a belt. The little girl was still lying motionless on the bed. Rader watched her for a moment and then got an idea.

"My grand folly," he later wrote about the moment. He headed off to search for the basement. A moment later, he was descending a set of steps into the darkness. After locating a light switch and flipping it on, he quickly found what he'd come looking for — a thick cast-iron water pipe. It ran the length of the ceiling. He slapped it with his hand. It definitely felt sturdy enough. He went to work preparing the pipe, then hurried back upstairs and fetched the girl. He carried her downstairs, lay her on the bottom step, pulled off her pants, and tugged her panties down.

Leaving her there, he returned to the bedroom to inspect the bodies. Never having seen a dead person before, he poked and prodded them. Next he gave the house a good going-over, making sure the place was completely clean of any evidence. Only after he felt positive that he hadn't left anything behind did he head back down to the basement, where he was surprised to find the girl awake and staring groggily up at the noose, dangling from the ceiling.

Dennis quickly tied rope around her ankles, then around her knees and stomach. He pulled up her sweater and used his knife to cut into her bra, exposing one of her breasts. It excited him that he was probably the first man ever to see this part of her body, besides her father. He ran back upstairs and scoured every inch of the house again, then returned to the girl.

"Are you going to do the same thing to me that you did to everyone else?" she asked.

"No," he lied. "Don't worry about them. They're all just asleep."

Picking her up, he carried her a few feet from the stairs, then lay her down on her back, directly beneath the pipe. The noose dangled overhead, and he pulled it down and pushed her head through the opening in the rope and pulled it tight. It suddenly dawned on him that it might be nice to record this moment, so he bent down and asked the girl, "You happen to know if your dad has a camera?"

She shook her head no, then asked him a question: "What's going to happen to me?"

Dennis smiled. "Don't worry, baby," he said. "You'll be in heaven tonight with the rest of your family."

All she did was stare at him. She never said another word. A split second later, he yanked the rope with all his might, hoisting her upright. She gasped, blinked several times as a shudder ran through her body. Then she died. Dennis lifted her shirt up again to get another look at her breast. With his other hand, he masturbated. After he finished, he reached out and touched her breast.

He heard a sound from upstairs and quickly realized that it was a postal worker rattling around in the mailbox. It suddenly occurred to him that he had no real idea what sort of schedule the Otero household ran by. For all he knew, somebody — a friend, relative, or another of their kids — might walk through the front door at any minute. He switched off the lights, hurried up the stairs, and shut the door behind him.

After gathering together his supplies, he cranked up the thermostat as high as it would go; he'd heard somewhere that this would make the bodies decompose faster, which would confuse the cops about exactly when the murders occurred.

As he walked out to the garage, he noticed the sweat — his clothes were completely drenched with it. His rubber gloves were so full of perspiration that they felt like water balloons. So much for being a cool, calm master criminal, he thought.

He climbed into the family's station wagon and started it. The gas gauge revealed that the tank was nearly empty, which annoyed him. He figured he had enough fuel to get back to the mall parking lot. A few minutes later he arrived at the mall, killed the engine, and did a quick inventory of all his gear. He quickly realized he'd left his knife behind.

"Damn it," he seethed.

If the police found it, he was screwed. So he raced back to the family's house in his own car, sped up their driveway, and slammed on the brakes as he pulled into their garage. He ran into the house, searching for his blade. His head was spinning. After a few minutes spent retracing his steps and combing through every room, it finally dawned on him what had happened. He darted out the back door and spotted it lying in the snow, just beneath the phone line he'd cut. Rader figured that he must have dropped it in all the excitement of seeing the boy suddenly appear outside the kitchen door. *Can't lose control like that,* he scolded himself. He grabbed it, wiped the snow off of it, and dropped it into his pocket. A moment later, he wrote, he was back in his car, driving toward his house in Park City.

And in his journal I read his description of how his brain was on fire. How he tried to think, but nothing came.

14

I'd been drifting for far too many hours on Dennis Rader's words and dark thoughts. I needed to feel something else move through me besides him and the terrible, curious images his writings caused to play out inside my head.

I was a bit like that little boy in the movie *The Sixth Sense.* I not only saw dead people — although, actually, they were corpses — but also people killing people. When I plunged myself into a case, I became someone else. I became the killer. I glimpsed the world through his eyes, seeing events I really had no business seeing.

Once, during an interview with a man convicted of murdering six people (authorities suspected he'd been responsible for twice as many), I listened as he recounted his crimes, and suddenly the visuals began to unfold in front of my eyes. I saw everything — or at least just enough. After a few minutes, I began speaking in the first person when talking about his killings, as though I were the one who had committed the crimes just described to me.

"Knock it off, man," he shouted, looking unnerved. "You're freaking me out."

"What are you talking about?" I asked, unaware of what I'd just done.

"You're not me. OK?" he said. "You're not me. So stop pretending to be."

And as I read Dennis Rader's notes about what happened after he returned home from murdering those four members of the Otero family, I began to sense a slight pressure behind my eyes. Which didn't really surprise me, because Rader wrote that his head was killing him. When he returned home, he felt as though he'd gotten his head stuck in a vise and someone was cranking the hell out of it. At least that was how he described it.

In all the stories he'd read about killers in his detective magazines, he'd never heard of this happening before. After an hour or two, he wondered just how much more of it he could take. Paula wasn't home from work, which was good. He couldn't find the Off switch for his brain. The cops were going to kick in the door at any minute, he convinced himself.

His only chance, he told himself, was to

pitch everything — his sketches, his stash of detective magazines, and all those stories he'd written. He combed through every blessed inch of his car, then cleaned out his desk and tossed everything into the trash pit in his backyard. He doused it with gasoline and flung a match on it. A few minutes later, the pile had been reduced to a mound of black ash.

He changed his clothes; piled whatever he'd worn during the murders, including his shoes, into a paper bag; and drove back across town to his parents' house. No one was home. He wanted to torch his clothes in their trash pit, but decided against it. Something about burning a pile of clothes in the middle of the day just didn't make sense. How the hell would he explain that if somebody spotted him back there? Instead, he stashed everything up in the top of his folks' decrepit backyard hen house. His stuff would be safe there, he reassured himself. He'd come back some other time and put a match to it. At the last minute, he decided not to pitch his parka — the bloodstains on it, he wrote in his journal, weren't all that visible.

When he made it back to his house, he felt a bit calmer. Just to play it safe, though, he hid all his weapons around the house — his pistols, hunting rifles, knives, even the hatchet he'd stolen back when he'd gotten laid off at Cessna. If the cops really were going to come for him, he'd be damned if they were going to take him without a fight.

But the cops never did come, and by February life slowly returned to normal. The paranoia had begun to ease. Before he knew it, his appetite had returned, and he'd begun looking for another victim.

Rader's reaction was typical of the feelings other serial killers had described to me. After a brief wave of intense paranoia, they begin to realize how easy it is for them to get away with murder — even if their MO was somewhat sloppy. Rader must have known that picking strangers as victims made it terribly difficult for police. The so-called smoking gun cases, involving family members, friends, or associates, are the easy ones to crack. But crimes without any apparent motive are tough to solve, particularly when they are well planned and thought out in advance by the perp.

One afternoon in March, Rader wrote in his journal, he was driving to lunch with his wife when he spotted a young woman with long blonde hair pulling some letters out of a mailbox on the front stoop of her house on

13th Street. Although he didn't know it at the time, the young woman's name was Kathy Bright. The moment he saw her, he couldn't get her out of his mind. All during lunch, the image of her jean jacket and beaded purse burned a black hole into his brain, he wrote in his journal. Later that afternoon, he climbed back in his car to try to locate her, but failed. Instead, he drove back to her house and looked it over. He liked what he saw. The place was situated by a vacant lot. On the other side, the neighbor's house looked deserted.

He parked a few blocks away, then walked back to the house with a dark stocking cap pulled down over his ears. In his pockets he carried a knife. Tucked into his belt was his .22-caliber pistol. It was hardly a menacing-looking weapon, I thought, the kind of firearm that — if he had to use it — would make a minimal amount of noise.

In his journal, Rader described pounding his fist on the front door, but no one answered. So he walked back to his car, telling himself he'd return some other time. Weeks passed. He was never quite sure how many. But every day he reviewed his "hit plan" in his head, going over every detail just as he imagined it unfolding.

"Little by little," he wrote, "my heart raced

as the hit came into focus."

He was never quite sure how many women lived in the house, but he had a hunch that there were at least two. On April 4, he decided to make his move after his morning classes at WSU. He later claimed to have been so excited during math class that he couldn't focus on anything the professor said. Yet, at the same time, he was "tensely aware" of everything going on around him — the other students dutifully scribbling notes, sunlight streaming in through the window, the sound the chalk made as it slammed against the blackboard. Never before had he felt so focused. Sweat drenched his clothing.

After class, he decided it was time to take action. He made one last pass of the house, to check out the location of the phone line and the back door. In front of the house sat the blonde girl's green Pinto, which led him to believe she was inside. He parked a few blocks away, then walked a meandering route back to the house. Tucked inside his heavy ski jacket were his ropes, cords, gags, knife, and two pistols.

As luck would have it, by the time he reached the house and pounded on the front door, no one was home. He walked around back, cut the phone line, and broke the glass on the back door with his wire-cutters. The place was empty, but he told himself he'd stick around awhile and wait for her to return. After a few minutes, he decided to check out the inside of the house, walking from bedroom to bedroom, plotting out exactly where and how the crime would all go down. He eventually decided that he'd tie her up in a back bedroom, using some of the panty hose and clothes he'd located in the house.

Then he sat down in a chair and waited for the woman with the long blonde hair and the beaded purse to arrive back home. His head was filled with all the images he'd created about what he wanted to have happen. The moment she walked inside, he envisioned choking her into unconsciousness, then dragging her into the bedroom. Once there, he'd tie her naked to the bed and rape her. When she awoke, he planned on either plunging an ice pick into her heart or strangling her. But on that particular morning as he waited for his victim, he couldn't stop thinking about what he later referred to in his journal as "anus intercourse." Perhaps he'd try that?

His daydream was cut short when he heard a car door slam. He raced to the front room and hid by the door. A second later, it swung open, and his victim's nineteen-year-old brother walked in. Thinking he was alone, Rader stepped out to confront him, brandishing his pistol. But a split second later, the young woman whose image he couldn't get out of his mind walked in. It was a bad moment, he later recalled. His whole plan seemed on the verge of being blown.

"She could have turn and run out screaming down the road," he wrote in his journal. But she didn't, and Rader quickly launched into his story about being a wanted felon in California and how he needed their car, money, and food in order to get to New York.

The combination of his bogus story and his pistol convinced them to go along with his demands. After tying the two up in separate bedrooms, Rader racked his brain trying to figure how he was going to handle this glitch in his plan. Once again, he hadn't foreseen the possibility of a man being at the house.

"How do you do away with one without the other knowing it?" he later wrote.

The next fifteen minutes were pure chaos. He was running back and forth from bedroom to bedroom, trying to keep control of a situation that was quickly deteriorating. Absolutely nothing was going according to his carefully rehearsed plan. In an attempt to kill the boy, he ended up shooting him two times in the head. His nerves were so frayed that he accidentally fired an additional round through the bathroom wall. He tried to strangle the young woman, but it seemed to be taking too long, so he grabbed his knife and began stabbing her. "I drove one in her back below the rib cage, hoping to hit the lungs," he wrote. Blood splattered everywhere. Rader later commented that he was amazed at how slick it felt when it got on his fingertips.

Just as he was just preparing to jab the blade into the woman's neck, he heard the front door open. He ran to the front window in time to see the young man he'd shot stumbling down the street, trying to flag down a car. In a flash, Rader grabbed his gear and ran like hell out the back door.

This time, Rader didn't bother to write what happened in the hours after the murder. In an entry penned weeks later, he did explain that he once again believed it to be just a matter of time before the police nabbed him.

He confessed to his journal that he'd been transformed into a nervous wreck. He couldn't recall ever reading about such a botched crime that didn't end with the guy who did it going to jail. But the cops never came. Even after weeks and months passed, Rader was still on edge.

One afternoon in October 1974, a high school buddy named Bobby Ormston picked up the phone and dialed Rader's phone number. I'd first heard about Ormston after a law enforcement source familiar with the details of Rader's interrogation passed his name on to me. Apparently, Rader told the cops that during the final days of his letter writing campaign in 2004–2005, he'd toyed with the idea of convincing the authorities that Ormston was BTK. He thought it would be funny to trick the police into kicking in Bobby's front door, then dragging him away in handcuffs. I spoke to Ormston on the phone a few days before hunkering down in this Wichita hotel room with Rader's journal.

Ormston told me that when he phoned Rader in 1974, nearly ten years had passed since they'd seen each other, and he was dying to catch up with him. During that time, Ormston had moved away from Wichita to attend college, earned an engineering degree, and gotten married, and was now in the midst of a divorce.

He and Rader chatted for a few minutes on the phone. Ormston recalled thinking that

Rader's voice sounded just as flat and serious as it had back in high school. By the time he hung up, they'd agreed to meet at the Blackout, a local tavern near the WSU campus, and catch up on life over a pitcher of beer.

It was around 5:30 in the afternoon when Ormston showed up at the bar. Dennis was already there, sitting at a table in the back, nursing his beer. He'd positioned his chair so that he was facing the door, allowing him to glimpse whoever entered long before they would be able to spot him. Ormston grabbed a glass and joined him at the table, excited to hear what he'd been up to over the past decade. But the moment he sat down, he was shocked at what he encountered.

"There was just this incredible hostility about him," he told me over the phone one afternoon a few weeks before my arrival in Wichita. "It made me real uncomfortable. A couple of times I thought he was going to come across the table at me. He was just so tense. Never in my life had I seen Dennis like that. It was like he was sitting on a spring and was ready to pop out of his seat. I've been around people who have been high on meth, and that look that he gave me had that same kind of teeth-gritted intensity to it."

Ormston explained to me that he tried his

best to ignore the tension and listened as Rader described his life since graduating from high school.

"He told me how he'd just gotten married and was big into the church and big into Jesus," his friend recalled. "I don't have anything against Jesus, it's just his fan club I sometimes have a problem with. Dennis knew that about me, and he also knew I was going through a divorce, so I figured that all the hostility I'd been sensing was on account of him thinking I was some wayward sinner. I chalked it all up to that."

Over three decades later, Ormston began sobbing when recounting that awkward meeting with his friend.

"I couldn't understand why he'd treated me that way," he said. "Even though I thought the world of him as a kid, I had no desire to see him again after that. That's how much he frightened me. I never could understand it. On the surface, he looked the same. But underneath his skin, something I'd never seen before had taken him over. Whatever it was, it scared me."

The two never spoke again, he told me.

In July 1975, Paula gave birth to the couple's first child, Brian Howard Rader. By then, Dennis had already landed a job as a construction and installation supervisor with

ADT Security, a firm that specialized in burglary alarms for residences and businesses. Three years later in June 1978, a daughter was born — Kerri Lynn Rader.

If Rader truly enjoyed the role of being a father — as many who thought they knew him said he seemed to — he certainly never mentioned it in any of his journals. In fact, in the countless pages of his writings, he makes reference to his family only a half dozen times at most. And even when he does write about them, it's only in the briefest, most cursory manner. Perhaps there was a good reason for this: his diaries focused on the most passionate loves in his secret life — bondage and death.

By all accounts, Rader was a doting father, the kind who would often romp in the family's backyard, where he eventually built a massive tree house with the kids. He made sure his son became a Boy Scout, eventually earning the organization's top honor of Eagle Scout, which had eluded Dennis back when he was a teen. But of course, back when he was growing up, the elder Rader had other things on his mind.

Kerri grew into an athletic girl, who eventually qualified for the Kansas state high school golf championships in 1996. Like her father, she had an insatiable appetite for horror stories. As she grew older, she devoured nearly every book she could find on monsters, zombies, ghosts, and ghouls. Whenever she finished one, her father would often walk into her room, pluck it off of her bookshelf, and read it himself.

But there was something else about Kerri that her father always found puzzling. When she was six or seven, she began being plagued by horrible nightmares that caused her to awaken in the middle of the night, shrieking in terror. Whenever this happened, her mother and father would plod into her room, sit on her bed, and try to convince her that it was all just a bad dream. Over time, Rader — who never had nightmares and normally drifted off to sleep within minutes of placing his head on a pillow — began to attribute Kerri's night terrors with her love of horror books and movies. But still, he found it all quite curious. She didn't just awaken, screaming, from her terrible dreams. More often than not, she awoke as if she were being attacked by something and were fighting off something or someone. Sometimes when her parents walked into her bedroom, she'd literally be pounding on a nearby table, or anything close to her, with her fists.

Although some might attribute this behavior to Kerri's somehow picking up on the dark psychic energy of her father, I think the explanation might be a lot less far-fetched. For starters, I believe she might have stumbled onto Rader's horrific stash of detective magazines and sketches of women in bondage. That, I had begun to understand, would be enough to warp any young, impressionable brain. I also think it would be safe to say that Rader was not as protective of his yearning for violent-themed books and movies as he should have been, and these obsessive appetites were unfortunately transferred into his young daughter's mind. The fact that she never said anything to her father about her bewildering discovery of his stash isn't surprising. Like most kids, the last thing she would have wanted to do was admit she'd been snooping in his stuff.

Kerri's birth in June 1978 coincided with a slowdown in her father's passion for murder. But in the fifteen months leading up to her arrival in the Rader family, her father had hunted down and murdered two additional women, bringing his total body count to seven. Shirley Vian, a mother of three young children, was garroted on March 17, 1977. Rader claimed the life of Nancy Fox on December 8 of that same year, just around the time Paula was three months pregnant with Kerri.

The convoluted story behind how Shirley Vian ended up as one of his victims started in "the early weeks of March," Rader wrote in his journal.

"The uncontrollable Factor X is saying kill," he wrote.

So Rader began once again to look for another victim. It didn't take long to find one — a single mother who he'd seen on a few occasions at the Blackout tavern, the same watering hole where he'd met his buddy Bobby Ormston three years earlier. He'd dropped by the popular tavern after one of his night classes at WSU. It wasn't Vian he spotted originally, however, but one of her neighbors. The neighbor was there with some friends, and Rader watched her, following her home on foot when she left. He soon began scoping out her house, trying to determine if she lived with a man or owned a dog.

On a couple of occasions, he walked the dimly lit alley behind her property. He decided to make his move on March 17, but reminded himself that he needed to remain "fexable" in case things didn't work out. In the three years since Kathy Bright's murder, he realized he shouldn't be so bullheaded about his crimes. If the conditions weren't right, he'd go home and wait for another chance. But if it "looks good — it's a hit."

Late that morning, he put on his tweed sport coat and a pair of dark slacks, drove into Wichita, and knocked on the front door of his intended victim's house. No one answered. He turned to walk back to his car, but he spotted a young boy on the sidewalk, carrying a sack of groceries. Rader decided to use his "detective ruse" on the young lad and pulled a picture out of his wallet of Paula and his young son, Brian.

"Do you know if these people live around here?" he asked.

The boy told him that he'd never seen them before, then continued on to his house, located just down the street. Rader watched him, paying close attention to which house he entered. Ten minutes later, he knocked on their front door. When the boy answered, he flashed his pistol, told him he was a detective, and pushed his way inside, where he spotted the boy's brother and sister watching TV.

In his journal, he noted how the boy's mother grew frightened and nervous when he told her that he intended to rape her. The kitchen seemed like a good place to do it, he said. She begged him to first let her have a cigarette.

"I grant that," he typed in his grammatically challenged account of the crime. But no sooner had she polished off the cigarette than she informed him that she felt sick. After glancing around the filthy, "junk"-filled house, the hyperneat and always organized Rader decided that it was no wonder.

He attempted to tie the wrists of Vian's older son, but the boy began sobbing. Within seconds, his younger brother and sister also broke out in tears. "You got some place where I can lock your kids up?" he asked Vian. But before she could answer, he decided to put them in the bathroom and managed to prevent the kids from getting out by blocking one of the doors with a bed and using a rope to tie another door shut.

With that out of the way, he wrote, he looked at Vian and said, "It's time."

She removed her blue housecoat and pink nightie, then lay down on her stomach, on top of the bed. In his entry, Rader noted that her head faced east and her feet pointed west. As he wrapped black electrical tape around her hands and arms, she vomited on the floor. He walked into the kitchen and fetched her a glass of water. She drank it and once again attempted to talk him out of raping her. Rader was unmoved by her plea and taped her feet to the railing at the west end of the bed, then continued wrapping more tape around her ankles and knees.

Suddenly the telephone rang. Vian explained that it was probably her friend, calling to inquire about when she should drop by to take her to the doctor. Something about the ringing phone caused the children to begin crying again.

"Plans changed . . . Plans changed," Rader noted.

He wrote that in a flash, he looped a piece of cord around Vian's neck, which seemed to surprise her. She moaned about the tension, begging for somebody to help her. But nobody could hear her except for Rader, who watched as her face changed from red to blue, then from purple to dark purple. He decided to wrap additional cord around her neck, observing that if he relied on what he'd originally used, she might "come too" in the same way that Josephine Otero had during his initial attempts to kill her.

After a few minutes, he pulled a plastic bag over Vian's head, then tied her nightie around her neck to keep it tight. He masturbated as she thrashed atop the dirty sheets, her life slowly seeping away. Then he fled the house.

He ended his write-up of the murder with a lament over not being able to kill Vian's children. If only he'd had more time, he fretted. If he had, he had intended to use "a rough hemp rope for the girl and more plastic bag for the boys."

Nine months later in December, he struck again. This time his victim was a twenty-five-year-old woman named Nancy Fox, whom he first spotted in November while trolling the streets for victims. He quickly learned her name and that she held two jobs — working at a local law firm and at a jewelry store — by rifling through the contents of her mailbox.

In an effort to get a close-up look at Fox, Rader tracked her to the store and purchased some cheap jewelry out of a display case from a clerk; all the while he eyed Fox working in a back room. For the next month, whenever he had time, he stalked the young woman, hoping to learn her routine. On a couple of occasions, he cased the outside of her duplex, trying to find a good entry point inside. Twice he undertook what he called a "dress rehearsal," and in both instances he was prepared to carry out his intended crime "if everything was a go."

The more he learned about Fox, the more

he decided she fulfilled all the requirements of the perfect victim. Because of his first few nearly botched attempts at murder, he'd come up with a list of criteria that every one of his "projects" needed to fulfill: they needed to live alone, have an established routine, and not have a boyfriend, husband, or any close male friends who might interfere with things.

The victim also needed to be "cute" and of the right age — although he never specified in his journals what that age should be. It was imperative that she live in the type of neighborhood where he believed he wouldn't stick out if he were observed or spotted. The location of her apartment needed to be such that he could break in without being seen by neighbors. But most important, the proper victim appeared to exude some ineffable quality that led Rader to believe he could "control her if things suddenly went to hell, like they'd had a tendency to do in the past."

On the night of December 8, Rader decided he'd give what he called Project Fox Tail one more try. He told his wife he had to work late on a term paper at the WSU library. So after work he headed back to Wichita in her red Chevelle. Knowing that he had nearly the entire night to himself filled him with confidence.

It had been dark for hours when he parked the car a few blocks away from Fox's apartment and walked to her duplex. It was 8:30 P.M. He was fairly confident that she'd still be at work, but just to play it safe he knocked on her front door. If she answered it, he planned on saying, "Oops, wrong apartment. I was looking for Joanne." Then he'd flash his pistol, tucked away in his shoulder holster. Provided she didn't go "ape shit" on him, he'd barge in.

But when no one answered his knock, he walked around back and quickly cut Fox's phone line. He smashed out one of her back windows, climbed inside, and waited. When Fox finally did arrive home around 9:20 P.M., he waited until she walked into the kitchen before confronting her. She attempted to reach for the phone, but he informed her that he had a knife, and pulled open his jacket to reveal his magnum. He informed her that he wanted to rape her and threatened to hurt her badly if she tried anything funny.

Just like Shirley Vian, she lit up a cigarette and asked him why he felt compelled to do this. Fox remained calm and cool as the two stood in the kitchen. After she finished the cigarette, she looked at Rader and said, "Let's get this over with so I can call the police." On the way to the bedroom, she asked if he'd allow her to use the bathroom.

"Yeah," he replied. "But you better not have any weapons in there or try to escape."

Just to play it safe, he wedged a shoe in the door jamb.

After a few minutes, he instructed her to come out with her "main clothes off." The first thing Fox noticed when she walked out of the bathroom, Rader wrote later, were the rubber gloves he'd just pulled over his hands.

As usual, he did his best not to alarm his victim and used his standard line: "I don't want to leave prints . . . I'm wanted by the cops in a couple of other states."

After instructing Fox to lie down on the bed on her stomach, he snapped a pair of cold steel handcuffs around her wrists. She turned her head, straining to look up at him.

"Why do you want to do that?" she asked.

"I don't want any scratches or problems," he said.

He walked across the bedroom and pushed the door closed. "Leave it open," she pleaded. He ignored her and quickly went to work trying to pull her sweater off. She begged him to leave it on. His heart was pounding as he fumbled to pull off his shoes, pants, and shirt, then tied a yellow night-gown tightly around her ankles and gagged her with a pair of nylons.

"Has your boyfriend ever fucked you in the butt?" he asked. But she just lay there, ignoring his question, no doubt hoping to get all this over with. It thrilled him, he wrote, to see that he had an erection. Before he knew it, he was tugging her panties down to her knees with one hand and grabbing his black leather belt off the floor with the other. In a flash, he slipped it over her neck and pulled it tight, trying to be careful not to use so much force that he killed her.

Fox's fingers managed to grab hold of his scrotum, and she squeezed it with every ounce of strength she had left in her. Rader felt no pain. Instead, he wrote, the sensation of "[my victim's fingernails] digging into my balls . . . increased my sexual thrill." He pulled the belt tighter and watched as Fox began to pass out.

As her eyes fluttered shut, he released the tension on the belt and waited as she came to. Bending over her, he whispered into her left ear that he was the man who killed the Otero family, along with several other women in Wichita. He then informed her that "she was next."

Despite nearly being choked to death moments before, Fox was conscious enough to quickly realize that she was in terrible trouble. Once again, she struggled as best she could against her attacker, but it was no use. Rader pulled on the belt with all his strength. After a few minutes, Nancy Fox was dead.

He looked down at her body and masturbated into her nightgown. Afterwards he loosened the belt, then tied several pair of panty hose around the young woman's neck. Then he unlocked the handcuffs and bound her wrists with red panty hose. He got dressed, tidied up the apartment, and rummaged through her possessions, looking for some suitable mementos, finally settling on her driver's license and several pieces of her lingerie and jewelry.

The last thing he did before leaving was to crank up the thermostat again in the belief that it would cause Fox's body to decay at a faster rate, no doubt making her autopsy more difficult. Rader probably learned about this in one of his criminal justice classes at WSU. He'd been told that one of the ways to determine a victim's time of death is to take his or her temperature with a rectal thermometer, then check the degree of rigor mortis in the body. Room temperature does have an effect on the rate of decomposition, but in many ways this didn't matter because Rader had no real link to the victim. Instead, this sort of measure would ordinarily be an act for a killer who knew the deceased and wished to alter the estimated time of death in order to establish an alibi.

By the next morning, the suspense was killing him. When the hell were the cops going to find her? When was the news of his latest kill going to hit the media? He hadn't slept much the night before, and the moment he awoke he grabbed that morning's issue of the *Wichita Eagle* and scanned it for some mention of Nancy Fox. His scrapbooks were stuffed full of articles he'd torn out of the local papers, discussing his previous three murders, and he no doubt was looking forward to adding to his collection. But he could find nothing about the murder in the *Eagle.* Suddenly it dawned on him that even if the cops had discovered her body some time in the night, it probably would have happened far too late to make the deadline for the morning paper.

He got dressed and drove to his job at ADT. At the time, he was working as a crew chief, overseeing the installation of a fire alarm in a large building in downtown Wichita. On the way there, he stopped off at a restaurant with a few of the guys from work and picked up some cinnamon rolls and coffee. That was when he spotted the pay phone on the side of a mini-market on the corner of Central and Saint Francis streets. For the next hour, he couldn't get the image of that damn phone out of his brain. He was dying to pick it up and tip off the cops about what he'd left them in that apartment on South Pershing Street. Even though he knew it would be a stupid move and that his voice would probably be recorded, he couldn't help himself.

No sooner did his men begin working on the fire alarm job than he announced that he needed to head back to the ADT office and pick up some supplies. A few minutes later he was standing beside that pay phone, telling himself that what he was about to do was both careless and bold. "It's probably the kind of thing you do when you're younger, the kind of thing you don't do if you really think things through," he said years later. But at that moment, the fire burning inside Rader was far too hot. He picked up the phone and dialed the police dispatch number.

"You will find a homicide at 843 South Pershing," he told the dispatcher. "Nancy Fox."

"I'm sorry, sir," the woman on the other end of the line replied. "I can't understand you. What is the address?"

At that point another dispatcher, who had been monitoring the call, interrupted: "I believe 843 South Pershing."

"That is correct," the man said. Then the phone line went quiet.

The entire call lasted fifteen seconds. In his journal he wrote that as he hung up the phone, he mumbled to himself afterwards, "Maybe no one will recognize my voice."

A few nights later, while watching TV with Paula, the recording of the call was played on TV for the umpteenth time. Brian was asleep, and Paula was tired. She listened as the voice of Nancy Fox's killer drifted out of their TV set.

After a few seconds of reflection, she commented, "He sounds just like you."

Dennis felt his heart begin thumping madly. He did his best to look cool and calm, as though the mere idea that his wife believed that his voice resembled that of the sick and twisted man responsible for Fox's death was too ludicrous even to be worthy of a comment. But deep down he was in a panic. When he finally glanced over at Paula, she was still gazing at the TV screen. Her comment, he concluded, was nothing more than a bit of idle chat. If she truly believed he was a murderer, she wouldn't still be sitting beside him in the family room. That phone call to police kept Rader on edge for years, he later claimed. He was forever paranoid that someday somebody would put it all together. But no one did, and as time passed, so did the paranoia.

In an entry penned months after the murder, he likened himself to a submarine loaded with deadly torpedoes. He had surfaced just long enough to claim another victim. But now that his mission was complete, he was ready to descend back into the depths and head back out into open water.

15

I needed a drink. By now it was the middle of the night; Landwehr had yet to return. I was still scrolling through Rader's writings, and I was thirsty. I needed a shot of something. Vodka would be nice. I wanted to feel something course through my body, to wake me up from this numbing world of words penned by a psychopath.

Years before, I shared a bottle of vodka with a Russian police chief. After polishing off nearly all of it, he recounted the story of a serial killer he once tracked.

"There had been many killings, all decapitations," he told me. "So we found a suspect, brought him in, questioned him, and, when it appeared we had found our killer, we walked him behind the police station and placed a bullet into his brain. But when the killings continued, we knew that perhaps we hadn't considered all the facts in the case. So we found another suspect, a good one. But still more killings we had. . . . Finally, after four suspects and four bullets, the killings, they stopped."

I felt sick to my stomach. "We don't do things like that here," I informed the official. He shook his head in disgust, waving my comment away as though it were a gnat.

"That, I think, is why you Americans have so many serial killers," he said.

I glanced across the room. The digital clock glowed 1:45. In fifteen minutes, the tavern down the street from my hotel room would shut its doors. I put my computer to sleep. Five minutes later, I was seated at the bar. Vodka, for some reason, didn't sound that appealing anymore.

"A glass of Chardonnay," I told the bartender, "and two cups of coffee."

I arranged the glasses in front of me and drank them down in quick succession, noticing how nice the liquids felt sliding down my throat.

Twenty minutes later, I was back at my desk, reading about Rader's descent into middle age. As I sifted my way through the scrawled pages of his journals, I could feel the empty desperation of his words, how he'd begun to sense that his days were ticking by like mile markers on I-135, one after another, running off toward a horizon that had begun to loom so close he could practically touch it.

If there was anything more pathetic than a serial killer, I thought, it's an aging serial killer.

The overall impression that I gleaned from Rader's journal entries from this period was that he'd begun to feel weighed down by life. Having to keep everything bottled up inside — all those horrible yet thrilling secrets — made his heart flutter with excitement whenever he let them play out in his brain. Most of the time, he felt like a spy, forever walking around undercover, watching and waiting, always ready for action, perpetually on the lookout, always wondering if the cops were closing in on him or if someone had stumbled on one of his "hidey holes," where he stashed all his journals and other mementos from his kills.

The life of a spy suited him, though. He'd grown used to it. After all, he'd spent most of his life keeping his real self bottled up inside him the way his grandmother used to put pickles in mason jars. It was one of the things that helped him survive this long. What bothered him, though, was that he needed to erect such a big façade around him. That was where his wife and children came in. That was where church came in.

And the Boy Scouts. And his job. He had so many damn social obligations, so many things pulling him away from the very thing he loved best.

People were his alibi, but they were also his greatest frustration. They slowed him down. They hamstrung him. They kept him from killing with the frequency he yearned for and spent his days fantasizing about. They made it impossible for him to be the lone wolf he'd always fancied himself. In the best of all worlds, he told himself, he'd enjoy living alone. He'd be able to come and go whenever he pleased, stalking victims until 4 A.M. on a weeknight without ever having to explain himself, without worrying about whether or not his wife suspected something. He wrote in his journals that sometimes he'd drive around in his truck and hold pretend conversations with the cops, telling them, "If I'd been a lone wolf, there'd be a lot more bodies around here."

Still, it wasn't a bad life. When he could find the time, he enjoyed hanging himself. All he needed was a quiet place to do it. That was the trouble with hanging, especially when you liked getting all dolled up for it the way he did. It was an all-or-nothing kind of affair. Much of the time he'd do it in his parents' basement. He liked the dark, dank feel of the room. It reminded him of some medieval dungeon. Other times, he'd go out into the woods and find a sturdy branch, then toss a nice thick rope over it. Not a cord, though — that would be far too thin. Besides, cord had the tendency to bite like a knife into the soft flesh of the neck. True, he'd have no qualms about using it on one of his victims. But for himself he preferred a thicker gauge rope — nylon, polyester, sisal, or hemp. He'd slip his head through the simple noose he'd fashioned, then put some weight onto it. Not enough to fully cut off the blood supply to his brain — just enough so that he could feel the biting pressure against his throat and up the side of his neck.

It was the pressure he enjoyed most of all. He never went all the way, though. Unlike some of the jokers he'd read about who accidentally died while hanging themselves, he always kept his feet planted firmly on the ground, and leaned into the rope. That was enough to do the trick. He could literally hang himself for hours at a time, dangling there, imagining himself to be one of his victims, feeling all the terror, confusion, and helplessness that must have coursed through their bodies before he put them down. More often than not, he'd be dressed in a frilly, intimate getup he'd stolen out of some woman's house. A few of the outfits came from his victims' lingerie drawers.

A source close to Rader told me that once, on a family fishing vacation to Colorado, Rader managed to secure an afternoon away from Paula and the kids, so he hung himself from a tree for hours. The problem was, he didn't bother putting any sunscreen on his neck, and the sun cooked him red — all except where the rope had been, which was white as the stripe that ran along the back of a skunk. He had a helluva time trying to explain that one the next morning, but he managed somehow. He always did. That was one of his strengths. He could play people the way some people played musical instruments.

But there was something peculiar about the way Rader hung himself. Plenty of people use a rope to cut off the blood supply to their brain in order to intensify an orgasm they've achieved either through sex with another person or by masturbating. But Rader did things differently. He didn't need to have sex or masturbate in order to reach an orgasm. In his mind, just being hung was enough. The longer he dangled from the end of that rope, the harder his erection would become, until eventually he'd explode.

For him, it was all about the rope.

■ ■ ■ ■

Marine Hedge lived five doors down from him. Whenever Dennis Rader would walk by her place, his journals revealed, he'd wave to her if she were out front gardening. Some time in early April 1985, something clicked inside his head, and he began to wonder what she'd look like with a rope around her neck and a gag in her mouth. When he learned that the fifty-three-year-old widow worked in a hospital coffee shop, he nick-named her Project Cookie. Deep down, he knew that targeting someone who lived so close to his house violated one of the cardinal rules of serial killing — never murder a neighbor. But he didn't care. Once he'd begun fixating on her, he couldn't shake her loose from his mind. After a few months spent fantasizing about all the things he yearned to do her, he started sneaking down to her house at night and peeking in through the venetian blinds as she read in bed. On one occasion, her cat spotted him looking in the window and flipped out, jumping off the bed and hissing.

He finally decided he would make his move on April 27, during a Saturday night Boy Scout camping trip with Brian. Logisti-cally, the murder would be his most complicated, involving what he later referred to as lots of "maneuverment." On that evening, the tents had all been pitched, the dinner was cooked, and the campfire was blazing when Rader began to complain to the other Scout leaders of a headache, and soon disappeared inside his tent. Not long afterwards, he sneaked out, fetched his hit kit, which he'd stashed inside a bowling bag, then hoofed it to a nearby bowling alley. He stayed just long enough to buy a beer, drink a bit of it, then splash the rest of it on his clothes. He walked outside, reeking of beer, and called a taxi from a pay phone.

A few minutes later, a cabbie was driving him back toward Park City. Along the way, Rader mumbled that he felt too tipsy to drive. When he finally reached the outskirts of his neighborhood, he announced that he needed some fresh air. He asked the driver to pull over and let him out so that he could walk it off. After paying the driver, he began walking, eventually taking a short cut through his in-laws' backyard, then walking past the swing sets in the tiny city park located behind his house. He jumped the chain-link fence, scrambled through Marine Hedge's backyard, then peeked around the side of the house.

Her car sat in the driveway, so Rader figured she was inside, asleep. Using a screwdriver, he jimmied open the back window, crawled inside the darkened house, and crept into Hedge's darkened bedroom. Her bed was empty, so he decided to stick around and wait for her to arrive home.

It was around 11 P.M. when Hedge finally returned from a night spent playing bingo. Much to Rader's dismay, a man accompanied her inside the house. Rader hid himself in a closet and listened as the two made what he considered to be "loving" remarks to one another. Finally he left, and Hedge got into bed. It was around 1 A.M., he later wrote, that he emerged from the closet, entered her room, and "pounced on her like a tiger," quickly clutching her throat with his gloved hands. The whole thing happened far too quickly for his liking. After all, he'd spent months fantasizing about exactly how he wanted to take her, then force her to submit to him. As he learned from past kills, however, his most obsessively thought-out plans often went awry.

Before he knew it, the petite Hedge had slipped into unconsciousness, never quite knowing what was happening to her — that her neighbor was the dreaded BTK and that he'd chosen her to be his next victim. Rader's realization that all she knew was that some dark stranger with powerful hands was choking the life out of her frustrated him. He quickly handcuffed her and, out of habit, slipped a garrote over her neck, then pulled it tight. He realized that he needn't have bothered — she was already dead. Afterwards, he rolled her up in a blanket and quickly began rummaging through her apartment for a few trophies he could take with him. He settled on her purse.

Afterwards, he did something that he'd never before done after killing someone: he moved his victim's body from the crime scene. Rader, it was now clear to me, had decided to change his MO. He didn't want this to look like a BTK killing; that way, the police couldn't link this murder to his previous crimes. Rader also knew that indoor crimes allow police to do a more efficient job collecting and processing evidence. Victims disposed of outdoors make forensic work much more challenging. Depending on weather conditions, evidence can be washed away. Dumping of the body also means that a corpse has more time to decompose — further obliterating evidence.

Rader loaded Hedge's body into the trunk of her car and drove to Christ Lutheran Church, where he and the family spent their Sunday mornings singing hymns, listening to sermons, and helping out with things. Because of all his work at the church, he had a key to the place. He carried Hedge downstairs to the basement and laid her out on the floor. A few days earlier, he'd put black plastic over the windows and taped everything up so that nobody could tell if he was down there with the lights on. He unrolled the blanket and spent the next few hours posing her body in a myriad of positions, snapping pictures of her. Playing the role of a deranged fashion photographer, he searched for the perfect shot. He'd tie and then remove his various bindings from around her lifeless limbs. Sometimes he'd tug her undergarments down in suggestive poses, he wrote.

Time slipped away from him. Before long, he noticed that the sun was coming up. So he stripped her body, loaded her back into the trunk, and drove roughly six miles, where he dumped Hedge into a ditch and covered her with leaves and branches. Next to her head he dropped a knotted panty hose. He dropped her car six miles away in a shopping center parking lot. Rader made it back to the campground before anyone woke up, and soon went to work scrambling eggs and cooking bacon over the fire for breakfast.

The murder of his neighbor Marine Hedge

sustained and nourished Dennis Rader for the next year and a half. But he soon grew hungry again.

The next time Rader put pen to paper to chronicle a kill was shortly after he strangled Vicki Wegerle on September 16, 1986. In his account of the crime, he wrote, "It had been a long time from the last time factor x exploded in my world and shatter someone else's. Mrs. Hedge's memories are still fresh in my mind."

All Rader had to do was shut his eyes, and the homicide came flooding back to him — the feeling of the damp air, the rain; the sensation of his hands on her flesh; that long, nerve-wracking wait in the dark for her to fall asleep. And now it was beginning again. Factor X, he wrote, was arising out of him like a ticking time bomb. He looked back over his kills and thought about the locations of all his murders, relative to Wichita: Otero was northeast, Bright was northeast, Vian was south-central, Fox was southeast, Hedge was north.

The time had come, he reasoned, to murder someone who lived west of the city.

He first spotted Vicki Wegerle when he stopped on her street one afternoon to eat lunch in his truck. That was one of his favorite things to do — eat and troll for victims at the same time. Although he had a handful of potential targets, Wegerle, a twenty-eight-year-old mother of two who supplemented her husband's income by teaching piano, quickly moved to the top of his so-called hit list.

This time, he decided to strike in the middle of the day, gaining access to his victim's home by pretending to be a telephone repairman. On the afternoon he struck, he'd glued a Southwestern Bell logo onto a yellow hard hat. On his shirt, he wore a name tag fashioned out of a phone company business card he'd found somewhere. He carried a briefcase containing some of the tools that he believed a repairman might be expected to use, along with his hit kit. Because he thought it would look less suspicious, he decided to first stop off at the home of her neighbor next door. An elderly woman answered the doorbell, and Rader quickly ran through his prepared lines.

"I'm from Southwestern Bell, ma'am," he told her. "We're having trouble with the phone line, and we're trying to track down the problem. Need to check it if you don't mind."

He stood there on her front step watching through the screen door as she listened to him. All at once, the thought flashed through his head that maybe he ought to kill her instead, but he decided she was too old. Instead of inviting himself inside her house, he told her he could check her line from outside, and quickly walked to the corner of her house and started fidgeting with her phone line. Through a nearby open window, he could hear Wegerle playing the piano.

A moment later, he was knocking on Wegerle's door, feeding her the same line as he had her neighbor. Vicki reluctantly let him inside, but watched him closely as he connected some wires to her interior phone jack. Her two-year-old son played on the floor.

After a bit of small talk, he pulled out his gun and told her, "I'm not going to hurt you or your baby." Then he demanded that she give him her purse and keys to the car. She looked terrified, he wrote afterwards. The dog was barking, and her child was watching him as he ordered Wegerle into the bedroom, leaving her son behind.

Wegerle began crying, insisting that she was having her period and that her husband would be home at any minute. Grabbing her arm, he dragged her into the bedroom and told her he needed to tie her up.

"I want to take some pictures of you," he said.

Once again, Rader relied on words, rather

than threats of physical violence, to convince his victim to do as he asked.

"You're sick," she replied, as he tied her hands with cord. "You need help."

She continued to argue with him, telling him that the woman next door had seen him, refusing to get undressed for his pictures. Rader believed he was once again on the verge of losing control of the situation. So he pulled a cord out of his pocket, looped it around her neck, and yanked hard. She began to yell, but the force of the cord crushing her windpipe silenced her. A moment later, the cord snapped, her hands shot up into his face, and she managed to suck a precious lungful of air into her body.

She tried to scream, but he placed his hand over her mouth. He was dumbfounded by her strength. Although her ankles were tied, she poked him with her fingers, slammed her head against his chest, and raked her fingernails across his neck. He winced as his sweat seeped into the wounds, then he gripped her throat so hard that his hands begin to cramp.

"She is a regular tiger," he wrote afterwards.

He finally managed to grab a pair of panty hose, wrap them around her throat, then tie them into a knot behind her neck. He stood there above her, watching as she died, then grabbed his camera and began snapping pictures — pulling her sweater up in one, her pants down in another, and finally rearranging the panty hose so that they resembled a gag. I clicked my way through his snapshot collection, included on the disc, and felt a stab of nausea sweep through me.

It dawned on Rader that if he stuck around any longer, Wegerle's husband might return, and Rader would be forced to kill him. So he picked up his gear, organized everything inside his briefcase, and placed his yellow hard hat and Wegerle's billfold into a paper bag. The dog was still barking in the backyard. On his way out of the house, he noticed that Wegerle's son sitting on the floor in front room, staring contentedly off into space.

"He looked on without sound," he wrote in his journal.

After grabbing the woman's car keys, he walked out the front door and climbed inside her bronze '83 Monte Carlo and drove away. At a nearby shopping center, he disposed of his hard hat in a trash can located beside an ice cream parlor. He combed through Wegerle's wallet, taking her driver's license and cash, then tucked it under the passenger's seat. A moment later, he decided to head back to within a few blocks of Wegerle's house in order to retrieve his car.

He parked, and as he walked back to it, he could see her house in the distance and noticed that her husband's truck was parked in front. The police had yet to arrive, he noted.

A moment later he heard the siren of an approaching ambulance. He drove away, and at one point found himself following a police car for several blocks. Finally, he pulled over, changed his clothes, then began driving north, tossing his gloves and other bits of clothing out the window. While heading across one of the city's many bridges that stretched across the Arkansas River, a gust of wind blew several pages of notes he'd compiled on his victim out the passenger window of his car. Instead of stopping to gather them, he drove back and forth across the bridge, convinced that the wind created from his car would blow the notes into the river.

"I hope the police don't find them — bad move on my part," he later wrote.

He was hungry. So he decided to grab a bit of lunch and made mental notes of his mistakes as he drove. As best as he could remember, he'd left a fingerprint from his left hand on the neighbor's gate. He was also fairly certain he'd touched Wegerle's door without wearing a glove. He told himself that the next time he killed, the first thing he needed to do was handcuff his victim and always remember to wear gloves when using a ligature. Last, he decided it would be nice to have a place in the country where he could drive after his kills, in order to store or dispose of his gear more efficiently.

From what I'd gleaned about how Rader's brain worked, I knew he must have been riding the high from his first five murders when he landed his job with ADT Security Systems in November 1974. At the time, he was still enrolled at night school at WSU, studying criminal justice. This meant that he'd work all day, often miles outside of Wichita, then head back into town for classes. Landwehr told me that what Rader loved most about the job was that it gave him the sensation of being a cop.

That was something I had sensed two and a half decades before when I first analyzed the case and wrote that BTK was more than likely a wannabe cop.

He also told Landwehr during his interrogation that he got to carry a gun, a long-barreled .22 pistol. And every so often, he got to hang out with police when they'd arrive at a break-in that had occurred at a home or a business he serviced. But the best part of the job was how it allowed him to float around the region like a ghost. He had a desk and an office, but in his line of work he was never tethered to one place for very long. He specialized in home security systems, which always tended to make him feel like a kid in a candy shop — albeit a very sick kid. More times than he can remember, he rifled through the bedroom of an ADT client and grabbed a few pairs of panties or women's socks — never anything that the owner would think had been stolen.

One of his most memorable scams occurred on a job he worked for a woman who, he later told police, was being stalked by "a guy just like me. He'd written and told her how he had scissors and tape and was going to do all sorts of things to her. So she hired our company to protect her."

Rader and his small crew installed alarms on every door and window of the house.

"We did a good job," he would later say.

Except for one minor detail. Before they completed all the wiring, Rader realized that he might one day enjoy paying this woman a visit himself.

"I rigged the home in a way that would allow me to get back inside," he later confessed to Landwehr. "All I had to do was hot-wire it in such a way that I'd be able to go around the alarm."

He claimed never to have taken advantage of the rigged alarm, but just knowing that it was there gave him a sick sense of comfort.

In his journal, he wrote that another perk of his job at ADT was the overnight trips he took to towns scattered around Kansas. Whenever he was out of town, Rader happily combined business with pleasure. At night, when whatever work was expected of him on these out-of-town assignments was finished, he'd either go out trolling for future victims or break into homes to steal lingerie, jewelry, and various types of IDs, such as driver's licenses or Social Security cards.

Once, in mid-1987, his bosses sent him to Belleville, Kansas, to install an alarm system in an old meat-packing plant. The place was filled with all sorts of dangerous machinery, and the owners wanted alarms installed to make sure nobody broke in and got injured by the equipment.

Initially Rader was ticked off that he'd been dragged away from Wichita for the job.

"I was a team leader and a supervisor," he later told Landwehr, "and my boss wanted me to go out and start installing alarms." But he quickly decided to roll with it. "I used it to my advantage," he said. "I thought, 'If you're gonna send me out of town, I'll go trolling and stalking on my free time.'"

And that was exactly what he did. One evening while in Belleville, he was "lone-wolfing" it, just cruising the streets looking for the right type of woman he might want to strangle or garrote, when he happened to spot a young mother through the front windows of her house, playing with her kids.

This just might work out, he chuckled to himself.

So he drove over to the town bowling alley, parked his truck, and walked back. It was the dead of winter, an ice-cold night. On the way over, he thought about what he wanted to do with the woman's body after he killed her. "I'm going to take her out, somewhere out in the woods," he recalled of that night. "They may not find her for a while. Basically, it'll look like a disappearance."

But, of course, by the time he made it back to her house, the place was empty. Just his rotten luck. He paced back and forth in front of the house, stomping his feet on the ground, trying to stay warm. After a while, he figured he might as well just break in and wait inside. But after sitting around in her house for two hours, his head began toying with him. He finally decided no one was coming home. So he grabbed some jewelry and a pair of fancy red bikini-style panties and headed back to the bowling alley.

■ ■ ■ ■

In July 1988, the ax fell, and Rader lost his job with ADT. He has always maintained that he was laid off. "It was an informal lay-off, you know. I got a nice letter from them and everything. It wasn't anything I did — just company policy."

But Landwehr told me that he'd heard from a source who worked at the company that Rader had been seen as mercurial and had a reputation for being highly argumentative. The source also claimed that Rader was fired from the job.

Whatever really happened, it didn't take Rader long to line up another job perfectly suited for his temperament. In 1989, he was hired as a field supervisor for the U.S. Census Bureau. Once again, he had found a job that gave him a priceless feeling of power over the countless underlings whose duty it was to collect census forms from local residents. His first territory was limited to the Wichita area, but by 1990 he did so well that he was promoted to the role of state supervisor. Getting to boss people around felt wonderful, but not as nice as it felt to be a freewheeler who was able to spend plenty of time by himself out on the road, living out of a suitcase as he traveled from one town to the next.

Just as he did while working for ADT, Rader quickly discovered a way to combine his two loves — being a boss and being a stalker. Just looking at a map of Kansas could bring a smile to his face. He had so many projects in so many towns — Topeka, Concordia, Hayes, Salina, Beaumont.

He wrote in his journal that on one occasion he tracked a woman in the town of Hayes, whom he eventually decided to kill. He nicknamed her Project Prairie. One afternoon, he dug a grave for her outside of town and, just as he envisioned doing in Belleville but never got the chance, broke into her home, then sat in a chair waiting for her to return.

But she never did.

So he grabbed her purse, which she'd left behind, and fled into the night. As he drove down the road, he placed the bag in his lap and plucked out a few choice trinkets — her license and her Social Security card — and pitched everything else out the window of his car.

16

The digital clock beside my bed read 3:47. I'd been wandering through Rader's chronicle of his life for over nine straight hours now.

I stood up and paced around the room, hoping to clear my head, to purge it for a few moments. I walked over to the bed, opened my briefcase, and fished out a snapshot taken eight years before on the day of my older daughter's wedding. I held it in my hand, and it all came back to me, how I'd nearly died a few days earlier from pulmonary embolisms and loss of blood after a doctor punctured my lung while attempting to place an IV in my chest. On that day, all I could do was sit in a wheelchair and watch as my ten-year-old son walked my daughter down the aisle for me.

I stared at my tired face in the photo, then studied the brave, uncertain expressions on the faces of my family, who wondered if I'd be alive next week. Life is fragile, I thought to myself. If you're not careful, it can be snatched away in the wink of a tear-glazed eye. And then all at once I remembered Dennis Rader and how he'd done that to one person after another until the number of lives he'd snatched away equaled ten.

I didn't want to look at my photograph after that. I turned it over, shoved it back into my briefcase, and walked back toward the desk, then continued reading the words of a monster who fooled everyone into believing he was human.

By July 1988, the rush Dennis Rader received from Vicki Wegerle's murder had long ago faded, leaving him feeling as empty and hollow as ever. The urge to take another life thrashed inside him as though he'd swallowed an anaconda. One afternoon he picked up his pen and wrote in his standard butchered English, "The desire are in me so strong now day. I have no ideal what keep them in check. Could it be my strong moral as a husband, father, trusted friend or the I-don't-want-to-be-caught side of me?"

This was definitely a worthy question for Rader to be asking. But like all worthy questions in his life, he felt no reason to wait around for an answer or even to continue probing. When you lack a conscience, simply asking such a question feels good enough. It quiets things just a bit. Perhaps in Rader's case it even paved the way for the next paragraph he wrote in his journal, in which he launched into a lengthy confession about what he wanted to do with a young blonde-haired girl he'd spotted at the pool earlier that day, on a trip he'd taken there with his kids.

According to his journal, he could barely take his eyes off her. She was eating candy, and something about the way the sunlight danced off her bronze body caused his head to go crazy concocting fantasies about this "innocent, childhood virgin."

Rader saw himself as a simple man with simple tastes. On that particular afternoon, all he wanted from life was some sort of lubrication for his "rod" and a few moments alone with this girl. He wrote that just thinking about the things he envisioned doing to her "small, delicate" body made his heart race wildly.

Yet no sooner had he concocted some dark scenario inside his mind wherein she found herself bound and gagged than he claimed to feel a sense of shame descend on him. He cautioned himself to be careful, to remember that these desires threatened to rip everything in his life away from him. The revelations of his secret life, he wrote, would destroy the heart and souls of everyone around him. "It must be kept a secret forever," he concluded.

Meanwhile, in the very next paragraph of his journal, the young blonde girl he'd spotted earlier in the day was now crying in pain, her body drenched in sweat. Although he had tried to be gentle while raping her a few sentences earlier, he now decided that it was time to be done with her. So he fashioned a garrote from a "loose coil" of rope, looped it around her neck, and pulled tight. But instead of feeling good about the kill, he expressed remorse in his next sentence, begging the "guardian of small ones" to give him the strength he needed to continue on with life.

His journal of more than two years later revealed that the urge to kill was as strong as ever. But the stirrings of guilt and shame over his secret world seem to have vanished. Rader hadn't taken a life in nearly four years, but by Halloween of 1990, he'd already begun planning the intimate details of Project Dogside, the code name he'd given to what would turn out to be his final murder. This one, which wouldn't take place for another two and one-half months, involved sixty-two-year-old Park City resident Delores Davis, who lived beside a dog kennel on Hillside Street.

Once again, I was reminded that when Rader disappeared from view after his gloating letter to police in 1978, he'd continued plotting. And, on three more occasions, he continued killing. In the pages of his journal, he described how during the afternoon before killing Davis, he acted out exactly what he desired to do with her. His journal described step-by-step how he pretended to be the victim.

This particular masturbatory session began with "heavy breathing and quick relax as he prepare for a trip into far way time zone."

Within minutes, he'd wrapped a leather belt around his ankles, then encircled his body in a leather web fashioned from various other belts he kept in his closet. After tying himself up, he pulled a plastic bag over his head, wrapped a slipknot around it, then pulled it tight and thrilled as his lungs slowly sucked what remained of the air from the bag.

"He lies there as she [Davis] would, bound, helpless," he wrote.

Rader first mentioned the thrill he experienced from self-imposed suffocation a couple of months earlier, in September. He still had his job with the Census Bureau at the time, and one afternoon he hung a sign on the door of his office, informing his coworkers that he'd stepped out to lunch. Then he locked the door, spread a plastic tarp over the floor, and rigged up a camera on a tripod with a long cord, allowing him to trigger the shutter from a distance.

Over the course of the next sixty minutes, he stripped himself, then pulled on a pair of panty hose, pink panties, and a bra, complete with padding. He bound himself in nylon straps and began snapping pictures of himself. Thirty minutes later, he'd finished wrapping his entire body in plastic. He eventually reached orgasm after being forced to "fight for air."

Afterwards, he remarked that the plastic was only part of the reason he experienced a "most satisfying climax." What really excited him was the notion of pulling off this stunt at the office, surrounded by his coworkers, and managing to knock out this entire fantasy (complete with the snapping of a handful of Polaroids) during his sixty-minute lunch break.

This was a fertile period for Rader's journal writing. With no one to turn to and years since his last kill, he dumped his thoughts onto the pages of his diary with furious passion. In November 1990, he wrote a short entry about standing in his house and watching "the blonde next door" gather evergreens from her yard for a holiday wreath. He loved the shape of her "butt" in her blue jeans. Later that day while taking a shower, he shut his eyes and masturbated as the fantasy of what he intended to do to her danced on the back of his eyelids.

Two days later he was combing through the *Wichita Eagle*, looking for pictures of women that he could use to "fit the sequence" of a fantasy he'd had the morning before. This one involved a girl between the age of seven and eight with "a nice firm ass."

In his mind, she was bound on a bed and petrified with fear. The "bogeyman," it seemed, had claimed another victim. Her name was Kirsten. When Rader climbed into the shower, he still didn't have all the details of the attack worked out, but by the time the water hit him and he covered his body with soap, the images began to come to him.

He had wrapped tape around her ankles and hands, then whispered, "Hi, I'm the bogeyman."

He sodomized her, then looped a nylon garrote around her throat and quickly got down to the business of strangling her.

All of this fantasy killing was detailed in his journal. Then he wrote about how he made the fantasy into a graphic representation. It took a bit of searching, but he finally located a photo of a model from an ad that looked like it would do the trick. He cut it out, laid a piece of paper over it, and went to work tracing the outline of the little girl — although unlike the ad, his picture, which he titled "Boogie Men Loves Little Girls," depicted her pants rolled down around her ankles.

Because the newspaper was chock full of ads on that particular day, Rader saw no reason to limit his art project to just one so-called slick ad. He quickly located another picture of what he felt was a suitably curvy preteen wearing some sort of a Halloween costume. His ink pen knew exactly what it needed to do, and twenty minutes later she became the "Devil's Delight." His art project, which he would later stash away in the far reaches of his bedroom closet, whipped him into such a frenzy that he sat back in his easy chair, and when he was sure that Paula and the kids were out of the house, he masturbated into a plastic baggie. That was one of the drawbacks of living in such horribly tight quarters — he was forever having to watch his back in order to have any fun. It wasn't until the late 1990s that he was able at least to move part of his cache of sketches and other memorabilia to some file cabinets at work.

In May 1991, with his temporary census job finished, Rader landed another job — as compliance supervisor for Park City. This time he got to wear a badge and a uniform, complete with a radio he clipped onto his belt. His main duties involved driving around the tiny suburb in a white truck and writing up tickets for residents who kept old refrigerators in their front yards or let their dogs run off-leash or let their grass grow too long. The job paid $16.62 an hour. For a guy who always wanted to be a cop and spent much of his waking hours dreaming about flaunting power over others, this was about as close to heaven as he could get without killing someone. He even got to carry a rifle in his truck, on the off chance that he had to put down a wild dog.

But the best thing about the job was that it allowed him to disappear for hours at a stretch in his truck, providing plenty of time to stalk victims, work on his slick ads, or fantasize about past kills while masturbating into plastic sandwich bags.

According to Landwehr, opinion is divided

over exactly how heavy-handed Rader was in his duties. Plenty of residents loathed the way he bullied them, showing up at their homes with a ruler to measure the height of their grass, then demanding they mow it or else he'd fine them. Others complained that he had their dogs euthanized purely out of his lust for power. And then there were those who insisted that Rader was doing only what was expected of him — enforcing city code.

Over time, the job even caused him to see the irony of a serial killer writing someone a ticket for leaving her trash can out on the curb for too many days wasn't lost on him.

"I work with code violators," he told Landwehr after his arrest. "Year after year, they keep doing the same old thing. They never change. People don't change."

He paused for a moment after saying this, as though his words were seeping into his brain. Then, Landwehr told me, he blurted out, "You are what you are, and I am what I am."

As I read on and on, I could see how Rader continued to dump his troubled thoughts out into the pages of his makeshift journals, which were often nothing more than random pages he'd torn from a notebook.

Few entries exist for the four-year period

that stretched between November 1990 and October 1994. The approaching death of his father from colon cancer in 1996 caused him to pick up his pen and scrawl a few comments onto a notepad, which he later shoved into his cache. In this particular entry, he seemed concerned that his old man would learn about his eldest son's murderous alter ego when he died and crossed over to the other realm.

"Will he know of my foul deeds?" Rader pondered. "I hope if there is a heaven or afterlife, he will forgive me. I wish no sorrow on his heart. He has been a good dad . . . He must understand that he did not raise a problem child." The real culprit responsible for his horrible appetite, Rader concluded, was Factor X.

Later that same day, it appeared that any sense of worry over his father's soul had vanished. He penned another entry about how he'd begun carrying photographs of girls around with him in the work truck. The females he chose were his "dream girls," and for hours at a time he'd cruise through the neighborhoods daydreaming about how he'd use rope and sexual molestation to mentally torture his victims. The fantasy, he claimed, broke the boredom of everyday life at work.

A few weeks later, Rader no longer described what he was doing as simply driving around town with tiny pictures of women in his truck. By mid-November 1990, he'd begun to consider these photographs glued to three-by-five cards as actual living creatures.

"Rode around with cute blonde in bikini today," he wrote. The next day, he claimed to have ridden with a "babe with a Jewish or Hispanic-looking face."

Two days after that, he took pop music sensation Madonna with him for a one-way tour of Park City. In her picture, she wore a bodysuit complete with cup-shaped brassiere. As he went about his duties that day, his mind exploded with angry thoughts about hanging her from a heavy wooden beam. He envisioned himself wrapping a coarse hemp rope around her neck. In her mouth was stuffed the obligatory gag. The only problem was that he couldn't decide whether he wanted to use a rope or a chain to spread her legs apart. But what he did know was that he wouldn't use his usual rope garrote to dispatch the Material Girl. For her, he opted to end his fantasy and her life with a "slow strangulation hold."

The following Sunday, after attending church, he wrote about shoplifting a book on a serial killer who lived in Hawaii. The next morning, he went to work with a redhead in the seat beside him. On Tuesday, she'd been replaced with a woman whom he would describe only as "the bitch." For the rest of that afternoon, he daydreamed that she'd kidnapped him, trussed him up in cord, placed a leather collar around his neck, and laid him out on a bed covered with red satin pillows.

A week later, in an effort to drum up some orders for the annual Boy Scout popcorn drive, he dropped by a church not far from his office. On his way back out to his truck, he happened to glance at a young boy and his sister playing in the grass by the parking lot. All at once, the telltale urge seemed to well up from deep inside him.

"The sexual predatory instinct kicks in," he wrote. His head was flooded by thoughts of "getting" the two young children. By the time he climbed inside his truck and started the engine, the kids had vanished, and he spent the next ten minutes cruising the streets around the church hoping to catch another glimpse of them. He wasn't exactly sure what he would have done if he had spotted them, but by this point in the day his head was going crazy with wild possibilities. He steered his truck toward the neighborhoods where his last two victims had lived before he'd paid them a late night visit, driving up and down the streets that surrounded their homes, letting his mind wander.

The need to take another life was rising up inside him, threatening to burst out. On the first weekend in December 1990, he attended an out-of-town Boy Scout camp with his son. Packed away in his truck was his hit kit, complete with plastic gloves, knife, .25-caliber pistol, mask, and cord. Exactly what he intended to do, he never specified in his journal, although he did write that he arrived at the camp "too late and was too tired to try anything."

A week before Christmas, he wrote that he and Paula had had sex for the first time "in a long time." For a guy who often filled page after page with detailed accounts of his imagined sexual conquests, he devoted precious little ink to the real thing. His only comment in his journal was that his session with his wife "felt very good and satisfying."

My sources insist that when it came to his carnal fantasies, Rader never crossed the line with his daughter.

"She was his best friend, and he claims it never crossed his mind to think those things about her," I was told. "But Kerri's friends . . . well, that was a different matter. They were definitely fantasy material for him."

Like plenty of violent offenders I'd spoken with, Rader had a boundary he wouldn't cross, and that gave him comfort. He told this same source that pornography nauseated him, that he was bewildered that anyone could think he might be a homosexual, and that it made him feel good to know that he never "cheated" on Paula by having sex with any of his murder victims.

During this period of his life, Rader lived for his so-called motel parties. According to his journals, he'd drive out of town, check into a room, lock the door, and spend hours alone, fondling the belongings of his victims, dressing in their clothes, wearing wigs and masks he'd prettied up with lipstick and mascara, then binding himself in ropes and tying plastic bags over his head.

Sometimes he'd cover the bed with scantily clad Barbie dolls, set up his camera on a tripod, and squat down beside the dolls. He'd position the camera far enough away so that when the shutter snapped he appeared to be the same size as the dolls — all of which he imagined were his real-life victims. It just didn't get any better than that, as far as he was concerned, because the Barbie doll was the symbol of the perfect female. I'd seen this type of behavior in men who would hang dolls, blow them up with M-80s, and smear red dye all over them to simulate blood. Surprisingly, some of these guys never progressed past the stage of torturing dolls. They seemed to sense what Rader later found out — that the fantasy, where they are forever in control, is always better than the actual crime.

One evening in October 1995, Rader took several decades' worth of drawings he'd sketched of women in the midst of being stabbed, drowned, buried alive, hung, strangled, shot, and tortured on various homemade devices of his own design, then spread them across the room. The collective image of all these nude, gasping, wincing, terrified women and girls covering the room was horribly breathtaking, he thought.

As he gazed at the drawings, it reinforced his belief that he definitely didn't want anything to happen to his cache of artwork. A few months earlier, he'd celebrated his fiftieth birthday, and at that time it had begun to occur to him that he needed to stop being so careless with his drawings, along with the rest of his cache of memorabilia. So he began to concoct a plan of how to copy his sketches over to three-by-five cards, then stick the original drawings in a safe-deposit box that he'd reserve by using the fake name

"Johnson." The way he envisioned it, the box wouldn't get opened until months after he died. Whether or not the bank employee who found it was able to piece together what the contents alluded to didn't concern him, he told Landwehr.

Because he had so much material to catalogue during that autumn night in 1995, he decided to organize it into categories, such as hangings, strangulations, torture devices, and so on. In his journal, he bitched that it "took a lot of work checking dates and sorting," but his recent milestone birthday had convinced him that the last thing he wanted to do was die and leave a "skeleton in the closet." It wasn't until late 2004 that he began digitizing his archives and copying them onto CDs. But the project was fraught with headaches because the CD burner on his decrepit home computer was broken. Even more frustrating was the fact that he didn't have a scanner at home, so he had to use the one at the office, which meant he had to do everything on the sly. By the time police caught up with him, he'd been able to transfer only a small handful of material onto discs.

His duties as an archivist soon sent him combing through his journals and scores of yellowed clippings from the *Wichita Eagle,* detailing BTK's various murders and efforts to catch him. For the first time since he'd begun killing, he suddenly realized that his cache of memorabilia could get him in trouble; he wrote, "[it would be] bad news for me if found, yet I can't let it go."

One of the reasons Rader couldn't let it go was because four years had elapsed since his last — and what would prove to be his final — murder. He desperately needed his various mementos to curb his lust for death, to sustain and recharge him.

Just as he had with his countless other projects, Rader had spent a couple of months driving past the home of Delores "Dee" Davis, a sixty-two-year-old retired secretary at an oil and gas company. Before long, he decided that she seemed to have everything going for her — all the qualities he required of his victims. For weeks on end during the closing months of 1990, he'd lie in bed and fantasize about all the things he wanted to do to her.

One afternoon in mid-January 1991, the fantasies had grown so real that he decided it didn't make sense to wait any longer. A few nights later on January 18, shortly after attending a Boy Scout function with his son, he changed out of his scouting uniform at a

Baptist church near his home, then drove out near her house on North Hillside Street in Park City. He parked a couple miles away.

It was so cold outside that the only thing that kept him warm on that moonless night during his twenty-five-minute walk to her house were the thoughts of what he was on the verge of doing.

Davis's bedroom light was still on when he arrived in her front yard. She was inside reading. He paced around in the darkness, waiting for her to go to bed. It occurred to him that he didn't have a clue about how he was going to get inside. The locks on her doors were all sturdy. It would come to him, he told himself. He just needed to be patient. It made him crazy to know that his victim was inside, oblivious to the wolf that lurked just beyond her walls.

After what felt like an eternity, Davis switched off her bedside light and climbed into bed. Rader waited for another thirty minutes, then decided the time had come to make his move. If there was some neat and orderly way to get inside, he couldn't figure out what it might be. He decided to wing it. He'd never done that before with one of his projects — at least not to gain entry. But, as he would later tell Landwehr, he was "hell bent for leather, and Factor X had kicked in."

According to his journal, he stood there in her backyard looking around for something, anything he could use to help him get inside. When he finally spotted a cinder block lying near the patio, he knew exactly what he needed to do. After slicing through the outside phone line, he picked up the block, gripping the sides of it firmly with his hands; he crept up on the back porch, then heaved the block through the large sliding-glass door. The sound of the glass shattering made one helluva loud noise.

Davis came running out of her bedroom to see what had happened and discovered Rader standing in her family room. She thought a car had slammed into the side of her house, but he quickly set her straight, telling her he was ex-con on the run.

"It's cold outside," he said. "I need some warmth, a car, and some food."

Then he told her to lie down on the bed; he pulled handcuffs out from a pocket in his coat and slipped them over her wrists. Davis began to panic, but Rader told her to relax. He explained that if she'd only tell him where her car keys were, he'd be gone in no time. He grabbed a pillowcase, went into the kitchen, and began filling it with cans of food, making as much noise as possible. This seemed to calm Davis down.

His journal detailed how he checked out where she kept her car, then got everything ready for what would happen next. In his mind, he felt confident that Davis believed he was preparing to leave. Next he walked back into the bedroom, unlocked her cuffs, and tied her wrists with rope. Once again, he apologized for breaking into her house, assuring her that he'd be gone in a minute and that someone would probably find her shortly. As she lay there on her stomach on the bed, he opened the drawer to her dresser and pulled out a pair of panty hose. She spotted him, but he once again attempted to convince her that everything would be okay; the last thing he wanted was for her to begin panicking.

"Are you comfortable?" he asked. "I need these to tie you a little more."

And that was when he decided there was no reason to wait any longer. In one quick motion, he looped the hose around her throat.

"Please," she pleaded. "I have children."

So did Rader, I thought. They were both home asleep in their beds, just down the hallway from his wife. But that didn't seem to matter. He pulled the hose tight and later wrote that it took her between two and three minutes to die. Rivulets of blood trickled from her nose, ears, and mouth. As he stared down at her body, the thought occurred to him that the moment he savored most when he killed happened at that instant when his victims had been bound and realized they were doomed. He could live off that moment for years, he wrote afterwards.

Rader later told police that he didn't masturbate at the scene, and because no traces of semen were found in the house, he might have been telling the truth. From the sound of it, he had other things on his mind, because after watching the life seep out of Davis, he wrapped her body in a blanket from the bed and dragged her out to the trunk of her car. Afterwards he darted back inside the house, grabbed some jewelry, lingerie, and a camera, then headed out to a remote highway several miles outside Park City and rolled Davis's corpse into a culvert, then hopped back in her car and found another spot beneath a highway maintenance shed to stash the various trinkets he'd stolen from the house, along with his hit kit. He'd come back for that later, he told himself. First, he needed to switch vehicles before any more time passed.

After returning the car to Davis's garage, he walked the two miles back to his truck. In his journal, he described how he felt cold, thirsty, and tired. His clothes were drenched in sweat.

Thirty minutes later, he was driving back out to the spot where he'd just deposited Davis, and retrieved her body. Fog had begun to roll in as he continued on to a remote part of the county, where he pulled over long enough to drag Davis's body beneath a tiny concrete bridge located beside an expanse of empty farmland. As he drove back home, he wrote that thoughts of sex and bondage flooded his brain. Knowing that the sun would be up in a few hours made him feel like a vampire, he later wrote.

As horrific as these Dear Diary confessions were, they didn't shock or surprise me. His words merely confirmed something I'd discovered years before: serial killers like Rader aren't human. They look like us, they train themselves to act like us, but just below the surface they are hideously different. That was why I expected nothing else out of a monster like Rader. All I felt was a terrible, heavy sadness for Delores Davis, along with the rest of Rader's victims. They didn't deserve any of this.

The night after the murder, Rader returned to the bridge to snap photos of Davis's partially nude body. Her feet, hands, and knees were still tied with panty hose. The first thing Rader noticed on arriving was that some sort of animal — perhaps a coyote, a rat, or a raccoon — had begun chewing on her body. Because he carried one of those clear plastic Halloween masks in his hit kit, which was still in his car, he retrieved it and placed it over her face. He smeared lipstick on it, trying to make her look more presentable, then snapped a few more photos. He would have stayed longer, but it was so bloody cold out that he decided to head home.

Besides, Paula would probably be wondering about him.

Two weeks later, a fifteen-year-old boy chasing a stray dog stumbled on what remained of Davis. The next day, a story about the murder appeared in the *Wichita Eagle.* Rader clipped it from the newspaper and placed it in his stash. Not long afterward, he picked up his pen and confided to his journal that he wanted Davis to be his last kill — although he seemed to realize quickly that this might be wishful thinking. He reminded himself that only two things could stop someone with his sort of appetite: incarceration or death.

Writing in the third person, he explained what he intended to do next and why.

"In the back of his brain a voice says, 'You can't quit. The drive is too strong. Cover your tracks and prepare for the next stalk.'"

17

The sun was coming up. I'd been at it all night. I was getting too old for this sort of thing, I told myself as I walked across the hotel room and opened a window, leaned my head out, and dragged a long, deep breath of the cool morning air into my lungs.

The leaves, a little yellower than the day before, clung to the branches of the crab-apple tree just outside my window. In a few more days, their tenuous grasp on the branches would weaken, causing them to tumble to the ground.

Before I knew what I was doing, I caught myself studying the limbs, looking to see if any might be strong enough to hold the weight of a full-grown psychopath in a white satin evening gown with a rope tied around his neck. But none appeared to possess the necessary girth for the task.

"Jesus," I muttered, "his journals are changing the way I look at trees."

A moment later, I dumped some coffee grounds into the tiny percolator on a shelf by the closet, filled it with water, then walked back to my desk, listening for my coffee maker to gurgle to life.

On my computer screen glowed a picture of a piece of notebook paper dated January 27, 1991. Rader was ruminating on how much he loved what happened after he killed. That feeling of being on edge, of running on pure adrenaline as he waited for the police to track him down was priceless, he told himself. It was as if every cell in his body were on red alert, waiting for the inevitable to happen.

The murder of Dolores Davis was no different. Afterwards, he did what he always did when the memory of a kill was still fresh in his head. He tried his best to melt back into everyday life.

"Don't drop the bucket," he urged himself in the pages of his journal. "Just keep going with the people around you." This wasn't all that difficult for Rader, because he imagined himself to be a wolf among sheep. A month after the murder, the paranoia passed, just as it always did. When the cops never showed up at his front door, he wrote of himself in the third person, "Maybe he was lucky again."

One afternoon, he penned an entry in his journal about the day he pulled out an old tape recorder he'd kept in the closet, popped in a fresh cassette, and spoke the details of his crime into the microphone. Before long, he realized that it felt good to talk all his fantasies out like that — so different than writing them down on a piece of paper. Verbalizing his kills and dark thoughts just made everything feel so much more real.

It was easier, too. The spoken word flowed out of him in a way written words never had. He tried to understand why, and the only reason he could think of was that maybe it was because he'd never been able to say those words aloud before.

He'd never before in his life dared let all those thoughts and memories — the ones he'd locked away inside his head — drift out of his mouth. The sensation proved so cathartic that after he finished speaking the memories of Davis into his tape recorder, he decided to forgo paper and begin chronicling his fantasies with his tape recorder. At least for most of the next year he did. But, like so many of his artificial substitutes for killing, recording his fantasies eventually grew boring. A few years later, he pitched his collection of cassettes into an incinerator — the same oven, he later told police, where he burned the bodies of dead cats and dogs during his stint as a compliance officer — and watched them melt away to nothing.

The murder of Davis also marked another turning point in Rader's life. The business of serial killing — which was how he referred to it in his journal and, after his arrest, to police — wasn't for the lazy. Yet when he looked back over his last two kills, he had to admit that he had been doing just that — being lazy. Of course, there was an undeniable element of risk that came from pulling off a project so close to his home. But he also realized that he was possibly leading the cops right to his back door.

After Davis's murder, he told himself that if he "did another one" so close to his house, the cops would most certainly begin connecting the dots. He told himself that the one surefire way to throw the cops off his trail would be to leave them some bodies in some other cities.

Before long, Rader was out trolling again, looking for other victims. In his notes, he likened himself to a seasoned tracker, combing the forest for game. All he really needed was patience and a good, sharp eye. He reminded himself that with ten victims under his belt, he couldn't afford to get sloppy.

He began to catalogue his projects with a fury: PJ (Project) Nails was a white female who often favored business attire and lived in the eastern portion of Wichita in a large house. PJ 2 Black involved two African American university coeds who lived a block away from Nails, the salon where Paula worked. PJ Mex was a Mexican family living on the south end of town. His list went on and on for good reason. To be a successful hunter, he reflected in the pages of his journal, it was crucial to have a list of potential victims. Then all he needed to do was keep moving around, checking up on them and waiting until the nuances of their schedules began to fall in sync with his.

Over the next few years, he had plenty of projects and just as many close calls. Project Twin Peaks involved an elderly couple who lived, appropriately enough, in the Twin Peaks neighborhood of Wichita. He spent close to a month staking them out, watching them. Then one day he decided it was time. That was back in the day when he wanted to use a shotgun in one of his hits. So he parked his car down the road, out in a field by a hedgerow, and started walking back toward their house. His gun was down at his side, and he was so focused on what was about to happen that he never even saw the "county mountie barging over the hill lickity split."

He had his lights off, and Rader figured the sheriff must have spotted him parking. All he could think was, "Man, I'm cold turkey." He dove into a culvert beside the road.

The sheriff roared past, no doubt in pursuit of someone else, and Rader climbed out of the mud, miffed that he'd scratched the barrel of his shotgun.

He walked back to his truck and drove home, cursing himself over his rotten luck.

Landwehr told me that Rader spoke of another so-called project that he called off at the last minute. It happened back one afternoon in August 1976, at a time when he'd begun locating potential victims by roaming through neighborhoods on the lookout for For Sale signs taped to an old car or a fishing boat in someone's front yard. He'd knock on the front door, and if a woman answered, he'd inquire about whatever it was she was attempting sell. During the conversation, he'd check out the inside of the house, trying to figure out if she lived alone or, God forbid, shared her place with a male. If that were the case, he'd stay the hell away.

One afternoon, he stumbled on a single

mother with two or three kids, who had a Coleman trailer for sale in her driveway. They chatted for a few moments, then Rader quickly went on his way. She was perfect in every way. He wanted to take her so badly it hurt.

A few days later he decided to strike. Late one morning, he stuffed all his gear inside his pockets and drove toward her house, parked his car nearby, and began walking back to Project Coleman's house. He stood out front to collect himself and rehearse how he wanted everything to go down. Then he took a deep breath and started up the walkway. But just as the sole of his shoe made contact with the concrete step that led to her front door, all hell broke loose. The air suddenly exploded with a cacophony of police and ambulance sirens. The sounds were so loud that they drowned out the fantasies playing inside his head.

"Something's up," he muttered to himself as he turned and hightailed it back to his car. He switched on the radio and learned that a sniper was hunkered down on the twenty-sixth floor of the Holiday Inn Plaza in downtown Wichita, picking off people in the streets below. The gunman ended up killing two men and wounding seven others. Rader drove back to Park City, feeling as though he'd just had a piece of candy snatched away from him.

One activity that always seemed to take the edge off was reading over his collection of headlines he'd clipped from old detective magazines or ripped from the covers of books. He fancied himself to be an intelligent man, one who was sensitive enough to be moved by words. That was why he'd started saving all this stuff in the first place. He'd read poetry — that is, of course, if limericks were considered poetry. But nothing he'd read before touched him like those words.

Part of it might have had to do with the typography — the big, bold letters, which nearly always seemed to be capitalized. And sometimes the images they conjured up struck him as a little too over the top. But it was these words that always got him. They cut into him like a knife and stirred things up inside him. They were something to aspire to. They made him proud of who he was and what he stood for. They were written about other guys just like him, guys who lived all around this great nation of ours, who all seemed to have this same thing living inside their heads that he had. They'd all done unspeakable, horrible things to other humans just as he had. Their crimes were big, bold, and daring — he had to give them that. But more often than not, they weren't particularly the kind of atrocities that he got off on.

Nevertheless, as corny as it sounded, his collection of headlines always felt to him as though they'd been written just for him. The words transported him to another place. They stood for everything he lived for but had always kept hidden away. Some of his favorite headlines included: NEVER KILL ANYONE YOU KNOW . . . SCHOOL GIRL STRANGLER . . . NEVER TEASE A SEX KILLER . . . SHE WATCHED HIM DIG HER GRAVE . . . SEXUAL HORROR FANTASIES BECAME REALITY . . . PRETTY WOMAN PLAYING GAMES FOUND OUT — YOU SHOULD NEVER TEASE A SEX KILLER.

Even the lowercase headlines never failed to excite him: "He used to 'practice' in his basement with stuffed dolls." "He liked to watch his young female hostages writhe painfully against the rope holding them tightly bound. He felt he could do anything he wanted to them — even blow them away." "The suspect's alibi, lawmen claim, is that he was engaged in a little karate mixed with bondage and he accidentally killed her. Then why rape her after she's dead, they wondered." "Look of innocence masks the mind of murderer whose obsession with bondage led to girl's strangulation." "An air-powered dart gun, several sharp darts, knives, twine and an assortment of various-sized vibrators — these told were all used by the sex fiend who ravaged many girls' lives with them."

Reading the longer pieces he'd clipped from books, magazines, and newspapers also helped feed Rader's hunger. From time to time, when it was safe, he'd thumb through his stack of articles and passages that allowed him to put everything inside his head into perspective. These weren't fantasy stories. They were articles written by scholars and others who had studied people just like him.

One of his favorite was an op-ed piece he clipped from a January 23, 1997, issue of the *Wichita Eagle,* titled "Children Without a Conscience Dangerous But Can Be Helped." Accompanying the piece was a moody sketch of a little boy with an angry, defiant glare in his eyes. Two adult hands appeared to be gripping the troubled young lad's shoulders.

"They are a parent's nightmare," the article stated, "society's worst fear come to life. They seem a mocking rebuke to our sacred, deeply held beliefs on the innocence and purity of childhood. And they do not exist only in pulp novels or B-grade movies such as *The Bad Seed.* Terrifyingly they exist in real life."

There was another entry, from a book titled *The Criminal Mind,* that he loved to read and reread, then think about because it showed just how confusing and contradictory killers like him could be. He'd even underlined various sections of it with yellow highlighter.

Even within a category of theories there can be contradictions. When evaluating which personality constructs lead to aggression, for example, many theorists proposed that low self-esteem is a key factor. Bullies and rapists were thought to be men who did not value themselves. However, another researcher said that there is increasing evidence that high self-esteem is instrumental in aggression. Many violent types have an inflated, albeit unstable, sense. If challenged or criticized, they react with violence to reestablish their self-esteem. Researchers who support this theory believe that studies of incarcerated offenders that measured a significant proportion with low self-esteem are a result of the offenders being locked up. The low self-esteem supporters counter that the so-called high self-esteem factor is actually narcissism, which is based on perceived superiority, not a healthy regard for self.

By the late 1990s, Rader was beginning to grow bored. Brian and Kerri had already graduated from high school and were out of the house. He immersed himself in his job, his duties at Christ Lutheran Church, periodic fishing trips, and, in the fall, driving over to Manhattan, Kansas, with Paula to attend football games at Kansas State, where Kerri attended college.

Most important, he still had plenty of projects, scores of them located all over the city, woman he fantasized about undressing, tying up in cord, and strangling.

Over time, one of these projects began to emerge as his favorite. Try as he might, he couldn't shake from his head the images of all the things he planned to do to her — not that he ever tried very hard. She was going to be his last one, he told himself. When he finished with her, he was going to shut down "his operation." Which was how he enjoyed referring to the past three decades of his life — as though it were some sort of business endeavor.

Part of him seriously doubted he'd ever get around to pulling this one off. He just wasn't sure he was physically up to it. What he did required plenty of brute strength, and now that he was getting older, he wondered if he still had it in him. Nevertheless, he realized he couldn't let this one slip through his fingers. He'd been stalking his potential victim for over a year. In that time he'd begun to realize that her days followed such a predictable pattern that he could set his watch by her comings and goings from her apartment. She never changed her routine. And, as he always used to say, people like that were in bad shape.

She was a large woman, probably tipping the scales at 160 pounds. She wasn't the type whom most people might assume a serial killer would target. Rader seemed to pride himself in that fact. It was another one of those things that made him different from those other killers — he didn't discriminate. When it came to victims, everyone was welcome — just as long as they were female, didn't live with any men, and adhered to a schedule that meshed with his.

He had big plans for her, which was why he wanted everything to be perfect. He wrote in his journal that he'd either strangle her or suffocate her, then spread her body out in the main doorway of her apartment in a wildly suggestive pose. He could only imagine what the cops would think when they saw her. Because of her size, he knew he'd have a heck of a time lifting her and securing her into the position he'd envisioned. He also couldn't quite figure out exactly how he'd hold her there — would he tie a rope around her feet or place a noose around her head?

Whatever method he chose, he realized he'd need some sort of a device to winch her up into the position he'd been fantasizing about. He stopped off at a hardware store near his house one afternoon during work and purchased a massive hook, a pulley, and a large screw. Rader had arrived at the conclusion that this was how he'd hoist her body up above the door frame. He'd grown so excited about this project that he began carrying his hit kit with him in his truck wherever he went. He even kept his portable drill with him in order to help him sink that screw into the door frame.

Over time, the killing began to grow grander and more elaborate in the secret fantasies of his sick mind. He eventually decided that after murdering her and stringing her up, he'd burn the building down by dousing a few of the rooms with kerosene, then rigging a time-delayed fuse out of a candle. The fuse was crucial, he wrote; the last thing he wanted was for billows of smoke to be rolling out from the windows as he backed out of her driveway.

It would be huge, he promised himself.

Yet not even this grand, bold fantasy could fill the empty hole inside him that threatened to swallow him up. Which was a bit ironic. After all, he'd spent a lifetime telling himself how badly he yearned to live the carefree life of a lone wolf. Yet now that he was free of the obligations brought on by raising children, he had no idea what to do with himself.

According to what Landwehr had told me yesterday while we were driving around Wichita, Rader finally understood what the next chapter of his life would entail on January 2004. The day was a Sunday, and he had just returned from church, picked up a copy of the *Wichita Eagle,* and read an article that used the thirtieth anniversary of the Otero murders as an excuse to run a retrospective article on the seemingly long forgotten serial killer named BTK.

The headline read, "BTK Case Unsolved, 30 Years Later." Besides rehashing his seven known murders, the 1,100-word article focused on the efforts of a Wichita attorney named Robert Beattie, who also taught a class in criminal justice at a local university. Beattie had taken it upon himself to pen a book on BTK, partly because he felt that most residents had forgotten this "significant chapter in the city's history."

Halfway through the piece, Beattie explained how the year before, he'd brought up the case in one of his classes "and was surprised by the reaction. 'I had zero recognition from the students,' he said. 'Not one of them had heard of it.'"

Rader read the piece and, according to what he told Landwehr during his interrogation, became disgusted that some local know-it-all attorney was going to write a book about him. He was flattered by the idea of it, but he'd be damned if he was going to let this guy have the final say on his life's work.

And that was when Rader decided he'd write his own damn story, explaining everything — how he worked, how he chose his victims, how he jumped from one project to the next. Nobody knew anything about that sort of thing. They knew about his victims and the facts surrounding his crimes — that stuff was pretty much all out in the public domain — but what he yearned to do was dump the contents of his brain out on the sidewalk for everybody in Wichita to shudder over. He wanted to stir the hornets' nest. He just hoped he didn't end up getting stung, although he told himself that the chances of that were slim. After all, he'd been thumbing his nose at the cops for three decades, and they'd never come close to laying a finger on him. He wasn't deluded enough to think that a publisher might actually take on his project and release his writings in the form of a book. What he had mind was more on the order of a public relations effort. He wanted to set the record straight, while also reminding the community that Wichita's infamous brand-name killer was still alive and plotting.

By then, Brian had joined the Navy as a seaman apprentice and was based at the Navy submarine base in Groton, Connecticut. Kerri had gotten married and moved to Michigan. Like a lot of tech-savvy couples, she and her husband maintained a blog about their life together, which they posted online. From the sound of it, her night terrors had continued into adulthood; whatever had crawled inside as a child and caused her so much pain whenever she shut her eyes at night was still alive and squirming.

A few months before my arrival in Wichita, I was doing a bit of Web sleuthing on Kerri's name and stumbled onto one particularly chilling entry from the couple's blog.

Kerri's husband had written it sometime in 2004. In it, he described what it was like to live with a woman who suffered from night terrors:

I think this is going to shorten my life. I am either waking up with no covers, waking up with a psychotic woman looking for a monster or for some Mexican person that could've broken in to murder us. Either that or she is screaming because she thinks, in my peaceful state of slumber, I am trying to mutilate her in some way. I have heard rumors that all women are completely insane when they sleep. I think the idea is to control every facet of their man's life. There was a week where I was woke up three times in a night to some sort of dream event of some kind or screaming. Let me tell you, it just about destroyed me.

My cell phone rang. It was Landwehr.

"You up yet?" he asked.

"Never went to bed."

"Got tied up last night," he said. "Homicide we're working. Couple things we'd been waiting to happen fell into place. Made some arrests."

"That always feels good," I said, remembering the rush that I'd sometimes get after helping take some dangerous scumbag off the street.

"Yeah. I'm hungry," he said. "You wanna grab some breakfast? I got some time before work."

"Sure," I said.

"You get a chance to look at that disc I left on the desk?" he asked.

"You might say so," I laughed, wearily. "He's one prolific son of a bitch."

"Yeah," Landwehr grumbled. "Just another poor frustrated artist."

"Twisted," I said. "Don't think I've ever stumbled across one quite like him."

"You don't know the half of it," he said. "I'll tell you all about it over breakfast."

"Meet you down in the hotel lobby," I said.

"Gimme fifteen."

18

The moment Ken Landwehr walked into Egg Cetera, nearly every head in the breakfast eatery turned to look. Some stared, others whispered. Landwehr took it all in. His face seemed to tighten just a bit; he looked annoyed.

"Let's take that booth in the back," he said. "Back in the corner."

As we navigated our way through the maze of tables, I noticed that he was clutching a folder stuffed with paper. One of the patrons stood up, grabbed his hand, and pumped it.

"Lieutenant Landwehr," the man exclaimed. "It's a pleasure, a real pleasure."

"How you doing?" Landwehr growled, sounding truly excited. "How you been?"

The man proceeded to tell him.

Afterwards, as we slid into our booth, I asked, "Friend of yours?"

"Never laid eyes on him before," he said. "Figured he was one of your fans and was just trying to be nice to me."

The waitress handed us menus, smiling at Landwehr the whole time. "I'm telling you, you oughta run for mayor," I laughed.

Landwehr's face went taut. "Yeah," he said. "Gonna put that one on my to-do list later today."

The waitress returned, took our order, filled our cups with coffee, and disappeared.

"So where were you when he resurfaced?" I asked. "I'm curious what the hell you were doing when he poked his head up."

Landwehr nodded at the waitress to come dump some more coffee into his cup. He was wearing a starched white shirt and black tie. He ran his fingers along his neck, just inside his stiff white collar. Then he told me. The morning it happened, he was standing beside his wife's hospital bed. She'd just had stomach surgery, and he was waiting for the anesthesia to wear off. It was March 17, 2004, the twenty-seventh anniversary of Shirley Vian's murder.

"My phone rang," he recalled. "It was a detective in my unit. 'We just got a letter,' he said. 'Looks like it could be from BTK.'"

"How'd that make you feel?" I asked, sipping my coffee.

"Sick to my stomach," Landwehr said. "I thought, 'We could be in a lot of trouble, here' . . . But the more I thought about it, the more I realized we had a chance to finally catch this guy."

A half hour later, he was holding the white envelope that had arrived in the morning mail at the offices of the *Wichita Eagle*. The sender's name, typed in the upper left-hand corner, was listed as Bill Thomas Killman. His return address — 1684 S. Oldmanor — didn't exist on any map of Wichita.

Inside the white envelope was a single sheet of paper containing three photocopied snapshots of a woman who appeared to be unconscious, lying on a carpeted floor. A photocopy of a driver's license belonging to a twenty-eight-year-old woman named Vicki Wegerle, whose 1986 murder had never been solved, also appeared on the page.

But the most chilling part of the letter were the letters B-T-K scrawled at the bottom of the page. It was penned with the same haunting, telltale flourish employed by the killer back in the 1970s — the letter B had been fashioned into breasts.

At the top of the page was a string of seemingly nonsensical numbers and letters. Police asked several experts to try to decipher the message, but no one was ever able to figure out what it meant. It wasn't until after Rader's arrest that they learned what the

465

message, supposedly written in a code used by the Germans in World War II, actually said: "Let Beatty [sic] know for his book." In other words, he wanted the man chronicling his crimes to understand that he was still very much alive.

Although this single piece of paper had all the makings of a bona fide communiqué, Landwehr knew damn well that he needed to proceed with caution. Because BTK had been featured in a lengthy newspaper article a couple of months before, it wouldn't be unusual to receive a copycat communiqué from some warped and perverted soul with too much time on his hands. The key is to review the document carefully, searching for references to factual data that would be unique to the case. This is one of the main reasons why police sometimes sit on information, preventing it from becoming public knowledge.

The moment I learned about that first communication from my FBI source, I knew that if it was legit, it was just a matter of time before police snared BTK. It had always been obvious to me that the more he wrote to the media and police, the more we could learn about him. He craved attention. In fact, I wasn't surprised that he'd resumed his writing career.

What stumped me was that he'd been able to stop for all those years. He craved attention, and now he wanted it again. What, I wondered, must be going on in his life at that moment to cause him to surface? He had to be around sixty years old. The only thing I could think of was that he'd grown bored with his life and yearned to recharge his batteries.

As Landwehr examined the contents of the letter, however, he realized that he had plenty of reasons to be guardedly excited over the communiqué. Why? Because the letter offered copies of evidence removed from the scene of the crime — those three haunting photocopied images of what appeared to be a recently strangled Vicki Wegerle lying on her bedroom floor.

The March 17 mailing also answered a question to which Landwehr had long suspected he knew the answer, ever since he arrived at Wegerle's home after the murder in 1986. The Wegerle homicide had never been directly attributed to BKT, but Landwehr had thought he knew better.

"I always thought it was a BTK kill," he told me, chewing a mouthful of scrambled eggs.

He remained so convinced that in 2000 he asked two of his detectives to dust off the case files of Wegerle, whose bound and strangled body had been discovered inside her house on West 13th Street by her husband, Bill. Beneath her fingernails, police discovered a man's DNA. Despite his never having been charged, her husband, who worked as a handyman at a number of apartment complexes in the area, had lived under a cloud of suspicion for years. Which wasn't exactly surprising — in most murder cases, the husband is the first and foremost suspect investigators look at.

Even though the DNA under Vicki's fingernails wasn't her husband's, investigators always found it suspicious that he'd spent so much time at the couple's home before telephoning police.

In 2003, investigators input a profile of that DNA sample into a recently created national database containing the genetic information compiled on hundreds of thousands of known criminals. They never found any samples in the registry that matched, which did nothing more than confirm to Landwehr and his detectives that the man they were looking for wasn't catalogued in any DNA database — nor had he been a known suspect in the case.

Within hours of realizing that the letter was authentic, Landwehr contacted the FBI and soon began consulting with my former unit to create a proactive strategy to reel the killer in. And, just as I'd first envisioned back in 1984, they created a super-cop to become the human face of the investigation — Landwehr. They couldn't have picked a better man for the role, although Landwehr admitted that he was hardly thrilled with the suggestion.

"I told them I didn't think the head of an investigation should be holding press conferences," he recalled. "I knew too much about the case, and I knew that if some reporter asked me a question, no matter what I answered they'd be able to read my body reaction. But they didn't want to hear about that. They kept telling me, 'Just stand up there, read your script and walk away. Don't get into any interplay with the reporters.'"

Six days after BTK's envelope arrived in the offices of the *Wichita Eagle,* Landwehr stood up in front of a bank of microphones in the fourth-floor briefing room of the city building and held the first of his twenty-two press conferences, none of which lasted more than four minutes. He definitely looked a bit uncomfortable up there in his dark suit, staring straight into the TV cameras, reading the press release crafted by the Wichita police chief's assistant.

But that hardly mattered. In fact, it only made Landwehr's performance all the more convincing. Somewhere out there, he knew the man he'd been hunting since 1984 was watching his every move, hanging on every word he spoke.

"The Wichita Police Department recently received information on the Vicki Wegerle homicide that occurred on September 16, 1986, in the 2400 block of West 13th Street," he told the crowd of print, TV, and radio reporters packed into the room. "Mrs. Wegerle was discovered in her home shortly before noon on that day by her husband. Her murder remains unsolved."

Even though word had begun circulating among the media about the nature of this press conference, the edgy tension in the room was palpable, Landwehr later told me.

"Investigations personnel now believe that this homicide could possibly be linked to the unsolved homicides that occurred in Wichita in the 1970s and were attributed to the BTK serial killer," Landwehr told reporters. "This is the most challenging case I have ever worked on, and the individual would be very interesting to talk with. We are working closely with the FBI, the KBI [Kansas Bureau of Investigation], the Sedgwick County sheriff's office, and the district attorney's office on this investigation. This case is a top priority with the Wichita Police Department, and we will be working this as a strong, unsolved case, and exploring all possible leads."

Landwehr did everything I'd recommended back in 1984, when I suggested that a close bond with the lead investigator on this case could create the kind of situation in which BTK would not only feel respected but also see himself as a consummate professional, playing a game of hide-and-seek with a collegial opponent. In the end, he might just let his guard down enough to give himself away or possibly even give himself up.

A few days after the contents of that first communiqué were released to the public, the seven phone lines in the BTK task force offices started ringing. Nearly a thousand tips came flooding in. A command post was soon established in the nearby offices of the FBI. Before long, police were driving around town with sterile Q-Tips, eventually taking DNA mouth swabs from nearly sixteen hundred local men in their late forties and fifties, including a number of retired police officers. Not surprisingly, this caused plenty of grumbling among former cops.

When Landwehr told me this, I could feel

the frustration he must have been enduring at the time. Clearly the police had no leads and were forced to resort to tossing out the widest high-tech net they could find in order to catch their killer. The reason retired cops were targeted was that investigators always believed that BTK possessed some type of law enforcement background and even may have once worked for the Wichita Police Department.

By April 2004, the offices of the BTK task force were buzzing. Not only had the killer surfaced after nearly twenty-five years of silence, but there was another cause for excitement. Crime lab technicians at the Sedgwick County Regional Forensic Science Center had managed to link the DNA extracted from a semen stain on the blue nightgown found at Nancy Fox's house with the skin fragments scraped out from beneath Wegerle's fingernails. The same killer, it seemed, was responsible for the murders of both women. This also meant that during the two-and-a-half decades that had elapsed since Fox's killing, BTK hadn't been dormant as many had suspected and hoped. He'd just managed to keep a lower profile than he had with his first series of murders. Exactly how many other homicides, they wondered, might he be responsible for?

On May 4, a second envelope, supposedly from the killer, arrived at the KAKE-TV studio in downtown Wichita. It contained three pages. The first sheet bore the title "The BTK Story." It resembled the table of contents from a biography the killer seemed to envision he was writing.

Landwehr reached across the table to the folder he'd placed atop the napkin dispenser. He opened it, quietly fished out a sheet of paper encased in plastic, and handed it to me. It looked like this:

1. A SERIAL KILLER IS BORN
2. DAWN
3. FETISH
4. FANTASY WORLD
5. THE SEARCH BEGINS
6. BTK'S HAUNTS
7. PJ'S
8. MO-ID-RUSE
9. HITS
10. TREASURED MEMORIES
11. FINAL CURTAIN CALL
12. DUSK
13. WILL THERE MORE?

The next page contained a computer-generated word-search puzzle that at first felt reminiscent of something that a diabolical mastermind like the fictional Hannibal Lecter might create to confound authorities. But the more investigators scrutinized it, the more they realized that this guy was no better at designing a puzzle (he couldn't quite seem to line the numbers up with the letters) than he was at spelling.

The puzzle contained words relating to the case, including *victim, serviceman, fantasies, lost pet,* and *officer.* On the final page were photocopies of two ID badges — one from a phone company in town, the other from the local school district.

One month later, BTK's third communication was discovered in a Ziploc plastic bag, duct-taped to a stop sign near an on-ramp to I-135, which bisected the city. On the outside of the enclosed brown envelope were the words "BTK Field Gram." It contained a disturbingly sophomoric account of the Otero murders, including a graphic description of his slaying of eleven-year-old Josie. The killer also included a sketch of a gagged, bound, nude woman dangling from a noose. The caption read, THE SEXUAL THRILL IS MY BILL.

On July 17, Wichita Public Library workers discovered a clear plastic bag marked BTK at the bottom of an outdoor book collection bin. This mailing consisted of five sheets of paper. Two of those pages detailed BTK's involvement in the death of a troubled nineteen-year-old young man named Jake Allen, whose suicide had been reported in the local press a few weeks earlier. Of course, everything Rader wrote in that communiqué was pure bullshit, but the Wichita police didn't know that at the time. According to Landwehr, Allen, a star athlete and high school valedictorian, had dreamed of becoming an optometrist, but weeks before his death he and some buddies had gotten caught by local cops for having beer in their car. Allen soon convinced himself that he'd blown his chances of ever getting into optometry school and, in the early morning hours of July 5, lay down on the train tracks near his home in tiny Argonia, Kansas, forty miles from Wichita. Not long afterwards, a passing Burlington Northern Santa Fe freight train barreled over his body, crushing it almost beyond recognition.

Hoping to send police off in countless directions, the killer wrote that he'd been responsible for the death of "Jakey" after meeting him in a computer chat room and convincing him that he was a private eye hunting for BTK. The young man, who he claimed "had fantasies about Sexual Masturbation in unusual ways with Bondage and Homosexual thrills," agreed to help him. Everything he wrote was pure make-believe. Rader had absolutely nothing to do with Allen's tragic death. But Landwehr couldn't take that chance, so his men began combing through Allen's computers, sifting through his e-mails and piecing together every word he'd ever posted in a chatroom. After a couple of weeks, it became evident that everything BTK had written about Allen had either been lifted from newspaper accounts of his death or fabricated.

"Of all his letters, I'd say that was the one that stood out the most," recalled Landwehr. "There he was telling us that he'd killed again."

"It confirmed everyone's worst fears," I said. "You knew about Vicki Wegerle, so you knew he'd been killing while he'd gone underground. But Wegerle was back in 1986. Suddenly he's telling you that he's still at it, he's still killing."

"Not only that, his letter led us off on a wild goose chase," Landwehr said. "Because when we dug into Jakey's background, we learned that he was studying to be an optometrist. That's what he wanted to do in college. But we also knew that eyeglasses were important to BTK, so we knew we had to run down that angle."

"The eyeglasses?" I said. "I'd forgotten all about that. He mentioned Josephine's glasses in the letter he sent police after the Otero killing, and he drew glasses on the bedside table when he sent you that picture of Nancy Fox in 1978."

Landwehr nodded. "And Cheryl Gilmore, the woman we believed he was after on the day he ended up killing Shirley Vian, worked for an optometrist," he said. "So when we learned about Jakey's optometry connection, the KBI guys started [DNA] swabbing every optometrist in town. I told them, 'I want to know who refuses, the second it happens, and we'll put an undercover on them.'"

"You must have thought this was your huge break," I said.

"But it gets better," Landwehr grumbled. "Turns out that the eye doctor Gilmore worked for also saw Jake. So now we've got a potential victim who didn't get hit and a kid who might be a possible victim both connected to the same guy."

"All you needed to do was go put cuffs on the guy," I laughed.

Landwehr stared at his empty coffee cup, then shook his head, slowly. "This investigation was filled with so many moments like that," he explained. "There were just so many points when you'd get so excited and think, 'This is it! We got him.' You're ready for the victory party . . . Everything is looking good and then you just get shot down. It all falls apart. You can't imagine how many times we had victory parties planned. I know of eight in 2004. The same thing happened back in the 1980s."

But there was something else about the Jakey letter that caused Landwehr's stomach to twist into knots. In it, the killer threatened that he had "spotted a female that I think lives alone and/or is a spotted latchkey kid. Just got to work out the details. I'm much older (not feeble) now and have to conditions myself carefully. Also my thinking process is not as sharp as it uses to be. . . . I think fall or winter would be just about right for the HIT. Got to do it this year or next! . . . time is running out for me."

Landwehr glared down at the table in front of him and pushed his plate aside, to the corner of the table.

"That's the part that really made me sick," he said. "I was so worried that he'd picked out another victim. To think he might targeting some kid was just too much. I never worried about me, you know. About how, if he struck again, it might effect my reputation professionally. But what ate at me was that he might claim another innocent life. And if he'd killed a kid, that would have been tough for all of us, too tough for the unit. It would have been very, very bad."

But for Landwehr, the worst thing about what happened after the so-called Jakey letter was that BTK went silent. "We didn't get another letter for about three months," Landwehr said. "I really thought he'd quit talking to us because he'd actually chosen his next victim and was working out all the details before the kill."

I could understand why Landwehr felt nervous and sick with frustration. I agreed with Landwehr that as long as this guy kept sending communications to the police and the media, he was doomed.

BTK's next correspondence didn't arrive until October. A UPS driver spotted an unsealed envelope left in a drop box at the Omni Center in downtown Wichita. He inspected the contents, which consisted of a plastic bag with another envelope inside. The words BTK FIELD GRAM were typed on the front. Tucked inside was a stack of three-by-five cards. Two of the cards were covered with what the killer called his "UNO-DOS-TRES THEORY," intended to explain the philosophical and mathematical underpinnings of the complicated universe he yearned to have police believe dwelled within his head.

"The BTK World, Works in Threes," he wrote, "and is base on the Eternal Triangle." He went on to list countless examples of this world, such as, "Sun — Light — Heat . . . Child — Mothers Love — Dad's Love . . . BTK — Victim — Police . . . Detective — Others — Landwehr."

But what Landwehr and his detectives instantly pounced on were the four index cards that contained what the killer hoped would be accepted as his biography. If his so-called Uno-Dos-Tres seemed bizarre, his purported bio read like the first draft of a novella penned by a sexually frustrated teen with some serious Oedipal issues.

CHILDHOOD REFLECTIONS: 1–8 Years Old: Only memories float around in the mind, but never seem to disappear, but you almost see them (possible sexual overtures or early childhood problems that develop into sexual variant later on in life). . . . Mother slept beside me at times, the smells, the feel of underclothes and she let me rub her hair. . . . 10–11 years old: If you masturbate god will come and kill you, mom words after she found seminal yellow stain in her underwear one day. She tried to beat me. I fought back. She held my hands behind my back and used the man's belt to whip me. Funny it hurt but Sparky liked it. Mother finally quit and said, 'Oh my god what have I done?' She kiss me. I was close to her, tears and moisture upon her and my cheeks. I could feel her heart beating and smell those wonderful motherly aromas.

After consulting with the FBI, investigators sat on the contents of the bizarre story for over a month before releasing them to the community.

"We assumed it was mostly lies," Landwehr said. "But we still had to comb through every single thing he wrote down, trying to track every bit of information down. We kept asking ourselves, 'What if he is actually telling the truth about something?' That's what kept all of us going."

On November 30, a twelfth press conference was held, and Landwehr distributed a media advisory, titled "BTK describes his background," that had been created over the previous few weeks.

In it, police laid out list of biographical factoids about BTK and urged residents to read it with a grain of salt. Releasing a list of his "claims," they reasoned, might allow someone, somewhere to make a connection that police couldn't hope to.

Because I'd never worked a case in which the perp told us the truth about himself, I had learned to ignore those kinds of "facts" and just concentrate on motive and what could be done proactively to rein in the UNSUB.

"What in God's name did you pull from his letter?" I asked. "Anything that turned out to be useful?"

Landwehr reached into his folder and plucked out a copy of the release police distributed. It read like this:

- He claims he was born in 1939, which would make his current age 64 or 65.
- His father died in World War II, and his mother raised him.
- His mother was forced to work, so his grandparents cared for him.
- His mother worked during the day near the railroad.
- He had a cousin named Susan, who moved to Missouri.
- His family moved a lot, but always lived near a railroad.
- His grandfather played the fiddle and died of a lung disease.

- His mother started dating a railroad detective when BTK was around 11 years old. This relationship would have occurred during the years 1950–1955.
- In the early 1950s he built and operated a ham radio.
- He has participated in outdoor hobbies including hunting, fishing and camping.
- As a youth he attended church and Sunday school.
- He had a female, Hispanic acquaintance named Petra, who had a younger sister named Tina.
- Around 1960, he went to tech military school. He then joined the military for active duty and was discharged in 1966.
- He has a basic knowledge of photography and the ability to develop and print pictures.
- In 1966 he moved back in with his mother who had re-married and was renting out part of her house.
- His first job was as an electro-mechanic, requiring some travel.
- After attending more tech school, he worked repairing copiers and business equipment; this sometimes required travel and he was away from home for

extended periods.

- He admits to soliciting prostitutes.
- He has a lifetime fascination with rail-roads and trains.

After immersing myself in his journals and talking to his friends, I could clearly see that nearly everything Rader purported to be biographical truth was anything but. He'd sprinkled a few tiny shreds of veracity into the "life story" he sent to police, but it was all so general and ambiguous that it gave investigators nothing to work with.

Why on earth Landwehr and his men spent any time and resources trying to make sense out of his nonsense initially escaped me. Clearly all Rader wanted to do was fling as much disinformation into the air as he could, then sit back and watch as the cops ran off in a million different directions, chasing wild geese. But Landwehr was desperate. He'd finally hooked his big fish, and this, he felt, was all part of the process of reeling him in.

Landwehr and I split the tab for breakfast, gulped down another cup of coffee, and headed back to my hotel room. Along the way, he continued to walk me through the next twist the case took.

It happened on January 25 with the arrival

of a postcard at the studios of KAKE-TV. The sender's name was listed as S. Killet, and his return address was the same as the Otero family home.

On the back of the postcard beneath the words COMMUNICATION #8, he explained where he'd tied a Post Toasties cereal box to a street sign on North Seneca Street. It was found to contain some jewelry from one of his victims along with a doll fashioned to resemble Josie Otero. Around its neck was tied a tiny noose attached to a bit of pipe.

The presence of this package in north Sedgwick County, Landwehr explained to me, began fueling rumors that two unsolved homicides in the area might be the work of the killer. In April 1985, the body of fifty-three-year-old Park City resident Marine Hedge was discovered near a rural dirt road several miles away from her home. Near her body, a knotted pair of panty hose was found. A coroner determined that she'd been strangled. Her 1967 Chevrolet Monte Carlo was later discovered in the parking lot of a local shopping center several miles away.

The area's next unsolved homicide occurred in January 1991 when Delores "Dee" Davis, sixty-two, disappeared from her Park City home. Like Hedge, Davis had been strangled and abducted from her residence and her phone line cut. Two weeks passed before her body was discovered on a dirt road. Her hands, feet, and knees were still bound in panty hose.

Just as Landwehr had always believed that Vicki Wegerle's murder could be the work of BTK, he had long suspected that the killer was responsible for the killings of Hedge and Davis. Yet because both cases apparently took place outside Wichita city limits, the homicides were handled by detectives working for the Sedgwick County Sheriff's Department. According to Landwehr, county investigators originally considered that BTK might be the killer of the two Park City residents, but they eventually discounted the possibility. One of the reasons was that the bodies had been discovered so far from their homes, which didn't appear to fit BTK's known MO.

The most perplexing part of this latest package was the killer's inquiry about whether or not police had discovered "#7 at Home Depot Drop Site 1-8-05." Landwehr and his detectives had no idea what he was talking about. Several task force members were dispatched to the local Home Depot, where they spent the next few hours scouring the inside and outside of the store, searching for what they assumed would be a package or letter.

They discovered nothing, but eventually hit pay dirt after the store manager played a security videotape for them from the late evening of January 8. The grainy black-and-white footage of the tape showed some sort of SUV pulling into the nearly empty parking lot and stopping beside a parked pickup truck. Because of the darkness and the quality of the image, detectives were unable to pinpoint the exact make of the SUV. However, after roughly calculating the vehicle's length and wheelbase and the amount of ground clearance, they felt confident that it was a Jeep Grand Cherokee.

But the most riveting part of the video unfolded just moments after the SUV parked and the driver's door opened. From out of the interior, a shadowy figure emerged, walked briskly across the parking lot, then appeared to toss something into the bed of the nearby truck. Once again, the detectives paused the tape and scrutinized the individual frames. But no matter how they tried to enhance the image, the man's face was too blurry and dark for any of his features to be visible.

Although the detectives wanted to yank their hair out in frustration, they were ecstatic over one thing: they were actually staring at the phantom whom the Wichita police had been trying to locate for three decades. And, if their calculations were correct and the vehicle wasn't stolen, he was one of nearly twenty-five hundred Sedgwick County residents who owned a Jeep Grand Cherokee.

But there was another question the police were unable to answer: What the hell had happened to whatever the killer had tossed into the back of that pickup truck? Detectives got their answer the next afternoon after the manager posted a notice on a bulletin board in the back of the store, inquiring if any employee had discovered a curious-looking package in his or her vehicle.

As it turned out, the roommate of an employee had discovered a Special K cereal box in the back of his truck. He'd pitched it in the garbage, but because the trash collector hadn't yet stopped by his apartment, he was able to fish the mystery package out of his trash and turn it over to police.

Among the contents was a two-page document that detailed how the killer's "lair" was booby-trapped with explosives. He also included a lengthy list of "PJs," which included "PJ — Little Mex, my 1 big hit . . . a good start as Serial Killer" and PJ Fox Tail . . . Nancy J Fox, My best Hit." But the part of the communication that caught Landwehr's eye was the pithy message BTK had tacked onto the final page. It read, "Look, be honest with me. If I send you a disk will it be traceable? Just put (the answer) in the newspaper under Miscellaneous Section 494 (Rex, it will be OK). Run it for a few day in case I'm out of town — etc. I will try a floppy for a test run some time in the near future — February or March."

This marked the beginning of the end for BTK. If the killer was being honest — and Landwehr certainly had no reason to believe he was — it appeared that a shift had occurred in their relationship. For the first time in three decades, BTK was no longer just barking at the cops. He was asking them a question. And this was huge. He wanted to know if it was safe to begin sending police his communications on a computer disk. It wasn't so much what he was asking. What mattered was the notion that BTK finally wanted to establish some sort of a dialogue with police. Landwehr, it seemed, had begun to wear his adversary down. Rader was playing right into his hands.

The killer had begun to trust the supercop — which was exactly what I had envisioned when I began suggesting this technique back in 1984.

■ ■ ■ ■

Landwehr grinned while recounting this part of the BTK story to me. "We didn't know what to think," he said. "The last thing we thought was that he'd use his own computer, because whenever you stick a floppy in a computer, it gets stamped with all the identification information of that computer, and it's pretty easy to trace. We figured he'd just use one at a library or some school. At the very least, we'd be able to analyze the floppy, and it would give us a better chance to see where he'd just been."

As Landwehr later learned when he interrogated him, BTK was growing frustrated with the elaborate, complicated logistics involved with dropping off his communiqués around the Wichita area. He wanted to go digital and begin submitting his messages to them via computer disk. Because the police knew about these high-tech matters, he truly believed he could trust them to give it to him straight.

So Landwehr decided to do exactly as the man he was trying to catch had requested. On January 28, a detective quietly placed a classified ad in the *Wichita Eagle,* informing Rex to go ahead and send them a floppy.

Then Landwehr sat back and waited.

19

Landwehr needed a smoke. "I'll meet you up in your room in a minute," he said. So I walked slowly back upstairs thinking over everything he'd told me.

BTK's reappearance in March 2004 had stirred up the proverbial hornets' nest, all right. Before long, it was as if the killer had never gone into hiding for the past two and half decades. By that summer, the entire city had gone on red alert — gun sales skyrocketed; so did the number of security systems. Police were being inundated with so many calls on their special hotline that they had to hire more operators. Suddenly it felt like 1978 all over again.

It was good to be back in the public eye, BTK told Landwehr after his arrest.

One evening a few months into his BTK 2.0 act, Rader recounted how he flipped on the TV and happened to catch an interview with Charlie Otero, Joseph Otero's eldest surviving son. Once BTK resurfaced, the media tracked Charlie down, and he had ended up doing lots of interviews over the past few months. He'd also been "pretty verbal" about the killings.

He was one angry dude, Rader thought. Big, too. He listened to the TV and quickly concluded — as he told the police after his arrest — that Charlie wanted to cut him up and feed him to the sharks.

Rader told Landwehr after his arrest that the more he thought about it at the time, he realized that that probably wouldn't be such a bad way to go. Sure as hell beat being locked up in prison for the rest of your life. All the same, he decided that if he had to be put away, he wanted to be hanged, as they had done to the killers of the Clutter family. But because they don't do that anymore, he resigned himself to the fact that he'd either rot in prison or, if it came down to it, commit suicide. He hoped it would never come to that.

Just a little while longer, he kept telling himself. A few more taunts to the police, then he'd disappear forever.

Rader told Landwehr that he found it interesting watching Charlie — not so much because he had any interest in learning how the murders had affected the families of his victims. What he found intriguing was the effect Charlie's TV appearance had on him. He was sitting with Paula at the time his interview came on, and the moment it started, he felt himself suddenly shift into what he referred to as chameleon mode.

"I had to pretend he was somebody else besides who he really was," he explained during his interrogation. "After all these years, this sort of thing was easy to do. He just kept telling himself, "Don't tip it . . . Don't tip it.'"

He had another close call a few days later. As Landwehr told me, Rader was at home writing a letter to his brother Paul, who was stationed over in "the big sandbox," which was how Rader enjoyed describing Iraq. Paula happened to walk by and glance over her husband's shoulder at the letter, reading the words he'd written. Suddenly, he heard her exclaim, "You know, you spell just like BTK."

Rader realized that like everyone else in Wichita, she'd been watching and reading all the coverage of his recent communiqués. He knew the case had been on her mind lately. So he didn't panic. Not like the time back in 1979 when she told him he sounded like the man who telephoned police to inform them where they could find the murdered body of Nancy Fox.

Instead, he joked around with her and said, "We [he and BTK] went to school before they were teaching phonics." Then he laughed, and she walked off into the kitchen.

He finished the letter and mailed it, he told police. But for the next few days he found himself wondering, *Does she have a clue?*

One Friday in February 2005, Rader met with Michael Clark, the pastor of Christ Lutheran Church, where Rader had recently been chosen to serve as congregation president. Over lunch at a local Park City eatery, the two discussed the agenda for the upcoming church council meeting. Early on in the discussion, Rader placed his briefcase on the table, opened it up, reached in, and without a moment wasted, quickly pulled out a notepad and pen.

Clark told me that he sat there dumbfounded, watching as Rader retrieved the items. He was astonished at how everything in his briefcase appeared to have been positioned in an exact, very precise position. He'd never seen anything like it.

"He didn't have to hunt for anything," Clark said. "He knew exactly where everything was — unlike me, who has to search through four different compartments in my briefcase before I can find anything. I thought to myself, 'I knew Dennis was organized, but not anything quite like this.'"

Over the course of the next hour, Rader took copious notes as Clark spoke. Afterwards, the pastor suggested that Rader give him the notes and he'd have the church secretary type them up in an agenda-style format and hand them out to the other church council members, so they could prepare for the meeting two weeks away.

"I'll type it up myself," replied Rader.

"As you wish," said Clark.

Just before they parted company, Rader told the pastor, "You know what? I don't really have a good place to print up any copies for you."

"No problem, Dennis," Clark told him. "Type it up on your home computer, load it onto a disk, then bring it into the church tomorrow and I'll show you how to load it onto the church computer. You can print it up from there."

Which is exactly what Rader did. The next morning at ten sharp, he showed up at Christ Lutheran Church. Clark showed him what to do, then disappeared into his office to work on his sermon. Fifteen minutes later, Rader poked his head in through Clark's door.

"He looked at me," Clark told me, "and said, 'I'm out of here.' "

In his hand was the computer disk.

Ken Landwehr pushed open the metal door of my hotel room and walked inside. He took off his suit coat, carefully draped it over the one chair in the room, and took a seat on the bed. A few minutes earlier, I had assumed my usual perch beside the desk, basking in the glow of my computer screen.

"So how'd it go down?" I asked him. "Walk me through those final days before you put the cuffs on him."

Landwehr explained that after Rader met with Clark, he returned home, placed the disk into his computer, deleted the agenda for the upcoming church council meeting and made the biggest mistake of his life — besides being born. He typed out the next installment of his message to police.

On February 16, a padded envelope arrived at the studios of KAKE-TV. Inside was the usual assortment of index cards, along with a locket attached to a gold chain, no doubt pilfered from one of his victims. But the envelope also contained something else — a purple computer disk. The communiqué was quickly turned over to the task force.

The moment Landwehr spotted the disk,

he dialed the extension for Det. Randy Stone, the department's computer crimes sleuth. Within minutes, Stone had popped the disk into a PC and began clicking his way inside it.

"There were seven of us there," recalled Landwehr. "We were all staring over his shoulder, watching what he was doing, and he was walking us through every step he took."

Stone quickly saw that the disk held only one file, which was titled "TestA.rtf." He clicked it open and read the message left by the killer: "This is a test. See 3 x 5 Card for details on Communication with me in the newspaper." Stone asked to see the index card and moaned after reading the message: "Any communications will have a # assigned from now on, encase one is lost or not found."

Landwehr explained to me that it was Rader's use of the word "encase" that put everybody in the room on alert. It turned out that Encase is the proprietary name for a sophisticated type of software used in forensic computer investigations. "With it, you can literally strip off all the identifying information we were hoping to find," Landwehr explained. "Randy said that it looked like it could be a setup, and his use of the word was some sort of clue he'd left for us."

Landwehr had begun to wonder the same thing.

But a few minutes later, Stone worked his way into a portion of the file that he hoped would contain some traces of identifying information about whoever created it, along with the computer's registered owner. Stone clicked open this portion of the file and read that the alleged creator of the file was someone named Dennis. The owner of the computer was listed as Christ Lutheran Church.

Stone called up Google on another computer and typed what he'd just learned into the search engine. In less time than it took to blink, the pieces of the puzzle began to fall into place. Christ Lutheran Church was located in Park City. Somebody named Dennis Rader was listed as the church president.

"So four task force detectives took off to Park City," Landwehr recalled, "to check out what they could find about this guy. And I'm standing there thinking to myself, 'Can it really be this easy?' "

Within an hour, they'd pieced together a rough idea of just who Dennis Rader was. He'd lived in the same house for thirty-three years, had been married to the same woman for thirty-three years, and every morning for the past thirteen years had gotten dressed in a brown uniform that made him resemble a park ranger — complete with a badge, cap, and two-way radio dangling off his jacket — and driven off to a job where he got to play make-believe and pretend to be a cop. The more Landwehr learned about the guy, the more he liked what he saw.

Fifty minutes later, on their first drive-by of Rader's tiny ranch-style home, located a half mile from the Park City municipal building, detectives spotted a black Jeep Cherokee in the driveway. It resembled the vehicle they'd spotted in the Home Depot security videotape and was registered to Rader's twenty-nine-year-old son, Brian, currently serving in the navy.

Undercover agents began loosely tailing Rader, watching his movements, but keeping an extremely low profile. Although Landwehr didn't post undercover detectives in front of his house or at the Park City Municipal Building, his men monitored Rader's activities on a regular, steady basis. During the day, they continually watched to ensure that he was at work. And at night when he was supposed to be at home, they performed hourly bed checks to make sure he didn't sneak out.

"But we were careful not to jump on him right away," Landwehr told me. "We'd had too many close calls before. So we stuck to him day and night, studying everything he did and, most important, making sure he didn't try and go after anyone else."

Within hours of discovering Rader's identity, the task force met to brainstorm what needed to be done to nail Rader to the BTK murders. After thirty-one years spent searching for their killer, the last thing investigators wanted was for their top suspect to slip through their fingers. Landwehr had other reasons for wanting to move slowly. He couldn't shake the sick feeling that BTK was setting them up, leading them straight to Dennis Rader in the hopes that they'd arrest him and become the laughingstock of the media for nabbing the wrong man.

"His use of the word 'encase,' " Landwehr told me, "was just something I couldn't write off to bad spelling."

And there was another reason. In one of BTK's early communiqués, he had threatened to blow up his house — or as he called it, his "lair" — if police tried to close in on him.

But Landwehr was far too smart a detective to let these obstacles slow him down. He'd spent a couple of years learning the ins and outs of DNA evidence while working in the department's high-tech crime lab back in the early 1990s. What he learned there convinced him that the next step in the investigation would involve obtaining a DNA sample from Rader and matching it with semen left behind at his crime scenes.

There was just one problem, Landwehr explained to me. How the hell could police do that without tipping Rader off that he was a suspect in the case? And it was during a brainstorming session the next morning at task force headquarters that one of Landwehr's investigators on loan from the KBI came up with a novel solution that sounded like something straight out of an episode of the hit TV show *CSI*.

If they couldn't get Rader's DNA, Landwehr reasoned, why not get hold of a sample from a relative? Landwehr had used that technique in the past to help ID murder victims whose identity they weren't sure of. If they could just locate a sample from a parent, sibling, or child, it should be close enough to Rader's to confirm whether or not police had the right man.

But Wichita was far too small a city for police to be able to waltz into a doctor's office with a court order asking for the medical records of someone related to Rader. Word would quickly leak out about what they were up to, and that was the last thing Landwehr or anyone on the task force wanted.

Ray Lundin, a KBI special agent, attended that task force meeting, held on the following Monday morning. Two weeks before I flew out to Wichita, Lundin's boss, KBI director Larry Welch, a longtime friend of mine, gave Lundin the green light to speak with me about those final days of the investigation.

Lundin told me that when he learned at the meeting that Rader's daughter, Kerri, had attended Kansas State University — which happened to be the same university he had attended — a light bulb went on inside his head.

"I remembered that at K-State everyone used the student clinic," he said. Lundin also knew that the school's medical center was far enough away from Wichita that his inquiries there about Kerri Rader's health records wouldn't send up so many red flags.

So on Thursday morning he drove to Manhattan, Kansas, 130 miles away from Wichita, and learned that Kerri had visited the clinic on several occasions. Lundin returned the next day with a court order for the young woman's medical records and spent the weekend combing through them, finding reference to a pap test.

The following Monday morning, Lundin

returned to Manhattan and confirmed that the tiny glass microscope slide containing a collection of cells scraped from Kerri's cervix still existed. It was stored, he learned, at a nearby lab. The next morning he showed up at the lab with another court order. Thirty minutes later, he began the drive back to Topeka to deliver the slide to the KBI's crime lab.

On Wednesday morning, he handed it off to the lab supervisor, who ended up spending hours trying to remove the thin, brittle glass cover from the top of the slide.

Thursday night, just around 7:30, Lundin was walking into Sam's Club in Wichita when his cell phone rang. He looked at the number and saw that the call was coming from the crime lab.

"I remember thinking, 'Well, here we go,' " Lundin told me.

He placed the phone to his ear. "I'm shaking," said the KBI's forensic lab supervisor Sindey Schueler.

"What'd you get?" Lundin asked.

"I can tell you this," said Schueler, "this girl is the offspring of BTK."

Landwehr was notified about the match, and he knew the hunt was finally over. He'd found his killer. Now all he had to do was go collect him.

■ ■ ■ ■

The same day Kerri Rader's pap smear was being examined by Schueler in Topeka, Park City resident Kimmie Comer was sitting on the couch in the front room of her house, watching Dr. Phil on TV.

Kimmie had just gotten home from her job as a dialysis technician. Her kids were off at school. And that was when something happened, something that still makes her queasy whenever she thinks about it. She tries not to.

Not long before I arrived in Wichita to interview Ken Landwehr, Comer tracked me down through my Web site, wondering if I might be interested in hearing her story.

I told her I was.

It happened on a Wednesday afternoon. Nice day. Sunny. Spring, it seemed, had arrived early. Comer left her front door open, and a warm breeze was seeping in through the screen door as Dr. Phil's twangy Texas voice drifted out of the TV.

"All of a sudden, I turned and looked up and he was standing there, staring at me," she recalled. "Dennis Rader had walked right in my house without knocking. He looked at me sitting there, then said in this calm, quiet voice, 'Oh, I wanted to make sure you didn't forget your court date . . . for the ticket I gave you.' "

Comer told me that she couldn't believe what was happening. For the past eight months, Park City's heavy-handed compliance officer had made her life a living hell — all because she'd parked two cars in her driveway. Both cars worked just fine, but Rader started giving her tickets — eight of them, to be exact — for having what he considered to be an inoperable vehicle on her property. Each time he'd pull up in front of her house to give her another one, she'd attempt to show him how both automobiles ran perfectly fine, but the officious Rader didn't want to hear about it.

"That's why we have courts," he'd tell her. "Take it up with the judge."

So on that balmy Wednesday afternoon in late February when she saw him standing in her family room, holding his goddamned ticket book, she lost it. "I jumped up from the couch and got right in his face and started cussing him out. I told him how dare he walk into my house like this, and he better get the hell out. And that's what he did. He didn't get angry. He just turned and walked out."

As Rader futzed around his truck, pulling papers in and out of his briefcase, Comer stood there on the doorstep shaking.

"You're an old pervert," she shouted at him. "Why won't you leave me and family alone? You're just a goddamned dog catcher."

Rader had began thrusting himself into Comer's life shortly after her move to Park City in November 2003. A single mother of two young children, Comer's second husband was murdered several years earlier. She'd come to the sleepy little bedroom community of Wichita because it seemed like a nice place for her young son and daughter to grow up.

"I'd only been there about an hour and a half, moving boxes inside the house, when I saw him walking up the driveway in that little uniform of his," she recalled. "I thought he'd stopped by to meet the new people, to say hello."

But, she told me, it quickly became apparent that Rader wasn't in the welcoming mood, and he certainly hadn't dropped by her house on a social visit. "Before I could even get a single word out of my mouth, he pointed to my washer and dryer that had just been unloaded from our moving truck and were sitting under the carport and snapped, 'You can't have these here. You're going to have to put those inside the house.' "

Comer was dumbfounded. "I thought, 'You gotta be kidding me.' I tried to tell him that we'd just unloaded them a few minutes before and were going to move them inside, but we hadn't had a chance yet.' But all he could say was, 'Just move them inside or I'm going to write you up.'"

Within a couple of months, she explained that Rader began showing up at her house with alarming, annoying regularity. In February 2004, he started writing Comer tickets for the vehicle in her driveway. On more occasions than she could recall, she'd arrive from work and find his white truck parked in front of her house. The moment he spotted her, he'd drive away. One Saturday afternoon, her two children walked into the family room and informed their mother that a man in white truck had just given them a ride home from the park where they'd been playing.

"What do you mean a man in a white truck gave you a ride?" she asked, alarmed.

"The man who always parks in front of the house," her son replied. "He said there was a dog with rabies running around and that's why he needed to take us home. He gave me his card."

He handed his mother a stiff white piece of paper that read, "Dennis Rader. Park City

Compliance Officer."

"After a while, it was like he knew my schedule," she said. "I'd come home from work, and my neighbors would tell me that he'd stopped by their house, asking them questions about me. Sometimes he'd be out in front of my house, measuring my grass. I am not kidding about that. He would actually measure grass with a little tape measure. I just thought he was a crazy old pervert. I know all this sounds crazy, but I think he used to come in here and take things. Pictures would be missing and . . . well, so would my underwear. It used to drive me crazy. I never could understand where my panties had disappeared to. It doesn't mean he did it, but I've never had things disappear like that. Not ever. One night, my dog — he was an old, blind racing greyhound I'd adopted — disappeared. I'd put him out in the backyard on the chain, and the next thing in knew he was gone. The only way that dog could have gotten loose is if somebody unclipped him from that chain."

On another occasion, Comer received a phone call at work from a neighbor, informing her that some "old guy in a brown uniform, who claimed to be a police officer" was looking for her. She rushed home on her lunch break and a few minutes later watched as Rader thrust his ugly head in through her open kitchen window.

"You fucked up, buddy," she yelled, picking up the phone and dialing 911. But the Park City police officer who arrived at her house a few minutes later told her that Rader was just performing his duties and that she really needed to chill out.

20

Landwehr had gone downstairs to snag a Mountain Dew, smoke a cigarette, and make a couple of calls. The guy needed to take some time off, I thought. Reminded me of me, back before I crashed and burned, then spent a week in a coma.

I turned on my laptop, clicked my mouse a couple of times, and began wading back through Landwehr's disc, looking for something I might have missed, something to help explain when the murderous short circuit inside Rader's brain occurred. Just as I stumbled on several pictures of Rader in a feminine mask, buried up to his neck in a grave, Landwehr marched back into my room and took a seat in the chair by the window.

"These damn journals of Raders," I said. "They really start playing tricks on your head if you spend too much time reading them."

"Yeah," he said. "But that's your specialty,

right? I don't need to read his diaries to know he's a sick little pervert."

"You have any idea what Rader was thinking about on the morning you arrested him?" I asked.

"Haven't a clue," he replied. "But I know he didn't have any idea what we had planned for him."

I recounted how Rader later told one of my sources that the morning before his arrest, Dennis woke up and started thinking about what his next move should be. Part of him wanted to send police another package. He was just dying to unload one more of his specially prepared dolls, which he stored in a closet in Brian's old bedroom. He wanted this one to represent Shirley Vian, and on his last morning as a free man, he was thinking about how he planned to tie a little plastic baggie over its head — just like he'd done to Vian in real life. But another part of him told him to back off for a bit, especially as it appeared that he could now start communicating via computer disk.

"Had a lot on his mind, didn't he?" Landwehr smiled.

Then he proceeded to tell me about the day it all went down: February 25, 2005.

The weather had held, he said. Winter appeared to have skipped town early. The sun glowed like a searchlight up in the blue sky. Shortly after 9:30 on that morning, Landwehr's cell phone rang. One of his buddies was calling, wanting to know if he had time to play a round of golf later that afternoon.

"No," Landwehr told him, trying not to chuckle at the understatement. "I'd love to, but it looks like I'm probably gonna be a bit tied up most of the day."

All morning long, a contingent of Landwehr's men, along with agents from the FBI and KBI, had been on edge. In other parts of Sedgwick County — and in the town of Farmington, Michigan, and Groton, Connecticut — FBI agents were in place, ready to serve search warrants and go to work interviewing Rader's relatives and coworkers.

Everything, it seemed, was ready. Now all they needed was for the guest of honor to arrive.

From what Landwehr's detectives had learned, Rader was a creature of habit. He left his office for lunch every day at precisely 12:15. Three minutes later he would arrive home to find that Paula had lunch waiting for him on the kitchen table. That morning was no exception. At 12:15, he walked out of his office, strode across the black asphalt, climbed into his GMC truck, and started the engine.

Less than thirty seconds later, after he turned right out of the Park City Municipal Building parking lot, Rader's life started coming apart.

"Click on the folder that says 'arrest photos,'" Landwehr told me, pointing to my computer screen.

I did. A moment later I was staring at thumbnails of roughly seventy photographs, aerial shots of what I assumed marked the progression of Rader's arrest.

"They were shot from a helicopter," he explained.

It was fascinating to click my way through the pictures, one after the other, knowing that it marked the last few moments that BTK would ever know freedom. The action started moments after he turned onto Frontage Road, a tiny side street that paralleled 61st Street, the busy four-lane arterial that led to I-135. A white sedan could be seen waiting for Rader to make the turn. The moment he did, I watched as it moved up behind him. One block away on a side street, four brown and black sedans stood ready.

The group sat in a tight little convoy on a side street, listening to their radios for a report of Rader's progress. Landwehr was in the backseat of one of the vehicles. Wichita's chief of police, Norman Williams, was in another. The consensus was that Rader might not go down without a bloody fight.

"I've faced a lot of these violent guys over the years, even some who don't want to go to jail for five years, and they try to force the cops to kill them," KBI special agent Ray Lundin told me a few days before my arrival in Wichita. Not that he had to. I knew from my own experience arresting fugitives just how dangerous the next few minutes could be. At a task force meeting the night before Rader's arrest, there was talk of using the city's SWAT team to take him down. The idea was scrapped when task force members voiced frustration over the idea of having some outside group put the cuffs on the man they'd spent so much time trying to catch.

"The last thing Ken said to us," Lundin told me later, "was, 'Be ready and be careful.'"

Word came over the radio that Rader was on the move. The moment his white truck drove past the side street, the group swooped after him like wolves. Lundin was piloting a black Crown Victoria. A swarm of butterflies was flapping inside his gut. Strapped to his side was a Sigsauer 9 mm semiautomatic.

Beside him in the passenger seat was Wichita police homicide detective Kelly Otis, a Remington 12-gauge shotgun rested in his lap. The lead car, an unmarked white Impala, roared up behind Rader and hit the lights, causing the grillwork to explode in flashing bursts of red and white. Another dozen officers waited on the next street in case Rader tried to make a run for it. He didn't. The moment he spotted the unmarked car behind him, he steered his truck to the side of the road as Lundin and others rolled into place, forming what resembled a wedge in the aerial photos.

Lundin pulled up so close to the chief's vehicle that Otis, a stocky former college football player, couldn't get his door open enough to hop out. So he propped it open, rested his shotgun on the door frame and took aim at Rader, who immediately pushed open his door and climbed out of his truck.

"I had barely stopped the car when Rader jumped out," Lundin said. "It happened much quicker than any of us thought it would, which is why I made a run for him. He had a pretty aggressive look on his face, and we still didn't know if he'd be armed. We figured he'd either shoot at us or flash a gun at us, trying to make us shoot him."

In the seconds it took Lundin to traverse

those thirty feet between his sedan and Rader, he marveled at how the man's uniform resembled the one worn by Wichita police. Lundin also told me that he couldn't shake the feeling that this arrest might turn violent, ugly.

"Rader knew why we were there," he said. "And he knew he was going to prison and not coming out."

Ray Lundin is the kind of man that most people wouldn't want to see charging toward them at full gallop. A former power lifter who competed nationally while in college, he stands six feet tall and weighs 225 pounds. In a flash, he grabbed Rader's right arm with one beefy hand, then quickly clenched the collar of his jacket in the other.

"I took him down to the asphalt," Lundin said. "He went quickly, without much effort."

A moment later, another officer slapped cuffs on Rader's wrists, and Lundin yanked him back upright. But as he tugged on Rader's body, lifting him upright, the eighteen-year veteran special agent noticed something peculiar.

"His heart wasn't racing," he recalled. "He wasn't breathing hard or perspiring in the least. I'd never seen anything like it, never seen anyone look so calm at a moment like that. It was pretty chilling, really. Kind of summed up everything about who this guy was. It was as though he felt absolutely nothing. When I got him back to his feet, he turned slowly and looked me straight in the eye. Everything about him was calm, cool, flat. He said, 'Tell my wife I won't be home for lunch . . . I assume you know where I live.' "

Lundin replied, "Yeah, we'll take care of it."

Lundin told me that he had tried to make sense of the expression he glimpsed in Rader's face on that afternoon. But what he saw there defied any permutation of evil he'd ever encountered.

"A long time ago, I heard someone describe a Nazi war criminal in a way that I think works for Rader," he said. "They referred to him as an 'unfinished soul.' I can't think of a better term — unfinished soul. Just seems to fit. This guy just doesn't have the capability to care, and I have no idea why. Normally, with these guys, you can link it back to their childhood. But his was so average and run-of-the-mill, it doesn't make sense. He was proud of what he did. Didn't have a single shred of sadness or remorse — not even for himself. He had nothing. Absolutely nothing."

It was all over in two minutes. Lundin handed Rader off to several officers in bulletproof vests who hustled the handcuffed man to a nearby brown Chevy Impala with tinted windows, parked up the street. Landwehr sat in the backseat. By this point, Rader's look of aggression had disappeared, and he appeared dazed.

Rader later told one of my sources that it had all gone down so quickly that he couldn't understand what had happened. He never saw it coming, he confided. He racked his brain, trying to figure out where he'd slipped up.

Landwehr told me that the moment he laid eyes on Rader, he thought the guy looked confused, lost in thought. When the back door to the Impala opened, Rader peered inside expectantly and looked relieved when he spotted the familiar-looking face he had seen on TV press conferences.

"What happened then?" I asked. "You were about to come face-to-face with the guy you'd been looking for for over two decades."

Landwehr took a deep breath and sighed. "He looked in at me and said, 'Hey, Mr. Landwehr.' So I replied, 'Good afternoon, Mr. Rader.' "

At that instant, for a few brief moments the world outside grew muffled and still. Suddenly it was just the two of them — Dennis and Ken. Just the way my source told me Rader had always hoped it would be. Just the way I'd always imagined he dreamed about.

One of Landwehr's detectives sat behind the wheel, and the car sped off toward I-135, racing back toward the Epic Center in downtown Wichita where the FBI had offices. An interrogation room on the fourth floor was about to get very busy.

There are moments in life when things become as clear as a freshly cleaned windshield. Landwehr told me that this was one of those moments. Because it was at that exact instant when Dennis Rader uttered his name that he knew the man he'd been pursuing for the last two decades was going to sing until someone told him to shut up.

For the first few minutes of the short drive, the three men sat quietly as the community that Rader had terrorized for over three decades rolled past the windows. Rader told my source that he tried to keep his eyes riveted on the passing scenery, doing his best to look cool and unflustered. He glanced up at the helicopter flying overhead.

After a few minutes, Landwehr told me, he turned toward Rader and said, "Nice day outside. Good golfing weather. You play golf, Mr. Rader?"

The expression on the handcuffed man's face instantly softened.

"No," he said, "Not much of a golfer. I garden and fish, mostly."

He paused, peered back out the window and up at the helicopter. He looked almost pleased, Landwehr told me.

"It certainly is a nice day," he continued, starting to open up now. "Spring is coming. I made some notes about that just the other day. The flowers are coming up. You know, I saw some robins in the area the other day. Canadian robins, I imagine. Probably just passing through the area. I feed the birds, you know. Just to keep an eye on them."

Within minutes of arriving at the Epic Center, Rader was taken to the fourth floor interrogation room, which was filled with computers, printers, radios, and fax machines. He was still wearing his compliance uniform. One of the men waiting for him in the room wiped the inside of his mouth with cotton swabs, gathering saliva for a DNA test. Crime technicians at the KBI's crime lab were anxiously awaiting the sample.

He was led to a chair and asked to take a seat.

Because a police wannabe and egomaniac like Rader would probably be excited to know that an FBI agent had traveled to Wichita from FBI headquarters just to interview him, Landwehr asked FBI behavioral analyst Bob Morton to join in on this phase of the interview. Morton sat at the table beside Landwehr. They both wore black suits.

"I'm from Quantico," Morton said. "I flew all the way out here for this . . . because this is a very, very interesting investigation for us. I mean, we've been looking at it off and on for thirty years."

As Rader nodded, the expression on his face softened. "Uh-huh," he mumbled. Morton continued stroking him.

"This is such a dramatic crime," he said. "Kind of an unheralded crime, if you want to think about it, in history. That's why there's so much attention about it."

Rader continued nodding like some bobblehead doll.

"Yeah, a lot," Rader said. "A lot. A lot of media attention. A lot of stuff going on."

A faint grin spread across Landwehr's face when I asked him about the incident. "At first, I thought it would be a good idea to have an FBI agent there," he told me. "But it started to become pretty evident that he was so excited to be there, to be the center of this much attention, that he would have talked anyway."

By now, the world knows that Rader eventually confessed to being BTK, but what I found most interesting were those hours that elapsed between the time when this dazed, handcuffed nobody from Park City, Kansas, was read his Miranda rights and when he finally began spilling his guts. During those hours, before Rader's dark, perverse world got thrust out into the light for everyone to see, Landwehr received a firsthand glimpse at the façade Rader had lived behind for decades.

"It's all there in one of those folders on your computer, the folder named 'interrogation,' " Landwehr told me. "It's a transcript of what happened."

After a few seconds spent searching for it, I found the folder, clicked it open, and began reading, noticing that Landwehr didn't waste much time in getting to the point about why he'd hauled Rader up to this room.

"Do you know why you're here?" he asked.

"Well, probably for the BTK thing," Rader

replied. "I assume I'm a suspect at this point in time."

"Any reason why we should think that you're BTK?" Landwehr inquired.

Rader nodded again, slowly. "Well, I live in Park City, went to WSU, served in the . . . Uhh. I'm in that age group. Kind of surprised you haven't been knocking on my door before, wanting a swab."

Rader grew quiet for a moment, then added, "I've been a BTK fan for years."

Morton, who had remained quiet, broke his silence: "Since the first murder?"

Rader seemed a bit flustered with the question. "Well, I don't know," he fumbled. "I've always . . . I've got a degree in administration of justice, so it's always been an interest."

I'm sure Morton must have been smiling at that moment. I would have been if I'd been sitting there with him, smiling one of those stern, no-nonsense smiles that would let Rader know we held all the cards. It would be important to Rader's ego to appear friendly, but not so friendly that it didn't ring true.

Then Morton asked, "Do you know why you're getting swabbed today?"

"Well, I assume I'm a main suspect," Rader replied.

"So," Morton continued, "if that swab we just took —"

Rader was getting so excited over what Morton was about to say that he interrupted him with a "Yeah . . . Uh-huh."

"If it comes back a match," Morton continued.

"Then I guess that will be it," replied Rader.

"You're BTK?" Morton asked.

"Well," Rader said, "if that's what the scientists say, you know."

"Do you think it'll come back that way?" Morton inquired.

"I don't know," Rader said. "Let's just leave it. I don't know at this point in time."

Morton did as Rader asked. He pulled back just a bit, although not much. "Dennis, I have a question to ask you," he said.

"Uh-huh," Rader grunted.

"How do you think we came to talk to you?"

Rader frowned and bit into his lip. "Well, I don't know. As a suspect I assume. You must have something on me, otherwise you wouldn't have brought me in."

Morton held up the floppy disk received by police nine days earlier, then Landwehr proceeded to recount exactly how they'd linked it to him.

"You know, every time you print or every time you save something, it registers in a header that's hidden, that you can't alter," Landwehr said. "So if we get something like that and it would come from BTK, then we can go in there, and we can find out that it came from Christ Lutheran Church. . . . And that's when we came to you."

Rader sat there staring at Landwehr, looking like someone had just hit him over the head with a golf club.

"Pretty sharp," he said, but the words came out faint, almost in a whisper.

It was still early in the party, but the guest of honor had begun to show signs of wear. So Morton decided to keep at it for just a bit longer. He'd hit him with a few more jabs, then give him a chance to catch his breath.

"So what do you think the motivation would be for all of this?" Morton asked.

A forced smile appeared on Rader's face, and he nodded as if lost in thought. "Motivation?" he asked, slowly rolling the word over and over inside in his brain. "Well, what's the motivation for a serial killer? I don't know what causes them to do what it is they do."

"I'd be curious to know what you think," Morton told him.

Rader flashed a serious, professorial look

at his inquisitors. "I think it's a . . ." He paused to organize the thoughts that I was sure he'd been mulling over for decades. "I don't know too much about the genetics, but I think they have one of those off genes. . . . I think that BTK guy said he had a 'Factor X' inside him, so I think they must have an extra chromosome or something. Somewhere along the line, if that gets out of kilter, they are going to go. It's like an alcoholic or something. They sooner or later just want to go. They can't stop. They can't stop. They might try to control it, but it's still there. That impulse is always still there. They are always planning, or thinking, or dreaming, or something. To me, it's a disease. You know, you've got your jails full of people who are hardened criminals. You let them out and they go right back to what they did. A few of them straighten out. They tell themselves, 'Oh, I'll never do it again.' But basically it's inside them and they are set."

Landwehr and Morton sat there and listened to Rader ramble. It was all beginning to bubble to the surface, just the way they hoped it would. Just a matter of time, they told themselves, before everything began to gush out of him like vomit. All they needed to do was sit there, keep spoon-feeding his ego, and let him continue talking.

"So what do you think they are dreaming about?" Morton asked. "You said 'It's in their dreams.'"

Rader nodded his head, pleased with the agent's question. He'd grown so intoxicated with all this attention that it never occurred to him that Morton already knew the answer to his question, that all he was doing was tossing bait into the water in order to keep Rader swimming near the surface.

"Well," Rader intoned. "If you'll allow me to use an example: let's say you're a bank robber. You're always going to be dreaming about your next big haul — like how you're going to pull it off. And then one day, you might drive by a bank and look at it, then figure out that what you had in mind might not work. So then you go looking for another one. I mean, it's always in the back of your mind, just clicking away there all the time, always asking you: 'How are you going to do it? How are you going to work toward pulling it off?'"

They let Rader collect himself for a few moments. He sat there, not saying a word, beginning to crack but not yet knowing it. "I think it's in his genes," he stammered. "I think, well, they call it Factor X. That's what he called it — Factor X. You don't have any control over it. You try and put it away, but that doesn't work. I mean, it's not accepted by society. But it's like an alcohol or a drug person. You know, they're going to blame it on the drugs or alcohol. They are going to say they couldn't control it."

He took a deep breath, then muttered, "People have problems and probably always will have problems."

A few minutes later, his terrible secret continued rising up like bile from that hidden place he'd let it fester his entire life. Landwehr could tell it was all starting to come out, and there was nothing Rader could do to stop it.

He looked straight at Landwehr and said, "Give me a pastor."

"A pastor?" Landwehr asked.

"Yeah," Rader replied.

But before Landwehr could leave the room, pretending to arrange for Rader's minister from Christ Lutheran to be shuttled to the federal building, the handcuffed man began to utter the words that police had been waiting to hear for decades:

"You guys have got me."

Yet that was all he said. Nothing more. And Landwehr knew he'd need much, much more from Rader.

In the next breath, Rader was trying to figure out whether Morton had taken a regular commuter jet to Wichita that morning or whether his case was a big enough for the FBI to charter a jet. Much to Rader's disappointment, he didn't warrant a charter flight. And this, for the next few moments, caused Rader to sulk just a bit, making him reluctant to connect the dots for the two men and admit that he was BTK.

He was inching closer, yet he refused to make that final leap. Simply saying, "You guys have got me" was a far cry from what prosecutors would need to build an ironclad case against Rader. Deep down, Landwehr wasn't worried. He knew it was just a matter of time before Rader came clean and confessed. But he also knew that getting Rader to admit that he was BTK was just part of what he needed to do.

More than anything, it was crucial that Rader copped to each of the ten murders police now suspected he'd committed, especially those three homicides he'd never publicly claimed responsibility for — Kathy Bright, Marine Hedge, and Dolores Davis.

But now that they'd sent his saliva off to be tested at a crime lab in Topeka, Rader also knew it was just a matter of time.

"I thank you for being so forthright," agent Morton said.

"Well," Rader replied, "with DNA folks

out there, not much I can do about it. Haven't really said I'm BTK, but pretty close, I guess."

"Close?" asked Morton.

"Close," Rader agreed.

"I think," Morton said, "you'll feel better if —"

"Yeah, it's going to be an emotional drain on me. It's going to hit me, starting right now."

But still Rader didn't say it, did not confess in a definitive way. So Landwehr, in an effort to keep things moving, began to explain the DNA evidence investigators had amassed against him. Rader listened thoughtfully, then asked, "Isn't any way you can get out of the DNA, right?"

"You can't get out of your DNA unless you have had a total blood transfer and lost every organ in your body," Landwehr smiled, slowly tapping the desk with his index finger.

"Wouldn't that be a bummer if the BTK copycat confessed and then it didn't match?" Rader asked.

Landwehr looked deep into Rader's eyes. "With the evidence I got, I know that there's somebody in your family that knows who BTK is," he said. "I knew this before we even walked in here, before I could get probable cause to arrest you."

The detective paused for a moment, then added, "I know that BTK is the father of your children. That's what brings me to you. That's why I know your DNA is going to match BTK's."

Morton, who had disappeared from the room a few minutes earlier, returned and interrupted the two men.

"The preacher is on his way," he said. "So why don't you just say it."

Rader took a deep breath and looked down at the floor. "I guess you guys got me," he mumbled. "What else can I say?"

Three and a half hours had elapsed since Rader had first been seated in that interrogation room. Morton looked at him and said, "Say who you are."

Rader lifted his gaze and stared at the wall behind the two men. After a few moments, he opened his mouth and finally said it:

"BTK."

And that was that. In a matter of seconds, it was all over.

But a moment later, Rader realized he needed to ask Landwehr something. He later told my source that it had been eating away at him ever since the lieutenant informed him that police had caught him by tracing his computer disk to Christ Lutheran Church.

To hell with the fact that he'd just confessed to being the man who had killed ten people. Deep down, part of him always knew that one day he might be caught. That was practically a given in his business.

What really bothered him, though, was how he'd been caught. It just didn't seem . . . fair, Rader told my source. Over that past year, he'd begun to feel that he and Landwehr had formed a professional bond. And why wouldn't he? Ken played the role of the no-nonsense super-cop just as I had envisioned it two decades earlier. For the past eleven months, Landwehr had appeared on the color TV set in Rader's family room and spoken directly to Dennis, stroking his oversized ego, slowly convincing him that theirs was a relationship built on trust and respect. The way Dennis saw it, they needed each other — Rader played the role of the bad guy, and Ken played the cop. They had a good thing going, a rapport.

"I need to ask you, how come you lied to me?" Rader said. "How come you lied to me?"

Landwehr listened to the question, but he told me that he couldn't quite believe what he'd just heard. Could Rader really be that dense? Was he so hopelessly deluded as to imagine that the past three decades had been nothing more than a big game? He bit his lip to keep from laughing. But Rader was serious. He sat there across the table, staring at Landwehr, not blinking, patiently waiting for an answer to his question.

Finally, the tired homicide detective shook his head and muttered, "Because I was trying to catch you."

Within minutes of the arrest, a half dozen Wichita police officers had descended on Rader's local family, rounding up Paula, her parents, and two of his brothers and taking them down to FBI headquarters, a few blocks from city hall. They were briefed on what had just happened to Dennis and peppered with questions, such as whether they could remember Rader ever doing anything suspicious.

"You got the wrong man," Paula Rader's mother and father kept saying. "There's no way Dennis would have done this."

The arrest and charges were clearly a terrible, disorienting blow to Rader's devoted wife.

Paula had arrived first, having been driven to the FBI office by police, who had resisted descending on the Rader home until after Dennis had been cuffed. She arrived at the building a few minutes after her husband was ushered inside, and spent the next four hours sitting there, listening to investigators paint a picture of a stranger they claimed was her husband. And all the while, she never appeared to stop believing in his innocence, insisting that what she really needed to be doing was hiring a lawyer for him.

But then she remembered something, "a coincidence" she'd called it.

"Dennis used to drive me to work in 1974," she explained. "And we'd always go past the Otero house. That was the route he'd always take.

"But you've got the wrong man," she told Lundin. "Dennis couldn't have done this."

Paula's mother excused herself to use the restroom. Her father, a World War II vet, stared down at his thick arms, and Lundin said he could practically hear "the wheels turning round and round in his head."

After a few moments he looked up at Lundin and said, "So . . . you got the goods on this guy."

"Yeah," Lundin replied. "No doubt about it. It's him."

After Rader's in-laws left, Paula excused herself to get a breath of fresh air and clear her head. Lundin told me that he walked out into the hallway and saw her leaning against the wall, dazed looking, with a cell phone pressed up against her ear. She was talking to her daughter, Kerri, in Michigan, who had just been interviewed by several FBI agents.

"No, no, no," she whispered. "Your daddy didn't do this. There's been some horrible mistake. You don't need to worry."

Lundin heard the same thing a few days later when he flew to a naval base in Connecticut to speak with Rader's son, Brian, who was there attending submarine training school. Like everyone else close to Rader, he told Lundin there had to be some mistake.

"We walked through things with him, and he was shocked," Lundin explained to me. "He seemed like a squared-away guy, solid. But he took it really super-hard. He told me, 'We had the *Leave It to Beaver* life. Mom was always at home and Dad was doing everything — the Scouts, church, helping out at school. Every summer we'd go on summer vacations.'"

But just like Paula's father, Brian grew quiet after a bit of time had passed.

"Then he looked at me and said, 'It just doesn't make any sense. . . . The only thing that ever gave me any cause of suspicion happened when I was a little kid and I was going through Dad's stuff. I found this drawing. It was of a woman in this horrible position. She was all bound up in ropes. It scared me. I put it away and never looked in his stuff again.' "

At the same time that Rader's family was being briefed on his secret life, he sat in a nearby interrogation room, relishing all the attention being heaped on him. He felt downright giddy with all those detectives rotating in and out of the room, asking him questions. Now that he'd confessed to being BTK, the next order of business involved getting him to walk police through each of his ten murders, step-by-step.

It felt as though they were talking shop, Rader later confessed to my source. The way he saw it, he was practically a cop himself. Of course, he knew what they were trying to do. But at the same time, it felt as though they were all soldiers, battle-worn vets who had once been sworn enemies but, now that the war was over, could come together to chew the fat.

Rader, I knew, was thrilled to be able finally to talk about everything he'd done — even if it meant the end of the line for him. He'd never been able to do that, to talk about that side of his life to anybody. And suddenly there he was, handcuffed in a room filled with cops, shooting the breeze with a group of guys who seemed to know everything about him, eager to ask questions about how he'd managed to pull everything off.

At the same time, though, a sense of weariness had begun to seep in.

Rader told my source that despite all the hoopla and excitement surrounding his arrest, after a few hours he'd begun to feel the gentle stirrings of fatigue and depression. The high he'd initially experienced had started to tiptoe away — just as all his highs did. But he didn't want to think about *that* right now. He wanted to sit there and talk about his crimes — he could do that forever. These guys were soaking up every word he uttered. But as more hours stretched on and on, the weariness became too pronounced to ignore.

At one point, he shook his head and muttered, "A little thirty-nine-cent piece of plastic floppy was my demise . . . That's what cooked my goose."

Roughly twelve hours into his interrogation, Rader looked across the table at his inquisitors and said, "Could one of you guys do me a favor? Just shoot me in the head. Put me out of my misery. I know you would be in big trouble for that. But just shoot me like a mad dog. Just shoot me and be done with it. Sneak up behind me and shoot me.

BOOM! I won't know what hit me."

The detectives seated across from him would have been happy to oblige, but they didn't. A bullet to the back of the head would be far too easy an out for Rader.

Landwehr let Rader keep blabbing off and on for thirty-two hours. Then he had him booked in the Sedgwick County Jail and placed him under suicide watch. When Rader awoke in jail the next morning, he told my source, he'd never felt so low in all his life.

"My heart goes out to him," Landwehr grumbled.

"Yeah," I replied. "Really chokes me up."

The two of us sat there in silence for a few moments, then I said, "You know what really eats at me is that I've still got so many unanswered questions about this guy, so many things I can't figure out. I gotta get in to see him. I need to sit down with him and pick his brain."

Landwehr shook his head, looking almost bored. "Getting into that prison is gonna be tough, even for you," he said, giving me one of those why-bother sighs. "I'm gonna be honest with you. I don't need to know why Dennis Rader killed all those people. I don't need to know where his mind was or how it got that way. That's not my forte. He killed them, he planned it, and my job was to nail him for ten murders. After I did that, I was done with him."

Part of me wished I too could be done with Dennis Rader. But for some reason, I felt as though I was only just beginning.

■ ■ ■ ■

ACT THREE
MEETING BTK:
AN EXCLUSIVE INTERVIEW

■ ■ ■ ■

21

On May 28, eight months after my last trip to Wichita to research the events leading up to Rader's arrest, I hopped another flight out to that city on the plains and booked a hotel room downtown by the old train station, at the same place I stayed last time — a newly renovated century-old former warehouse for a company that manufactured scythes, axes, and butcher knives. The sidewalks and the buildings in that part of the city had a tired, ancient smell. Everything there appeared to be constructed from bricks made from day-old dried blood. Just thinking about that color brought back memories of the thousands of grisly crime scene photos I'd spent my career wading through while attempting to reconstruct events I now wanted to forget.

It was late May, but even at midnight the air felt hot and damp, the kind of syrupy heat that made me wish I could shake my compulsion to wear button-down shirts. But

543

old habits die hard.

I'd returned to Wichita to interview Dennis Rader, now known to the staff of the El Dorado Correctional Facility as Inmate no. 0083707. Getting permission to see him hadn't been easy. In fact, it had been damn near impossible. Most people think that all I have to do is show up at the front gate of a prison and the warden will meet and escort me to the cell of whatever inmate I want to speak with. Truth is, there are countless bureaucratic hoops I'm forced to jump through before I can talk with an inmate — particularly *this* inmate.

Back in the days when I was in the FBI, things were different. All I needed to do was walk in, flash my credentials, and ask to speak with an inmate. Not anymore. I lost that luxury when I retired from the agency in 1995. But even if I still had my credentials and the warden's support, Rader wouldn't have to speak with me, and I couldn't force him to.

Six months ago, I'd learned that a woman named Kris Casarona had formed a special relationship with Rader in prison. They had a signed contract between them that gave her power as his official gatekeeper over who could see or interview him. She evidently had plans to write a book about him.

I began communicating with Kris Casarona, calling her, writing her, talking to her at great length, trying to convince her to approve my interview with Rader. I needed her blessing before he'd agree to speak with me. Since his arrest, he'd been contacted by hundreds of journalists, TV producers, behavioral scientists, authors, and screenwriters, all of them requesting — and, in many cases, begging — for an interview. So far, the only people to have gained access to Rader at his new home in the El Dorado Correctional Facility were the Wichita police, members of his state-appointed defense team, and, of course, Casarona herself.

So far we had never met in person, but on this evening when I got back to Wichita, Casarona came over to the hotel, and we sat together in the hotel lobby. Casarona turned out to be a frazzled-looking thirty-nine-year-old woman in a floral-print dress. I sipped Chardonnay as she drank a Jack Daniel's and cola. Several, to be exact. But that was partially because the past week had been so hellish. It seemed as though every time she picked up the telephone, her lawyer was on the other end of the line, giving her more bad news.

Hardly surprising. For the past thirteen months, Casarona had become increasingly involved in the world of Dennis Rader. Shortly after his arrest, she succeeded in befriending him, convincing him that she was on his side, that she understood. At the time, he was still incarcerated in the Sedgwick County Jail. The relationship, however, had taken a terrible toll on her, turning her life upside down, sinking her deep into debt, leading to her vilification by many in this part of Kansas. Nobody said that dancing with the devil was easy.

Casarona drained what was left in her glass. Her eyes looked nervous, as though she was already regretting what was going to happen the next morning when, thanks to her help, I would be allowed to speak with Rader.

"Tell me about the dream," I said, trying to get her to think about something else.

She crinkled up the skin around her nose, which gave her a look that conveyed both bewilderment and amusement. Several weeks earlier, she'd briefly alluded to the dream, and now seemed like the perfect time to have her tell me about it.

"So you wanna know how all this has affected me, right?" she asked.

I nodded.

Casarona took a deep breath, then launched into a scene that had played itself out inside her head one night as she lay tossing and turning in her troubled sleep not too long ago. For some unknown reason, she had traveled to Venice with Rader. They sat together at a rickety little metal table on the edge of the Piazza San Marco. Out across the massive public square loomed the gothic stone columns and delicate arches of the Palazzo Ducale. Tourists milled about with shopping bags and cameras. She felt uneasy sitting there with him like this. Even as she was dreaming it, she could feel her skin crawling. It didn't feel right, and her eyes remained locked on him, much the way an animal, such as a chipmunk or a squirrel, might watch a human offering it a scrap of bread.

He knew she was nervous. He didn't care. It was all part of the game for him. She knew something bad was about to happen. It was only a matter of time. And sure enough, after a few minutes, he did it. He dropped his right arm down toward his waist and began fumbling with his black leather belt that he intended to wrap around her throat.

In the dream, Casarona stood up and walked quickly out into the massive open-air plaza. It would be safer out there among the tourists, she believed. But Rader quickly followed her, and soon he was standing behind her, gripping both ends of the belt with his hands. She began to run, frantically searching for someone to protect her. But wherever she went, he followed. She couldn't shake him.

"I never told Dennis about that dream," Casarona said, chewing on a piece of ice. "I mean, I told him I had a dream about the two of us in Venice, but I didn't tell him about the belt part. It's just too creepy. . . . Dennis is really into dreams, you know. He thinks it's possible, if two people are dreaming at the same time, that they can appear in each other's dreams. I don't like thinking about that sort of stuff."

Casarona's journey to this hotel lobby had been fraught with plenty of drama, headache, and frustration. We'd first bumped up against each other in December 2005 when I wrote Rader to request an interview for this book. He'd forwarded my letter to her, and she promptly telephoned my office, leaving a curt message that instructed me to cease and desist. Rader was hers. She'd bagged him. She had exclusive access to him, and it was this access that was going to net her a book contract, which she would use to jump-start her writing career.

She had a point, of course. A very good one. But if I had been the type of guy who backed down whenever someone told me to go away, I'd still be a FBI field agent, working the streets back in Detroit. I didn't bother telephoning her back — I decided to let her come to me. Three weeks later, I sent Rader another letter reiterating my same request and expressing my surprise over his decision to pass my first letter on to Casarona. I wanted to push a few buttons — both Rader's and Casarona's. She wasted no time getting back to me and fired off a private e-mail to me through my Web site, repeating how she had an exclusive deal with Rader and that he would speak to no one but her. She also mentioned that she'd read all my books and was, for lack of a better word, a fan of my work. I decided not to respond.

A few days later, Casarona once again telephoned my office. I picked up the phone, and we had a brief conversation. I listened as she told me how she'd become interested in the case and why she wanted to write a book on Rader. But I'd begun to grow a bit miffed at Casarona and the way she was preventing me from gaining access to Rader — something that had never happened to me before.

I told her how I first started working on the BTK case in the late 1970s, explaining that I used the knowledge I'd gleaned from decades spent in the trenches researching violent offenders to enlighten my readers about what made these guys tick, educating them in ways she never could.

"I know," she said. "I've read all your books. . . . But I just can't let you talk to Dennis. I've got bills piling up, and I need the money from a book deal to pay off all my lawyers."

"So you don't have a book deal yet?" I asked.

"Well . . . no," she said. "But I will."

"Tough business, publishing," I told her. "I've written several best sellers, and I can tell you that selling a book to a publisher isn't easy. Not even for me."

"Yeah," she groaned. "I know."

A week passed and we had another conversation. Then another. And, like I said, when it comes to speaking with people, I'm not half bad. The two of us struck up a weird friendship. After five months of back-and-forth — during which I often played the role of therapist as she vented all her frustrations — Casarona finally caved in. She agreed to give up her precious exclusive access to Rader. She would tell her man to speak with me.

It was a gracious, generous act on her part. The only catch was that she wanted to be present during the interview and then afterwards compare my impressions of Rader with hers.

I was far from excited about her stipulations, so I contacted the state's Department of Corrections and informed them that Rader had agreed to speak with me. An official there quickly nixed the idea of Casarona coming with me to the prison. She was furious with their decision, but insisted that she'd stand by her agreement to let me talk to Rader.

"When I give my word about something, I stick to it," she said. "But maybe we could meet afterwards and discuss what you learned?"

"Of course," I told her. "It's the least I can do for you."

Kris Casarona couldn't recall exactly when her fascination with Dennis Rader started. But she had told me during numerous telephone conversations we'd had over the past months that she'd been able to narrow it down to the year 1974, the same year I first learned about BTK from those homicide detectives in Detroit. She was six at the time of the Otero murders, but the memory of her parents whispering about it became one of those indelible moments in her childhood — just like the sound of locust or the wail of a tornado siren on a spring afternoon. Although her dream was to become a veterinarian (just like Rader, just like me), Casarona also toyed with the idea of one day becoming a detective. By the time she turned ten, she had decided that her first case would be the mysterious BTK homicides.

By this point in her life, the precocious Casarona was regularly devouring the *Wichita Eagle* from the front page to the back. And just like everyone else in the city, she soaked up every word written about the unknown killer who was terrorizing the city.

One Saturday afternoon, she and a friend hoofed it to the Wichita Public Library, hoping to catch a glimpse of the killer. She figured that because he'd once left a letter for police on a bookshelf in the library, it only made sense that he'd be there lurking in the aisles, just waiting to be discovered. The two girls combed every aisle looking for the killer, whom they both had a hunch they'd recognize the moment they laid eyes on him, but they never did.

Twenty years later, Casarona was working as an oil and gas analyst for the state of Kansas, wading through piles of state statutes and federal regulations in order to write detailed reports on pipeline safety in

Topeka, wondering why life hadn't turned out quite the way she'd dreamed it would when she was younger. Over the past few years, she'd survived a rape, battled osteoporosis, and weathered a divorce, and now was in the midst of watching her second marriage crumble.

She yearned for change. Nothing terribly dramatic, just something small and meaningful. One morning in February 2005, she picked up the newspaper and read an article about how the bogeyman from her childhood had been apprehended by the Wichita police.

At first she didn't know what to think. But after a few weeks had passed, she decided to write him a letter, the kind of letter you send to someone without necessarily expecting ever to receive a reply. In her two-page note, Casarona explained how his awful crimes had left a mark on her childhood that she could never quite wash away. She dropped the letter in the mailbox and never gave the matter much thought. Seven days later, she came home from work and pulled an envelope out of the mailbox with a return address from the Sedgwick County Jail.

She and Rader became pen pals, firing off an endless volley of letters to one another. This was three months before I even considered writing a book on BTK. By the middle of April, he began telephoning her at home. Two weeks after that, she drove to Wichita and visited him in the county jail, where access to a prisoner is much easier to get than in a state prison. It was during this first face-to-face meeting that it became obvious what she needed to do.

Casarona decided that she would write a crime book. She would wade in the muck and filth of Rader's past and attempt to figure out what had transformed him into a heartless killer. Although she'd never had any of her work published, she'd won a handful of writing contests and had spent a couple of years penning speeches for a Kansas senator. She was confident that she could craft a readable sentence on paper. More important, she'd also become something of an armchair crime buff and amateur profiler, devouring countless true-crime books (including all of mine), plowing through them the way most of her friends polished off romance novels.

But here was the most peculiar part of her plan: whatever money she earned from the book — minus expenses — she planned to donate to the families of Rader's victims. Casarona wanted to do the right thing for these people who had endured such an unending loss. But she was also savvy enough to realize that if her book on Rader went big, her next one could also earn substantial royalties as she continued her career as a successful writer.

"That first time we met, there was a piece of glass between us," she told me. "I wasn't scared. But I definitely wasn't excited or thrilled either. I had no feelings either way. Except that I found him utterly repulsive, so I guess that was my only feeling. I really just tried to disassociate myself like I read that you do when you go to interview one of these guys. I figured I had a job to do, and that was to get him to trust me."

Between late April and mid-June, they had met seventeen times face-to-face, and on each occasion Casarona wore skirt-suits with high-collar shirts or suit jackets, always buttoned high. She wanted the guards to assume she was an attorney. Every time they met, she smiled, laughed, listened with a sympathetic ear, and exuded a strange intensity that transformed Rader into a type of dopey teddy bear — if that was possible for a homicidal psychopath.

Four months after that first letter to him, she asked Rader to sign over the rights to his story to her. He eagerly agreed.

And that was when Casarona's real troubles started. The media learned of her relationship with Rader when he forwarded their interview requests to her and she'd reply, declining all their requests on Dennis's behalf. Then, starting in June 2005, three months after Rader's arrest, the local and national media, hungry for any news about Rader, began writing about her relationship with the killer. Word leaked out that she was writing a religious type of book, which angered many in the region who believed her to be some sort of bleeding-heart kook, the type who was probably coddling Rader, telling him he'd be forgiven for his transgressions.

"It wasn't long before I became known as 'that crazy woman from Topeka,'" Casarona moaned.

But being written off as a kook was one thing. Her legal problems were even worse.

Casarona's legal nightmare began to unfold in January 2006 when the families of Rader's victims sued her for an unspecified amount because of the book contract Rader signed. They alleged that Rader had made a deal with her that would allow her to profit from his crimes. The fact that she originally wanted to turn over the proceeds from her book to these same families didn't seem to matter. A jury trial was tentatively set, but the case was dismissed in March 2007 when both Rader and Casarona signed an agreement requiring her to do exactly what she'd intended to do all along.

Before I spent time getting to know Kris Casarona, I'd written her off as a loony. In all probability, I told myself, she was just another serial killer groupie who would end up being a nuisance and possibly a hindrance to investigators.

In fact, the Wichita police worried about Casarona because when news first leaked that she was about to write a book, Rader had yet to enter a formal plea in court in the ten murder charges filed against him. The authorities still had no idea how many people Rader might have killed. Because law enforcement depends on the public for potential leads and other information, their greatest frustration was that Casarona might end up concealing information for her book about a murder Rader had committed after 1994, when Kansas reinstated the death penalty.

When I finally caught up with Casarona in Wichita in May 2006, she claimed to be nearly $100,000 in debt to the attorneys she'd been forced to hire to defend her against her various lawsuits. Her bold dream of writing a crime book, she told herself, had been stabbed through the heart. She doubted that any of the insight she'd gleaned from her hundreds of hours of phone calls, letters, and jailhouse visits would ever find their way onto paper.

"All I wanted to do was write a crime book, just like everyone else was doing, and now look what happened," she moaned in the hotel lobby. "I get letters from people telling me I'm going to hell for doing this. And for what? I didn't want a dime from this book. Not a dime. If I could get out of this contract with Dennis and be done with all this, I would. But the families of Rader's victims don't care. They're suing me anyway. So I'm stuck."

Ever since I first wrote that letter to Rader in December 2005, requesting an interview for this book, Casarona had been a never-ending source of headaches in my life. But, as strange as it now seems for me to write this, over time she'd become something of a delight. She was a whip-smart, bullheaded woman with a knack for getting herself into tight scrapes. But for those who took the time to get to know her, she was also a generous, good-natured soul, the type to give a stranger in need the last dollar out of her purse.

"Of course, he disgusts me," Casarona said, staring at her empty glass. The ice had melted long ago. "If he were to somehow get out of prison and show up on my front doorstep, I'd pump as many slugs into his body as I could. I've got a forty-five, you know. Got a nice kick to it. Picked it up after failed marriage number one."

Casarona laughed.

I believed her.

Ever since we'd begun communicating, Casarona had been guarded about most of the intimate details she'd learned about Rader's childhood. That was what interested her the most. *When did it happen? When did he know he was different?* Something told me she'd yet to unearth the answer. Every so often, she'd drop hints about what she'd learned, but it wasn't anything that I didn't already know. And from the few morsels she'd told me, my gut had confirmed one important, disturbing observation: Casarona had become Rader's next victim. He might be locked behind steel doors, several feet of concrete, and glistening razor wire, monitored by surveillance cameras and watched over by countless heavily armed guards, but he was still up to his old tricks. Somewhere inside his brain, he was plotting to kill Casarona, torturing and strangling her, day after day, week after week, imagining her lifeless naked body fallen before him as he masturbated.

The two of them had forged a symbiotic relationship. He needed her as fodder for his fantasies, and she needed him as grist for her book and to solve the riddle that many people were asking: Was Rader born a serial killer and those ten murders he committed an example of genetic destiny? Or was he shaped and molded by some sort of horrible childhood trauma? Of course, this question was nothing more than the age-old nature-versus-nurture enigma, pushed to its moral outer limit.

Like me, she'd discovered no examples of sexual or physical abuse in Rader's past. Although he steadfastly denied ever being victimized as a child, I didn't buy it. Either he didn't want to admit it or his psyche had been so shattered by the trauma that he couldn't retrieve the memory. I refused to believe that Rader was a natural-born killer. It was far too easy an explanation.

It was late. I wanted to get some sleep. My body was running on East Coast time, where it was closing in on three in the morning. "If I'm gonna do this interview tomorrow, I gotta get some shut-eye," I mumbled. Casarona nodded wearily, looking almost as exhausted as I felt. We said good-night, and as I headed off to my room, she called out, "I forgot to tell you the code word."

"The code word?" I asked.

"Yeah, the code word. Because I wouldn't get a chance to speak with Dennis on the phone between the time I met you in person tonight and when you showed up for your interview tomorrow morning, I came up with the idea of having you give him a prearranged word that just Dennis and I would know."

"Oh, I see," I said, convinced she'd been watching far too many spy movies.

"Depending on how much I trusted you and what I thought of you, Dennis and I had several passwords," she said. "Depending on what you tell him, he'll know how freely he can talk to you, how open he can be." She paused for a moment, staring down at the stains on the hotel carpet. "You know, he doesn't understand why I'm letting you speak to him. He really wants me to save everything for *my* book."

I stood there looking at her, too tired to summon up the energy to tell her how idiotic I felt muttering some stupid code word to a convicted serial killer.

"So, what is it?" I asked, starting to feel annoyed.

"I'm still trying to decide," she said.

"Look, I'm really beat. Why don't you phone me in the morning when you decide on something."

She started to look a bit embarrassed by all the cloak-and-dagger precautions she was taking. "Tell Dennis when you see him . . . tell him that the lion is strong," she said.

"That's my password?" I asked. "The lion is strong."

"That's right."

"This is ridiculous, you know."

Casarona smiled. "Tell him the lion is strong, and it is very positive."

"The lion is strong, and it is very positive," I said. "Anything else?"

"That's it."

"Good night, Kris," I mumbled.

"Good luck," she said.

I stumbled upstairs to my room, wondering about what I was getting myself into. If my meeting with Rader did go down — and I still wasn't convinced it would — the interview conditions would be far from perfect.

A few days before I flew in to Wichita, an official at El Dorado informed me that Rader and I wouldn't be allowed to sit together in the same room or even across from one another at a table separated by a slab of bullet-resistant glass. Instead, I'd be required to park myself in the visitor center while he sat in a room in another wing of the facility, staring into the lens of a video camera. The two of us would watch one another on TV screens and communicate with microphones and speakers.

The warden could have allowed me to interview Rader in the same room, but he apparently refused. After all, I wasn't in law enforcement anymore, and he didn't want to be seen as giving me any "special treatment" or perks, especially when he had a box on his desk stuffed full of requests from people wanting to speak with Rader. Even my good friend Larry Welch, director of the KBI, tried to get me a face-to-face interview, but the warden wasn't inclined to make any exceptions. It pissed me off something awful, but I respected his decision.

Yet the most frustrating stipulation was that I would be allowed to spend only two and a half hours with Rader. That may sound like plenty of time to engage in a one-on-one conversation with a homicidal psychopath, but it was woefully inadequate. To date, all of my interviews had been open ended. They finished either when I obtained all the information I needed or when the prisoner got so ticked off that he called for a guard and demanded to be taken back to his cell.

I fell back onto my bed and lay there, staring up at the ceiling, trying to figure out the lines I'd use on Rader in the morning. Shouts echoed up from the street below. A bottle, perhaps two or three of them, shattered. A bar fight, I figured, was spilling out into the night. Listening to the din, my mind raced backwards two decades to an interview I'd somehow managed to pull off, despite being told to hit the goddamned road. The memory of that afternoon I walked through the rusted gates of Stateville Correctional Institute in Joliet, Illinois, to pick the ugly, disturbed brain of mass murderer Richard Speck, caused my mood to lighten.

As mass murderers go, Speck was at the top of the cesspool. One hot July morning in 1966 in South Chicago, he butchered eight student nurses, raping several of the women before beating and stabbing them.

Speck had been sentenced to twelve hundred years in prison. When I arrived on his cell block, he was in a foul mood. In the months prior to my visit, he'd managed to capture one of the sparrows that used to fly in and out of the broken windows of Stateville. He tied a string around one of its legs and turned the bird into his pet. The guards would watch him sitting in his cell for hours at a time talking to it, feeding it scraps of bread.

Prison officials were mildly astonished to observe this cold-blooded killer's kinder, gentler side. Over time, however, the novelty wore off, and Speck, who was violating prison rules prohibiting inmates from having pets, was informed that the bird would have to go. So he untied the string from its tiny leg, held the animal in his hand for a few brief seconds, and just when it appeared that he would set it free, crushed the bird in his hands, tossing the bloodied carcass into a large fan, sending feathers and bird guts throughout the cell block.

"GO FUCK YOURSELF" were the first words out of Speck's mouth when I entered the chain-link holding pen where he sat on a filing cabinet, waiting for me.

After a few more obscenity-laced descriptions of all the activities he wanted to perform on my mother, I looked at him and said, "It's OK, Richard. I don't have to be here. I've got plenty of other things to do."

I stood up, preparing to leave, then glanced over at one of the prison administrators who organized the interview. "Damn," I said with a wink. "I wanted to ask this son of a bitch how the hell he fucked all those eight nurses.

Because whatever Richard's eating, I want some of it."

Speck shut his big dirty mouth and looked at me as though he couldn't believe what he'd just heard me say. He took the bait almost as soon as I tossed it at him.

"I didn't fuck all eight of them," he said, alarmed that I didn't have my facts straight. "Who the hell fucks eight women in one sitting?"

By the time I finally walked out of that holding cell, Speck had blabbed for nearly seven hours, walking me through all the wretched days of his life, providing me with an intimate look into the evolution of this twisted killer.

Something told me that I wouldn't enjoy the same luxury with Dennis Rader. I was fairly certain that he'd pretend to weep over the memory of his victims. And odds were that he'd also be respectful and polite because he believed the two of us shared some sort of professional camaraderie. But the bottom line was this: if he grew miffed or upset at any moment during the interview — which often happened during these sessions — he could pull the plug, and I'd be unable to do anything to stop him. All he'd need to do would be to shout for a guard, who would walk over and flick a switch on the video camera. And that would be it. Game over.

Welcome to the brave new world of criminology, I mumbled to myself, then felt the soft tug of sleep pull me away.

22

A few hours later I awoke, showered, and pulled on a pair of trousers, a sport coat over my tan plaid shirt, and loafers. On the way out of my room, I glanced at my reflection in the mirror.

"Jesus," I laughed. "You look just like a prison shrink." Even though Rader knew my background, I'd discovered years ago that wearing casual clothes helped grease the skids during these prison interviews.

Incarcerated felons, it seems, can smell a cop two hundred feet away. Dressing down gave me the appearance of being either a social worker or a member of the prison's psych staff, two categories that tended to put inmates at ease.

I grabbed my briefcase and headed down to the hotel lobby for a cup of coffee, then took a seat at a rickety table.

Tucked away in my briefcase was a folder containing five pieces of yellow paper yanked from a legal pad. The pages were a gift from Casarona, handed to me the previous night. Rader had mailed them to her a few days earlier. Turned out that when he learned I was writing a book about him and that Kris had given him her blessing to speak with me, Rader decided to contribute an essay of sorts.

As Landwehr had told me during my last visit to Wichita, Rader was a fan of my books. Predictably, his favorite was *Obsession,* no doubt because the first chapter was a thinly veiled account of the BTK case.

According to Casarona, Rader was impressed at what I seemed to know about him long before police apprehended him. Over the years, he had gone back to that chapter again and again. He had told Kris that reading what I'd written gave him a sense of perspective about himself he'd never had, allowing him to better understand the forces that writhed and squirmed within him, compelling him to kill. Not that this insight did him a lick of good. But because he could never turn to a psychiatrist or a psychologist for help, what I'd written in *Obsession* felt as close to a therapy session as he'd ever had. The words on the pages of that chapter forced him to ask questions about himself. Of course, he never figured out any answers.

But, as I've said before, for someone as shallow and empty as Rader, just asking the questions was good enough.

I spread Rader's "essay" out across the table. I'd never had a serial killer send me a piece of writing quite like this before. Neither had any of my colleagues.

At first glance, the pages looked to be nothing more than scribbled notes culled from that first chapter of *Obsession.*

Rader's words were printed in black ink in the same tiny, hopeless chicken scratch employed in his journals. I'm no handwriting specialist, but his contained, tight lettering reminded me of just how controlled and withdrawn Rader was. His scrawl looked hollow, flat in a way I'd never seen before when reading the handwritten words of a killer. It was almost as though Rader had been attempting to write something else, but this came out instead, and it made me feel as though I were peering into his brain.

He intended this document to be a type of chart. Across the top of the first page he'd written the words OBSESSION (CASE STUDIES). Down the middle of the page, he'd printed out a list of qualities and attributes that I'd discussed in the book as ones he shared with other serial killers, all of which he must have felt were relevant to him. On

the left side of the yellow paper, he refer-
enced the page number and paragraphs
where these traits had been described in *Obsession.* The words appeared on the page in
quick bursts, jumping from one disturbing
topic to the next, never remaining in one
place for very long.

Manipulation, domination, control
. . . . Locate and identify — profile victim. . . . Knows how to get inside victim's
head. . . . Manipulation, domination,
control of that victim. . . . He can and
does the same to law enforcement. . . .
Background of virtually all of them [se-
rial killers] came from abusive or otherwise severely dysfunctional background,
but that doesn't excuse what they do. . . .
Compelled to commit violent predatory
crime. . . . Sexual predators and child
molesters do enjoy their crimes. . . . Signature aspect — better than MO. MO is
what an offender has to do to accomplish
a crime. The signature, on the other
hand, [is what the] offender has to do to
fulfill himself emotionally. It's not
needed to successfully accomplish the
crime. But it is the reason he undertakes
the particular crime in the first place. . . .
Predator in the night and always on the

hunt for victim of opportunity. . . . Voyeurism, which would be consistent with hunting, getting ready for next assault. . . . Geographic comfort. . . . The sadistic killer anticipates his crime. In fact, he has perfected his MO over his criminal career. Fantasy evolves and he gains more experience. . . . Bring weapon. . . . Torture kit, whip, manacles, etc. . . . Place to take his victim, not disturbed. Obscure cabin in woods outfitted w/ sound proof. . . . Uses ruse. . . . May take photographs or record the scenes . . . . Take souvenirs — jewelry, underwear. . . . Most often ends in murder. . . . Killing the victim may be the integral part of the sadistic fantasy scenario. . . . Sadistic type — white, above-normal intelligence, may be college educated with good middle class job. He will have a dominant personality and collect bondage and sadomasochist bondage. He may collect related items, such as knives, guns, read military, law enforcement or survivalist literature. He may have a large attack-type dog. . . . Because of his intelligence and planning, he will be difficult to apprehend.

On each of the next four pages, he created

another type of chart, comparing himself with other serial killers, the ones with whom he yearned to share equal billing. This was another example of Rader's bloated ego at work. His murders made him somebody, although he seemed to have forgotten that they started out as a secret, something he wanted no one to know about. But the moment he realized how much attention his crimes were receiving from the media, he reveled in the notoriety.

Suddenly he wanted the world to know that the BTK Strangler was badder than bad and utterly unstoppable. The same thing happened to David Berkowitz, Ted Kaczynski, and the Zodiac Killer. (This last case ranks as one of the nation's major unsolved serial murder cases.) The rush created by seeing and hearing his name in the media gave Rader a far better buzz than the one he received from actually killing another human being.

Across the top of the pages, he'd listed the names Ted Bundy, Son of Sam, Ed Kemper, Steven Pennel (Delaware's first serial killer, a case I was called in to work due to my expertise in the field of torture), the fictional killer Buffalo Bill from the movie *Silence of the Lambs,* and Gary Heidnik, a serial killer from Philadelphia who kept women in his cellar in a pit filled with water, and electrocuted them. Rader also included a column for BTK.

Extending down the left side of the page, he'd listed a smorgasbord of biographical and psychological traits, then answered yes or no beside each killer's name, depending on whether or not they possessed that specific quality. I found it interesting that beside the entry for "overbearing mother," he scrawled "1/2 ." I assumed that this meant she was only half overbearing and made a note to ask him about this if I got the chance during our interview.

Next to the entries for "Arrogance," "Self Centered," and "Inside voices," he wrote "No."

Yet when he pondered the question of whether or not he was "Intelligent," he decided that the answer was yes.

In fact, he concluded that each of the serial killers on his chart — with the exception of Berkowitz and the fictional Buffalo Bill (both of whom he wasn't sure about) — also possessed what he considered to be intelligence.

In a note above the final page of his chart, he wrote: "KEY: Predator don't care what happens to victims as long as he gets what he wants."

These words were perhaps the most honest

Rader had ever written, cutting straight to the heart of who he was and what he stood for. I couldn't imagine a better epitaph for this heartless killer.

It was just after 8 A.M. when I climbed into my rental car to begin the drive to El Dorado, steering north on I-135 past Park City, past the off-ramp that Rader took to get to his house.

It was green and lush this time of year in Kansas. In two short months, most of these fields would be baked golden brown by the fierce Kansas sun. It was Sunday morning. Every cemetery I drove past had American flags fluttering in the warm morning breeze.

Since Rader's transfer to this state facility following his sentencing in August 2005, the only family member to visit him was his youngest brother, Paul, the same one Dennis used to defend in grade school when the other kids would torment him because of his size. Paul brought their mother with him, but she was so hopelessly lost in the fog of Alzheimer's that she couldn't grasp what her oldest son had done and why he'd been locked away in prison. From what my source told me, the two brothers cried when they saw each other, and the bulk of the visit re-volved around Paul telling Dennis what his relatives had been doing since his arrest.

Neither his wife, Paula, her parents, nor any of his children had visited Rader. Kerri sent him a few letters at first, but hadn't written in over a year. Paula has never communicated with her now former husband since he's been at El Dorado, but Dennis told my source that he dreams about the day she finally does. In one of the only letters she penned to him right after his arrest, she told him that she'd have to forgive him one day in order for God to forgive her for her sins. So Rader tells himself he has that going for him. His son, Brian, writes occasionally, telling him about his life in the Navy and filling him in on family matters. In one letter, Brian commented, "You're not right in the head and people don't understand that."

The drive to the prison from Wichita takes roughly forty minutes, but it felt longer to me.

I didn't know what I expected to take away from this interview. Truth is, I'd had a fairly good understanding about what went on inside Rader's head long before I reimmersed myself in this case. But after digging through his journals, talking to his friends, and interviewing the cops who had chased him, I found that Rader had begun to grow blurry again for me, becoming almost mysterious. The sensation was similar to that of driving into a fog bank. As you approach it, you can make out its shape and dimensions, but within seconds of entering it, you grow disoriented, confused.

I still had unanswered questions.

Could I truthfully say I understood why he'd gone so long between killings?

Did I really know how he was able to compartmentalize his life with such absolute precision?

Why did he resurface at the age of fifty-nine, an age when most serial killers are incarcerated, dead, or smart enough to understand that serial killing isn't a pastime for old men?

And last, what could we in law enforcement learn from Rader to help stop other serial killers earlier in their careers?

Meanwhile, I was lost. After what seemed like hours spent on the road, I told myself I must have taken a wrong turn somewhere along the way. When I spotted an old man in baggy overalls walking across the gravel parking lot of a diner, I pulled over.

"You happen to know where a prison is around here?" I asked, leaning out the window of my car.

The old man gave me the once over, trying to figure out if he knew me or if I looked to be from these parts. "What sort of business you got up there?" he asked.

"Somebody I've been wanting to talk to for a long time is waiting for me."

"Well, ain't that just something," he grinned, then pointed back at the highway in the direction I was already going. "Keep going down the road a ways. You can't miss it."

I thanked him and continued on my way. A few minutes later as I crested a hill, the prison complex loomed enormous in the distance, squat, ringed with what appeared to be miles of glistening chain-link fence. A bone-white water tower resembling a mushroom cloud jutted up into the sky above the facility. The massive compound looked like something out of a sci-fi flick, the kind of place where one might expect to find an evil scientist holed up in a laboratory making poison.

I turned off the highway and followed the long, meandering road that led to the parking lot. A wind, warm and furious, blew across the prairie out of the south, bending the tiny saplings along the road. I pulled into a space and parked. From the window of my car, I stared at the dozens of crows and sparrows hunched over on the ground, leaning into the gusts, straining to keep from being blown away. A brass clip dangling from a rope on the massive aluminum flagpole by the guard tower clanged out a rhythm, strangely hypnotic, permeating everything.

I made my way toward a concrete walkway, trying not to stare at the stern-faced women sitting inside the dozen or so cars and trucks, preening themselves in their rearview mirrors. The doors of the prison were constructed from thick glass. Because of the wind, I had to tug on them with all my strength in order to coax them open.

Once I was inside, the first thing that caught my eye was a glass case filled with handicrafts made by the residents of El Dorado. On one of the shelves sat a collection of dream-catchers made from yarn and sticks, for sale. According to the lore, various Native American tribes used these as protection against bad dreams. You simply hang one up over your bed, and the nightmares get caught in the yarn before reaching your head.

I wondered if Rader's daughter had ever resorted to using one of these. When I heard through some sources that she was a cop buff, I'd written her a letter, letting her know that I wanted to ask her some questions about her father. I never received a reply.

God knows she could use one of these, I told myself. *Maybe I'll pick one up for her on the way out and mail it to her.*

I made my way over to a large counter where a young woman stood; I told her why I'd come, and she handed me several sheets of paper.

"You gotta fill these out," she said.

I took a seat on a wooden bench and went to work on the forms. All around me, visitors were feeding dollar bills into machines mounted on the walls, transforming their cash into tokens that could later be used in the commissary. The room sounded like the slots section of a Las Vegas casino.

A few moments after I returned the visitation forms to her, the clerk motioned me back to the counter and pointed at them. She had questions about what I'd written.

"What's your relationship with the inmate?" she asked.

"Friend," I told her, feeling ridiculous telling someone I was Dennis Rader's friend.

"What's your occupation?"

"Former FBI agent."

She wrote the word "investigator" in the blank, read over the form, then excused herself, disappearing through a door into a back office with several people in it. A moment later, she returned.

"Seems to be a bit of problem," she said.

Even though I half expected her to say this, I felt my heart begin to pound. Doing my best to look utterly unconcerned, I smiled. She trotted back into her office again, only to reappear thirty seconds later.

"Actually there are two problems," she said.

I wasn't interested in hearing what either of them might be. I wouldn't be leaving El Dorado without talking to Rader. If he wanted to shut down the interview, so be it. But I'd waited too long, traveled too many miles, and jumped through too many hoops to get here. So I dropped the names of some heavies in the state's law enforcement and Department of Corrections world who had either tried to get me in here themselves or were aware of my intentions to do so.

"Why don't you give them a call," I suggested, hoping she wouldn't. "I have all their numbers. I think they'd be interested to hear about the runaround I'm getting here."

She made several more trips in and out of her office.

"That way," she said, pointing to a metal door in a corner of the room.

I opened it, walked through a metal detector, and proceeded down a hallway lined on either side with bullet-resistant glass. Compared to Attica or San Quentin, El Dorado hardly felt intimidating. It was a clean, well-lit place that gave off a just-built vibe. It reeked of fresh paint instead of stale urine. And unlike nearly every facility I'd ever visited, it had actually been landscaped.

A guard met me at the end and stamped some sort of invisible ink on top of my hand, and I made my way into a room that resembled a community college cafeteria. Men and women sat across from one another at long tables, holding hands, speaking in hushed tones. A few of the men, all dressed in prison-issue jeans and blue T-shirts, bounced children on their knees. Violent offenders like Rader posed far too great a risk to be allowed the luxury of a face-to-face meeting with visitors. *These guys,* I thought to myself, *must be the best of the worst.*

Another clerk, standing behind another desk, waved to me. After handing her the piece of paper I carried with me, she studied it and announced, "You got two and a half hours."

Her words didn't sit well with the heavyset woman in Lycra shorts, standing nearby. "Hey, that's not fair," she shouted. "How come I only get one hour and he gets two and a half?"

I looked into her angry eyes as she gripped the hand of a chubby-cheeked toddler in a dirty NASCAR T-shirt.

"I've been waiting thirty years to get in here to talk to this guy," I told her, then watched the expression on her face soften.

The clerk handed me a key to a locker, directing me to place my sunglasses and wallet inside. Another guard led me to a row of four tiny wooden three-sided cubicles in a far corner of the room, each just wide enough to fit a chair. I took a seat and noticed the two TV screens, stacked one on top of the other, on the table in front of me on a wooden shelf. On top of the monitors was perched a tiny camera with a lens that resembled the barrel of 12-gauge.

The top screen displayed my image, the same one Rader would be seeing. On the lower monitor, I glimpsed a nondescript room painted the color of week-old custard. An empty chair sat in the middle of the floor. Dull white light shone in through a steel-barred window on a distant wall. I was dying to ask the guard where on the grounds of this massive prison facility the room on my monitor was located, but I decided against it. Everyone in here seemed so paranoid about security that I knew my question would only make them more nervous.

The room was empty. So I sat there for several minutes, marveling at how hot and sticky the air felt. Patches of sweat, I could feel, had begun to seep through my shirt.

Minutes passed . . . *Where the hell was Rader?* I wondered. A guard walked over and apologized for the delay, explaining that something had gone screwy with the audio feed between the two rooms.

Waiting for the guest of dishonor to appear, I thought back to something Casarona had mentioned the night before. Rader's mood had grown dark lately. A few days earlier, one of his violent fellow inmates thought it would be funny to forge Rader's signature on a "Do Not Resuscitate" form. Prison humor, I suppose. Not long afterward, one of the guards showed up at Rader's cell to make sure he had actually signed the form. Rader apparently stood there in the middle of the cell, staring at the piece of paper and reading the legal jargon over and over again, then informed the guard that the signature was bogus.

"Kind of thought as much," the man told him, then turned to leave.

"Wait," Rader said. He walked over to the tiny desk bolted into the wall, grabbed a pen, crossed out the imposter's scrawl, then wrote his name across the form.

"Here," he said. "Now I signed it."

I attempted to hold in my head that image of Rader standing there, reading that document. He was beginning to settle in. The novelty of his new life behind bars was starting to wear off, and that do-not-resuscitate form reminded him that the only way he would ever leave El Dorado — outside of being transferred to another prison — was zipped up in a rubber body bag, atop a gurney.

Fifteen minutes later, the screen of the lower monitor showed a door opening. Rader shuffled into the room, led by a guard. His wrists were handcuffed, and his legs were shackled in chains.

It hit me that Rader was far thinner and more gaunt than I could ever recall seeing him in photographs or on TV. He must have lost a lot of weight since he had been incarcerated. Maybe he didn't like the prison food.

Rader dropped down onto the chair and squinted in the direction of the camera. The blank expression on his face told me that the monitors on his end must still be black. He had no idea I was watching him.

I moved closer to the screen and observed beads of sweat glistening on his face. After a few moments he attempted to wipe away the wetness, but because of the thick steel chain extending upward from his legs to his wrists, he was unable to lift his hands more than an inch or two up from his lap. Instead, he was forced to double over and place his head into his knees in order to rub away the perspiration by sliding his face back and forth across his hands.

You'd think that for a guy who loved bondage, he'd be enjoying himself but the bored scowl on his face certainly didn't give any indication of that. A minute later, the sound of human breathing erupted from the speakers positioned in front of me. Judging by the self-conscious shift in Rader's void demeanor, I could tell that he was now staring at my image on the screen in front of him.

"Hello, sir," he said.

His use of the word *sir* startled me. It seemed terribly naïve and a bit calculated, especially considering that we were both the same age.

"Call me John."

Rader nodded.

"A mutual friend of ours sends her regards," I said.

He nodded again, no doubt conjuring up Casarona's image inside his head. "She's a very sweet woman," Rader said. "She's . . . she's been quite helpful to me."

"Yes," I told him, wondering if he'd already tortured and murdered her in his mind this morning. "I'm sure she has."

Rader's face went blank again as though he hadn't heard me, but I continued.

"There's something I'm supposed to tell you . . . The lion is strong, and it is very positive."

Rader squinted into the camera, then bent down, twisted his head sideways, and tapped his right ear with his hand. I could still hear his heavy breathing, but I had a hunch he was attempting to tell me that the sound on his end had gone on the fritz. Once again, we stared into each other's image on the screen in front of us, waiting in silence until the audio began working.

The moment the sound came back on, his face lit up as if a thought of great importance had just materialized in his mind. "Hey," he said. "Don't you have some sort of a code for me?"

This was getting more idiotic with each passing moment. "Yes," I replied. "The lion is very strong, and it is positive."

Rader nodded slowly, letting the words soak in. His mouth hung open slightly, causing him to look almost befuddled. I had a sneaking suspicion that he'd already forgotten what Casarona's damn code was, but decided to wing it.

"Very good," he said. "That's very good about the lion."

23

Dennis Rader sat in the black plastic chair, ramrod straight. The dark circles of sweat on his blue T-shirt were growing larger by the minute around his armpits and beneath his neck. In the past, I'd always paid close attention to the way my interview subjects perspired. It often meant they'd begun to lose control. But here in El Dorado all bets were off. The place felt like a goddamned sauna, and I was dying to take my sport coat off, but decided to keep it on. Rader no doubt was impressed by my feeling compelled to put on a sport coat for him.

"Sorry to hear about your mother," Rader said, squinting as he peered into the camera. His words hit me like a sucker punch to the gut. I figured Casarona might have told him about my mother's death three months earlier, but I never imagined that he'd bring it up. Something about a serial killer handing out condolences over the death of a loved one just seemed ironic. Not only that, he didn't mean it — because he couldn't mean it. At least not the way most people do. But he said it anyway, because it was one of those things that normal people said to one another, and Dennis Rader had long ago mastered the art of trying to do and say all the things that were expected of normal people.

"Thanks," I said.

Rader sat there and listened with a pensive, somber look plastered on his face as I continued to speak about my mother's death. He appeared as though he were trying to fathom what I was telling him, but I knew he could not. It was physically and psychologically impossible. And after a few moments, a thin, dull glaze had begun to descend over his eyes, so I decided to steer the conversation back to him.

"I had a hell of a time getting in to see you," I told him.

"Yeah," he replied. "There were a few people who rather we didn't talk. Two FBI agents came here a couple of months ago and told me that I didn't need to be speaking to you. They kept telling me, 'Forget about John Douglas. Talk to us' . . . I think they're jealous of you."

"They're not jealous," I told him. "They're just sore. I've butted heads with the FBI a few times since my retirement in cases where I believed they'd made a mistake. The Jon-Benet Ramsey murder was one of them."

I spoke slowly, trying not to appear too anxious to talk about his crimes. I wanted to establish myself as a guy who looked at all sides of a case, the kind who wasn't out to please either prosecutors or defense attorneys. I wanted him to know that I would give him a fair shake.

Rader peered intently into the camera and nodded his head slowly. "You don't think her parents had something to do with it?"

"No, I don't," I told him. "At different times during the investigation I was brought in by both the defense and the prosecution, but I walked away from that one convinced there was no way the family could have committed that murder."

"Why not?" he asked.

"When a parent kills a child, the body generally doesn't look like that little girl's did," I said. "After the murder, they usually attempt to undo the scene and make it appear more comfortable and peaceful for the victim. But JonBenet had been viciously garroted. Duct tape covered her mouth. Her hands were bound over her head. And shortly before she died, her skull was smashed with a blow that would have brought down a two-hundred-pound man."

Rader looked bored, fidgety. He'd begun to slouch just a bit. All this talk about some murder he'd played no part in had begun to annoy him, I could tell. He wanted this to be all about him.

Fearful he was on the verge of growing bored because I wasn't properly stroking his ego, I decided to switch gears and compliment him. I told him that I'd always been impressed with his ability to describe his crime scenes with such uncanny precision. Rader appeared happy to play along with me. His face once again took on that serious look. His head rocked up and down, and his back straightened.

"I remember every detail from every crime," he replied. "I remember every detail like most people do their favorite movie, and I play it over and over again inside my head. That's really how it all started back when I was a child. I had these thoughts and images that played out inside my head. The more I thought about them, the stronger they became. I just got so caught up in them that pretty soon . . . they took me over. I couldn't fight them anymore."

"I always felt you had to have had a camera in order to remember all that detail," I said. "You must have an amazing memory."

Rader turned his face away from the camera and stared off at a distant wall in the room where he was sitting. For all I knew he was daydreaming; perhaps he had just imagined wrapping a rope around Casarona's throat. Rader had spent a lifetime doing just that sort of thing — fantasizing not only about murder and torture but also about being famous, powerful, influential, and superior to everyone. When he finally returned and once again made eye contact with the camera, he quickly went to work trying to hoodwink me into believing he was a changed man.

"I'm trying not to think those thoughts anymore," he said. "I'm trying to have more control over my life, trying to stay away from all those fantasies. It's the only way for me now. When I wake up each morning, that's when the fantasies start — that was when they were always the most powerful and uncontrollable. Paula always got up before me, and I'd lay in bed thinking about all that stuff. But now I try and block out the images. I try and think about Paula and the kids and all the things I'm going to read and write for the rest of the day. And instead of drawing bondage pictures, I draw happy faces. And I read the Bible. Ask Kris. I often mention the Bible to her when we talk or when I write her letters.

"I'm a Christian, you know," he went on. "Always have been. After I killed the Oteros, I began to pray to God for help so I could fight this thing inside me. My greatest fear, even more than being caught, was whether God would allow me into heaven or would I be condemned forever. All my life I thought about that — even before I killed anyone. I wonder if God might not accept me because of my deeds, no matter how many times I ask for forgiveness."

All this blather about God, the hereafter, and forgiveness made me want to laugh, but I didn't dare. Religion was part of his façade he had used to fool those around him. Most people were shocked when the news broke that Rader was president of his church congregation, but I wasn't. When I learned about his longtime ties with Park City's Christ Lutheran Church, I wanted to shout: "Of course he was!"

Our landmark ten-year study on serial killers revealed as much. We learned that if these guys could choose a profession, it would be minister, police officer, or counselor.

Why? Because of the perks, of course. The single most obvious one being that all these professions involve some type of power and control over others. It's not surprising that in prison many violent offenders gravitate toward religion — not merely to be a member of a group, but rather to lead the group. Charles "Tex" Watson of the Charles Manson family and David Berkowitz (aka Son of Sam) are now jailhouse preachers.

But now I could sense that Rader had begun to loosen up, allowing himself to get comfortable with the idea of speaking to someone such as myself who represented the law enforcement community. According to Casarona, he still harbored resentment toward the cops, telling her he was upset with the way they allowed him to figuratively hang himself during his marathon interrogation session.

"I know about you," he said, chuckling. "I know about what you think of me."

"Do you?" I asked.

"Somebody sent me the newsletter from your Web site, the one you wrote last winter," he said. "You don't like guys like me. You think that all of us make choices, so we have to take responsibility for our actions. You said I deserved the death penalty."

He paused for a moment, chewed on his

lip, then continued. "I believe in capital punishment too, you know. And I suppose I deserve the death penalty. But since I never killed anyone after 1994, I'm not eligible for it."

"Is that what kept you from killing after Dolores Davis's murder?" I asked, not completely convinced that he hadn't taken another life after Kansas reinstituted capital punishment in 1994.

"No," he said.

Rader's words reinforced my belief that he knew exactly what he was doing when he committed his savage murders. It had nothing to do with any split personality, evil twin, or monster living within him. I thought back to how Rader's pastor at Christ Lutheran Church wanted to attribute what happened to his parishioner as an example of how a demonic force can corrupt an otherwise healthy, caring, well-adjusted man. I suppose that was the difference between me and a man of the cloth like Rader's pastor.

"It's not so bad in here," Rader went on, switching the subject. "They've got me in a twelve-by-nine cell. I have a little window that looks out over the fields. I can see robins out there in the grass. Sometimes I can even see butterflies. I watch a lot of sunsets, too. Every night I try and write up a little entry in my journal about the sunset I just watched.

"I do a lot of writing in here — letters mostly. I get a lot of mail. I miss being outside and getting to work in my garden. I had a pretty big garden at my house, out in the backyard. Maybe one day I'll be able to go out into the yard, here. That might be nice. But I guess it could probably be dangerous too. So I don't know . . ."

"You'd probably be a celebrity out in the yard," I said.

"Yeah, I know," he smiled. "Kind of like a rock star, I guess."

He paused again, bent down and wiped sweat — or maybe it could have been tears — out of his eyes, then continued. "This is Memorial Day weekend, isn't it? . . . You know, ever since my dad died, I'd drive out to the cemetery and stick flowers on his grave. Good guy, my old man. I asked Kris to do it for me. To ask him to forgive me, to tell him he didn't have anything to do with the way I turned out, to ask if he'd tell all my victims up in heaven to forgive me, but I'm not sure if Kris will."

"She's under a lot of pressure," I told him.

"I know she is," Rader said. "But I really like her. I really do. Not in a lover sort of way. It's nothing like that. She's had a hard time because of me, but she's stuck in there for me."

I clenched my teeth together. It amazed me how delusional this guy was. The only reason Casarona stuck in there with him was because she had no choice. The people suing her didn't care if she broke her contract with Rader or not. In their eyes, she'd cast her lot with the devil, and those lawsuits were her just deserts. She could crawl into a corner and try to wish it all away (I'd lost count of how many times she'd claimed to have done that). Or she could keep going and attempt to somehow finish this book that had made her life even more unbearable than it already was. What did she really have to lose?

"I want to thank you for the essay you wrote," I told him. "Kris gave it to me last night. Very interesting. But I've got something to ask you. Beside that question about whether or not your mother was overbearing, you wrote the number one-half."

"I can't tell you any more about that," he replied. "That's for Kris's book. I'm saving that for her. Are you going to help her get that published? She said you were."

"Yes," I assured him. "I'm going to try to help her. But I can't promise anything. Publishing is a tough business."

Rader's gaze dropped to the floor. A scowl

crept across his face. Silence. Casarona was correct: Rader looked depressed. His flat, monotone voice and his lifeless eyes were giveaways. Whatever rush he experienced by coming clean to the cops and from the media circus that ensued had begun to fade. The depression he'd grappled with for most of his life had no doubt returned, and now he had no way to hide from it.

I realized now that Rader hated himself with a passion. He always had. He may not have acted like it or revealed his self-contempt to another person, but deep down he loathed every molecule in his body. And because of that he was psychologically unable to love others or be loved. I'm confident that over time, he grew fond of Paula and his two kids, but the emotion he experienced when he was around them or thought of them had nothing to do with love. At best, it was a feeling of intense familiarity.

Rader was talking again, but the sound had gone screwy. I heard crackling coming out from my speaker, but I decided to keep talking until Rader indicated that he could no longer hear me.

"Something else I wanted to ask you," I told him. "I had this theory about why you started to cry over the Nancy Fox murder during your sentencing hearing. None of your other kills seemed to affect you, but that one did. You want to hear what I think?"

"Go ahead," he said. "Tell me."

"I've heard of this sort of thing happening from other guys I've spoken with," I told him. "Something happened during that murder. You always said Nancy Fox was your perfect victim, but after I watched you wipe away those tears, I figured it was because she said something to you, something that really got to you, and at that moment you suddenly didn't want to kill her, but you knew you had to. You knew you'd gone too far to allow her to live."

Rader scrunched up his face into the most serious look I'd seen all morning, appearing to mull over what I'd just told him. He stared into the camera, but somehow avoided looking at it with his eyes.

"I was pretty robotic during that whole day in court. I was on autopilot," he said. "I wasn't feeling much of anything. The reason I cried after Nancy's father's testimony was because I started thinking about Kerri, my daughter, and I thought about how I'd feel if something like what happened to Nancy Fox happened to her . . . That made me cry."

24

I stared at Rader's image on my screen. His mouth was moving, but the damn speaker appeared to have gone dead again. Because the only thing that ever came out of Rader's mouth was emptiness cloaked in words, I tried to convince myself that the malfunctioning sound system didn't matter. But I motioned for a guard to come over and fix it anyway. After a few moments spent shaking some wires and tapping the side of the TV monitor, the guard coaxed the speaker back to life, catching Rader in the midst of a ramble about what compelled him to commit his first murder.

"You already know what the precipitating event was," he said. "It was all because of my getting laid off at Cessna. I wasn't having any sexual problems with my wife or financial problems. It was all because of unemployment. It didn't seem fair. It just didn't seem fair. I really loved that job."

"Back up a minute, " I said. "The sound went on the fritz for a few minutes, just as you were about to tell me what it was that drove you."

A tiny smile returned to Rader's face. He seemed to be enjoying this.

"It was all psychological," he said. "My whole thing when I went into someone's house was based on a fantasy of bondage. I was especially into self-bondage. I wasn't a sadist. I never pulled the fingernails or toenails out of anyone. Sex was never part of my fantasy, either. I wanted power. I guess that's what I was really looking for. That's why Nancy Fox was my most perfect victim. I got to spend plenty of time with her without any interruptions."

"Tell me about your neighbor — Marine Hedge?" I asked, hoping to get him talking about his various murders. "You carried her to the basement of your church."

Rader twisted his face into another one of his ridiculous pensive expressions. "Yes, she was a good one," he said after a few moments of thought. "I really enjoyed that one. But you know what? Over the years, all the burglaries I began doing were almost as satisfying as the killing. I broke into a lot of houses, stole watches and jewelry and underwear. But it's just like you wrote in your books. The fantasy is better than the crime — because in my fantasies, everything was always under control. I played the director and the lead actor. Like I told you before, it's just like watching a movie. I see myself committing the crime, doing all the things I did in real life, only without all the headache or frustration. Because in real life things never quite turned out the way I wanted them to, the way I expected. My victims always seemed to react in ways I didn't plan."

Then Rader said, "You know, if there was one killer who I could identify with, it was Harvey Glatman."

I knew whom he meant. I said, "Yes, he was into binding and psychologically torturing his victims just like you. He was also the first serial killer we know of who chronicled every aspect of his murders with a camera and later developed the pictures in his home darkroom."

Rader's smile grew larger. The memory of this kindred spirit appeared to have lifted his mood.

"Kris told me about the book," I said. "Last night, she told me all about it."

"You mean Glatman's book, right?"

"Yeah," I replied. "Glatman's book. You told her that if she really wanted to understand you, all she needed to do is read the back cover of the book, the last couple of sentences."

"Kris told you that?" he asked, looking alarmed that she would have leaked this bit of information to me.

"You remember what the back of the book says?" I asked. "Because I do. I memorized it."

"You did?" he asked, obviously flattered that I'd gone to the trouble of memorizing something that I'd been told was so important to him.

" 'For decades,' " I said, reciting the copy from the back cover, " 'these infamous deeds would inspire television and movie plots. But until now, there has been no definitive account for the forces that drove one of America's most legendary serial killers. And never before has it been explained why, for Harvey Glatman, his crimes weren't about killing, raping and torturing at all — they were all about the rope.' "

Rader sat there, moving his lips as though he were repeating the words I'd just recited to him. I waited for him to say something, but he remained silent. So I spoke.

"So all you really cared about was binding your victims with rope?" I asked. "Was the hunting for victims, even the killing, just secondary? Your fantasy was to look at someone who you had totally immobilized and made powerless, someone who you were in total control of, free to do as you pleased."

He nodded, listening to me as though I were a doctor describing some type of physical condition that had troubled him for most of his life.

"So you never really wanted to sexually assault them. That would almost be like cheating on Paula, and you certainly didn't want to do that . . . What you wanted to do was masturbate as you looked down at the crime scene you'd created for yourself."

I waited for Rader to say something, but he remained silent. Judging from the look on his face, I wasn't telling him anything he didn't already know about himself. But he'd never heard it come from someone else's mouth before, and he seemed almost stunned by it, as if I'd held up a mirror in front of his face and the image he glimpsed staring back confused him.

A few moments later, he stammered, "But I was a little bit different than Glatman. He didn't communicate with the police and he didn't have a wife, a family, and all my social obligations."

Next, I brought in another serial killer, as I knew he loved the comparisons.

"I once mentioned your case to convince David Berkowitz, that Son of Sam guy, to speak with me."

Rader's face brightened when he heard that. "You used me to get to Berkowitz?" he asked. "When would that have been? What year?"

"That was in 1981," I told him. "Back when you were still working for ADT."

"You know a lot about me," he said, smiling. "But you know Berkowitz was also different than me. He was after lovers in the park — and his crimes, like you wrote in one of your books, were impersonal. . . . You know they have another serial killer in here named John Robinson."

"I know all about John Robinson," I told him. "I wrote a book about him several years ago."

"You did?" he asked. "I never saw that one."

"Nobody did," I said. "Nobody wanted to read about John Robinson."

"He was sort of like me because of all the bondage stuff he was into," Rader said. "But he was into that whole discipline and masochistic stuff which I'm not. He was more sophisticated than me when he chose his victims. He often used the Internet to lure them in . . . I found mine the old-

605

fashioned way. I got in my car and started driving.

"You know, I used to love driving around with classical music on, looking for projects in areas where I felt comfortable, where I knew my way around and felt familiar with the streets. I can't tell you how many times I cruised past the homes of my past victims over the years. I'd slow down and stare at the house and felt this feeling of accomplishment settle over me because that house was my trophy. It reminded me of what I'd gotten away with, of a secret I knew and nobody else did."

"Did you ever visit the graves of any of your victims?" I asked.

"No, but I cut their obituaries out of the newspaper and read them over and over again. But I never went to the cemeteries, though. I'd read that the cops sometimes staked out those places, so it didn't seem to be a safe place to go."

"What about if the police had organized a community meeting for residents, in order to update them on the killings and ask for citizen volunteers. Would you have attended?" I asked.

"No way," he said, shaking his head. "I'd know for certain that the place would be filled with police just waiting for me to show up."

I told him about my super-cop theory, explaining how the intended goal was to make the UNSUB identify with a single officer instead of an entire police force. As he listened, his eyes grew wide, and his tongue darted over his top lip as if he were trying to wet it.

"Yes," he said, grasping what it was I was speaking about. "Ken Landwehr was kinda like that. For the longest time I really liked him. He seemed like a good cop, a straight shooter. The two of us would have had a lot to talk about. You know, before they caught me, I sometimes thought about what it would be like to sit down with him and have a good long talk about everything.

"But then he lied to me about the computer disk and called me all those names. Said I was a sick pervert and all that. I respected him, but I don't respect him now . . .

"I think the guy I liked best was Richard LaMunyon. He was the chief of police back in the 1970s. Seemed like a real nice guy. I was hoping that he and I could sit down and have a cup of coffee at the jail after my arrest. But he never came."

Amazing. Rader still believed that he and the police shared some sort of professional camaraderie. I'd suspected that BTK was a wannabe cop back when I first looked at the case in 1979, but until sitting here and listening to him speak, I hadn't realized how entrenched his delusion was. If only we'd been able to better capitalize on this frailty of his, to use it against him. Part of me wanted to reach through the TV monitor and beat some sense into his brain. Talk about paradoxes. Rader was too savvy to visit one of his victim's graves or attend a community meeting, yet he somehow believed that Landwehr or LaMunyon would actually sit down to have a cup of coffee with him and chew the fat.

"How did it make you feel when LaMunyon stood up at that press conference in 1979 and announced that the police had no leads in the killings?" I asked.

"That felt good," he laughed. "No, that felt great. It meant the police didn't know anything. It meant I could relax and stop looking over my shoulder every two minutes. That was tiring. But something I didn't like was when that district attorney said I used to hang myself at Boy Scout outings. That's just not true. I wish you could clear that up for me in your book. I never did that. I never would have done that. That's one of the things that really bothers me. I love the Boy Scouts far too much to have ever done anything like that during a camp-out."

The fact that Rader strangled his neighbor during a Boy Scout camp-out didn't bother him in the least. Like every criminal, violent and nonviolent, he had his own twisted code of ethics. Murder was one thing. He just didn't want anyone to think he was the type who might do something weird like hang himself during a Scout outing.

Rader, of course, didn't know what I knew about him. I'd read an entry in his journal detailing his late-night exploits in the back of his truck during a camp-out during the mid-1980s. On that autumn night, Rader didn't wrap a rope around his throat, but he did strip off his clothes, pull on a pair of women's underwear and a bra, wrap himself up in ropes and dog collars, and clamp a pair of handcuffs over his hands. Problem was, the damn lock got jammed, and he couldn't remove the cuffs. So he lay there in the back of his truck, thrashing and grunting, sweating like a pig as he desperately tried to free himself.

He wrote in his journal that at one point he feared he might have to begin shouting for one of his young Scouts to help extricate him from his bindings. But then, at the last moment, all that perspiration lathering his body allowed his wrists to slide out of his cuffs. He removed the rest of his bindings, cleaned himself up, then returned to the campfire to listen to ghost stories and instruct whoever might be interested on some advanced knot-tying tips.

Rader's mouth was primed and ready now. Even if he didn't want them to, the words had begun to spill out of his mouth. I could push a bit harder, lean on him with just a little more force in order to get him to take me where I wanted to go.

Next I decided to ask him about his earliest victims — the animals. Since his arrest, Rader had flip-flopped over the issue of whether he bound, tortured, or killed any animals while he was growing up. His diaries touched on the subject. During his marathon gabfest with police, he confirmed as much, explaining that he'd often take the animals to a barn near his house and kill them. But lately Rader had changed his tune, telling Casarona that he never would have taken the life of an animal because he loved them far too much.

"Tell me about the animals, Dennis," I said. "How did you kill them, and why always in the barn?"

The face of the man on my TV monitor went stern. His thick, bushy eyebrows arched downward.

"I know where you're going with this," he said. "It's part of that homicidal triangle — along with bedwetting and starting fires. But I never killed any animals. I would never have done that. You know, at one time I wanted to be a vet? So I just couldn't do something like that to an animal."

I knew he was lying. But I also knew that I didn't dare call his bluff. All I could do was try to salvage a part of the truth. "OK, so you didn't kill them, but you tied a few dogs and cats up, right?" I asked. "And why always in barns? What was it about barns?"

For the first time all morning, he looked almost embarrassed. In his mind, torturing and killing humans was one thing, but performing the same atrocities on animals was something else altogether.

"I just always felt safe in a barn," he said. "Just something about them. Maybe because barns are always detached from the house, separate, off away by itself. You can do things in a barn and no one will interrupt you. It's more private than a basement, and I always liked basements. Did a lot of stuff in my parents' basement."

He stopped talking. Judging from the angle of his eyes in relation to the video camera in front of him, he was once again staring at the floor. He looked ashamed.

"I never killed any animals," he said. "But I did tie some up and then I masturbated next to them."

Why wouldn't he cop to it? I wondered. *Why couldn't he admit to torturing and killing an animal?* Part of the answer had to do with the contradictory, unsettling nature of violent criminals. They'll elaborate on the goriest details of a case, but then turn evasive over some minor point. In other words, Rader was embarrassed. I'd spent enough time working on farms in high school, hoping to earn school credits to get into a vet school, to know what sort of unspoken things sometimes occurred on a farm when no one was watching.

At Montana State University, where I spent a few years as an undergraduate, the coeds had a motto that went something like "Montana State. Where men are men and sheep are nervous."

That pretty much summed things up. Seeing Rader's shamed expression, I not only realized that had he killed his share of animals as a youth but also wouldn't have been surprised if he'd engaged in a bit of sexual experimentation with them as well.

That was what led me to my next question: "Tell me about your fascination with autoeroticism," I asked.

Rader's green eyes did a double take. His face went blank. "What's that — autoeroticism?" he asked. Once again, I realized we'd given him far too much credit. He appeared to have no idea that the activity he performed with a rope during his "motel parties," out in the privacy of the woods, or down in his parents' basement actually had a name. For all he knew, when I used the term "autoeroticism," I was talking about inserting a portion of his anatomy into the exhaust pipe of a car. So I explained the clinical definition of the term, and Rader once again shook his head back and forth, claiming he'd never hung himself because it was too risky.

"I just wouldn't do that," he said, his head now turned sideways. "That's far too dangerous. People die doing that sort of stuff, and that was the last thing I wanted to have happen."

He was lying, of course. Not only had several reliable sources confirmed as much, but I also knew that he'd written about this activity far too many times in his journals for it not to be true.

Yet Rader's twist on autoeroticism was unique. Unlike all the other case studies I'd researched, he didn't hang or suffocate himself in order to intensify an orgasm. It turned out that his sense of what caused him to get aroused was so tweaked that merely the sensation of being hung or suffocated was enough to induce an orgasm. I'd never heard of anything like this. Sitting there thinking about Rader stringing himself up made me think about Paula Rader. Plenty of the killers I'd tracked were married to women all cut from the same cloth — placid, easy-to-please, the kind of woman who wouldn't snoop around in her husband's belongings.

Then a new thought occurred to me: I would have wagered a case of Corona (Rader's favorite beer) that at least once in his thirty-plus years of marriage to her, Paula had walked in on Dennis in the midst of one of his kinky necktie parties.

"Man," I said. "This has got to be really rough on your wife."

Knowing that I'd made it this far without Rader walking out on me or shutting down made me a bit bolder. But I still didn't want to burn any bridges. If I played my cards wisely, I could pump him for information long after this interview wrapped up, using Casarona as an intermediary.

So I just grinned at him, one of those I-might-know-more-than-you, shit-eating kind of smiles. He knew damn well I was working him. He couldn't be that dense. He understood that I was beginning to sense something about Paula, something nobody else knew. His ugly face glared intently at the camera. When interviewing killers like Rader, I always tried to imagine what their faces looked like during one of their homicidal frenzies. I wondered if the expression I was staring at on my monitor was the same face his victims saw.

"Paula never knew anything," he said in a low growl. "She didn't know a thing . . . And they're punishing her. She deserves to get some compensation from the sale of the house, but they don't want her to. I hope some day she'll forgive me for all this."

Tears poured down his cheeks. Touching, really — that is, if one didn't understand that Rader wasn't crying for Paula. His tears were still exclusively for himself.

I gave him a few moments to wallow in self-pity.

Finally, I said, "No, I don't think Paula knew anything exactly, but I'm wondering if she ever saw anything. There's a difference, you know . . . There's a difference between knowing and seeing."

"Yeah" was the only word Rader uttered. His gaze appeared to be focused to the left of the video camera, somewhere front of him. He appeared dazed, lost inside the world behind his eyelids. I let him have a few minutes for himself to think things over, to let the seeds I'd just dropped into his brain take root.

"Anything else you want to tell me?"

I watched Rader double over again, attempting to smear what I knew to be tears from his eyes. By the time he raised his head back up, he looked more composed.

"You know, lately I've been thinking about what people can do to protect themselves from guys like me, and I came up with a little list," he said. "I guess most of it is pretty obvious, but I'll tell it to you if you like."

"I'm all ears," I said.

"The first thing I'd suggest for a woman living alone is to get a security system," he said.

"I have ADT," I told him, remembering how Rader once rigged a home alarm system he helped install for ADT such that if the mood struck him, he could break in and kill the female occupant.

"You do?" he exclaimed. "They're a really great company. I worked for them for years, you know. I really liked that job."

"I imagine you did," I replied.

"Back to my list," he said, aware that the clock was ticking. "For women living alone, I think the most important thing they can do is give the impression that they live with a man. Maybe have some men's clothes scattered around the house or leave a toiletry kit out in the open, just in case someone breaks in to scope the place out. It would also be wise to have two dogs — one outside and another one inside. And on the answering machine, have a man's voice on the outgoing recording. And you know how I used to cut the phone lines of houses? People should always check their phones whenever they enter their house . . ."

His voice trailed off, realizing how antiquated that piece of advice sounded.

"Since everybody seems to have cell phones these days, maybe that's not so important . . . But I do think it's a good idea to always leave the radio on in your house and avoid routines. Never take the same route to and from work or someplace like the grocery store. And the last thing would be for women to be extra suspicious of vehicles they see parked out in front of their house or apartment. I often used to drive back to my victims' homes over and over again and park out in front."

Rader's face once again went blank. His sweat-drenched head bobbed up and down.

"Is that it?" I asked, not exactly overwhelmed by his crime safety tips.

"Yeah," he said. "Just off the top of my head that's what came to me."

A guard walked toward me, tapping his wristwatch.

"I think we've got to wrap this up, Dennis," I told him.

"Yeah," he said. "I guess you and I have run out of time."

We stared at one another's image on our monitors. Neither of us spoke a word.

I thought about a line from Truman Capote's classic book *In Cold Blood,* detailing the 1959 farmhouse slaying of a family that lived in a small Kansas town west of Wichita. In it, Capote wrote of his strange bond with one of the killers — Perry Smith. "It's as if Perry and I grew up in the same house. One day, I went out the front door and he went out the back."

I sure couldn't say that about Rader and me, despite the uncanny biographical similarities we share. (We were born the same year; both of us wanted to be veterinarians; and we graduated from high school the same year, joined and were discharged from the Air Force the same year, and were married the same year.) I felt not a shred of kinship with the man. Nothing except a professional curiosity about the way his brain worked and what I might be able to learn to help the authorities keep someone like him from going so long without detection.

I'd like to think that if Rader and I had grown up in the same house, I would have had the courtesy to find some way to drop a cinderblock on his head and put him out of his misery, long before he began inflicting his nightmare on others.

"I'm trying to control it — I am," he said. "But the scary thing was how quickly the urge could come over me. I could be staring out the window, looking at something, and it would suddenly be on me and it would take me over . . . But I'm trying to get the upper hand now, now that I'm in here. You know, the other day the guards were walking me to the shower, and a bunch of the guys in the cells I passed by began chanting, 'BTK . . . BTK . . . BTK.' I listened for a couple seconds, then I stopped dead in my tracks and looked right at them and I told them, "I'm not BTK . . . I'm Dennis Rader.' Then I walked on to the shower."

I watched as Rader's eyes move deftly and subtly from the camera down to the screen, no doubt studying my reaction to what he'd just told me.

"Nice story, Dennis," I told him, because that was just what I believed it to be: a piece of fiction created solely for my benefit. For however much time Rader had left on this planet — and, if you ask me, he was living on borrowed time — he would forever be BTK. Being BTK was all he knew, all he ever did know. The Dennis Rader bit was just another gimmick, another ruse. Like some frustrated former high school quarterback sliding into middle age, he would forever be reliving his conquests until that day he took his last breath — something that couldn't come soon enough, as far as I was concerned.

"You know, I really liked speaking with you," he said. "It felt good to talk about this stuff. Maybe when all this dies down, you can come back and we can talk face-to-face, without all the cameras."

"Maybe," I told him. "I'll see you later, perhaps."

"Good-bye, sir," he said.

The screen went gray, then black, and the image of Dennis Rader disappeared.

25

A few hours later back in Wichita, Kris Casarona had a smile plastered on her face as she walked into the lobby of my hotel and took a seat in the tiny lounge.

"It's over," she said. "It's so over. I can't believe I just threw away my exclusivity like that. I just got off the phone with one of my friends. They can't believe I did this. Now I have nothing."

I sat there watching her, sipping my Chardonnay, not saying a word.

"You want a drink?" I asked.

"Yeah," she said. "Jack Daniel's and Coke . . . You know, the code word that Dennis and I use for you is Daniel because you've got the same initials as Jack Daniel's — JD."

"Why in God's name do you need a code name for me?" I asked.

"It was Dennis's idea," she said. "But we were both convinced that whenever we spoke to one another, the police were listening to us."

"They probably were," I told her. "Or they should have been. You know, they want to be able to pin another murder on Dennis. Something after 1994, so they can stick him on death row."

"I know," she said. "If he doesn't deserve the death penalty, who does? But I don't think he killed anyone after 1991."

"Neither do I," I told her. "He certainly never wrote about it in any of his journals. And he seemed to write about everything. I don't think he would have been able to leave something like that out."

Casarona's drink arrived. She raised her lips to the glass and drained part of it, shutting her eyes for a few brief moments as it slid down her throat. We both sat there in silence, listening to the old man in a tuxedo playing show tunes on a piano.

"I need to ask you something," I said. "Something I've been wondering about since Ken Landwehr mentioned it to me. Did Dennis ever tell you what happened just before he killed Julie Otero?"

"What do you mean?"

I told her what I'd learned about that January morning back in 1974 as he straddled Julie Otero's body on the bed and wrapped his sweat-drenched hands, sheathed in rubber gloves, around her throat. On the floor nearby, Joseph lay dead with a pillowcase tied over his head. In her heart, Julie must have known that her eleven-year-old daughter and nine-year-old son would probably soon be joining him, if they hadn't already. She was next. She must have known that. She didn't have a chance, and I couldn't imagine a more hopeless, powerless situation. Yet something inside this doomed woman allowed her to gaze up into Rader's face and whisper, "May God have mercy on your soul."

How does someone summon up such grace at such a terrible, horrifying moment, I've often wondered. It was a question I'd thought about from time to time, a question I never had been able to answer.

"So, did he ever tell you anything about that?" I asked. "Did he ever tell you how her words affected him?"

Casarona polished off her drink and motioned for the waitress to bring her another.

"Yeah," she said. "He told me about that. He told me that Julie's words dazed him. He told me that several days passed before he even remembered what she'd said to him."

"And then what?" I asked.

"And then he didn't think about it again for another three decades," she said, "but lately he has."

"Prison can do that to a guy," I said. "Lot of bush league philosophers in prison."

"What he told me was that he's begun to see Julie as a saint," Casarona said. "Which is also how he's started to see Paula."

"Nothing like hindsight, I suppose," I said.

"Yeah," she said, taking a sip out of her new drink, then chewing on a chunk of ice. She placed the glass back on the table.

"So," she said, "tell me what Dennis said to you. Tell me everything . . . Tell me everything."

So I did. It was the least I could for Kris Casarona.

By the time I started back to my room, it was nearly nine o'clock. I placed the key in my door, twisted it, then pushed it open. The first thing I noticed was a white envelope sitting on the burgundy carpet. Nothing was written on the front of it. I opened it and pulled out three typewritten pages. Whoever had written the letter felt the need to make one thing clear up front. None of what appeared on the pages that followed were to be quoted in my book. The reason I'd been sent this material was so that I might have all the facts. Whether or not I chose to use them in my book was up to me.

I fumbled for my reading glasses, then sat down on the edge of my bed and started reading. Slowly. One word at a time. Backing up every few words and going over what I'd just ingested. Ten minutes later, I'd finished. I folded the letter up, placed it back in the envelope, then lay down on the bed to think.

Whoever had written this was either close to Dennis or a confidante of Paula. Exactly why it came to be sitting inside my hotel room was hardly surprising. Wichita may be the largest city in Kansas, but gossip still moves through it the way it does in a small town. No doubt word had leaked out fast that I was coming here to interview Dennis, and someone had decided to help me in a way not unlike anonymous tipsters do when they phone police with a scrap of crucial information to help solve a crime.

I sensed that whoever wrote this note wanted to provide law enforcement with some useful, concrete information that would shed light on one of the most enigmatic unanswered questions about BTK — namely, why he went underground for so many years. It's only by understanding the answer to that question that we can find better, more effective ways to ensure that we never have another Dennis Rader.

My hunch was spot-on. It had gone down

much the way I'd imagined. According to my letter, the first time Rader had to go underground was in the autumn of 1978, when Paula walked into the tiny bedroom she shared with her husband and found herself staring at something that just about killed her.

Her husband.

Dennis had tied a rope around his neck and was hanging himself from a door in front of the bathroom mirror. He wore a dress, probably stolen during one of the countless home burglaries he had committed.

Nothing in Paula's sheltered, cloistered life spent in sleepy Park City could have prepared her for that strange sight. Rader told my source that this happened a few months after Kerri's birth in June 1978.

By then, Shirley Vian had been dead for roughly eighteen months. Ten months had passed since Nancy Fox's murder, which he considered his homicidal masterpiece. In February 1978, he had penned his infamous screed to police, announcing that there was a new serial killer on the block and that he was unstoppable. Fear and paranoia gnawed at the heart and soul of every resident of Wichita. Rader must have prided himself that he was at the pinnacle of his career as a serial killer. Then he seemed to vanish into the hot, humid air of western Kansas.

I'd never been able to answer why he'd disappeared. But now I could.

According to the letter, Rader claimed that Paula's discovery marked the most humiliating, embarrassing day of his entire life. Far worse, he said, than his arrest twenty-five years later.

He told this source that he had been prepared to get down on his knees and beg her for forgiveness, but it never came to that. His wife reportedly wasn't so much angry as she was sickened and concerned that something was terribly wrong with her husband's brain. She'd never heard of anyone doing something so downright disturbing and strange.

You need help, she reportedly told him.

The only problem was that she had no idea whom to turn to, especially as she was so embarrassed by it all — far too embarrassed ever to have the stomach to tell anyone about what had happened. This no doubt must have pleased the hell out of Rader, who described his wife to one of my sources as "sweet, sincere, naïve and the most reserved woman he'd ever known."

Obviously it was her naiveté that Rader found most attractive about Paula. Because even though the cat was out of the bag, Dennis couldn't have picked a better person with whom to have accidentally shared his secret. She was close to her mother, her two sisters, and a friend in Missouri, but he was fairly certain she'd never breathe a word of what she'd seen him doing to a single living soul. Who knows? Perhaps this was the real reason why this always calculating, perpetually plotting psychopath chose Paula to be his wife in the first place.

Having Rader speak with a therapist or a counselor was out of the question, Paula informed Dennis. It petrified her to imagine what people might think if word ever got out — and Lord only knows that it would in a town as small as Wichita. So, in a matter of days, Paula decided to summon up enough courage to telephone the VA Hospital in Wichita, where she'd once worked as a bookkeeper back during the Otero murders. Without identifying herself, she asked to speak with a therapist over the phone, confiding that a friend of hers had a problem with her husband and wondered whether they had any suggestions on how it might best be handled.

Whomever she spoke with gave her a list of several self-help books that addressed the issue she'd described. She bought every single title she could find and gave the books to Dennis, telling him he'd better read them and memorize every single page.

According to my source, he attempted to do just that.

Rader claimed that his biggest fear was that Paula would leave him, the source insisted. This made perfect sense. Without Paula, he would have no one running interference for him, no one to cover for him — even though Paula had no earthly idea that this was what she was doing. Rader knew that without Paula, it might be just a matter of time before people began wondering about him, giving him second looks and possibly starting to point fingers at him. Paula's departure from his life, he guessed, could very well be the beginning of the end.

Rader told my source that for the next two years he tried to clean up his act — at least when it came to practicing his unique form of autoeroticism. He did his best to go cold turkey from the rope. I have no idea what Rader did to quench his terrible, destructive hunger for the next two years. All I know is that one afternoon in 1980, it happened again. Paula walked into the bedroom and caught him with another rope around his neck.

This time, Rader told my source, his wife was no longer concerned that something might be wrong inside her husband's head. Instead, she was angry. Just plain ticked off. Mad as a goddamned hornet. This was obviously a reaction Rader hadn't foreseen. So he took what was a very calculated gamble. He informed Paula that he'd be willing to move out of the house, no doubt keeping his fingers crossed that she'd let him to stay.

Instead, Paula reportedly replied that she'd contemplate his offer, and for the next few weeks she barely uttered a single word to him.

Eventually she came around, although I think this was probably because she realized that allowing Dennis to leave would cause people to begin asking questions, something Rader knew his wife would not want. She told him that he could stay, but issued an ultimatum that even he knew he could never violate.

Paula, according to my letter, tersely informed her husband that he had better *never* do it again.

And Rader didn't. At least that's what he told my source. He never again put on a dress and hung himself from the bathroom door. The inside of the Rader home became off-limits for that sort of overt, blatantly strange activity. Instead, he waited for one of his "motel parties" or when he was alone out in the woods to break out his rope.

He knew that Paula would probably never give him another chance. Even worse, he feared, she might begin connecting the dots that would link his bizarre actions with those of the mysterious strangler everyone in Wichita seemed to be talking about.

It was late, and I was wiped out. I picked up the phone and dialed the front desk. "Did somebody drop off a letter for me at the front desk?" I asked the clerk.

"Hold on," she said. A moment later, she returned to the line. "No. We're you expecting one?"

I awoke the morning after my trip to El Dorado with a dream about death still fresh in my head. I couldn't recall the specifics, but I knew I'd been murdered some time in the night when my eyes were shut. I've always believed that of all the ways to go out, that would be the easiest — simply to shut your eyes and never open them again. Far kinder and more humane than most of the murder cases I had worked in my lifetime, in which victims begged to be killed rather than endure another moment of the torture session at the hands of their psychopathic captors.

After toast and a cup of coffee, I decided to drive back over to Rader's abandoned house in Park City. A beat-up wooden bench in his backyard was calling me. I'd spotted it seven months earlier on my first visit to the property, perched amid an overgrown tangle of weeds and grass. I wanted to sit on it and have a nice, long think.

The streets and highways of Wichita were empty, barren on that Monday morning. The place felt like a ghost town. From my hotel, the drive to Park City took less than ten minutes. On the way, I couldn't get last night's letter out of my mind. It had come from someone who would only identify himself or herself as close to Rader, although this could be anyone from Casarona to the handful of pen pals Dennis had attracted since his arrest. I wondered if it might be the same person who had contacted me months earlier with some inside information about Dennis. This time, the source wanted to pass on some answers to me about Paula, answers to the question I'd posed to Rader regarding what his wife would have known about his terrible, destructive appetite. If this letter was correct, it turned out that Paula didn't know anything about her husband's being a killer, but she had seen something to upset and anger her about his sexual acting out.

I also speculated that probably Rader himself was behind the letter. Perhaps he'd phoned the source after our prison meeting because a few of my questions had wormed their way into his thick head, and it concerned him that some people out there might still suspect that Paula had somehow covered up for him during those years he was on the lam. Then again, it could have been any of a number of people. A handful of folks knew I'd come to town this weekend in order to interview Rader.

From my conversations with his friends, police, and other sources, Rader had never once stopped to consider the ramifications his murders would have on his family. According to Casarona, the couple had roughly $7,000 in savings at the time of Rader's arrest, leaving Paula with precious little to live off of when her husband was promptly sacked from his job a few days later.

Judging from Rader's comments he made to me at El Dorado the morning before, the wake-up call about the mess he'd made of his wife's life came when Paula tried to sell the family's house in July 2005. The would-be buyer, who happened to be a well-intentioned, publicity-savvy owner of a popular strip club in the area, backed out of the deal upon learning that a civil lawsuit on behalf of the surviving family members of Rader's victims would block any of the cash from ever going to Paula.

Now the house I was driving toward sat in limbo, and Paula worked as a bookkeeper at a nearby Park City convenience store to make ends meet. So far, people have chosen to respect her privacy and leave her alone, including me. Ever since her husband's arrest, she's spent most of her time living with her parents and said she had no interest in ever again stepping foot in the house where she and Dennis lived for over thirty years.

Shortly before reaching Rader's house, I decided to take a short detour and stop by Rader's place of employment to see if there was anything I might have missed during my visit there with Landwehr months before. For fourteen years, Rader's job in Park City's city hall served as his refuge. The freedom his position granted him, not to mention the ego gratification, was one of the factors that kept Rader from killing with the frequency that he longed for. I think it would be safe to say that Rader's being a compliance officer might actually have saved a handful of lives in the community because the job allowed Rader's imagination plenty of room to breathe. Other than being incarcerated, there was perhaps no safer way for him to occupy his time for eight hours each day, five days a week.

The parking lot was empty when I arrived. Waves of heat radiated up from the vast expanse of black asphalt as though from a skillet. The only vehicles in the lot were two bone white Chevy pick-up trucks in which Rader often tooled around the streets of Park City. I pulled up next to one of the trucks, rolled down the window of my car, and touched the tiny sticker over the rear quarter-panel; it read CODE ENFORCEMENT. It felt as though it had been cooked with a blowtorch. I pressed my hand against it and thought about how Rader used to crank up classical music on the stereo inside these vehicles and head off across the community, fantasizing about strangling people, while talking dirty to the "slick ad" he'd brought with him and placed in the passenger seat.

I rolled the window up and sat back in my car with the air conditioner on high, staring out through my windshield, reminding myself that this was the exact view Rader took in each day as he pulled in and out of this parking lot. In order to get to his office on the left side of the squat brick building,

Rader had to walk across the parking lot and follow a little concrete sidewalk around the side of the structure.

But seated there in the sweltering late morning heat, I realized something. On the far right side of the building, completely opposite to where Rader's office was located, sat the headquarters of Park City's ten-officer police force. As often as Rader told himself that he loved his job as a compliance officer, deep down he knew it was an ill-fitting substitute for what he truly yearned to be doing: working as a cop. Every morning, instead of heading to the right side of the building, to the police station, Rader was forced to follow the little sidewalk that stretched to the left, to his job as a dog-catcher. It was just one more disappointment in a life filled with disappointments.

The drive to Rader's house took only about three minutes. To get there, I drove past the city's tiny public library, located in a run-down mini-mall, where he often did much of his research for his final barrage of communiqués to police.

Rader's neighborhood felt like a cemetery. At this hour, the sun burned so hot overhead that nobody bothered watering their lawns. Hours would pass before the hoses and sprinklers were turned on. I parked, walked up Rader's cracked, crumbling concrete driveway, and noticed a sign in the plate-glass window of his neighbor's house advertising piano lessons. Could this be the same neighbor mentioned in his journal? I wondered. The one he fantasized over as she clipped evergreen boughs from her shrubs to make a holiday wreath?

There was nothing out of the ordinary about his place. It was roughly the same size as all his neighbors' homes and — besides having an overgrown yard — resembled every other residence on the street. People always seem surprised whenever I tell them how unremarkable the home of a killer can be. Of course, it's only human nature to want anything associated with a monster to stand out, much as everyone wanted Rader to resemble some sort of hideous ghoul with blood dripping from his teeth, someone who could be easily plucked out of a crowd.

The problem is, they look like us and to some degree can act like us. The only time they don't occurs during those horrifying few moments when they morph into their true identity as a secret killer. But precious few people ever get a glimpse of that side of the killer's personality. And those who do seldom live long enough to tell anyone about it.

I made my way to Rader's backyard and stood there in the middle of the brown, dead grass, surveying the space that stretched off behind Rader's house. I've always felt that if you wanted to understand someone, all you need do was spend some time in his backyard; it is there, hidden by the façade-like front of his home, that a person dares to act out all those things he keeps hidden away from the rest of the world.

The yard was large and comfortable, roughly the area of two tennis courts laid side by side. Tall, leafy hickory trees bordered much of the perimeter of the yard, but in the center the sun had baked the ground into hard clay. When I spotted Rader's empty, battered aluminum storage shed, I poked around inside, searching for something I figured I'd know when I saw it. But the shed had long since been picked over — no doubt by the police or someone looking to make a few bucks on eBay. I made a note to myself to check the Web site to see if any of his belongings turned up there.

Rader kept his fishing gear back there in that shed, a source had told me, but it was gone now — except for a few hooks scattered on the floor, a couple of sinkers, and a tiny ball of knotted-up nylon fishing line.

Standing there, it occurred to me that this was perfect fishing weather, and I found myself wondering if Rader was standing at the window of his prison cell, looking out across the prairie, thinking this exact same thought.

I recalled another story I'd heard from Casarona about Rader that happened on a day similar to this one. He was gazing out his cell window, daydreaming about God only knows what. He noticed a prison employee picking up trash in a stretch of grass near one of the many fences that encircled the facility. Rader's attention turned toward the man's slow, languid movements as he picked his way across the tough, wind-burned blades of grass. His head was fairly quiet. Rader wasn't thinking about much of anything, but suddenly everything turned to shit, just the way everything did in his life. Because when the garbage man turned and spotted the familiar-looking visage of Dennis Rader staring at him through one of the prison's thick bullet-resistant windows, it was clear that he didn't like what he saw one bit.

In the time it took Rader to blink his eyes, the garbage man held up his middle finger, flipping Rader off. This rubbed Rader the wrong way.

Who the hell did that guy think he was? Rader heard himself think. *That idiot is an employee of the state's Department of Corrections. His behavior certainly isn't the type of conduct taxpayers should tolerate. It's not only disrespectful; it no doubt violates some sort rule of conduct for state employees.*

So Rader turned away from his prairie vista and put out a call for a guard. When the guard arrived at Rader's cell, Rader told him what had just transpired and how he didn't much appreciate being flipped off. The guard wrote up a report and disappeared. A few minutes later, Rader heard the cellblock's speaker system crackle to life.

"Whoever flipped off BTK," the voice intoned, "needs to stop. He finds it disrespectful . . . Again, whoever flipped off BTK, please stop this disrespectful behavior at once."

Rader smiled and shook his head. *That ought to take care of that,* he told himself. A split second later, the cellblock exploded into a cacophony of laughter, jeers, and whistles. Before Rader knew it, he was laughing too.

It was a peculiar image, I thought. Because at first glance it almost appeared that Rader was laughing at himself. But he wasn't. This would have been impossible for an egomaniac like Rader. He would never have mentioned this incident to Casarona if he had understood that those other inmates were laughing at him. Instead, he interpreted the event as yet another example of how, for a brief instant, he'd become the center of the universe, the guy everybody was thinking and talking about.

He was BTK, he told himself. Even in prison, he was the guy giving orders, and, narcissistic sociopath that he was, he expected special treatment.

I poked around the backyard a bit longer, kicking at the dirt and dead grass, checking out what remained of Rader's vegetable gardens, where he claimed to enjoy futzing about on summer evenings after work. His two black plastic compost bins were nearly covered over by vines and weeds. Of all the low-life psychopaths in whose lives I'd immersed myself, Rader had his role down pat. No wonder it took police so long to catch him. He could out-normal even the most normal person. If they gave out awards for alter egos, he'd be a contender for an Oscar.

I tried to imagine Rader back here, playing with his kids, pushing his daughter, Kerri, on the now rusted swing set or sitting up on the now splintered planked floor of the treehouse with Brian. No matter how I attempted to picture a scene out of an idyllic Norman Rockwell painting, the images of Rader interacting with his family always lapsed into something hellish, terrifying, something resembling a canvas by Hieronymus Bosch. The vision caused me to experience yet another deep pang of pity for Rader's wife and kids. What could compel a man to play charades like that with the three people who trusted him most?

The rickety aluminum and wood bench sat in a corner of the yard near the swing set, facing away from the house. I dropped down on it, feeling it nearly collapse beneath my weight, then closed my eyes for a moment, listening to the pulsing sounds the locusts made in the hot, still air. Off in the distance to the west, I could see a bank of dark storm clouds forming.

I thought back to that sweltering afternoon in August 2005 when millions of Americans glued themselves to their TV sets as BTK detailed his murders. Listening to how calculated and planned each of his homicides were, hearing him discussing his crimes like a chef discussing a menu, sickened me — even with all my experience with guys like this. I've often wondered about the impact it must have had on regular folks. Standing there in that Sedgwick County courtroom in the suit he'd last worn to church, Rader became our nation's newest, darkest anticelebrity.

Tucked away in the front pocket of my shirt was the letter I'd found in my room last night. I rubbed my fingers over the fabric to make sure it was still there before pulling it out, unfolding it, then spending the next few minutes reading over the three pages of text again.

I wondered if Paula ever sat out here on those Saturday mornings when, I was told, Dennis used to shoo everybody out of the house so that he could "tidy" the place up, leaving him alone to rummage through his stash of mementos from his kill.

I wondered if this might have been where she went the first time she caught her husband hanging himself in drag. I tried to picture her out here, confused, hurt, wondering how the man who always told her he loved her could do such a thing. In her own way, Paula Rader performed a minor miracle. Although this is of no consolation to the families whose relatives her husband murdered, when Paula stumbled on Dennis hanging from the bathroom door, she inadvertently forced him to go into a type of low-grade hibernation. Outside of being arrested or killed, this was potentially the best thing that could have happened to Rader, preventing him from killing with even greater frequency. Who knows how many lives Paula may have saved?

It was nearly one in the afternoon. I had a night flight to catch back to Dulles International that left from Kansas City, so I decided it was time to start my four-hour drive to the airport. Walking back across Rader's yard, part of me wanted to put a match to his house, to erase this ugly monument to the lie he lived for decades. I doubted any of his neighbors would care.

But, as interesting as I'd always found arson to be from a criminology standpoint, I hurried to my car, climbed inside, and cranked up the air conditioning. A few minutes later I was speeding past Wichita, making my way back to the interstate that would take me to Kansas City. Fields of wheat and corn rushed past my window for nearly an hour before I noticed the message light flashing on my cell phone.

I looked at the numbers and saw that Casarona had just called, so I retrieved the message.

"I can't take this anymore," she moaned. "Last night, I talked to Dennis. I swear to

God half the time I feel like I'm talking to a little boy, not the monster I know he is.

"You know what he tells me? He tells me that he's felt depressed all day and says, 'I know I have no room to say this, but I really miss McDonald's. I really miss their hamburgers and fries.' I almost dropped my phone. Can you believe that? He killed ten people and he feels bad that he can't have a cheeseburger and fries. What do you say to that? I wanted to throw up. I made myself stay calm. I felt like his mother or something.

"I said in this really patient voice, 'Dennis, you really need to remember why you're in there. You need to remember that.'

"He got all silent after that, then he said, 'Yeah, I guess you're right.' I can't take this anymore, John. Why did I ever write him that damn letter? I have no idea how can you stand doing this . . .'"

Casarona's voice faded away. I figured I must have hit a dead zone.

I continued my trek east as my head churned through everything I'd absorbed over the past few days. Ten people were dead; countless other lives had holes torn out of them, holes that would forever remain empty.

All because of one man.

For just over three decades, I'd been trying to understand the man who called himself BTK. I'd now spent the past year immersing myself in his world, interviewing the cops who tracked him, talking to his friends, reading his journals, pouring through the words and images he left behind on paper. Here was what I had learned:

What was his motive? Initially, Rader's motive for killing was simply to act out his bondage fantasies with a victim, then kill her. Nothing too complicated about that. But his reasons for killing began to evolve when he realized what effect his actions had on the men and women of Wichita. The adrenaline rush proved intoxicating. The community feared him. Overnight, he'd gone from being a pathetic nobody to an all-powerful puppet master. He pulled the strings and everybody danced. Before long, terrorizing the community and outwitting the police became as satisfying as acting out those dark fantasies on his victims.

How did he pick his victims? What Rader really sought were women who were vulnerable. Nothing more. His victims could be any age. All that mattered was that he could bind and dress them exactly the way he wanted. Rader really didn't care what his victims looked like, because once he'd taken their lives, they became virtual entities existing only his mind, where he could sexually assault them over and over again, embellishing all the details of the crime or their physical features in any way he wanted.

How was he able to elude law enforcement for so long? Rader was a former criminal justice student and a police buff. He was an "organized type" of serial killer, meaning that he carefully thought about and planned each of his homicides. All of his victims — besides his neighbor Marine Hedge — were total strangers. For law enforcement, these so-called stranger homicides are the most difficult to solve. Something else he had going for him was patience. This is a quality not often found in the other serial killers I've studied. He didn't murder with regularity. He could go years between killings because he was able to sustain his fantasies by taking personal items from his victims, then using them during his masturbation sessions while reliving his crimes.

Why had Rader resurfaced after all these years? In January 2004, the *Wichita Eagle* ran a thirtieth-anniversary story on the Otero homicides. The article chronicled the efforts of a local attorney who was in the process of writing a book about BTK. I learned that these two events worked together to flip a switch inside Rader's fragile ego. He'd be damned if someone else was going to pen a book about him when he was the only one who knew what his motivation was; what drove him into bondage, torture, and killing; what really happened during each of his homicides. So he decided to write his own book, and eventually began sending messages to the media and police. In the end, his ego turned out to be his downfall; we in law enforcement should have used it against him much sooner.

What made Dennis Rader a serial killer? It has always been my opinion that killers like Rader aren't born bad. From what I'd learned, Dennis wasn't physically tortured as a child. His ideas about bondage stemmed from an experience he had had as a young boy, walking into his mother's bedroom and finding her entangled in her bed. The image lodged inside his head and festered. Several years later, he began tying up animals, drawing pictures of torture chambers, and sketching portraits of women bound in ropes and chains. Later in life, Rader began to devour detective magazines filled with stories about women being bound and tortured, along with true crime books. None of this material caused him to kill, but the material did fuel the preexisting fantasies that festered inside his head.

How can we prevent another BTK? It's much too late to stop the pain and horror caused by BTK. But understanding where we went wrong in our investigation is the best way to prevent another BTK from enjoying such a long reign of terror and carnage. To answer that question you only have to start with that image of Rader's wife walking in on her husband hanging himself in full drag. Both times this happened it scared the hell out of Dennis — not enough to keep him from killing again, but enough to spook him. He feared that Paula would be able to connect the dots and gulp, "Oh my God, my husband is BTK!"

But another part of him knew that he had little to worry about. Why? Because in those early years of the case, law enforcement agencies released precious little information about the UNSUB's probable behavior, traits, and characteristics.

That was where I now believed we should have handled things differently.

We knew from BTK's writings that at the very least, he was a police buff. More than likely, he was a wannabe cop. He described the scenes of his crimes as though he were a veteran member of CSI. I remember telling myself the first time I read his writings that in all probability, the UNSUB was a student of criminology. Knowing that Wichita State University offered such a program would have been a logical lead early on in the investigation.

We also knew from the crime scenes that BTK was heavily into bondage, an interest that doesn't blossom overnight. Therefore it seemed logical that BTK would possess a stash of pornographic material containing a fair share of bondage photos.

His artistic ability was another trait that didn't just sprout one day. Of course, he was far too careful to sketch women wrapped in ropes and chains while he was watching the nightly news with his family. But surely someone had witnessed him drawing human figures, possibly even women — perhaps it was something as simple as tracing a picture out of a magazine. Perhaps a family member had stumbled on a couple of Rader's drawings of women in bondage, strapped to some torture device, or depictions of his crime scenes. Maybe that's what his son saw. Yet because members of the community were unaware of all the specifics of Rader's crimes, they couldn't be expected to connect the dots even if they did find some of his drawings.

That's one of the most important things I learned regarding proactive police techniques. Once the leads begin to dry up, law enforcement departments need to begin releasing more information. It's crucial to get the community involved, to give people enough background into the case that they can better understand what drives the UNSUB, allowing them to become extra eyes and ears for law enforcement.

Police also had examples of BTK's handwriting and did, at one point, release a sample of the writing to the media. That Paula, who once noted the similarities between BTK's poor spelling and that of her husband, reportedly never saw this sample tells me that this release should have been handled in a different manner.

Several years ago, one of my former profilers working a triple homicide in the Tampa area came up with the idea of plastering a portion of a note written by the UNSUB on billboards in select parts of the city. Within twenty-four hours, someone recognized the handwriting, and the perp was arrested not long afterwards.

I strongly believe that Rader's wife and children, his colleagues at work, his friends at Christ Lutheran Church, and other fathers in his Boy Scout troop could have recognized the behavioral characteristics of Dennis Rader had we released this information sooner, in a systematic, controlled way. The problem was that in the 1970s and 1980s, we were still learning. That sort of thing just wasn't done. Today I believe we've accumulated the smarts and experience to nip a serial killer like Dennis Rader in the bud.

Releasing this sort of information would have had a profound effect on Rader — or any UNSUB that law enforcement would be attempting to identify in an ongoing investigation. Turning up the heat in this way would have created a tremendous amount of stress, causing Rader to become even more nervous and preoccupied with the case. Once that happened, he'd begin exhibiting behavior that those around him would probably have never witnessed before.

This could include buying every available newspaper he could get his hands on, channel surfing the TV, and constantly switching between radio stations while listening for updates in the case. He might have begun either growing facial hair or shaving it off, losing weight or putting it on, drinking more than usual, becoming more prone to arguments, or experiencing difficulty falling asleep and then waking up in the middle of the night and listening to late-night news. Perhaps he would have been looking for a legitimate reason to leave town for short periods, or his behavior might morph from appearing incredibly rigid and overcontrolled to seeming sloppy, careless, and disorganized.

More than anything else, what the BTK case did was reinforce my belief that the authorities need to supply information to the general public the moment they've exhausted all logical leads. More often than not, this can occur within a few days or sometimes within a few hours of launching an investigation.

The key here, however, isn't to release every bit of information known about the UNSUB — merely certain telling, helpful bits. The rest should be held back, lest the authorities be inundated with false confessions from people looking for some sort of perverted notoriety. Those select bits and pieces of the crime analysis that are released, along with interviews with investigators and press releases, should be distributed in piecemeal fashion. If no credible leads develop, the information should be periodically rereleased, along with fliers about the case, containing characteristics about the UNSUB.

Monetary rewards are another good idea. They seem to work best when the informer can remain anonymous. The informer is given a "code," which is nothing more than an identifying number or a word, when he or she supplies a possible lead or suspect name. Money will be paid if there is an indictment, which tends to be more effective than saying that payment will be "based on a conviction." Because this approach is designed purely for its "lead value," it doesn't require the informant to testify in court, another incentive, as in most cases the person being informed on is a family member, an associate from work, or a friend.

Another strong tool for law enforcement is the media. Although I've often been in the minority, I've always believed that the press can serve as a powerful ally of law enforcement. In many of the cases I worked on, I attempted to develop a strong bond with investigative reporters in the towns and cities where that particular crime had been perpetrated.

Unfortunately, even decades later, there are still some police departments and other law enforcement agencies whose only comment to the media is "No comment." Big mistake. The media, if properly managed, can be good friends to a criminal investigation.

In the case of BTK, I believe police might have been more effective in their efforts to catch him if they'd played things a bit differently. Of course, back in the 1970s, that wasn't how things were done. Police kept a tight lid on case information, releasing it only when absolutely necessary. But now we know differently, and I'm convinced that if the authorities had taken a more proactive approach, disseminating very specific details about BTK to the public, someone who was acquainted with Rader might have recognized him and tipped off police that they knew of someone who seemed to fit the description of the man they were seeking.

What sort of details would have allowed the public to make this connection? First, it would have been crucial to let the community know what sort of pre- and post-offense behavior someone like BTK would have exhibited. Second, his interest in detective magazines and bondage-oriented porn and his "gift" of drawing people, particularly women, would have been a useful bit of information to release. Another useful data point that should have been shared with the public involved BTK's fascination with law enforcement and the likelihood that he might have attended Wichita State University. Finally, the likelihood that he practiced autoeroticism should have been circulated to the community. We now know that Paula caught her husband hanging himself on at least two occasions, but she was never quite clear on what he was actually doing and how it could have connected Dennis to the BTK murders.

Paula Rader had been a loyal and loving wife. But if she had somehow received more detailed information about the behavioral traits of the UNSUB terrorizing her community, I believe she would have notified law enforcement, telling them everything she knew — even if she had done so anonymously.

But that was then, and this is now. Since 1974 we've learned volumes from the Dennis Raders of the world. There will always be violent offenders, but today law enforcement has a much better understanding of the motives and the minds of violent offenders.

One of our greatest and most underused tools is the FBI's Violent Criminal Apprehension Program, known as VICAP. What this computer analysis does is determine, for example, if two cases that occurred years apart and in different areas of the nation might have been perpetrated by the same offender.

In 1985, I was present when French Smith, then the U.S. attorney general, cut the ceremonial ribbon, launching VICAP. Over two decades later, the program still depends on departments voluntarily submitting their unsolved cases for review and analysis.

The fact that VICAP isn't a mandatory program not only saddens me but sometimes keeps me awake at night. Our nation has more than seventeen thousand different law enforcement agencies operating within its borders. For whatever the reason, precious few communicate with one another, nor do many feel compelled to share information. This needs to change — and fast. We desperately need a mandatory VICAP program in this country. It won't eradicate serial violent offenders, but it will allow the authorities to intercept them much earlier in their criminal careers.

Shafts of white sunlight shone down on the fields dotted with alfalfa rolled up in tractor-sized clumps resembling giant pieces of shredded wheat. The odor of skunk hung in the air. Warm blasts of highway wind slammed against my elbow as I drove with it jutting out the window. In the distance, that dark bank of clouds I'd first spotted hours earlier in Rader's backyard loomed closer. Their color reminded me of a deep, painful bruise.

I was trying to put Dennis Rader far behind me, but couldn't. I was too tangled up inside my head, sifting though the past few days. It isn't wrong for us to be interested in heartless predators like Rader, I thought to myself. What is wrong and pathetic is the deep, powerful craving we have to get inside their skin.

People often ask me why I want to write books about inhuman monsters like Dennis Rader. My answer is always the same: I've always believed that by taking the sensationalism out of the crimes, I can destroy the myth. I describe the gory details of their crimes, but never try and sensationalize their actions.

By recounting the story of the coward and loser that Rader — and every other serial killer — really is, I hope to cut the "legend" down to size.

Most of all, I believe that by explaining how the mind of a serial killer works, I can begin to help readers understand how to avoid ending up as a victim of violent crime.

Another hour had passed. I'd been so lost inside my head that I hadn't noticed the sky. It had turned the darkest shade of black I'd ever seen. I pulled over to the side of the highway, realizing that everything around me was illuminated by a greenish glow.

My heart began pounding. I killed the engine and climbed out of the car. Such stillness. The air felt dead. Nothing moved. I stared at the iridescent black sky above, trying to remember the last time I'd seen it go so dark in the middle of the afternoon. I climbed back into the car and switched on the radio.

Further on down the road, I began to see jagged veins of lightning flashing, causing the radio to crackle. According to a news report, flash floods had just torn through several nearby towns. Looking out the passenger window, I noticed the vague outline of tiny shadowy funnels dangling beneath a ceiling of roiling clouds on the horizon.

Tornado, I thought to myself.

There was nothing to do but sit there and watch the shapes forming overhead. From out of nowhere, a thought swirled inside my brain, and I found myself thinking about a dream Rader had recited to Casarona a few days before my arrival.

The first portion was blurry in my memory, but what I remembered most was the tornado. According to Rader, a twister had just ripped through Wichita, and afterwards he found himself walking through the wreckage, picking his way through the debris strewn across the ground. Everywhere he looked, houses, cars, and trailers had been smashed into millions of tiny splintered pieces. And every few feet he walked, he stopped to pick up a tattered photograph or what had once been a child's toy from the rubble. He held the torn, ripped bits of life in his fingers, inspecting each piece, wondering . . .

If any single image summed up the devastation Rader inflicted on the community of Wichita, and on his own family, this was it. He was that dark, dirty, swirling twister, dropping out of the sky, destroying whatever he touched.

The thought of it made me tired. I wished I could be done with Rader and put him behind me completely, although I knew that would never happen. He and those like him were my calling. Like it or not, I'll be attempting to understand how their minds work for as long as blood and air flow through my body.

The rain had come; it poured down in thick sheets. The highway was empty. I sat there on the side of the road, thinking about nothing and everything at the same time. A tiny ribbon of blue sky and golden sunlight shimmered on the horizon, just below the curtain of black clouds. So I twisted the ignition, stomped on the accelerator, and drove like hell straight toward it, straight for the light.

ABOUT THE AUTHORS

John E. Douglas, Ed.D., entered duty with the FBI in 1970 after serving four years in the U.S. Air Force. He gained investigative experience in violent crime in Detroit and Milwaukee field offices and also served as a hostage negotiator. In 1977 Douglas was appointed to the FBI Academy as an instructor in the FBI's Behavioral Science Unit, where he taught hostage negotiation and applied criminal psychology.

In 1990 he was promoted as unit chief within the FBI's National Center for the Analysis of Violent Crime. Serving in that capacity, he had overall supervision of the Violent Criminal Apprehension Program, the Criminal Investigative Analysis Program (better known as criminal profiling), and the Arson and Bombing Investigative Services Program.

Douglas was a coparticipant in the FBI's first research program of serial killers and, based on that study, coauthored *Sexual Homicide: Patterns and Motives.* The University of Virginia awarded Douglas the prestigious Jefferson Award for academic excellence for his work on that study.

In 1992 Douglas coauthored the first edition of the *Crime Classification Manual (CCM),* the first study of violent crime to define and standardize techniques and terminology to be used by the criminal justice system and academia. Douglas again received the Jefferson Award for this research and the publication of the *CCM.*

Douglas has consulted on thousands of cases worldwide, providing case analysis, interview and interrogation techniques, investigative strategies, prosecutorial strategies, and expert testimony. Included in the list of Douglas's cases are Seattle's "Green River Killer," Wichita's "BTK Strangler," the O. J. Simpson civil case, and the JonBenet Ramsey homicide.

Since his retirement in 1995 from the FBI, Douglas has been providing pro bono assistance whenever possible to police and victims of violent crime.

Douglas has coauthored both fiction and nonfiction books, including two New York Times best sellers, *Mindhunter* and *Journey into Darkness.* He also has coauthored *Ob-*

session, *Anatomy of Motive, Cases That Haunt Us, Anyone You Want Me to Be,* and *Broken Wings.*

Douglas does numerous public presentations yearly, belonging to the Greater Talent Network agency in New York. His personal Web site, johndouglasmindhunter.com, contains crime information as well as an active online discussion board.

Johnny Dodd has been a writer at *People* magazine for over a decade. He has reported on some of pop culture's biggest stories — and some of its most tragic crimes. From the savage murder of Nicole Brown Simpson to the cold-blooded killing of Laci Peterson, he has written about a wide assortment of thugs, cads, and psychopaths. His work, which has won numerous journalism awards, has appeared in dozens of publications. Johnny grew up in Kansas City, a three-hour drive from where BTK lived, plotted, and murdered. He now lives in Santa Monica, California. More information on Johnny's writing projects can be found at his Web site — www.acmewordcorp.com.